Lecture Notes in Computer Science 16401

Founding Editors

Gerhard Goos
Juris Hartmanis

Editorial Board Members

Elisa Bertino, *Purdue University, West Lafayette, IN, USA*
Wen Gao, *Peking University, Beijing, China*
Bernhard Steffen, *TU Dortmund University, Dortmund, Germany*
Moti Yung, *Columbia University, New York, NY, USA*

The series Lecture Notes in Computer Science (LNCS), including its subseries Lecture Notes in Artificial Intelligence (LNAI) and Lecture Notes in Bioinformatics (LNBI), has established itself as a medium for the publication of new developments in computer science and information technology research, teaching, and education.

LNCS enjoys close cooperation with the computer science R & D community, the series counts many renowned academics among its volume editors and paper authors, and collaborates with prestigious societies. Its mission is to serve this international community by providing an invaluable service, mainly focused on the publication of conference and workshop proceedings and postproceedings. LNCS commenced publication in 1973.

Nada Amin · Joaquín Arias

Editors

Practical Aspects of Declarative Languages

28th International Symposium, PADL 2026
Rennes, France, January 12–13, 2026
Proceedings

 Springer

Editors
Nada Amin (iD)
Harvard University
Allston, MA, USA

Joaquín Arias (iD)
Universidad Rey Juan Carlos
Madrid, Madrid, Spain

ISSN 0302-9743   ISSN 1611-3349 (electronic)
Lecture Notes in Computer Science
ISBN 978-3-032-15980-9   ISBN 978-3-032-15981-6 (eBook)
https://doi.org/10.1007/978-3-032-15981-6

This Springer imprint is published by the registered company Springer Nature Switzerland AG
The registered company address is: Gewerbestrasse 11, 6330 Cham, Switzerland

If disposing of this product, please recycle the paper.

Preface

This volume contains the papers presented at the 28th International Symposium on Practical Aspects of Declarative Languages (PADL 2026). The symposium was held on 12–13 January 2026 in Rennes, France, co-located with the 53rd ACM SIGPLAN Symposium on Principles of Programming Languages (POPL 2026). PADL is a well-established forum for researchers and practitioners to present original work emphasizing novel applications and implementation techniques for all forms of declarative programming, including functional and logic programming, databases and constraint programming, and theorem proving.

Originally established as a workshop (PADL 1999 in San Antonio, Texas), the PADL series developed into a regular annual symposium; other previous editions took place in Boston, Massachusetts (2000), Las Vegas, Nevada (2001), Portland, Oregon (2002), New Orleans, Louisiana (2003), Dallas, Texas (2004), Long Beach, California (2005), Charleston, South Carolina (2006), Nice, France (2007), San Francisco, California (2008), Savannah, Georgia (2009), Madrid, Spain (2010), Austin, Texas (2012), Rome, Italy (2013), San Diego, California (2014), Portland, Oregon (2015), St. Petersburg, Florida (2016), Paris, France (2017), Los Angeles, California (2018), Lisbon, Portugal (2019), New Orleans, Louisiana (2020), online (2021), Philadelphia, Pennsylvania (2022), Boston, Massachusetts (2023), London, UK (2024), and Denver, Colorado (2025).

The 12 papers in this volume, including 11 regular papers and one short paper, were selected by the Program Committee from 24 submissions. Each of the PADL 2026 submissions received at least three reviews and was discussed electronically, using the HotCRP conference system, by the Program Committee before a final decision was made. The reviewing process for PADL 2026 was double-anonymous, and only authors of the eventually accepted papers were revealed.

The accepted papers span a range of topics related to functional and logic programming, including some novel applications of Answer Set Programming, language extensions, runtime monitoring, program transformations, type checking, and applications of declarative programming techniques to networks, artificial intelligence, and machine learning, among others.

The symposium was supported and sponsored by the Association of Logic Programming. We thank all who contributed to the success and the exciting program of PADL 2026. This includes the authors of submissions; the external reviewers, who provided timely expert reviews; and, of course, the 34 members of the Program Committee. We are particularly grateful to Marina De Vos, Marco Gavanelli, and Enrico Pontelli for their invaluable advice and support.

November 2025

Nada Amin
Joaquín Arias

Organization

Program Committee Chairs

Nada Amin	Harvard University, USA
Joaquín Arias	Universidad Rey Juan Carlos, Spain

Program Committee Members

Özgür Akgün	University of St Andrews, UK
Patrick Bahr	IT University of Copenhagen, Denmark
Marcello Balduccini	Saint Joseph's University, USA
Aaron Bembenek	University of Melbourne, Australia
Clara Benac Earle	Universidad Politécnica de Madrid, Spain
Malgorzata Biernacka	University of Wrocław, Poland
William E. Byrd	University of Alabama at Birmingham, USA
Laura M. Castro	University of A Coruña, Spain
Jesper Cockx	Delft University of Technology, Netherlands
Youyou Cong	Institute of Science Tokyo, Japan
Esra Erdem	Sabanci University, Turkey
Matthew Flatt	University of Utah, USA
Simon Fowler	University of Glasgow, UK
Martin Gebser	University of Klagenfurt, Austria
Gopal Gupta	University of Texas at Dallas, USA
Michael Hanus	Kiel University, Germany
Daniela Inclezan	Miami University, USA
Yusuf Izmirlioglu	University of Roehampton, UK
Michael Leuschel	University of Düsseldorf, Germany
Y. Annie Liu	Stony Brook University, USA
Giuseppe Mazzotta	University of Calabria, Italy
Alexandra Mendes	University of Porto & INESC TEC, Portugal
José Morales	IMDEA Software Institute, Spain
Magnus O. Myreen	Chalmers University of Technology, Sweden
Enrico Pontelli	New Mexico State University, USA
Mukund Raghothaman	University of Southern California, USA
Zeynep G. Saribatur	TU Wien, Austria
Tom Schrijvers	KU Leuven, Belgium
Paul Tarau	University of North Texas, USA

Joost Vennekens	KU Leuven, Belgium
Johannes Wallner	Graz University of Technology, Austria
Sam Westrick	New York University, USA

Additional Reviewers

Ignacio Ballesteros González	Universidad Politécnica de Madrid, Spain
Abhiramon Rajasekharan	University of Texas at Dallas, USA

Contents

Interpretable Configuration Optimization for Static Program Verification via Rule-Based and Counterfactual Reasoning

Jaeseong Lee[✉] [iD], Sopam Dasgupta[iD], Gopal Gupta[iD], and Shiyi Wei[iD]

The University of Texas at Dallas, Richardson, TX 75080, USA
`{jxl115330,sopam.dasgupta,gupta,swei}@utdallas.edu`

Abstract. Static program verification tools are essential for ensuring software correctness and reliability without executing the code. However, their effectiveness relies heavily on precise configuration, which must be tailored to specific project requirements, coding standards, and quality objectives. Selecting appropriate configurations is challenging due to the unique properties of each codebase and the need for an in-depth understanding of the analysis techniques. Current methods often default to standard settings or rely on random exploration, leading to sub-optimal results. In this paper, we introduce ConfigTuneX, a novel rule-based machine learning approach that optimizes configuration settings in static program verification tools through composite FOLD-SE rules. These rules simultaneously address two critical challenges: (1) reducing inconclusive outcomes by distinguishing unresolved cases from resolved outcomes, and (2) improving verification accuracy by separating correct outcomes from incorrect ones. The extracted rules are transformed into stratified answer set program (ASP) compatible with the s(CASP) solver, which systematically generates counterfactual configurations to avoid undesired outcomes. This targeted reasoning narrows the search space to the most promising configurations, reducing computational overhead while enhancing both interpretability and effectiveness. Experimental results show that ConfigTuneX with composite FOLD-SE rules consistently outperforms the state-of-the-art baseline across verification tools. On Jayhorn, CBMC, and Symbiotic, ConfigTuneX improves success rates by 76.34%, 10.73%, and 3.17%, respectively, and achieves a 76.4% success rate on JBMC where the baseline fails completely. ConfigTuneX also reduces runtime by 76.42%, 14.66%, and 48.83% on Jayhorn, CBMC, and Symbiotic, while JBMC shows a 73.69% increase due to the additional computation required for newly verified cases.

1 Introduction

Static program verification tools analyze software to ensure correctness and reliability without execution. Their effectiveness depends heavily on configurations, which tailor the analysis to program characteristics and quality objectives. For

N. Amin and J. Arias (Eds.): PADL 2026, LNCS 16401, pp. 1–20, 2026.
https://doi.org/10.1007/978-3-032-15981-6_1

instance, CBMC allows adjusting the solver type (*solvert*) to balance precision and performance [24]. However, choosing appropriate configurations is challenging due to diverse program features and the need for deep understanding of underlying analysis techniques [6,15,17,23,28–30,35]. As a result, configuration tuning often requires expert knowledge and iterative effort, and many users default to developer-recommended settings for typical scenarios [15,23]. This challenge is further compounded by prior work showing that the effectiveness of static program verification tools is highly dependent on their configurations. Koc *et al.* [23] demonstrate that improper settings can degrade accuracy, causing missed defects or excessive false positives. Therefore, careful configuration tuning is crucial to fully leverage these tools and ensure software reliability. To search best configurations in large and complex configuration spaces, prior work implemented learning-based approaches to predict software performance on configurations [7,17–19,23,33,34]. However, it is limited in identifying which configurations to adjust, relying instead on random exploration [23]. Consequently, existing strategies for configuration optimization in program verification tools often perform sub-optimally and are time-consuming.

To address these challenges, we employ a rule-based machine learning (RBML) technique to explain the behavior of software verification tools for targeted exploration of configuration spaces. The technique identifies the input features that most strongly influence verification outcomes, enabling focused search over promising configurations while reducing computational cost. Specifically, we develop ConfigTuneX, an approach for automatically tuning large configuration spaces of verification tools. The goal of ConfigTuneX is to identify which configurations of a program verification tool should be modified to improve verification outcomes. First, we extract interpretable default rules [40] from tool-specific datasets to explain verification behaviors. Second, we generate counterfactual configurations by converting the rules associated with undesirable outcomes into a format compatible with the s(CASP) stratified ASP solver [12] and executing the solver to identify minimal changes that yield corresponding counterfactual configurations leading to desirable outcomes.

Overall, this work makes the following contributions.

- We present **ConfigTuneX**, an interpretable RBML approach that automates configuration optimization for static program verification tools through explainable reasoning.
- We introduce a **rule-based interpretability module** that identifies which configurations most influence verification outcomes, enabling users to understand why specific configurations succeed or fail.
- We develop a **counterfactual generation module** that extracts human-understandable default rules describing undesirable verification outcomes and leverages the s(CASP) goal-directed ASP system to derive counterfactual configurations leading to desirable outcomes.
- We empirically evaluate ConfigTuneX on four representative software verification tools using the SV-COMP benchmark [2], comparing it with baselines.

Results demonstrate that ConfigTuneX significantly improves both the success rate and runtime performance.

The artifact accompanying this paper, which includes all data and source code, is provided in a repository.[1]

2   Background

In this section, we introduce the background of RBML, the FOLD-SE algorithm and counterfactual reasoning, which ConfigTuneX uses to optimize static program verification tools.

Rule-Based Machine learning (RBML) and FOLD-SE.

```
1   survived(X, no)  :- gender(X,male).
2   survived(X, no)  :- class(X, 3),
3       gender(X,female), not exception(X).
4   exception(X)  :- fare(X,Y), Y=<23.25.
```

Fig. 1. Default Rule showing the prediction if someone will perish on sailing the Titanic.

RBML is a paradigm that focuses on learning interpretable models based on rules derived from data. The rules capture the logic of how a label depends on the features in the dataset. These rules make the model interpretable and the prediction process explainable, bringing transparency in the process. FOLD-SE [40] is an efficient and explainable RBML algorithm that learns a set of default rules [16] from data containing both numerical and categorical features. These default rules also capture exceptions. For example, Fig. 1 shows rules generated by FOLD-SE for the Titanic tragedy dataset [1] where one has to predict who will perish. The default logic rules (shown in logic programming syntax) state that a person X would have perished either if (1) they were male or (2) if they had a Class 3 ticket and were female *unless* the fare was less than 23.25. FOLD-SE constructs these rules incrementally to cover instances of a target class while avoiding misclassifications, with adjustable hyperparameters, *ratio* and *tail*, to balance false and true positives. The *ratio* parameter helps speed up training and reduces the number of learned rules, while the *tail* parameter constrains the minimum number or percentage of training examples that a rule must cover, preventing overly specific rules and promoting sufficient generalization. This integration of RBML and logic programming allows for sophisticated reasoning with default rules, enabling robust interpretability and explainability. FOLD-SE is an iterative RBML algorithm that first learns the features (represented as predicates) that determine the label (also represented as a predicate) as a default conclusion based on the examples in the data. Next, it looks at the examples not covered by the default to learn exceptions, followed by learning

---

[1] Repository link: https://github.com/UTD-FAST-Lab/configtunex.

exceptions to exceptions, then exceptions to exception to exceptions, and so on. FOLD-SE's learned rule set is much more succinct than decision trees, and its accuracy is comparable to state-of-the-art tools such as XGBoost and multi-layer perceptrons [40].

Counterfactual Reasoning. Representing a machine learning model as a set of rules allows us to perform counterfactual reasoning [13], where a counterfactual is a statement or scenario describing what would have happened under different circumstances. Consider the Titanic survival example above. Given the rules that tell us who perished, and given that a certain individual I is predicted to perish, we can analyze the rules to figure out the changes in feature values (counterfactual) for individual I that would have led to I's survival instead. An example counterfactual would be: if I was not traveling with a Class 3 ticket, I would have survived.

Counterfactual reasoning is pivotal in understanding causal relationships by exploring "what-if" scenarios for obtaining a desired outcome given one is initially subjected to an undesired outcome [13]. The P2C (Path-to-Counterfactuals) framework [12] builds upon existing logic programming based counterfactual approaches [9–11,13,14], to *automatically* generate such counterfactuals, producing step-by-step explanations for changes that need to occur to move from an undesired outcome to a desired one. P2C incorporates symbolic reasoning to maintain causal dependencies among features, ensuring that counterfactual explanations are realistic and adhere to the underlying causal model. The P2C framework's solution for counterfactual generation provides a structured path from an initial state to a counterfactual state. FOLD-SE and the P2C framework together support the methodology discussed in this work, combining rule-based learning, symbolic reasoning, and counterfactual analysis to guide the users of software verification tool to move away from configuration choices that do not work for them to those that work.

3   Approach

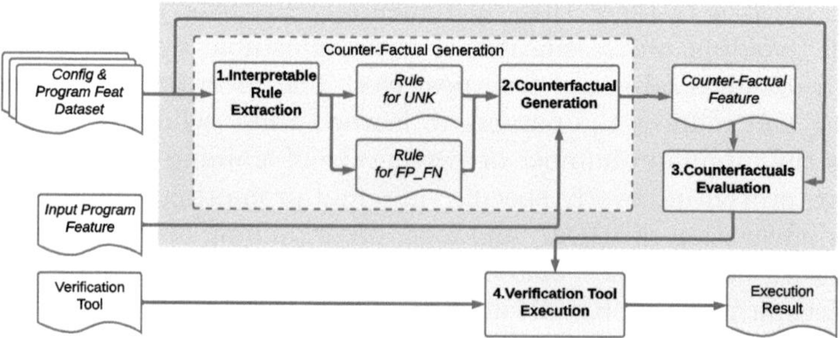

Fig. 2. Overview of ConfigTuneX.

We develop an automated framework, named ConfigTuneX, to optimally generate configurations for static program verification tools. ConfigTuneX pursues two main objectives. First, it automatically derives rules that identify configurations most influential to the incorrect verification outcomes. This rule set explains how tools verify input programs under specific configurations, particularly in cases leading to undesirable outcomes (*FP, FN, UNK*). Second, ConfigTuneX leverages these rules to generate counterfactual configurations that transform undesirable outcomes into desirable ones through appropriate configuration adjustments. Figure 2 depicts an overview of ConfigTuneX, which consists of four primary components. *(1) Interpretable Rule Extraction:* We extract interpretable rules that capture logical relationships among configurations for the undesirable verification outcomes. *(2) Counterfactual Generation:* Using the extracted rules, we generate candidate configurations through the s(CASP) solver, ensuring that they are likely to result in desirable outcomes. *(3) Counterfactual Evaluation:* We evaluate the quality and effectiveness of the generated counterfactuals in improving verification outcomes and rank them according to their quality. *(4) Verification Tool Execution:* Finally, we run the target verification tools with the adjusted configurations to produce correct verification outcomes. We now describe each component in detail.

3.1   Interpretable Rule Extraction

The goal of this step is to identify which configurations contribute to undesirable outcomes, enabling targeted adjustments rather than relying on random exploration over the entire configuration space. To enable interpretable reasoning about verification outcomes, we first extract structured features from both input programs and their associated configurations. For this purpose, we use the dataset collected by Koc *et al.* [23], which includes a set of programs along with their verification outcomes. Program-level features are extracted using a Bag-of-Words model [27], representing each program as a frequency vector over instructions, control-flow constructs, and data types. This representation effectively classifies verification outcomes [23]. The verification tool's configuration values, such as the choice of underlying SMT solver and parameters that limit the search space (e.g., timeout bounds) are encoded into a separate vector and concatenated with the program features to form the final input feature.

Using this combined features, ConfigTuneX automatically derives an interpretable set of default logic rules that captures relationships between features and verification outcomes. Specifically, we use the FOLD-SE rule interpreter, selected for its interpretability and strong predictive performance, to derive two levels of composite rules represented as stratified ASP [40]. The first type, *UNK rules*, distinguishes unresolved (*UNK*) from resolved outcomes (*TP, TN, FP, FN*) by relabeling all resolved cases as NOT_UNK and learning rules for UNK versus NOT_UNK. The second type, *incorrect-outcome rules*, separates incorrect (*FP, FN*) from correct (*TP, TN*) outcomes by grouping them as FP_FN and TP_TN, respectively, while ignoring unresolved cases. Rules are then extracted for this binary classifications to capture patterns leading to incorrect versus correct verification outcomes. These composite rules provide fine-grained inter-

```
1    label(X,'UNK')  :- not -solver(X,'spacer').
2    label(X,'UNK')  :- -solver(X,'spacer'),
3        ssaloadmetadatainstruction(X,N1), not(N1=<12.0).
4
5    label(X,'FP_FN')  :- numfundamentaltypes(X,N1), not(N1=<38.0).
6    label(X,'FP_FN')  :- -solver(X,'spacer'),
7        numvars(X,N2), N2>14.0, N2=<24.0,
8        ssaconditionalbranchinstruction(X,N3), N3=<2.0,
9        ssaarrayloadinstruction(X,N4), N4=<2.0,
10       ssabinaryopinstruction(X,N5), not(N5=<4.0).
```

Fig. 3. Rules extracted from FOLD-SE for Jayhorn [22,40].

pretability, revealing which configurations most influence verification outcomes and how they jointly determine correctness or uncertainty.

Figure 3 shows example composite rules. Among their predicates, *ssaloadmetadatainstruction* denotes the number of load operations with metadata describing how values are read in the program's static single-assignment (SSA) form. Other features include *numfundamentaltypes* (primitive data types), *numvars* (total variables), *ssaconditionalbranchinstruction* (conditional branches), *ssaarrayloadinstruction* (array reads), and *ssabinaryopinstruction* (binary arithmetic or logical operations). This rule set can be interpreted as follows: a program is classified as *UNK* if the solver option (*-solver*) is not set to *spacer*. Furthermore, even when the solver is set to *spacer*, the program still belongs to the *UNK* if it contains more than 12 SSA load metadata instructions (*ssaloadmetadatainstruction*). Otherwise, the program is classified as *NOT_UNK* because the example does not satisfy any *UNK* predicates in this binary classification setting. Additionally, the program is classified as *FP_FN* under two conditions: (1) when the program contains more than 38 fundamental data types (*numfundamentaltypes*) (2) when the solver is set to *spacer*, programs with a number of SSA variables between 14 and 24 (*numvars*), few conditional branches and array loads (less than 2 for *ssaconditionalbranchinstruction* and *ssaarrayloadinstruction*), and binary operations more than 4 (*ssabinaryopinstruction*). Otherwise, the program is classified as *TP_TN*.

3.2 Counterfactual Generation

Based on the interpretable rule set derived in Sect. 3.1, we generate counterfactual configurations aimed at altering undesirable verification outcomes.In this stage, the extracted rules are manually translated into executable s(CASP) code to ensure correct and reliable generation of counterfactual configurations. The resulting s(CASP) program includes four components: (1) valid value ranges for each feature, (2) predicates for UNK rules, (3) predicates for incorrect-outcome rules, and (4) predicates for the expected correct outcomes.

The input to the s(CASP) code includes both configuration and program features, represented as a single combined feature vector. Upon execution, the s(CASP) solver first checks whether the input vector satisfies any predicates associated with UNK or incorrect-outcome rules. If such conditions are triggered, the solver automatically searches for an alternative feature vector that (1) satisfies the valid value ranges of all features and (2) does not activate any of the UNK or incorrect-outcome conditions. During this search process, only the configuration features are modified, while program features remain fixed since the program itself cannot be altered. Consequently, the s(CASP) solver identifies counterfactual configurations by inverting the conditions that lead to undesirable outcomes.

For instance, in the first rule set in Fig. 3, when input features are classified as either *UNK* or *FP_FN*, the corresponding counterfactual configurations are generated by adjusting configuration features such as the solver, while program features remain fixed. In addition, due to potential suboptimality in rule-based predictions, the s(CASP)-derived counterfactuals may lead to limited exploration of uninvolved configurations that can still influence verification performance. To mitigate this issue, for each solver-generated counterfactual, we randomly sample the uninvolved configurations N times, resulting in N distinct counterfactual feature vectors associated with the same solver-derived counterfactual. This strategy broadens the set of candidate counterfactual configurations while maintaining logical consistency with the composite rules and improving robustness against imperfect rule accuracy.

3.3   Counterfactual Evaluation

To identify and execute the most promising counterfactual configurations, we estimate each candidate's likelihood of producing a correct verification outcome. First, we train a random forest classifier, consistent with SATune, on the same dataset used for FOLD-SE rule extraction to distinguish desirable from undesirable outcomes. Next, the classifier scores each counterfactual configuration, represented as a combined configuration-program feature vector, with a likelihood of producing a correct outcome. Finally, these likelihood scores are used to rank and select the most promising, rule-consistent counterfactual configurations for verification.

3.4   Verification Tool Execution

The goal of this step is to empirically evaluate each candidate configuration by executing the verification tool and collecting its actual outcomes. In this step, we execute a target verification tool with the prioritized counterfactual configurations obtained from the counterfactual evaluation step (Sect. 3.3). However, because rule-based predictions can be sub-optimal, counterfactual configurations may still receive low likelihood scores. To refine these candidates and discover more effective ones, we apply a simulated annealing algorithm that treats each counterfactual feature vector as a candidate state and evaluates its quality using the likelihood score. Unlike SATune [23], which uses two composite fitness functions to guide configuration exploration, our approach employs a single model to estimate the quality of counterfactual configurations. The simulated annealing

---

Algorithm 1: Simulated Annealing for Searching Counterfactuals.

Input: default configuration $config_{default}$, cost of the $config_{default}$ $cost_{default}$, counterfactual configuration set $CONFIG_{cf}$, Input Program P, Verification Tool F_{verif}, Initial temperature T_0, Cooling rate R, Stopping temperature T_s

Output: Final verification result Res

1   $config_{best} = config_{default}$;
2   $cost_{best} = cost_{default}$;
3   $config_{cur} = config_{best}$;
4   $cost_{cur} = cost_{best}$;
5   $T = T_0$;
6   **for each** $(config_{cf},\ cost_{cf})$ **in** $CONFIG_{cf}$ **do**
       // $config_{cf}$ denotes counterfactual configuration and
       // $cost_{cf}$ represents its associated cost
7      $delta = cost_{cf} - cur\_cost$;
8   **if not** $(delta \geq 0$ **and** $random.random() > e^{-delta/T}$ **and** $T > T_s)$ **then**
9         $config_{cur} = config_{cf}$;
10        $cost_{cur} = cost_{cf}$;
11   **if** $cost_{cur} < cost_{best}$ **then**
12           $config_{best} = config_{cur}$;
13           $cost_{best} = cost_{cur}$;
14           $Res = F_{verif}(P, config_{cur})$;
15   **if** Res is $conclusive$ **then**
16   **return** Res
17     $T = T - R * T$;
18 **return** Res

---

algorithm optimizes counterfactual configurations by minimizing a cost function defined as the inverse of the likelihood from Sect. 3.3, where a lower cost indicates a higher likelihood of correct verification. It follows the standard simulated annealing acceptance rule governed by the temperature parameters: initial temperature T_0, cooling rate R, and stopping temperature T_s, which control the balance between exploration and exploitation during the search.

The practical implementation is presented in Algorithm 1. The algorithm takes as input a default configuration and its associated cost, a set of counterfactual configurations, the input program P, a target verification tool F_{verif}, and the parameters of simulated annealing: the initial temperature T_0, cooling rate R, and stopping temperature T_s. It begins by initializing the default configuration as both the best and the current configuration, assigns their corresponding costs, and sets the temperature to T_0 (lines 1–5). For each counterfactual configuration in the candidate set, the algorithm evaluates whether to accept it as the new current configuration. If the candidate has a lower cost (*i.e.*, higher quality), it is accepted directly. Otherwise, if the candidate is worse (*i.e.*, higher cost), it may still be accepted with probability $e^{-\Delta/T}$, where Δ is the cost difference (lines 7–10). This acceptance rule allows the algorithm to escape local optima in the early stages of the search. Whenever a newly accepted configuration achieves a lower cost than the best configuration found so far, the best configuration is updated and its verification outcome is recorded by executing F_{verif} on program P with the accepted configuration (lines 11–14). If the verification outcome is conclusive (either positive or negative), it is returned immediately as the output of the algorithm (line 16). If the candidate is not accepted, the temperature is reduced according to the cooling rate (line 17).

4   Evaluation

4.1   Experimental Setup

Research Questions. In this evaluation, we aim to answer four research questions (RQs):

RQ1 Effectiveness: How effective is ConfigTuneX in improving verification outcomes compared to existing approaches?

RQ2 Efficiency: How efficient is ConfigTuneX compared to existing approaches?

RQ3 Ablation Study: How does the counterfactual generation using composite rules contribute to the overall performance of ConfigTuneX?

RQ4 Qualitative Analysis: How interpretable and useful are the extracted rules and counterfactual configurations for real verification scenarios?

Verification Tools. We conducted experiments using four representative software verification tools that participate in the annual software verification competition [2]: Jayhorn [22] and JBMC [8] for Java programs, and CBMC [24] and Symbiotic [36,37] for C/C++ programs.

Datasets. We trained both the binary classification model and its FOLD-SE rule interpreter using the dataset provided by SATune [23]. This dataset comprises five folds, each containing input features formed by concatenating program features with configurations, paired with verification outcomes labeled as *TP*, *TN*, *FP*, *FN*, or *UNK*. These outcomes were produced by four verification tools applied to Java and C/C++ programs, as detailed in Sect. 4.1.

In addition, we evaluated ConfigTuneX on benchmark suites from SV-COMP [2], which cover a broad range of verification tasks for Java and C/C++ programs. The SV-COMP benchmarks span multiple property classes, including safety, reachability, and correctness, and contain programs with diverse levels of complexity, control structures, and data types. Similar to the SATune dataset, the SV-COMP benchmarks were divided into five folds, and we report the performance of ConfigTuneX as the average across evaluations on these five folds.

Binary Classification Model. We employ a random forest model [4] to evaluate counterfactual configurations. The Gini impurity is used to measure the quality of splits within the model [5]. Nodes are expanded until all leaves are pure or contain fewer than two samples.

Table 1. Comparison of ConfigTuneX and the baseline (SATune) across four verification tools. The number of true positive, true negative, false positive and false negative, unresolved verification results, success rate and runtime are denoted as #TP, #TN, #FP, #FN, #UNK, SR and RT, respectively.

Tool	#Data	Method	#TP	#TN	#FP	#FN	#UNK	SR [%]	RT [sec]
Jayhorn	73.6	SATune	16.8	9	1.8	1.2	44.8	35.1	220.027
		ConfigTuneX	**34.6**	**20.2**	8	**0.2**	**10.6**	**74.5**	**51.893**
CBMC	200	SATune	82.6	0	**24.2**	0	93.2	41.3	96.228
		ConfigTuneX	**83.4**	0	33.4	0	**83.2**	**41.7**	**82.123**
JBMC	73.6	SATune	0	0	0	0	73.6	0	**7.625**
		ConfigTuneX	**31.6**	**24.6**	**6.2**	8	**3.2**	**76.4**	13.243
Symbiotic	125	SATune	28.4	**25.6**	0	5	**72.6**	37.4	164.793
		ConfigTuneX	**30.6**	23.6	0	**3.2**	75	**40.9**	**84.33**

Hyperparameters for FOLD-SE and Simulated Annealing. We used the default FOLD-SE settings, with the *ratio* set to 0.5 and the *tail* set to 5×10^{-3}. For simulated annealing, we set the initial temperature to 1.0, use a cooling rate of 1×10^{-4} and a stopping temperature of 1×10^{-5}, following the configuration used in baseline for comparison.

Baseline. In our evaluation, we compare ConfigTuneX against the state-of-the-art configuration search methodology for software verification tools, SATune [23]. SATune employs two fitness functions to predict verification outcomes and applies simulated annealing to search for improved configurations. In particular, it iteratively explores random variations of the default configuration and uses simulated annealing to identify candidate configurations for which the fitness functions predict acceptable verification outcomes. In addition, we include a baseline variant of ConfigTuneX that does not utilize the composite rules extracted by FOLD-SE during counterfactual generation, enabling us to isolate the contribution of the interpretable composite rules.

Metrics. To evaluate ConfigTuneX's effectiveness and efficiency, we use the following metrics:

- **Number of Correct Outcomes (#TP+#TN):** The total count of verification tasks that produce correct outcomes (TP and TN).
- **Number of Incorrect Outcomes (#FP+#FN):** The total count of verification tasks that produce incorrect outcomes (FP and FN).
- **Success Rate (SR):** The percentage of correct outcomes (TP and TN) relative to the total number of verification tasks.
- **Runtime (RT):** The total time required to verify each task using the configurations identified by the respective approach, reflecting the computational cost of verification.

4.2   RQ1: Effectiveness

Our results show that *ConfigTuneX improves predictive accuracy and reliability in verification outcomes*. Table 1 presents the experimental results comparing

ConfigTuneX with the baseline across the four verification tools. The first column lists the tools, and the second column reports the average number of input programs executed with each tool configuration over 5 folds. The third column indicates the configuration search method (ConfigTuneX or SATune). Columns four through eight present the average number of True Positives, True Negatives, False Positives, False Negatives, and unresolved outcomes across folds. Finally, the ninth and tenth columns report the average success rate (in %) and runtime (in seconds) for each tool and method.

Compared to the baseline, ConfigTuneX consistently increases the number of correct outcomes across verification tools. With Jayhorn, ConfigTuneX achieves significantly higher numbers of true positives and true negatives (34.6 TP and 20.2 TN) compared to SATune (16.8 TP and 9 TN), resulting in a success rate of 74.5% versus 35.1%. Similarly, with JBMC, ConfigTuneX reaches a success rate of 76.4%, while SATune fails to produce any correct outcomes. In addition to increasing correct outcomes, ConfigTuneX also reduces the number of unresolved cases. In Jayhorn, unresolved outcomes decrease from 44.8 with SATune to 10.6 with ConfigTuneX, and in JBMC from 73.6 to 3.2. These reductions demonstrate that ConfigTuneX not only improves accuracy but also produces more resolved and reliable verification outcomes. For CBMC, ConfigTuneX slightly outperforms baseline in terms of correct outcomes (83.4 TP for ConfigTuneX versus 82.6 TP for SATune) and unresolved cases (83.2 versus 93.2), although it produces a higher number of incorrect outcomes (33.4 FP versus 24.2 FP). As a result, the overall success rates of the two methods are comparable, with ConfigTuneX achieving 41.7% and SATune 41.3%. Finally, for Symbiotic, ConfigTuneX achieves a modest improvement in success rate (40.9% for ConfigTuneX versus 37.4% for SATune) by yielding a higher number of correct outcomes (30.6 TP and 23.6 TN versus 28.4 TP and 25.6 TN) and fewer incorrect outcomes (3.2 FN versus 5 FN), even though the number of unresolved outcomes increases slightly (75 versus 72.6). Overall, these results confirm that ConfigTuneX delivers more effective verification outcomes across diverse verification settings.

4.3 RQ2: Efficiency

ConfigTuneX Demonstrates Significantly Faster Runtimes Across Most Verification Tools. As shown in the last column of Table 1, ConfigTuneX consistently reduces runtime compared to the baseline. For Jayhorn, average runtime decreases from 220.0 s with SATune to 51.9 s with ConfigTuneX; for Symbiotic, from 164.8 s to 84.3 s; and for CBMC, from 96.2 s to 82.1 s. These reductions highlight the efficiency of ConfigTuneX in navigating the configuration space more effectively. In contrast, for JBMC, runtime increases moderately from 7.6 s with SATune to 13.2 s with ConfigTuneX. This increase is expected, as SATune typically returns unresolved outcomes almost immediately without deeper exploration, whereas ConfigTuneX performs a more thorough analysis that leads to substantially higher success rates. Overall, these results demonstrate that ConfigTuneX achieves significant efficiency gains on three of the four verification tools, while maintaining acceptable runtime overhead in the one case where execution time increases. This confirms that ConfigTuneX not only improves effectiveness but also delivers practical performance benefits in configuration search.

Table 2. Ablation study comparing ConfigTuneX with and without FOLD-SE rules across four verification tools.

Tool	#Data	Method	#TP	#TN	#FP	#FN	#UNK	SR [%]	RT [sec]
Jayhorn	73.6	w/o Rules	33.6	**20.6**	8	0.2	11.2	73.6	52.137
		w Rules	**34.6**	20.2	8	0.2	**10.6**	**74.5**	**51.893**
CBMC	200	w/o Rules	62.8	0	**20.8**	0	116.4	31.4	**41.468**
		w Rules	**83.4**	0	33.4	0	**83.2**	**41.7**	82.123
JBMC	73.6	w/o Rules	**35.4**	22.8	8.2	**2.6**	4.6	**79.1**	32.895
		w Rules	31.6	**24.6**	**6.2**	8	**3.2**	76.4	**13.243**
Symbiotic	125	w/o Rules	30.6	23.2	0	3.2	75.4	40.6	84.508
		w Rules	30.6	**23.6**	0	3.2	**75**	**40.9**	**84.33**

4.4   RQ3: Ablation Study

To further assess the contribution of individual components within ConfigTuneX, we conduct an ablation study. We evaluate the performance of ConfigTuneX when composite FOLD-SE rules were excluded and compared it against Config-TuneX across the four verification tools, as shown in Table 2. The table columns represent the same metrics as those in Table 1.

Effectiveness. On Jayhorn, composite rules reduce unresolved results and improve the number of correct outcomes, resulting in a higher success rate (74.5% versus 73.6%). For CBMC, the rules are more impactful, forcing the tool to resolve more cases (shifting UNK into TP and FP), which boosts the success rate (41.7% versus 31.4%) though it increases the number of incorrect outcomes. On JBMC, the rules reduce both FP and UNK but trade some TP for additional FN, leading to a small drop in success rate (76.4% versus 79.1%). For Symbiotic, composite rules lead to improvements in TN and UNK, yielding an increase in success rate (40.9% versus 40.6%).

Efficiency. On Jayhorn, composite rules slightly reduce runtime, reflecting lower overhead in configuration search (51.893 s versus 52.137 s). On CBMC, runtime increases with composite rules, due to the cost of resolving more counterfactual configuration introduced by the rules. In contrast, JBMC shows improved efficiency, with runtime reduced from 32.9 s to 13.2 s. For Symbiotic, runtime is also slightly reduced (84.3 s versus 84.5 s). Overall, the ablation study shows that composite FOLD-SE rules are most impactful for CBMC, substantially reducing unresolved cases and improving success rate despite longer runtime. They also provide improvements for Jayhorn, JBMC and Symbiotic.

4.5 RQ4: Qualitative Analysis

```
1  label(X,'UNK')  :- not -solver(X,'spacer'), not ab1(X,'True').
2  label(X,'UNK')  :- -solver(X,'spacer'), ... .
3  ab1(X,'True')  :- -heap-mode(X,'auto'),
4       -initial-heap-size(X,N2), N2=<10.0, ... .
5
6  label(X,'FP_FN')  :- -solver(X,'spacer'), ... .
7  label(X,'FP_FN')  :- ..., -heap-limit(X,N6), not(N6=<-1.0).
8  label(X,'FP_FN')  :- -heap-limit(X,N6), N6>-1.0, N6=<1.0, ...
```

Fig. 4. FOLD-SE rules on data fold 1 for Jayhorn. The ellipses (...) denote additional predicates over input program features that are omitted for brevity.

To illustrate how ConfigTuneX improves verification outcomes beyond numerical metrics, we examine two case studies where it corrected unresolved outcomes returned by SATune. Both examples highlight how rule-guided adjustments of configurations lead to more reliable verification.

Figure 4 shows the FOLD-SE rules extracted on data fold 1 for Jayhorn. The first three rules indicate that parameters such as solver choice ($-solver$), heap encoding mode ($-heap\text{-}mode$), and the initial value of the bounded heap size ($-initial\text{-}heap\text{-}size$) contribute to unresolved outcomes. In addition, the solver choice and the maximum heap allocation for the Spacer solver ($-heap\text{-}limit$) contribute to incorrect outcomes. Beyond marginal effects, the rules reveal structured dependencies between these configurations and verification outcomes:

Rule1 An unresolved outcome (UNK) arises (1) if the solver is not set to Spacer and (2) either the heap encoding mode is not auto or the initial heap size exceeds 10 (lines 1 and 3–4).

Rule2 If this condition is not satisfied, then UNK still arises when the solver is Spacer under the specific condition on program features (lines 1–4).

Rule3 Under certain program feature conditions, the Spacer solver produces incorrect outcomes (FP_FN) (line 6).

Rule4 If the first rule fails, FP_FN occurs when the maximum heap allocation for Spacer is limited, given specific program feature conditions (lines 6–7).

Rule5 If neither the first nor the second FP_FN rules applies, FP_FN arises when the maximum heap allocation is set to 1 (lines 6–8).

Table 3 compares the corresponding configurations and their verification outcomes between SATune and ConfigTuneX across two input programs, illustrating how ConfigTuneX successfully adjusts heap-related configurations to avoid the unresolved and incorrect outcomes characterized by these rules in Fig. 4. The first column lists the input programs, while the second column specifies the configurations identified from the FOLD-SE rules (Fig. 4). The third and fourth

Table 3. Comparison of Jayhorn configuration settings highlighted in Figure 4 and their corresponding verification outcomes.

Input Program	Configuration	ConfigValue (SATune)	ConfigValue (ConfigTuneX)	Verification Outcome
jpf-regression/ ExSymExeBool_true	-heap-limit	100	−1	SATune: UNK ConfigTuneX: TN
	-heap-mode	unbounded	unbounded	
	-initial-heap-size	1000	1	
	-solver	spacer	spacer	
jbmc-regression/ SubString03	-heap-limit	−1	−1	SATune: UNK ConfigTuneX: TP
	-heap-mode	bounded	unbounded	
	-initial-heap-size	10	1	
	-solver	spacer	spacer	

columns report the values selected by SATune and ConfigTuneX, respectively, and the final column shows the resulting Jayhorn outcomes.

The first row demonstrates that SATune produced a configuration with $-heap\text{-}limit = 100$ and $-initial\text{-}heap\text{-}size = 1000$. The program heap is a region of memory used by programs to store dynamically allocated objects at runtime, and in Jayhorn's verification, these configurations control how the heap is represented and explored. Specifically, the heap limit imposes an upper bound on the number of objects the solver may consider, while the initial heap size specifies the starting allocation for bounded analysis. Under these configurations, Jayhorn performs a bounded under-approximation, reasoning over a finite, concrete heap model. Since the program is safe and no counterexample arises within this constrained space, Jayhorn reports an unresolved outcome, meaning that the analysis cannot establish safety but merely indicates that no violation was discovered within the given bound. In contrast, the counterfactual configurations generated by ConfigTuneX configure Jayhorn to employ an unbounded, invariant-based analysis that reasons abstractly over all heap sizes ($-heap\text{-}limit = -1$ and $-initial\text{-}heap\text{-}size = 1$). In this setting, the solver is able to infer inductive invariants that establish program safety, thereby yielding a desirable outcome.

In addition, the second row shows that SATune produced a configuration enforcing bounded heap encoding, which restricted Jayhorn to a finite and shallow exploration of heap states. Heap encoding determines how the program heap is represented during verification: in bounded mode, the heap is modeled concretely up to a fixed limit, whereas in unbounded mode it is abstracted symbolically to represent all possible allocations. Because the assertion-violating sequence in the input program lies beyond the restricted scope of the bounded encoding, the analysis could not establish correctness and again returned an unresolved outcome. By contrast, the counterfactual configurations from ConfigTuneX directed Jayhorn to use unbounded heap encoding, where invariant inference failed to establish global safety. This failure indicated the presence of a violation, and Jayhorn therefore reported the program as unsafe, yielding a resolved and correct verification outcome as well. Overall, These case studies demonstrate the effectiveness of ConfigTuneX in guiding verification tools toward rule-consistent configurations that improve both reliability and explanatory power.

5   Threats to Validity

Internal. Internal threats may arise from discrepancies between the actual behavior of a verification tool and the default logic rules generated by FOLD-SE to approximate that behavior. Such differences can affect ConfigTuneX's accuracy in interpreting and explaining verification outcomes, which in turn may influence the guidance provided for configuration optimization. To mitigate this gap, we implement random exploration of configurations not captured by the extracted rules, along with the simulated annealing algorithm, to broaden the search space and reduce potential biases introduced by imperfect rule representations. Furthermore, we plan to enhance the robustness of the rule-based explanations, ensuring closer alignment between learned rules and the underlying tool behavior.

External. External threats include limitations in generalizing our manual translation of default logic rules into s(CASP) code. This process requires specific knowledge of s(CASP), potentially restricting ConfigTuneX applicability across contexts and verification tools. Despite validating our implementation, potential errors may remains. Future work to automate this translation could and improve the approach's generalizability and mitigate this threat.

6   Related Work

Configuration of Static Program Verification Tools. Prior studies have demonstrated that configurations can significantly affect verification outcomes. Lhoták and Hendren [25] investigated the trade-offs inherent in different design decisions by instantiating multiple variants of context-sensitive points-to analysis for Java. Xu et $al.$ [42] demonstrated with SATzilla that per-instance solver selection solved significantly more benchmarks than any individual solver, underscoring the strong effect of solver configuration on outcome. Beyer et $al.$ [3] introduced CPAchecker, a highly configurable software model checker, and showed that combining different abstract domains, precisions, and block-encoding strategies leads to substantial variation in both efficiency and precision of verification outcomes. Smaragdakis et $al.$ [38] refines object-sensitive points-to analysis by introducing a full-object-sensitive analysis. In addition, Wei et $al.$ [41] conducted a study examining the trade-offs across 162 different configurations of numerical static analysis for Java programs. Additionally, Koç et $al.$ [23] examined several popular verification tools to investigate the effects of different configurations on them, revealing a significant impact on verification outcomes. Our development of ConfigTuneX was inspired by these works that assessed configurations of static program analysis tools.

Software Configuration Optimization. Software configuration optimization involves fine-tuning the configurations of software to enhance performance, reliability, and other non-functional properties. Nair *et al.* [28] introduced a rank-based approach that learns performance models from configuration ranks without needing exact performance measurements. In subsequent work, Nair *et al.* [29] analyzed previously evaluated configurations to determine the next optimal configuration to explore. Oh *et al.* [30] employed random sampling and recursive search within the configuration space to directly identify near-optimal configurations in software product lines. Chen *et al.* [6] optimized configurations aiming at robust performance optimization across multiple objectives. Dorn *et al.* [15] modeled uncertainty in option influences, providing confidence intervals for each configuration's performance prediction. These approaches primarily serve as optimizers and offer limited interpretability compared to ConfigTuneX, which produces explicit rule-based explanations of configuration influence in verification tools. Additionally, Machine learning techniques also have been employed to predict software performance, including regression models [35], classification models [17,18,23,33], deep neural networks [7,19,34,43]. Our work extends these research by focusing on explaining verification performance prediction based on configurations, enabling users to identify the most influential configurations for the verification tools.

XAI for Software Engineering. XAI techniques aim to make ML models more transparent and understandable. In software engineering, XAI has been employed to interpret software defect detection models [20,21,31,39,44]. Techniques like LIME [32] and SHAP [26] provide insights into what input features influence model predictions. Wang *et al.* [40] extends these by generating logical relationships among these features in the form of default rules. Building on this, our work leverages a RBML method not only to identify the importance of various configurations within the ML-based fitness function but also to systematically adjust configuration features to achieve desirable outcomes.

7   Conclusions

This paper presents ConfigTuneX, an RBML-based approach for explaining and optimizing configuration settings in static program verification tools. Config-TuneX extracts rules that capture tool behavior, identifies configurations causing undesired outcomes, and transforms these rules through the s(CASP) solver to generate counterfactual configurations leading to desired results. Experiments show that ConfigTuneX significantly enhances predictive accuracy and reliability, yielding more correct and conclusive verification outcomes than the baseline. Notably, ConfigTuneX with composite FOLD-SE rules consistently outperforms the state-of-the-art across multiple verification tools. On Jayhorn, CBMC, and Symbiotic, ConfigTuneX increases success rates by 76.34%, 10.73%, and 3.17%, respectively, and achieves a 76.4% success rate on JBMC, where the baseline produces no successful results. In terms of efficiency, ConfigTuneX reduces runtime by 76.42%, 14.66%, and 48.83% on Jayhorn, CBMC, and Symbiotic, whereas JBMC exhibits a 73.69% runtime increase due to the additional computation needed for newly verified cases. Overall, the results show that ConfigTuneX enhances both effectiveness and efficiency, providing an interpretable and actionable framework for configuration optimization in program verification.

Acknowledgments. This work was partly supported by NSF grant CCF-2047682, NSF grants IIS-1910131, and grants from industry through the UT Dallas Center for Applied AI and Machine Learning.

References

1. Titanic - machine learning from disaster (2012)
2. Beyer, D.: State of the art in software verification and witness validation: SV-COMP 2024. In: Finkbeiner, B., Kovács, L. (eds.) TACAS 2024. LNCS, vol. 14572, pp. 299–329. Springer, Cham (2024). https://doi.org/10.1007/978-3-031-57256-2_15
3. Beyer, D., Keremoglu, M.E.: CPAchecker: a tool for configurable software verification. In: Gopalakrishnan, G., Qadeer, S. (eds.) CAV 2011. LNCS, vol. 6806, pp. 184–190. Springer, Heidelberg (2011). https://doi.org/10.1007/978-3-642-22110-1_16
4. Breiman, L.: Random forests. Mach. Learn. **45**, 5–32 (2001)
5. Breiman, L., Friedman, J.H., Olshen, R.A., Stone, C.J.: Classification and regression trees. Wadsworth International Group (1984)
6. Chen, T., Li, M.: Multi-objectivizing software configuration tuning. In: Proceedings of the 29th ACM Joint Meeting on European Software Engineering Conference and Symposium on the Foundations of Software Engineering, ESEC/FSE 2021, pp. 453–465. Association for Computing Machinery, New York (2021)
7. Cheng, J., Gao, C., Zheng, Z.: HINNPerf: hierarchical interaction neural network for performance prediction of configurable systems. ACM Trans. Softw. Eng. Methodol. **32**(2) (2023)
8. Cordeiro, L., Kesseli, P., Kroening, D., Schrammel, P., Trtik, M.: JBMC: a bounded model checking tool for verifying java bytecode. In: Chockler, H., Weissenbacher, G. (eds.) CAV 2018. LNCS, vol. 10981, pp. 183–190. Springer, Cham (2018). https://doi.org/10.1007/978-3-319-96145-3_10
9. Dasgupta, S.: Generating causally compliant counterfactual explanations using ASP. In: Proceedings 40th International Conference on Logic Programming, ICLP 2024, University of Texas at Dallas, Dallas Texas, USA, 14–17 October 2024. EPTCS, vol. 416, pp. 306–313 (2024)
10. Dasgupta, S., Arias, J., Salazar, E., Gupta, G.: CoGS: model agnostic causality constrained counterfactual explanations using goal-directed ASP. CoRR, abs/2410.22615 (2024)
11. Dasgupta, S., Halim, S.M., Arias, J., Salazar, E., Gupta, G.: MC3G:: model agnostic causally constrained counterfactual generation. In: Gilpin, L.H., Giunchiglia, E., Hitzler, P., van Krieken, E. (eds.) Proceedings of The 19th International Conference on Neurosymbolic Learning and Reasoning. Proceedings of Machine Learning Research, vol. 284, pp. 926–937. PMLR (2025)

12. Dasgupta, S., Halim, S.M., Arias, J., Salazar, E., Gupta, G.: P2C: path to counterfactuals. CoRR, abs/2508.20371 (2025)
13. Dasgupta, S., Shakerin, F., Arias, J., Salazar, E., Gupta, G.: C3G: causally constrained counterfactual generation. In: Erdem, E., Vidal, G. (eds.) PADL 2025. LNCS, vol. 15537, pp. 215–232. Springer, Cham (2025). https://doi.org/10.1007/978-3-031-84924-4_14
14. Dasgupta, S., Shakerin, F., Salazar, E., Arias, J., Gupta, G.: Causally constrained counterfactual generation using ASP. In: Workshop Proceedings of the 40th International Conference on Logic Programming (ICLP-WS 2024) co-located with the 40th International Conference on Logic Programming (ICLP 2024), Dallas, TX, USA, 12th–3th October 2024. CEUR Workshop Proceedings, vol. 3799. CEUR-WS.org (2024)
15. Dorn, J., Apel, S., Siegmund, N.: Mastering uncertainty in performance estimations of configurable software systems. In: Proceedings of the 35th IEEE/ACM International Conference on Automated Software Engineering, ASE 2020, pp. age 684–696. Association for Computing Machinery, New York (2021)
16. Gelfond, M., Kahl, Y.: Knowledge Representation, Reasoning, and the Design of Intelligent Agents: Answer Set Programming Approach. Cambridge University Press (2014)
17. Guo, J., Czarnecki, K., Apely, S., Siegmundy, N., Wasowski, A.: Variability-aware performance prediction: a statistical learning approach. In: Proceedings of the 28th IEEE/ACM International Conference on Automated Software Engineering, ASE 2013, pp. 301–311. IEEE Press (2013)
18. Guo, J., et al.: Data-efficient performance learning for configurable systems. Empir. Softw. Eng. **23**(3), 1826–1867 (2018)
19. Ha, H., Zhang, H.: DeepPerf: performance prediction for configurable software with deep sparse neural network. In: 2019 IEEE/ACM 41st International Conference on Software Engineering (ICSE), pp. 1095–1106 (2019)
20. Humphreys, J., Dam, H.K.: An explainable deep model for defect prediction. In: Proceedings of the 7th International Workshop on Realizing Artificial Intelligence Synergies in Software Engineering, RAISE 2019, pp. 49–55. IEEE Press (2019)
21. Jiarpakdee, J., Tantithamthavorn, C.K., Grundy, J.C.: Practitioners' perceptions of the goals and visual explanations of defect prediction models. In: 2021 IEEE/ACM 18th International Conference on Mining Software Repositories (MSR), pp. 432–443 (2021)
22. Kahsai, T., Rümmer, P., Sanchez, H., Schäf, M.: JayHorn: a framework for verifying java programs. In: Chaudhuri, S., Farzan, A. (eds.) CAV 2016. LNCS, vol. 9779, pp. 352–358. Springer, Cham (2016). https://doi.org/10.1007/978-3-319-41528-4_19
23. Koc, U., Mordahl, A, Wei, S., Foster, J.S., Porter, A.A.: Satune: a study-driven auto-tuning approach for configurable software verification tools. In: 2021 36th IEEE/ACM International Conference on Automated Software Engineering (ASE), pp. 330–342 (2021)
24. Kroening, D., Tautschnig, M.: CBMC – C bounded model checker. In: Ábrahám, E., Havelund, K. (eds.) TACAS 2014. LNCS, vol. 8413, pp. 389–391. Springer, Heidelberg (2014). https://doi.org/10.1007/978-3-642-54862-8_26
25. Lhoták, O., Hendren, L.: Evaluating the benefits of context-sensitive points-to analysis using a BDD-based implementation. ACM Trans. Softw. Eng. Methodol. **18**(1) (2008)
26. Lundberg, S.M., Lee, S.-I.: A unified approach to interpreting model predictions. In: Proceedings of the 31st International Conference on Neural Information Processing Systems, NIPS 2017, pp. 4768–4777. Curran Associates Inc., Red Hook (2017)

27. Manning, C.D., Raghavan, P., Schütze, H.: Introduction to Information Retrieval. Cambridge University Press, Cambridge (2008)
28. Nair, V., Menzies, T., Siegmund, N., Apel, S.: Using bad learners to find good configurations. In: Proceedings of the 2017 11th Joint Meeting on Foundations of Software Engineering, ESEC/FSE 2017, pp. 257–267. Association for Computing Machinery, New York (2017)
29. Nair, V., Yu, Z., Menzies, T., Siegmund, N., Apel, S.: Finding faster configurations using flash. IEEE Trans. Softw. Eng. **46**(7), 794–811 (2020)
30. Oh, J., Batory, D., Myers, M., Siegmund, N.: Finding near-optimal configurations in product lines by random sampling. In: Proceedings of the 2017 11th Joint Meeting on Foundations of Software Engineering, ESEC/FSE 2017, pp. 61–71. Association for Computing Machinery, New York (2017)
31. Pornprasit, C., Tantithamthavorn, C.K.: Jitline: a simpler, better, faster, finer-grained just-in-time defect prediction. In: 2021 IEEE/ACM 18th International Conference on Mining Software Repositories (MSR), pp. 369–379 (2021)
32. Ribeiro, M.T., Singh, S., Guestrin, C.: "Why should i trust you?": explaining the predictions of any classifier. In: Proceedings of the 22nd ACM SIGKDD International Conference on Knowledge Discovery and Data Mining, KDD 2016, pp. 1135–1144. Association for Computing Machinery, New York (2016)
33. Sarkar, A., Guo, J., Siegmund, N., Apel, S., Czarnecki, K.: Cost-efficient sampling for performance prediction of configurable systems (t). In: 2015 30th IEEE/ACM International Conference on Automated Software Engineering (ASE), pp. 342–352 (2015)
34. Shu, Y., Sui, Y., Zhang, H., Xu, G.: Perf-AL: performance prediction for configurable software through adversarial learning. In: Proceedings of the 14th ACM/IEEE International Symposium on Empirical Software Engineering and Measurement (ESEM), ESEM 2020. Association for Computing Machinery, New York (2020)
35. Siegmund, N., Grebhahn, A., Apel, S., Kästner, C.: Performance-influence models for highly configurable systems. In: Proceedings of the 2015 10th Joint Meeting on Foundations of Software Engineering, ESEC/FSE 2015, pp. 284–294. Association for Computing Machinery, New York (2015)
36. Slabý, J., Strejček, J., Trtík, M.: Checking properties described by state machines: on synergy of instrumentation, slicing, and symbolic execution. In: Stoelinga, M., Pinger, R. (eds.) FMICS 2012. LNCS, vol. 7437, pp. 207–221. Springer, Heidelberg (2012). https://doi.org/10.1007/978-3-642-32469-7_14
37. Slaby, J., Strejček, J., Trtík, M.: Symbiotic: synergy of instrumentation, slicing, and symbolic execution. In: Piterman, N., Smolka, S.A. (eds.) TACAS 2013. LNCS, vol. 7795, pp. 630–632. Springer, Heidelberg (2013). https://doi.org/10.1007/978-3-642-36742-7_50
38. Smaragdakis, Y., Bravenboer, M., Lhoták, O.: Pick your contexts well: understanding object-sensitivity. In: Proceedings of the 38th Annual ACM SIGPLAN-SIGACT Symposium on Principles of Programming Languages, POPL 2011, pp. 17–30. Association for Computing Machinery, New York (2011)
39. Tantithamthavorn, C., Hassan, A.E., Matsumoto, K.: The impact of class rebalancing techniques on the performance and interpretation of defect prediction models. IEEE Trans. Softw. Eng. **46**(11), 1200–1219 (2020)
40. Wang, H., Gupta, G.: FOLD-SE: an efficient rule-based machine learning algorithm with scalable explainability. In: Gebser, M., Sergey, I. (eds.) PADL 2024. LNCS, vol. 14512, pp. 37–53. Springer, Cham (2024). https://doi.org/10.1007/978-3-031-52038-9_3

41. Wei, S., Mardziel, P., Ruef, A., Foster, J.S., Hicks, M.: Evaluating design tradeoffs in numeric static analysis for java. In: Ahmed, A. (ed.) ESOP 2018. LNCS, vol. 10801, pp. 653–682. Springer, Cham (2018). https://doi.org/10.1007/978-3-319-89884-1_23
42. Xu, L., Hutter, F., Hoos, H.H., Leyton-Brown, K.: SATzilla: portfolio-based algorithm selection for SAT. J. Artif. Int. Res. **32**(1), 565–606 (2008)
43. Zhang, X., et al.: An efficient transfer learning based configuration adviser for database tuning. Proc. VLDB Endow. **17**(3), 539–552 (2023)
44. Zheng, W., Shen, T., Chen, X., Deng, P.: Interpretability application of the just-in-time software defect prediction model. J. Syst. Softw. **188**(C) (2022)

A One-Pass CPS Transform
with Simulation on the Nose

Pascal Y. Lasnier[1]([✉]) [iD], Jeremy Yallop[1] [iD], and Magnus O. Myreen[2,3] [iD]

[1] University of Cambridge, Cambridge, UK
pyl37@cantab.ac.uk
[2] Chalmers University of Technology, Gothenburg, Sweden
[3] University of Gothenburg, Gothenburg, Sweden

Abstract. Danvy & Nielsen's one-pass CPS transform has a straightforward definition, but clashes between the names of variables it introduces make it difficult to mechanically prove correct. Existing mechanical proofs either side-step the issue by using nameless representations, or rely on tedious α-equivalence relations between target terms. This paper presents a new formulation of the transform using evaluation contexts that allows deterministic introduction of fresh names, eliminating the need to work up to α-equivalence. We use our formulation to present a new and straightforward simulation proof of the correctness of the one-pass CPS transform, which we have mechanised in the HOL4 theorem prover.

1 Introduction

Continuation-passing style (CPS) transforms have many useful properties: they make evaluation order explicit, turn all calls into tail calls, name intermediate computations, and support simulation of non-standard control flow. These properties make the CPS transform a key technique in many applications, from defining control operator semantics [7] to intermediate representation in functional languages compilers [12] and languages with first-class continuations [2,13,22].

The classic CPS transform developed by Plotkin [18] introduces many *administrative redexes*, i.e. function applications which are trivial to evaluate and do not correspond to source program reductions. For example, the program fragment $x_1\,x_2\,(x_3\,x_4\,x_5)$ CPS-transforms into the following:

$$\lambda k.\,(\lambda k.(\lambda k.k\,x_1)\,(\lambda m.(\lambda k.k\,x_2)\,(\lambda n.m\,n\,k)))$$
$$(\lambda m.\,(\lambda k.\,(\lambda k.(\lambda k.k\,x_3)\,(\lambda m.(\lambda k.k\,x_4)\,(\lambda n.m\,n\,k)))$$
$$(\lambda m.(\lambda k.k\,x_5)\,(\lambda n.m\,n\,k)))$$
$$(\lambda n.m\,n\,k))$$

Reducing applications of the form $(\lambda k.k\,x)(\lambda y.e)$, to $[x/y]e$ (i.e. e with x substituted for y) straightforwardly produces the following reduced term:

$$\lambda k.(\lambda k.x_1\,x_2\,k)\,(\lambda m.(\lambda k.(\lambda k.x_3\,x_4\,k)\,(\lambda m.m\,x_5\,k))\,(\lambda n.m\,n\,k))$$

N. Amin and J. Arias (Eds.): PADL 2026, LNCS 16401, pp. 21–38, 2026.
https://doi.org/10.1007/978-3-032-15981-6_2

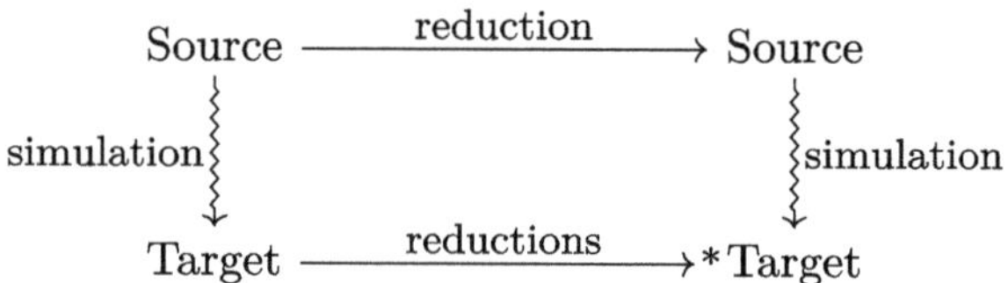

Fig. 1. Simulation as a commutative diagram.

There are three further administrative redexes that can be eliminated in this program. However, reducing these redexes requires renaming one of the m variables to avoid clashes. After reduction and renaming, the result is as follows:

$$\lambda k.x_1\, x_2\, (\lambda m.x_3\, x_4\, (\lambda m'.m'\, x_5\, (\lambda n.m\, n\, k)))$$

There are several optimised CPS transforms [4,9,21] that eliminate these administrative redexes and produce CPS programs such as the final version above. The state-of-the-art for the call-by-value lambda calculus is the first-order one-pass CPS transform by Danvy & Nielsen [9].

Proof of correctness of the CPS transform, which is typically formulated as a simulation proof, involves establishing a relation between source programs and CPS programs which the CPS transform satisfies, and proving that the relation is closed under source and target reductions. Figure 1 portrays this statement as a commutative diagram. Simulation is simple to prove for the classic CPS transform, but the name clashes seen in the example above introduce challenges in the proofs for the optimised variants.

In their hand-written correctness proof, Danvy & Nielsen simply assert that introduced variables are unique [9]. In contrast, in a typical mechanised proof, binders require explicit reasoning. A naive fresh binder naming scheme will result in CPS programs that do not strictly reduce in the simulation diagram, but instead reduce to α-equivalent programs [15], complicating the simulation proof with a new notion of equivalence.

Paraskevopoulou & Grover [16] summarise the accumulated literature on the variable binder issue for mechanised proofs of the optimised CPS transform. Proofs which represent variable binders with explicit names require establishing some notion of equivalence over programs in CPS, with Minamide & Okuma [15] using an α-equivalence relation, and Paraskevopoulou & Grover [16] developing a more general logical relation over CPS terms. These approaches complicate verified implementation of the CPS transform, since constructing an equivalence relation and proving it for a target language involves significant additional verification work, especially if the target language is complex. Other developments use nameless variable binding system such as de Bruijn indices [10,19] or higher-order abstract syntax [3,23].

This paper contributes a new approach to the problem of name generation in an optimised CPS transform, with a mechanised simulation proof that both uses named variable binders *and* completes the simulation diagram without requiring an additional notion of equivalence. Our approach to the problem consists of three components:

Evaluation-context-based optimised CPS transform. We refactor Danvy & Nielsen's optimised CPS transform [9] using evaluation contexts, following Sabry & Felleisen's non-compositional optimised transform [21], but preserving compositionality. Reframing the transform in this way highlights a critical feature of variable name introduction: name clashes are *local to the lexical scope* of source language terms. This observation is an instance of a general principle that freshness should not be treated as a global property, but determined relative to some local context [17]. We apply the principle to the challenge at hand, using it to design a name generation strategy that is deterministically dependent *only* on the evaluation context of the local scope.

Modified CEK-machine with lexical scopes. Using the insight that variable binder names may be allocated locally to the lexical scope of the source language, we modify the CEK-machine small-step semantic definition of the call-by-value lambda calculus by rephrasing evaluation contexts as a nested sequence of scopes, where each scope has a distinct, *local* environment and evaluation context. At the top level of the semantic state, the new abstract machine operates on a sequence of scopes, with the innermost evaluation context containing the control string in its hole.

Simulation. We construct a simulation relation between semantic states of the modified CEK-machine for the call-by-value lambda calculus to CPS terms through our evaluation-context-based optimised CPS transform, using the evaluation context of the local scope from the semantic state directly in the transform. Because variable binder names are deterministic from the local lexical scope, the exact variable name can be deduced directly from the simulation relation, and simulation can be easily proven without requiring a notion of equivalence.

We have mechanised our proof in the HOL4 theorem prover, and include the development as supplementary material.

2   Call-by-Value Lambda Calculus CEK-Machine

$$
\begin{aligned}
e &::= t \mid s &&\in \text{Exp} \\
t &::= x \mid \lambda x.e &&\in \text{Triv} \\
s &::= e_1\, e_2 &&\in \text{Comp} \\
x & &&\in \text{Ide}
\end{aligned}
$$

Fig. 2. Lambda calculus grammar

We first present the lambda calculus which we use in our mechanised proof (Fig. 2). Terms e are either trivial terms t, which include variables x and abstractions $\lambda x.e$, or serious terms s, which are applications $e_1\, e_2$.

$$\text{Cont}[\text{Ctrl}] \longrightarrow \text{Cont}[\text{Ctrl}]$$

$$v ::= \Lambda x.\{\rho\}e \qquad \in \text{Val}$$
$$\rho : \text{Ide} \rightharpoonup \text{Val}$$

$$E ::= [] \mid E\,\{\rho\}e \mid v\,E \qquad \in \text{Cont}$$
$$c ::= \{\rho\}e \mid v \qquad \in \text{Ctrl}$$

$$E[\{\rho\}x] \longrightarrow E[\rho(x)]$$
$$E[\{\rho\}\lambda x.e] \longrightarrow E[\Lambda x.\{\rho\}e]$$
$$E[\{\rho\}e_1\,e_2] \longrightarrow E[[\{\rho\}e_1]\,\{\rho\}e_2]$$

$$E[[v]\,\{\rho\}e] \longrightarrow E[v\,[\{\rho\}e]]$$
$$E[(\Lambda x.\{\rho\}e)\,[v]] \longrightarrow E[\{\rho[x \mapsto v]\}e]$$

Fig. 3. CEK-machine

Figure 3 shows the call-by-value semantics for the calculus as a small-step CEK-machine semantics. The CEK-machine operates on control strings which may be either terms with an attached environment, which we denote similarly to substitution $\{\rho\}e$, or values v, which may only be closures which capture an environment $\Lambda x.\{\rho\}e$. Environments ρ simply map variables to values.

The semantic state of the CEK-machine includes an evaluation context E, which is a nested sequence of stack frames. There are two types of stack frame: fn frames $E\,\{\rho\}e$ enclose an unevaluated function term in an application, where the evaluation context holds the argument term and associated environment $\{\rho\}e$, and arg frames $v\,E$ enclose an unevaluated argument term, where the evaluation context holds the previously evaluated function value v.

The complete definition of the CEK-machine is a relation between semantic states consisting of an evaluation context E with its hole filled by a control string c. We denote the type of a filled evaluation context by figuratively filling the hole of the Cont type, i.e. the type $\text{Cont}[\text{Ctrl}]$ is that of evaluation contexts with their holes filled by control strings $E[c]$.

3   Revisiting the Optimised CPS Transform

3.1   Classic Transform

Figure 4 shows Plotkin's classic CPS transform [18]. To distinguish the source and target domains, we write target terms in **bold**. The proof of Plotkin's classic simulation theorem is simple and well-understood, and has been mechanised by Minamide & Okuma [15] and Dargaye & Leroy [10].

A simulation proof technique which has proven quite effective is to relate CEK-machine source semantic states to CPS terms in the target domain. This relation is not arbitrary, but rather arises from the nature of small-step semantics as a *defunctionalisation* of the continuation-passing style [1,5,6,8,20], and it underscores the nature of CPS as a *simulation* of control structures (i.e. evaluation contexts in a small-step semantics) by terms in a target domain. This relation generalises to larger source languages: Lasnier, Yallop, & Myreen [14] use the relation to prove simulation for Scheme, including first-class continuations.

$$[\![x]\!] = \lambda k.k\,x$$
$$[\![\lambda x.e]\!] = \lambda k.k\,(\lambda x.[\![e]\!])$$
$$[\![e_1\,e_2]\!] = \lambda k.[\![e_1]\!]\,(\lambda m.[\![e_2]\!]\,(\lambda n.m\,n\,k))$$

Fig. 4. Plotkin's classic CPS transform.

3.2 One-Pass Transform

Figure 5 shows Danvy & Nielsen's first-order, compositional, one-pass formulation of the optimised CPS transform [9], with an explicit naming scheme we motivate in the following sections. The subscript K in the expression transform $\mathscr{E}$ corresponds to the top-level continuation of a given scope: it may be only either the identity continuation $\mathbf{I}$ or a continuation variable k. In contrast, in the serious transform $\mathscr{S}$, the continuation argument K may be an arbitrary continuation. The complete transform of a program p is $\mathscr{E}_{\mathbf{I}}[\![p]\!]$.

$$\mathscr{E}_{\mathbf{I}}[\![t]\!] = \mathscr{T}[\![t]\!]$$
$$\mathscr{E}_{k}[\![t]\!] = k\,\mathscr{T}[\![t]\!] \qquad \mathscr{T}[\![x]\!] = x$$
$$\mathscr{E}_{K}[\![s]\!] = \mathscr{S}[\![s]\!]_0\,K \qquad \mathscr{T}[\![\lambda x.e]\!] = \lambda x k.\mathscr{E}_{k}[\![e]\!]$$

$$\mathscr{S}[\![t_1\,t_2]\!]_i\,K = \mathscr{T}[\![t_1]\!]\,\mathscr{T}[\![t_2]\!]\,K$$
$$\mathscr{S}[\![t_1\,s_2]\!]_i\,K = \mathscr{S}[\![s_2]\!]_i\,(\lambda n.\mathscr{T}[\![t_1]\!]\,n\,K)$$
$$\mathscr{S}[\![s_1\,t_2]\!]_i\,K = \mathscr{S}[\![s_1]\!]_i\,(\lambda m_i.m_i\,\mathscr{T}[\![t_2]\!]\,K)$$
$$\mathscr{S}[\![s_1\,s_2]\!]_i\,K = \mathscr{S}[\![s_1]\!]_i\,(\lambda m_i.\mathscr{S}[\![s_2]\!]_{i+1}\,(\lambda n.m_i\,n\,K))$$

Fig. 5. Danvy & Nielsen's one-pass CPS transform

3.3 Clash of Variable Names and α-Equivalence

Minamide & Okuma [15] observe that it is not possible to implement Danvy & Nielsen's optimised transform without variable renaming, since it may introduce multiple conflicting instances of the variable m. They highlight this property with the example transform for $x_1\,x_2\,(x_3\,x_4\,x_5)$, in which one of the m variables must be renamed:

$$x_1\,x_2\,(\lambda m.x_3\,x_4\,(\lambda m'.m'\,x_5\,(\lambda n.m\,n\,k)))$$

Implementations of the optimised transform must consequently generate fresh variable names. Minamide & Okuma [15] generate names via a counter i attached to the transform similarly to Fig. 5, and Paraskevopoulou & Grover [16] allocate globally fresh names using a state monad. However, Danvy & Nielsen's simulation proof is complicated by these fresh variable name generation schemes, which only fit the simulation diagram up to α-equivalence. Consider Danvy & Nielsen's simulation theorem, which states that if a serious source term reduces to a new term, the CPS transform of the serious term must also reduce to the CPS transform of the new term. Using our definition from Fig. 5 and splitting cases for either a trivial or serious reduced source term, the theorem is formally stated as follows:

$$s \longrightarrow t \implies \mathscr{S}[\![s]\!]_i \, K \longrightarrow^+ K \, \mathscr{T}[\![t]\!]$$
$$s \longrightarrow s' \implies \mathscr{S}[\![s]\!]_i \, K \longrightarrow^+ \mathscr{S}[\![s']\!]_i \, K$$

Decomposing s into an evaluation context and a redex $E[t_1 \, t_2]$, the proof [9] follows by induction over E. This proof deals with the lambda calculus using term rewriting with substitutions rather than an abstract machine with an environment, so the evaluation context does not contain environments ρ.

Let us consider the case for an fn stack frame $E \, e$ where the argument expression is also a serious term, so that our source term may be written as $s_1 \, s_2$. The CPS transform for this term is $\mathscr{S}[\![s_1]\!]_i \, (\lambda m_i. \, \mathscr{S}[\![s_2]\!]_{i+1}(\lambda n. \, m_i \, n \, K))$.

If s_1 reduces to a trivial term $s_1 \longrightarrow t$, we may apply our induction hypothesis for the reduction to a trivial term, so our CPS term will reduce to $(\lambda m_i. \, \mathscr{S}[\![s_2]\!]_{i+1}(\lambda n. \, m_i \, n \, K)) \, \mathscr{T}[\![t]\!]$, then further to $\mathscr{S}[\![s_2]\!]_{i+1}(\lambda n. \, \mathscr{T}[\![t]\!] \, n \, K)$. This CPS term, though indeed the CPS transform of the reduced source term $t \, s_2$, does not satisfy the simulation theorem, because the fresh variable name counter i has been incremented.

It would be incorrect to increment the counter i in the starting simulation theorem as a way to compensate for this mismatch, because applying the induction hypothesis to the $s_1 \, s_2$ case where s_1 reduces to another serious term $s_1 \longrightarrow s_1'$ results in the reduced CPS term $\mathscr{S}[\![s_1']\!]_{i+1} \, (\lambda m_i. \, \mathscr{S}[\![s_2]\!]_{i+1}(\lambda n. \, m_i \, n \, K))$, which is strictly not the CPS transform of $s_1' \, s_2$ and breaks simulation.

It is therefore required, when proving simulation with explicit binder names, to establish α-equivalence over the CPS transform for incrementing fresh variable counters $\mathscr{S}[\![s]\!]_i =_\alpha \mathscr{S}[\![s]\!]_{i+1}$ as described by Minamide & Okuma [15].

3.4 Optimised CPS Transform as Static Reduction

The core issue with existing implementations of the optimised transform is that fresh variable names of an arbitrary program fragment in simulation cannot be determined by the simulation relation from the fragment alone, instead depending on a floating variable counter i or some global fresh variable allocator. In order to eliminate the need for an equivalence relation, we seek a transform with a variable name generation method which is deterministic, whilst still avoiding clashes.

With this aim in mind, we reformulate the optimised transform to more closely correspond to the source semantics, with the goal of facilitating a suitable simulation relation. Our starting point is the evaluation-context-based optimised transform presented by Sabry & Felleisen [21]. Drawing on the observation that the optimised transform reduces administrative redexes at the point of the transform, we construct the optimised transform as a kind of partial evaluator based on evaluation contexts like the CEK-machine source semantics, which is given in Fig. 6. Whereas evaluation contexts in the source semantics carry values v for arg frames, in the transform evaluation contexts carry trivial terms t in the target domain. We highlight this distinction by denoting evaluation contexts in the transform with a star $E^\star$.

$$\mathscr{E}_{\boldsymbol{K}}[\![E^\star[x]]\!] = \mathscr{C}_{\boldsymbol{K}}[\![E^\star]\!]\,\boldsymbol{x}$$

$$\mathscr{E}_{\boldsymbol{K}}[\![E^\star[\lambda x.e]]\!] = \mathscr{C}_{\boldsymbol{K}}[\![E^\star]\!]\,\boldsymbol{\lambda x k}.\mathscr{E}_{\boldsymbol{k}}[\![e]\!]$$

$$\mathscr{E}_{\boldsymbol{K}}[\![E^\star[e_1\,e_2]]\!] = \mathscr{E}_{\boldsymbol{K}}[\![E^\star[[e_1]\,e_2]]\!]$$

$$\mathscr{C}_{\mathbf{I}}[\![[]]\!]\,\boldsymbol{t} = \boldsymbol{t}$$

$$\mathscr{C}_{\boldsymbol{k}}[\![[]]\!]\,\boldsymbol{t} = \boldsymbol{k}\,\boldsymbol{t} \qquad\qquad \mathscr{K}_{\boldsymbol{K}}[\![[]]\!] = \boldsymbol{K}$$

$$\mathscr{C}_{\boldsymbol{K}}[\![E^\star[[]\,e]]\!]\,\boldsymbol{t} = \mathscr{E}_{\boldsymbol{K}}[\![E^\star[\boldsymbol{t}\,[e]]]\!] \qquad \mathscr{K}_{\boldsymbol{K}}[\![E^\star[[]\,e]]\!] = \lambda\boldsymbol{m_i}.\mathscr{E}_{\boldsymbol{K}}[\![E^\star[\boldsymbol{m_i}\,[e]]]\!] \quad i = \mathsf{fresh}\ E^\star$$

$$\mathscr{C}_{\boldsymbol{K}}[\![E^\star[t_1\,[]]]\!]\,\boldsymbol{t_2} = \boldsymbol{t_1}\,\boldsymbol{t_2}\,\mathscr{K}_{\boldsymbol{K}}[\![E^\star]\!] \qquad \mathscr{K}_{\boldsymbol{K}}[\![E^\star[\boldsymbol{t}\,[]]]\!] = \lambda\boldsymbol{n}.\boldsymbol{t}\,\boldsymbol{n}\,\mathscr{K}_{\boldsymbol{K}}[\![E^\star]\!]$$

Fig. 6. Our evaluation-context-based optimised CPS transform

In viewing the optimised CPS transform as partial evaluation, we conceptually split continuation applications into static and dynamic variants. In a static application $\mathscr{C}_{\boldsymbol{K}}[\![E^\star]\!]\,\boldsymbol{t}$, the argument is a trivial term in the target domain $\boldsymbol{t}$ rather than a value, and is directly substituted into the continuation bodies at the point of the transform. In a dynamic application $\boldsymbol{k}\,\boldsymbol{t}$, $\boldsymbol{k}$ maps to a closure evaluated from $\mathscr{K}_{\boldsymbol{K}}[\![E^\star]\!]$. The definitions of both these continuation transforms derive from the continuation steps of the CEK-machine from Fig. 3, i.e. steps from a value control string with a particular evaluation context.

The evaluation contexts used to form these static and dynamic continuations are grown from the shape of the program by the expression transform $\mathscr{E}$, which operates on an evaluation context filled with an expression, and whose definition is derived from the expression steps of the CEK-machine from Fig. 3.

One key distinction between our $\mathscr{E}$ transform and the transform by Sabry & Felleisen [21] is that $\mathscr{E}$ explicitly recurses into the evaluation context $E^\star$ of an expression, while Sabry & Felleisen's transform does not. Sabry & Felleisen instead implicitly arrive at an evaluation context via unique decomposition [24], the same notion relating CEK-machines and term-rewriting systems [11], and in effect squash our $\mathscr{E}$ and $\mathscr{C}$ transforms into a single $\mathscr{C}$ transform. A second distinction is that $\mathscr{E}$ is compositional, preserving the adjustments Danvy & Nielsen [9] made to the transform.

Benefits of the New Transform. As Sect. 5 shows, constructing the transform using evaluation contexts benefits the simulation proof by allowing us to directly relate the source language semantic evaluation state, including its evaluation context, to a CPS-transformed expression in the target language. We believe that this same construction can be applied to more complex languages with small-step semantics that use evaluation contexts, such as Scheme.

Constructing the transform as we have done also more clearly highlights the name clash issue encountered by Minamide & Okuma [15]. Note the continuation closure definition for an fn continuation $\mathscr{K}_K[\![E^\star[\![]\,e]\!]\!]$; this closure introduces a variable $\boldsymbol{m}$ containing the resultant value of application function term to fill the hole in the evaluation context $E^\star[\![]\,e]$. However, this variable is not immediately dispatched, and is instead stashed into the new evaluation context from which the next term e is transformed. Consequently, there can be multiple variables $\boldsymbol{m}$ present in the evaluation context; for example the transform of the $x_1\,x_2\,(x_3\,x_4\,x_5)$ expands as follows:

$$
\begin{aligned}
\mathscr{E}_k[\![x_1\,x_2\,(x_3\,x_4\,x_5)]\!] &= \boldsymbol{x_1}\,\boldsymbol{x_2}\,(\boldsymbol{\lambda m}.\mathscr{E}_k[\![\boldsymbol{m}\,[x_3\,x_4\,x_5]]\!]) \\
&= \boldsymbol{x_1}\,\boldsymbol{x_2}\,(\boldsymbol{\lambda m}.\boldsymbol{x_3}\,\boldsymbol{x_4}\,(\boldsymbol{\lambda m}.\mathscr{E}_k[\![\boldsymbol{m}\,[\boldsymbol{m}\,[x_5]]]\!]))
\end{aligned}
$$

The result is multiple $\boldsymbol{m}$ variables present in the same evaluation context, which would clash in the result of the transform if not appropriately renamed.

As Minamide & Okuma state, this clash is not clear from the definition of the optimised CPS transform presented by Danvy & Nielsen; our transform makes it clear by how the introduced variables interact with continuations. This clarity is important, as it enables us to thoughtfully design fresh variable name generation which simplifies the simulation proof.

The transform of Fig. 6 introduces new variables in three places. The first, the lambda abstraction $\lambda x.e$ case for $\mathscr{E}$, introduces $\boldsymbol{k}$, which never clashes because the transform only ever considers at most one $\boldsymbol{k}$ at a time, in the subscript of the transform functions. The second, the arg continuation $E^\star[\boldsymbol{t}\,[]]$ case for $\mathscr{K}$, introduces $\boldsymbol{n}$, which never clashes because it is immediately dispatched after its introduction, rather than stashed in the transform parameters for later use. The third, the fn continuation $E^\star[\![]\,e]$ case for $\mathscr{K}$, introduces $\boldsymbol{m}$, which is stashed in the evaluation context $E^\star[\boldsymbol{m}\,[]]$ passed to the next $\mathscr{E}$ transform, and hence may only clash with other $\boldsymbol{m}$ variables present in that evaluation context. What is important is that, when transforming a lambda abstraction $\lambda x.e$, we transform its body without the surrounding evaluation context of the abstraction. Intuitively, this means that $\boldsymbol{m}$ variables may only clash within a particular lexical scope. Consequently, variable naming need only depend on the evaluation context of the current scope, and the names of these introduced variables may also be determined uniquely from a program fragment in simulation. We will use this fact to build a simulation relation that can determine the name of introduced variables without depending on an external variable counter or allocator.

The function fresh on the evaluation context $E^\star$ allocates names that are fresh for the context, the simplest implementation being to count the number of existing $\boldsymbol{m}$ variables in the evaluation context $E^\star$. Including fresh variable naming, the transform of $x_1\,x_2\,(x_3\,x_4\,x_5)$ becomes:

$$
\boldsymbol{x_1}\,\boldsymbol{x_2}\,(\boldsymbol{\lambda m_0}.\boldsymbol{x_3}\,\boldsymbol{x_4}\,(\boldsymbol{\lambda m_1}.\boldsymbol{m_1}\,\boldsymbol{x_5}\,(\boldsymbol{\lambda n}.\boldsymbol{m_0}\,\boldsymbol{n}\,\boldsymbol{k})))
$$

With this particular implementation of fresh, our transform (Fig. 6) is the same as Danvy & Nielsen's with an equivalent naming scheme (Fig. 5), as seen by considering the expression transform on an expression in an empty evaluation context $\mathscr{E}_{K}[\![e]\!]$. We prove this property by induction over terms through the mutually recursive definitions of Danvy & Nielsen's transform functions $\mathscr{E}$ and $\mathscr{S}$, with an additional induction lemma establishing that our transform for an application expression with an arbitrary evaluation context $E^\star$ is the same as Danvy & Nielsen's serious term $\mathscr{S}$ transform with a continuation generated by our $\mathscr{K}$ transform, and an appropriate name counter index:

$$\mathscr{E}_{K}[\![E^\star[e_1\,e_2]]\!] = \mathscr{S}[\![e_1\,e_2]\!]_i\,\mathscr{K}_{K}[\![E^\star]\!] \quad i = \mathsf{fresh}\ E^\star$$

We have mechanised this proof alongside our simulation proof.

4   Adjusting the Semantics

Having analysed the nature of introduced variable name clashes in the optimised transform, we now turn our attention back to the semantics which inspired the analysis. In order to enable a suitable simulation relation from the side of the source semantics, we divide the evaluation contexts of the source semantics abstract machine into *scopes*, where environments are attached to particular scopes rather than stack frames in an evaluation context.

This division reflects the structure of evaluation contexts in the optimised CPS transform, where each transform function operates on a scoped evaluation context $E^\star$ and an underlying continuation K (which may be either the identity continuation I or a continuation variable k). New scopes are introduced into CPS by the transform for a lambda abstraction $\mathscr{E}_{K}[\![E^\star[\lambda x.e]]\!] = \mathscr{C}_{K}[\![E^\star]\!]\,\lambda x k.\mathscr{E}_{k}[\![e]\!]$, where the expression transform is applied to the lambda body e with an empty evaluation context, but with an underlying continuation captured by variable k which will eventually map to some continuation closure evaluated from $\mathscr{K}$.

We hence may formulate evaluation contexts in the source semantics as a nested sequence of scopes, where each scope has a distinct environment ρ and evaluation context $E^\star$. At the top level of the semantic state, the abstract machine operates on a sequence of scopes, with the innermost evaluation context containing the control string in its hole $O(\{\rho\}E^\star[c^\star])$. We formalise this notion of scopes and define the adjusted abstract machine semantics in Fig. 7. Each step in the semantics corresponds to a step in the original CEK-machine with the scopes flattened into one evaluation context, except for CBV-CONT-ID which is a CEK-machine no-op.

We equip our new, environment-less evaluation contexts $E^\star$ with a parameter α, which corresponds to the class of terms that may reside in an arg stack frame $a\,E^\star$, i.e. α ranges over the term sets Val, Exp, etc. This parameterised evaluation context allows us to share the same evaluation context construction with the evaluation-context-based optimised transform, by instantiating it with **Triv**, the set of trivial terms in the target domain, rather than Val, the set of values used in the new source semantics. We may hence preserve our optimised transform

$$E_\alpha^\star ::= []_\alpha \mid E_\alpha^\star\, e \mid a\, E_\alpha^\star \qquad \in \mathrm{Cont}_\alpha^\star, a \in \alpha$$
$$O \ ::= () \mid \{\rho\} E_{\mathrm{Val}}^\star\, O \qquad \in \mathrm{Scope}$$

$$p \ ::= \{\rho\} E_{\mathrm{Val}}^\star \qquad\qquad \in \mathrm{EnvCont}$$
$$c^\star ::= e \mid v \qquad\qquad\qquad \in \mathrm{Ctrl}^\star$$

$$\mathrm{Scope}(\mathrm{EnvCont}[\mathrm{Ctrl}^\star]) \longrightarrow^\star \mathrm{Scope}(\mathrm{EnvCont}[\mathrm{Ctrl}^\star])$$

$$O(\{\rho\}E^\star[x]) \longrightarrow^\star O(\{\rho\}E^\star[\rho(x)]) \qquad\qquad \text{(CBV-EXP-VAR)}$$
$$O(\{\rho\}E^\star[\lambda x.e]) \longrightarrow^\star O(\{\rho\}E^\star[\Lambda x.\{\rho\}e]) \qquad\qquad \text{(CBV-EXP-LAM)}$$
$$O(\{\rho\}E^\star[e_1\, e_2]) \longrightarrow^\star O(\{\rho\}E^\star[[e_1]\, e_2]) \qquad\qquad \text{(CBV-EXP-APP)}$$

$$O(\{\rho\}E^\star[[v]\, e]) \longrightarrow^\star O(\{\rho\}E^\star[v\,[e]]) \qquad\qquad \text{(CBV-CONT-FN)}$$
$$O(\{\rho\}E^\star[\Lambda x.\{\rho'\}e\,[v]]) \longrightarrow^\star O(\{\rho\}E^\star(\{\rho'[x \mapsto v]\}[e])) \qquad \text{(CBV-CONT-ARG)}$$

$$O(\{\rho'\}E^\star(\{\rho\}[v])) \longrightarrow^\star O(\{\rho'\}E^\star[v]) \qquad\qquad \text{(CBV-CONT-ID)}$$

Fig. 7. Our adjusted semantics, defined on sequences of scopes

definition from Fig. 6 and assign the transform functions types based on Cont, with types representing terms from the target domain in **bold** to differentiate from source terms:

$$\mathscr{E}_K : \mathrm{Cont}_{\mathbf{Triv}}^\star[\mathrm{Exp}] \quad \to \mathbf{Exp}$$
$$\mathscr{C}_K : \mathrm{Cont}_{\mathbf{Triv}}^\star \times \mathbf{Triv} \to \mathbf{Exp}$$
$$\mathscr{K}_K : \mathrm{Cont}_{\mathbf{Triv}}^\star \qquad\quad \to \mathbf{Triv}$$

We will omit α for the evaluation context $E^\star$ when it is clear from the context.

5   Simulation Relation

Using our adjusted semantics, we construct a simulation relation between semantic abstract machine states and CPS terms built from the optimised transform. The relation is defined inductively over components of the semantic state.

Values and Trivial Terms. The aspect of the optimised transform that enables it to eliminate administrative redexes is that it directly substitutes trivial terms into continuation bodies, which corresponds to statically applying a continuation to a trivial term at the point of transform through $\mathscr{C}_K[\![E]\!]\, t$. However, this static substitution amounts to deferring of evaluation of these trivial terms until they are used in a serious computation, whereas the corresponding reductions in the source semantics involve the value evaluated from these terms. We must therefore relate values from the source semantics to corresponding trivial terms in CPS to prove simulation.

$$\frac{\rho \sim \rho}{\Lambda x.\{\rho\}e \sim \boldsymbol{\Lambda x.}\{\rho\}\lambda k.\mathscr{E}_{\boldsymbol{k}}[\![e]\!]} \text{ CPS-VAL} \qquad \frac{\forall x \in \mathrm{dom}(\rho).\rho(x) \sim \boldsymbol{\rho(x)}}{\rho \sim \boldsymbol{\rho}} \text{ CPS-ENV}$$

$$\frac{v \sim \boldsymbol{\rho(x)}}{v \rightsquigarrow \{\rho\}\boldsymbol{x}} \text{ SIM-TRIV-VAR} \qquad \frac{\rho \sim \boldsymbol{\rho}}{\Lambda x.\{\rho\}e \rightsquigarrow \{\rho\}\boldsymbol{\lambda x k.}\mathscr{E}_{\boldsymbol{k}}[\![e]\!]} \text{ SIM-TRIV-LAM}$$

Fig. 8. Value relations.

Figure 8 defines our simulation relations for values from the source semantics. The $\sim$ relation, which we call *CPS equivalence*, relates equivalent semantic constructs between the source and target semantics. The CPS-VAL rule relates closures to CPS closures, ensuring that their respective captured environments are also related. The corresponding environment relation rule CPS-ENV requires all values mapped to by variables in the source semantics to be related to an equivalently mapped value in the target semantics.

The simulation relation $\rightsquigarrow$, which may be read as 'simulated by', relates source semantics constructs to the target CPS terms that simulate those constructs. For values, the simulation relation is the relation described above between source semantic values and target semantic trivial terms. Whereas the CPS equivalence relation $\sim$ on values is primarily used to ensure variables appropriately map to CPS values that have already been evaluated and bound, the simulation relation $\rightsquigarrow$ is used for values in the control string. Depending on how the value was introduced, the relevant trivial term is either a variable by SIM-TRIV-VAR, or a literal lambda abstraction by SIM-TRIV-LAM. The simulation relation $\rightsquigarrow$ includes the target semantics environment, in order to establish the conditions for the simulating terms to evaluate to the correct values. It is trivial to prove the lemma that these trivial terms evaluate under the included environment to values satisfying the CPS equivalence relation:

Lemma 1 (Simulated values evaluate to CPS-equivalent values).

$$\vdash \forall v \boldsymbol{\rho t v} . v \rightsquigarrow \{\rho\}\boldsymbol{t} \implies (\{\rho\}\boldsymbol{t} \longrightarrow \boldsymbol{v} \wedge v \sim \boldsymbol{v})$$

Evaluation Contexts. Our eventual simulation relation on semantic states is built on the transform functions $\mathscr{E}$, $\mathscr{C}$, and $\mathscr{K}$ from Fig. 6, and these functions operate on evaluation contexts parameterised by trivial terms in CPS $E^{\star}_{\mathbf{Triv}}$. We must therefore define a relation between the value-parameterised evaluation contexts of the source semantics $E^{\star}_{\mathrm{Val}}$ and the trivial CPS term-parameterised evaluation contexts used by the transform (Fig. 9).

The empty context and fn stack frames $E^{\star}[[]\, e]$ trivially relate to their counterparts, as they do not contain any values. For arg stack frames $E^{\star}[v\,[]]$, there are two possibilities for the stashed trivial term. The SIM-CONT-ARG-TRIV rule captures the case that the value was evaluated from a trivial term, and the resultant arg context $E^{\star}[v\,[]]$ arises from a static application of a fn continuation to a trivial term $\mathscr{C}_{\boldsymbol{K}}[\![E^{\star}[[]\, e]]\!]\,\boldsymbol{t}$.

The SIM-CONT-ARG-COMP rule instead captures the case that the value resulted from a computation, i.e. an application. In this case, it is a dynamic

$$\frac{}{[]_{\mathrm{Val}} \rightsquigarrow \{\rho\}[]_{\mathrm{Triv}}} \text{ SIM-CONT-ID} \qquad \frac{E^\star_{\mathrm{Val}} \rightsquigarrow \{\rho\} E^\star_{\mathrm{Triv}}}{E^\star_{\mathrm{Val}}[[]\,e] \rightsquigarrow \{\rho\} E^\star_{\mathrm{Triv}}[[]\,e]} \text{ SIM-CONT-FN}$$

$$\frac{E^\star_{\mathrm{Val}} \rightsquigarrow \{\rho\} E^\star_{\mathrm{Triv}} \qquad v \rightsquigarrow \{\rho\} t}{E^\star_{\mathrm{Val}}[v\,[]] \rightsquigarrow \{\rho\} E^\star_{\mathrm{Triv}}[t\,[]]} \text{ SIM-CONT-ARG-TRIV}$$

$$\frac{E^\star_{\mathrm{Val}} \rightsquigarrow \{\rho\} E^\star_{\mathrm{Triv}} \qquad v \sim \rho(m_i) \qquad i = \mathsf{fresh}\ E^\star_{\mathrm{Triv}}}{E^\star_{\mathrm{Val}}[v\,[]] \rightsquigarrow \{\rho\} E^\star_{\mathrm{Triv}}[m_i\,[]]} \text{ SIM-CONT-ARG-COMP}$$

Fig. 9. Evaluation context relation.

application of a fn continuation given by the closure evaluated from $\mathscr{K}_K[\![E^\star[[]\,e]]\!]$ which gives rise to the resulting arg continuation. The computed value is bound to the variable m_i and, importantly, only depends on the context of the local scope $E^\star$, as per the definition of $\mathscr{K}$.

Note that, though the simulation relation $\rightsquigarrow$ usually relates source semantic constructs to CPS terms with an attached environment, the relation on evaluation contexts only goes halfway, relating to similar evaluation contexts but with CPS terms in their value slots. It is the CPS transform applied to these evaluation contexts that produces the final simulating CPS terms, as we show in the following sections.

Scopes. Consider how the value bound to m_i in the relevant case of the evaluation context relation above arises, as the result of a computation. In the optimised transform, such values are bound to introduced variables such as n and m_i in continuation closures evaluated from $\mathscr{K}$, and arise from the application of an underlying continuation k being applied to a trivial term from the definition of $\mathscr{C}$ for an empty evaluation context $\mathscr{C}_k[\![[]]\!]\,t = k\,t$. Note, then, that this application of an underlying continuation must correspond to the case in the source semantics of an empty evaluation context with an underlying scope:

$$O(\{\rho'\} E^\star(\{\rho\}[v])) \longrightarrow^\star O(\{\rho'\} E^\star[v])$$

hence it is *changing scope* which results in a value becoming a computation. The SIM-SCOPE-CONT rule in Fig. 10 captures this correspondence by relating scopes to underlying continuation closures evaluated from $\mathscr{K}$ which are bound to k.

$$\frac{}{() \rightsquigarrow \{\rho\}\mathbf{I}} \text{ SIM-SCOPE-ID}$$

$$\frac{O \rightsquigarrow \{\rho'\} K \qquad \rho' \sim \rho' \\ E^\star_{\mathrm{Val}} \rightsquigarrow \{\rho'\} E^\star_{\mathrm{Triv}} \qquad \{\rho'\} \mathscr{K}_K[\![E^\star_{\mathrm{Triv}}]\!] \longrightarrow \rho(k)}{O(\{\rho'\} E^\star_{\mathrm{Val}}()) \rightsquigarrow \{\rho\} k} \text{ SIM-SCOPE-CONT}$$

Fig. 10. Scoping relation.

Semantic State Relation. Combining the relations covered in this section, we arrive at a full simulation relation which relates source semantic states to CPS terms and an appropriate environment to simulate those semantic states. The relation is given in Fig. 11.

$$\frac{O \rightsquigarrow \{\rho\}K \qquad \rho \sim \rho \qquad E^\star_{\mathrm{Val}} \rightsquigarrow \{\rho\}E^\star_{\mathrm{Triv}}}{O(\{\rho\}E^\star_{\mathrm{Val}}[e]) \rightsquigarrow \{\rho\}\mathscr{E}_K[\![E^\star_{\mathrm{Triv}}[e]]\!]} \ \text{SIM-EXP}$$

$$\frac{O \rightsquigarrow \{\rho\}K \qquad \rho \sim \rho \qquad E^\star_{\mathrm{Val}} \rightsquigarrow \{\rho\}E^\star_{\mathrm{Triv}} \qquad v \rightsquigarrow \{\rho\}t}{O(\{\rho\}E^\star_{\mathrm{Val}}[v]) \rightsquigarrow \{\rho\}\mathscr{C}_K[\![E^\star_{\mathrm{Triv}}[]]\!]\,t} \ \text{SIM-TRIV}$$

$$\frac{O(\{\rho'\}E^\star_{\mathrm{Val}}()) \rightsquigarrow \{\rho\}k \qquad v \rightsquigarrow \{\rho\}t}{O(\{\rho'\}E^\star_{\mathrm{Val}}[v]) \rightsquigarrow \{\rho\}k\,t} \ \text{SIM-COMP}$$

Fig. 11. Semantic state relation.

The resultant CPS expressions of the simulation relation are constructed from the definitions of the optimised CPS transform that we began with, each rule corresponding to each transform function. The first, SIM-EXP, relates an expression to its CPS transform by $\mathscr{E}$ in the corresponding evaluation context. The last two rules relate values to either their static application by $\mathscr{C}$ (SIM-TRIV) or dynamic application (SIM-COMP) by the closure evaluated from $\mathscr{K}$.

We choose to include SIM-COMP rather than attempt to use $\mathscr{C}$ with computed values as well as trivial ones, because it allows us to always relate the control string value to a directly related trivial term by the value simulation relation instead of having to also consider the possibility of binding the related value to an introduced variable such as n. As a result, this also allows us to ignore introduced variables if they are not stashed in the evaluation context, i.e. we never need to consider the presence of n in the relation.

6   Simulation Proof

Theorem 1 (Simulation).

$$\vdash \forall O\, O'\, \rho\, \rho'\, E^\star\, E^{\star\prime}\, c^\star\, c^{\star\prime}\, \rho\, e\,.$$
$$O(\{\rho\}E^\star[c^\star]) \longrightarrow^\star O'(\{\rho'\}E^{\star\prime}[c^{\star\prime}]) \wedge O(\{\rho\}E^\star[c^\star]) \rightsquigarrow \{\rho\}e$$
$$\implies$$
$$\exists n\, \rho'\, e'\,.\,\{\rho\}e \longrightarrow^n \{\rho'\}e' \wedge O'(\{\rho'\}E^{\star\prime}[c^{\star\prime}]) \rightsquigarrow \{\rho'\}e'$$

Static Reductions. The majority of the cases of Theorem 1 for small steps in the source semantics result in no reductions in the target semantics, which is consistent with the nature of the optimised transform. For example, the CBV-EXP-VAR and CBV-EXP-LAM steps for evaluation of trivial terms to values correspond only to expansions from the expression transform $\mathscr{E}_K[\![E^\star[t]]\!]$ to the static continuation application transform $\mathscr{C}_K[\![E^\star]\!]\,t$ where the source trivial term t evaluates to a value which is simulated by the target trivial term $v \rightsquigarrow \{\rho\}t$. In effect, these steps which do not involve dynamic reductions instead correspond to static reductions.

Another case where there are no reductions in the target semantics is for the CBV-CONT-ID reduction, which is the application to a value of an empty evaluation context with an underlying scope, as the simulation relation explicitly captures the introduction of a value as a computation by changing scope. The semantic state $O(\{\rho'\}E^\star(\{\rho\}[v]))$ relates either to $\{\rho\}\mathscr{C}_k[\![[]]\!]\,t$ which simply expands $\{\rho\}k\,t$ without reduction, or to $\{\rho^+\}k\,t$ with a different environment which maps k to the evaluation of $\mathscr{K}_k[\![[]]\!]$ under ρ, which is again just whatever k maps do under ρ, hence we similarly arrive at $\{\rho\}k\,t$.

Computations. The simulation proof becomes interesting when considering a dynamic application of a continuation to a value, i.e. the value was a computation. The starting point for such a step is from a semantic state under the SIM-COMP rule, where the continuation closure in k is applied to term. Let us consider the case for the CBV-CONT-FN step, where the evaluation context is $E^\star[[]\,e]$; by applying the corresponding closure in k, we arrive at the term $\mathscr{E}[\![E^\star[m_i\,[e]]]\!]$ where the value that the continuation was applied to is bound to m_i.

To satisfy the resultant simulation relation, we must ensure that the environment with the newly bound variable $\rho[m_i \mapsto v]$ is consistent with the conditions on it imposed by the subrelations of the simulation relation, i.e. we need to prove that various relations on values, evaluation contexts, etc. are monotonic with respect to the additional binding to the introduced variable m_i. For the environment CPS equivalence and value simulation relations, this is simple to prove if the transform ensures that variables from the original semantics are always distinct from introduced variables such as m_i, k, etc.

Lemma 2 (Environment relation monotonicity).

$$\vdash \forall \rho\,\boldsymbol{\rho}\,\boldsymbol{x}\,\boldsymbol{v}\,.\,(\forall x\,.\,\boldsymbol{x} \neq x) \implies \rho \sim \boldsymbol{\rho} \implies \rho \sim \boldsymbol{\rho}[\boldsymbol{x} \mapsto \boldsymbol{v}]$$

Lemma 3 (Value simulation monotonicity).

$$\vdash \forall v\,\boldsymbol{\rho}\,\boldsymbol{t}\,\boldsymbol{x}\,\boldsymbol{v}\,.\,(\forall x\,.\,\boldsymbol{x} \neq x) \implies v \rightsquigarrow \{\boldsymbol{\rho}\}\boldsymbol{t} \implies v \rightsquigarrow \{\boldsymbol{\rho}[\boldsymbol{x} \mapsto \boldsymbol{v}]\}\boldsymbol{t}$$

Proof. Trivial.

Monotonicity for the scoping relation is similarly trivial, as that relation depends only on the binding of k.

Lemma 4 (Scoping relation monotonicity).

$$\vdash \forall O\,\boldsymbol{\rho}\,K\,\boldsymbol{x}\,\boldsymbol{v}\,.\,\boldsymbol{x} \neq k \implies O \rightsquigarrow \{\boldsymbol{\rho}\}K \implies O \rightsquigarrow \{\boldsymbol{\rho}[\boldsymbol{x} \mapsto \boldsymbol{v}]\}K$$

Proof. Trivial.

The interesting monotonicity lemma, and really the pin holding together simulation for an optimised transform, is the monotonicity lemma for evaluation contexts. Not only must introduced variables not clash with source variables, but they must also not clash with the *other* introduced variables in the evaluation contexts, i.e. other m_i variables as per the SIM-CONT-ARG-COMP rule. Using the implementation of fresh described in Sect. 3.4, which counts the number of m variables in $E^\star$, the variable index must simply be at least fresh $E^\star$ to not clash. We then arrive at the evaluation context lemma of monotonicity:

Lemma 5 (Evaluation context relation monotonicity).

$$\vdash \forall E^\star_{\mathrm{Val}}\, \rho\, E^\star_{\mathbf{Triv}}\, \boldsymbol{x}\, \boldsymbol{v}\, .$$
$$(\forall x\, .\, \boldsymbol{x} \neq x) \wedge (\forall i < \mathsf{fresh}\ E^\star_{\mathbf{Triv}}\, .\, \boldsymbol{x} \neq m_i)$$
$$\implies E^\star_{\mathrm{Val}} \rightsquigarrow \{\rho\} E^\star_{\mathbf{Triv}} \implies E^\star_{\mathrm{Val}} \rightsquigarrow \{\rho[\boldsymbol{x} \mapsto \boldsymbol{v}]\} E^\star_{\mathbf{Triv}}$$

Proof. By induction over the SIM-CONT rules.

This lemma is the crux of our proof. The deterministic nature of the introduced variable names in the simulation relation, as a result of the local evaluation-context-based fresh name generation in our reformulated transform, enables us to prove monotonicity of the simulation relation with respect to the binding of introduced variables, even with multiple m variables already introduced into the scope.

Application. The CBV-CONT-ARG step, on the evaluation context $E^\star[v\,[]]$, always produces reductions in the target domain, regardless of if the continuation is applied to a trivial or computed term. Indeed, to simulate the source semantics, a completed reduction of an application expression in the source domain must correspond to a reduction of an application in the target domain; the transform produces the application $t_1\, t_2\, \mathscr{K}_K[\![E^\star]\!]$ in CPS which must be reduced.

By the simulation relation, t_1 will always evaluate to a closure $\Lambda x.\{\rho\}\lambda k.\mathscr{E}_k[\![e]\!]$, hence the application leads to the expression $\mathscr{E}_k[\![e]\!]$ with $\boldsymbol{x}$ and $\boldsymbol{k}$ freshly bound to the passed value and underlying continuation evaluated from $\mathscr{K}_K[\![E^\star]\!]$ respectively. The corresponding environment in the source semantics similarly has the variable x bound, and we may trivially prove that the environment relation is preserved when binding a source variable.

Lemma 6 (Environment relation synchronisation).

$$\vdash \forall \rho\, \boldsymbol{\rho}\, x\, v\, \boldsymbol{v}\, .\, v \sim \boldsymbol{v} \implies \rho \sim \boldsymbol{\rho} \implies \rho[x \mapsto v] \sim \boldsymbol{\rho}[\boldsymbol{x} \mapsto \boldsymbol{v}]$$

Proof. Cases on $x \in \mathrm{dom}(\rho)$.

Before Lemma 6 may be applied, we must first apply the environment monotonicity lemma, Lemma 2, to disregard the binding of $\boldsymbol{k}$.

Note that, in the case that the continuation was applied to a computed value, the value is bound to $\boldsymbol{n}$ then very quickly dispatched. We must then also apply the environment, scoping, and evaluation context monotonicity lemmas, Lemmas 2, 4, and 5, to disregard the binding of $\boldsymbol{n}$.

7   Conclusion

We have presented a reformulation of Danvy & Nielsen's one-pass CPS transform [9] in the style of Sabry & Felleisen's optimised transform based on evaluation contexts [21]. Our transform highlights the nature of the name clashes encountered in Minamide & Okuma's mechanised correctness proof [15]: clashes are local to the lexical scope, and may be reasoned about by the inclusion of the offending variables in the local evaluation context. It is hence possible to use a fresh variable generation method that depends only on the local evaluation context, and allows introduced variable names to be uniquely determined by the simulation relation.

We have proposed a modified CEK-machine to represent the source semantics, with evaluation contexts rephrased as nested sequences of lexical scopes, each with its own local environment and evaluation context. In combination with our new transform, this semantics builds naturally into a simulation relation which can determine introduced variable names, that consequently enables a straightforward simulation proof, with no need to consider α-equivalence. The modified CEK-machine represents only a small departure from a typical CEK-machine or alternative semantics and is easy to prove equivalent, hence we believe that it is a beneficial trade-off for the more difficult proof of α-equivalence.

The nature of our transform to use evaluation contexts from the semantics should allow it to be applied more generally to richer languages. We would particularly like to investigate the use of an evaluation-context-based CPS transform to languages with control operators such as `call/cc` or delimited continuations, which would likely have interesting variable clashing and fresh naming challenges for captured continuation variables.

Acknowledgments. We thank the PADL 2026 reviewers for helpful comments.

References

1. Ager, M.S., Biernacki, D., Danvy, O., Midtgaard, J.: A functional correspondence between evaluators and abstract machines. In: Proceedings of the 5th ACM SIGPLAN International Conference on Principles and Practice of Declaritive Programming, PPDP 2003, pp. 8–19. Association for Computing Machinery, New York (2003). https://doi.org/10.1145/888251.888254
2. Baker, H.G.: Cons should not cons its arguments, part ii: Cheney on the M.T.A. SIGPLAN Not. **30**(9), 17–20 (1995). https://doi.org/10.1145/214448.214454
3. Chlipala, A.: Parametric higher-order abstract syntax for mechanized semantics. In: Proceedings of the 13th ACM SIGPLAN International Conference on Functional Programming, ICFP 2008, pp. 143–156. Association for Computing Machinery, New York (2008). https://doi.org/10.1145/1411204.1411226
4. Danvy, O., Filinski, A.: Representing control: a study of the CPS transformation. Math. Struct. Comput. Sci. **2**(4), 361–391 (1992). https://doi.org/10.1017/S0960129500001535

5. Danvy, O.: On evaluation contexts, continuations, and the rest of computation (2004)
6. Danvy, O.: Defunctionalized interpreters for programming languages. In: Proceedings of the 13th ACM SIGPLAN International Conference on Functional Programming, ICFP 2008, pp. 131–142. Association for Computing Machinery, New York (2008). https://doi.org/10.1145/1411204.1411206
7. Danvy, O., Filinski, A.: Abstracting control. In: Kahn, G. (ed.) Proceedings of the 1990 ACM Conference on LISP and Functional Programming, LFP 1990, Nice, France, 27–29 June 1990, pp. 151–160. ACM (1990). https://doi.org/10.1145/91556.91622
8. Danvy, O., Nielsen, L.R.: Defunctionalization at work. In: Proceedings of the 3rd ACM SIGPLAN International Conference on Principles and Practice of Declarative Programming, PPDP 2001, pp. 162–174. Association for Computing Machinery, New York (2001). https://doi.org/10.1145/773184.773202
9. Danvy, O., Nielsen, L.R.: A first-order one-pass CPS transformation. Theoret. Comput. Sci. **308**(1), 239–257 (2003). https://doi.org/10.1016/S0304-3975(02)00733-8
10. Dargaye, Z., Leroy, X.: Mechanized verification of CPS transformations. In: Dershowitz, N., Voronkov, A. (eds.) LPAR 2007. LNCS (LNAI), vol. 4790, pp. 211–225. Springer, Heidelberg (2007). https://doi.org/10.1007/978-3-540-75560-9_17
11. Felleisen, M., Friedman, D.P.: Control operators, the SECD-machine, and the λ-calculus. In: Formal Description of Programming Concepts (1987). https://api.semanticscholar.org/CorpusID:57760323
12. Kelsey, R.A.: A correspondence between continuation passing style and static single assignment form. In: Papers from the 1995 ACM SIGPLAN Workshop on Intermediate Representations, IR 1995, pp. 13–22. Association for Computing Machinery, New York (1995). https://doi.org/10.1145/202529.202532
13. Kranz, D., Kelsey, R., Rees, J., Hudak, P., Philbin, J., Adams, N.: Orbit: an optimizing compiler for Scheme. In: Proceedings of the 1986 SIGPLAN Symposium on Compiler Construction, SIGPLAN 1986, pp. 219–233. Association for Computing Machinery, New York (1986). https://doi.org/10.1145/12276.13333
14. Lasnier, P.Y., Yallop, J., Myreen, M.O.: BRACK: a verified compiler for Scheme via CakeML. In: Proceedings of the 15th ACM SIGPLAN International Conference on Certified Programs and Proofs, CPP 2026. Association for Computing Machinery, New York (2026)
15. Minamide, Y., Okuma, K.: Verifying CPS transformations in Isabelle/HOL. In: Proceedings of the 2003 ACM SIGPLAN Workshop on Mechanized Reasoning about Languages with Variable Binding, MERLIN 2003, pp. 1–8. Association for Computing Machinery, New York (2003). https://doi.org/10.1145/976571.976576
16. Paraskevopoulou, Z., Grover, A.: Compiling with continuations, correctly. Proc. ACM Program. Lang. **5**(OOPSLA) (2021). https://doi.org/10.1145/3485491
17. Pitts, A.M.: Nominal logic, a first order theory of names and binding. Inf. Comput. **186**(2), 165–193 (2003). https://doi.org/10.1016/S0890-5401(03)00138-X
18. Plotkin, G.: Call-by-name, call-by-value and the λ-calculus. Theoret. Comput. Sci. **1**(2), 125–159 (1975). https://doi.org/10.1016/0304-3975(75)90017-1
19. Pottier, F.: Revisiting the CPS transformation and its implementation (2006)
20. Reynolds, J.C.: Definitional interpreters for higher-order programming languages. In: Proceedings of the ACM Annual Conference, ACM 1972, vol. 2, pp. 717–740. Association for Computing Machinery, New York (1972). https://doi.org/10.1145/800194.805852

21. Sabry, A., Felleisen, M.: Reasoning about programs in continuation-passing style. In: Proceedings of the 1992 ACM Conference on LISP and Functional Programming, LFP 1992, pp. 288–298. Association for Computing Machinery, New York (1992). https://doi.org/10.1145/141471.141563
22. Steele, G.L.: Rabbit: a compiler for Scheme. Technical report, USA (1978)
23. Tian, Y.H.: Mechanically verifying correctness of CPS compilation. In: Proceedings of the Twelfth Computing: The Australasian Theory Symposium, CATS 2006, vol. 51, pp. 41–51. Australian Computer Society, Inc. (2006)
24. Xiao, Y., Sabry, A., Ariola, Z.M.: From syntactic theories to interpreters: automating the proof of unique decomposition. High. Order Symb. Comput. **14**(4), 387–409 (2001). https://doi.org/10.1023/A:1014408032446

Property-Based Testing for Asynchronous Functional Reactive Programming Using Linear Temporal Logic

Christian Emil Nielsen[(✉)], Mathias Faber Kristiansen, and Patrick Bahr

IT University of Copenhagen, Copenhagen, Denmark
`{cemn,matkr,paba}@itu.dk`

Abstract. Functional reactive programming (FRP) is a programming paradigm for implementing software that continuously interacts with its environment and manipulates highly dynamic data. *Asynchronous* FRP, in particular, is very expressive and can be used to implement graphical user interfaces and other reactive systems interacting with data streams and events that are not synchronized. Testing such asynchronous FRP programs is difficult since a program's behaviour depends not only on the concrete data it receives from its environment but also the *relative timing* of when each piece of data arrives.

In this paper, we propose *PropRatt*, a property-based testing framework for asynchronous FRP. The key component of PropRatt is its specification language, which extends basic linear temporal logic with a means to express properties of several concurrent signals. This allows us to express temporal properties that relate data coming from different signals at different points in time. PropRatt is implemented in Haskell and targets a recently introduced asynchronous FRP language embedded in Haskell. We demonstrate the utility of PropRatt through a case study testing a signal combinator library as well as a graphical user interface, in which we suggest how the strategy for generating signals can be modified to better model specific domains.

Keywords: Property-based testing · Functional Reactive Programming · Linear Temporal Logic

1 Introduction

Reactive systems continuously respond to external inputs received from their environments. Examples of these include graphical user interfaces (GUIs) that react to a stream of mouse clicks and keyboard inputs, or control software for robots that continuously read input from hardware sensors. The key idea behind functional reactive programming (FRP) [7] is to model the input from the environment as a *signal* that can be manipulated as any other first-class value. This programming paradigm enables writing reactive systems in a declarative and compositional style. In the model of FRP we are considering here, signals are

N. Amin and J. Arias (Eds.): PADL 2026, LNCS 16401, pp. 39–56, 2026.
https://doi.org/10.1007/978-3-032-15981-6_3

values of type `Sig a` that represent a stream of values of type `a` that arrive incrementally over time. These signals can then be composed and manipulated using higher-order functions to build complex reactive systems. *Async Rattus* [1] is an asynchronous FRP language embedded in Haskell that enables this programming style. The asynchronous nature of the language allows for signals to update independently with respect to a *local* clock attached to each signal, as opposed to synchronous languages where all signals update according to a *global* clock. This model is favourable for GUIs, where subcomponents frequently need to be recomputed *independently* of most of the rest of the GUI. To illustrate such asynchronous behaviour, consider the `zip` function on signals in Async Rattus (instantiated to signals of integers and characters for the sake of this example):

```
zip : : Sig Int -> Sig Char -> Sig (Int :* Char)
```

A call to `zip` may produce the execution trace illustrated in Fig. 1. For each of the three signals, the figure shows a value whenever the signal updates. For example, at time t_5, the signal s_2 still has value `'c'`, while the other two signals have been updated to the values 4 and (4, `'c'`). The `zip` function combines two signals into a signal of (strict) pairs containing the two last observed values of the two signals. That means, it must update whenever either of the two argument signals updates. For example, at time t_5, only signal s_1 updates and s_2 remains unchanged. Accordingly, `zip` s_1 s_2 updates to the new value (4, `'c'`). As a sidenote, `zip` uses the strict product type `Int :* Char` rather than Haskell's standard lazy pair type `(Int, Char)`, because Async Rattus uses an eager evaluation semantics to make guarantees about the absence of space leaks.

time t_i	t_1	t_2	t_3	t_4	t_5	t_6	$\cdots$
$s_1 =$	1		2	3	4		$\cdots$
$s_2 =$	`'a'`	`'b'`	`'c'`			`'d'`	$\cdots$
`zip` s_1 $s_2 =$	(1, `'a'`)	(1, `'b'`)	(2, `'c'`)	(3, `'c'`)	(4, `'c'`)	(4, `'d'`)	$\cdots$

Fig. 1. Execution trace for `zip`.

From the trace in Fig. 1 we can see how the number of test cases explodes. Given two input signals s_1 and s_2, there are $3^5 = 243$ possible different outcomes for `zip` s_1 s_2 in the first 6 time steps just due to the different timings of s_1 and s_2! And that is before we even begin to consider the number of different values the signals can take. This combinatorial explosion renders conventional unit testing that uses known input/output pairs highly impractical for sufficient testing.

Property-based testing (PBT) [3] is a tool which may aid in addressing these challenges. Instead of writing test cases as input/output pairs, the user specifies a predicate that must hold *for all* input/output pairs. A testing framework then automatically checks the predicate against many randomly generated inputs, thereby testing a more general property of the system under test. This approach is well-suited for complex or combinatorial input spaces, as it can explore a broad range of inputs that would be impractical to write manually otherwise. To test a representative subset of execution paths, the generation of signals cannot be completely arbitrary. Instead, it must be carefully constrained to ensure fairness for all signals under test, to avoid a signal never updating during a test run.

However, predicates written exclusively with propositional logic are insufficiently expressive to specify the expected behaviour of signals, as it can only represent a static notion of truth. The value produced by a signal at a given instant is of limited use, since it cannot express how signals evolve dynamically *over time*. This naturally leads us to temporal logic, which allows properties to be formulated with temporal operators. In particular, linear temporal logic (LTL) [16] provides operators such as $\mathbf{G}$ ("always") and $\mathbf{F}$ ("eventually") to express statements relative to time. For example, we can express the property that the first component of a zipped signal $s_3 = \mathtt{zip}\, s_1\, s_2$ always reflects the current value of s_1 whenever s_1 produces a value:

$$\mathbf{G}(\checkmark s_1 \Rightarrow s_1 = \mathit{fst}(s_3)) \tag{1}$$

Here, $\checkmark s_1$ denotes a tick of the clock tied to s_1, capturing the idea that the property is only relevant when s_1 updates. Using the temporal operators offered by LTL allows for more expressive predicates and, in turn, properties of a system that we wish to test. Exactly how an LTL-based specification language should be designed to express specifications for *asynchronous* FRP has remained an open question so far.

In this paper, we present PropRatt[1], a PBT library for Async Rattus. PropRatt builds on top of QuickCheck [3], a PBT library for Haskell, to generate arbitrary signals and to check temporal properties. The key contributions of this work are as follows:

- We devise an LTL-based specification language to express temporal properties that involve multiple asynchronous signals.
- We implement an API that allows specifications to interact with several signals of heterogeneous types in a type-safe manner using Haskell's advanced type system features.
- We combine this API with an execution model that produces finite well-typed traces of parallel, asynchronous signals.
- We implement a testing harness that integrates the specification language and execution model into QuickCheck.
- We demonstrate the expressiveness of the specification language, its use, and its limitations in practice with a number of examples.

The remainder of this paper is structured as follows: In Sect. 2 we give a short introduction to the Async Rattus language and property-based testing. In Sect. 3 we present the LTL-based specification language, and in Sect. 4 we give an extended example of its use in PropRatt. In Sect. 5, we give an overview of the

---

[1] Available as a Hackage library, including all examples presented in this paper [12].

most important parts of the implementation of PropRatt and its specification language. Finally, we give an overview of related work in Sect. 6 and conclude in Sect. 7 with an outlook on future work.

2   Background

In this section, we give a brief introduction to functional reactive programming in the Async Rattus language and property-based testing.

Async Rattus. Async Rattus is an FRP language embedded in Haskell that enables programming with asynchronous signals. It uses modal types to reflect the temporal availability of expressions and values at the type level. To this end, Async Rattus introduces two type modalities: a *later* modality O and a *box* modality Box. The later modality classifies data that is available at some future time, while the box modality classifies time-independent data that can be moved unchanged across time. By encoding timing constraints at the type level, Async Rattus guarantees that only time-appropriate values are accessed at each step. For example, a computation cannot accidentally use a value before it is received at some later time. But these modalities also aid resource management: The runtime only needs to keep the current values and the deferred computations awaiting future input, freeing any older data that is no longer needed, thus avoiding space leaks, which are notoriously difficult to debug. The core FRP abstraction provided by Async Rattus is the signal type. A signal of type `Sig a` represents a (possibly infinite) stream of values of type `a`. It is defined in Async Rattus as a recursive type:

```
data Sig a = a ::: O (Sig a)
```

Here we use `:::` as a cons-like constructor operator. A value of type `Sig a` carries a head of type `a` and a tail of type `O (Sig a)`. The head is available right away, while the tail is a delayed computation that becomes available in the next time step, according to some clock.

Each value `d :: O b` consist of a *clock* `cl(d)` and a delayed computation, which produces a value of type `b` whenever the clock `cl(d)` ticks. In the case of a signal, the tail is of type `O (Sig a)` and thus has an associated clock, which determines when a new value of type `Sig a` is available, i.e. when the signal updates. Concretely, a clock is a set of *channels*, and each such channel is an address from which the program can receive input. When an input arrives on one of those channels, we say that the associated clock ticks and the deferred computation is executed. In the case of the tail of a signal, such a tick yields the next value of the signal. Thus, each `O (Sig a)` is essentially a promise to compute the next signal element as soon as the clock ticks. For example, in a GUI application, each button has an associated channel that receives data whenever the button is pressed. If a signal's clock includes the channel associated with a button, then each button press causes the signal to advance by one step.

This design lets different signals operate on independent clocks, unlike purely synchronous FRP where all signals share a single global clock.

Async Rattus provides two primitives for working with the later modality: `delay` and `adv` (advance). The `delay` primitive is the constructor for the later modality. It wraps a computation so that it does not execute until the signal's clock ticks. Conversely, `adv` is the eliminator. It retrieves the value from a delayed computation when its clock allows it. The typing rules of Async Rattus ensures that every `adv` must be nested under the scope of a corresponding `delay`, preventing the use of values that do not exist. For instance, consider the following function, that subtracts one from a delayed integer:

```
subtractOne :: O Int -> Int
subtractOne laterN = laterN - 1
```

This function does not type check since `laterN :: O Int` is not an integer but rather a delayed integer that arrives at some point in the future. We cannot subtract 1 in the current time step. Instead, we have to await the clock of the integer and only then subtract 1. A valid function could instead use the `delay` and `adv` primitives to delay the computation according to the clock of `laterN`.

```
subtractOne :: O Int -> O Int
subtractOne laterN = delay (adv laterN - 1)
```

In this way, we correctly await the input, before executing the computation, which also changes the type of the function so that it returns a *delayed* integer.

When we bind a variable x and use it in the scope of a `delay`, such as in \x -> delay x, we effectively move the data referenced by x into the future. Async Rattus requires that any value moved into the future be time-invariant. To this end, the language features the notion of *stable types*, which includes basic types like integers and recursive types like lists, but it excludes any types that contain the later modality or function types. Values of stable types are time-independent and consequently can be safely moved arbitrarily far into the future without risk of space leaks. To illustrate, consider a naive `map` implementation on signals:

```
leakyMap :: (a -> b) -> Sig a -> Sig b
```

This type would requite `leakyMap` to move the function of type a -> b arbitrarily far into the future in order to apply it to the signal at any time. However, function types are inherently not stable, as function closures may capture temporally-dependent data. Instead, `map` can be defined with the following type:

```
map :: Box (a -> b) -> Sig a -> Sig b
map f (x ::: xs) = unbox f x ::: delay (map f (adv xs))
```

The `Box` modality ensures that the function `f` is of a stable type and thereby temporally-invariant, which allows us to use `f` nested under a `delay`. To apply `f` as a function, we must first unbox it using `unbox :: Box a -> a`.

When constructing boxed values using the introduction form `box`, Async Rattus enforces a restriction similar to that for `delay`: We can only move values into a `box` if they are of a stable type. For example, `\x -> box x` only type checks if `x` has a stable type.

Property-Based Testing. Testing reactive and asynchronous programs written in Async Rattus is challenging because of the enormous space of possible event sequences. Property-based testing (PBT) offers a promising alternative to traditional testing. Instead of writing fixed test cases, the programmer states properties that the program should satisfy, and the testing framework checks them against many automatically generated inputs. This approach aligns well with the high-level nature of specifications and can uncover edge cases that handwritten examples might miss. PBT libraries allow the programmer to write compact specifications, such as the following specification that reversing a list twice produces the original list:

```
prop_rev : [Int] -> Property
prop_rev xs = reverse (reverse xs) == xs
```

A PBT library such as *QuickCheck* can generate random inputs for the argument `xs` and check whether these satisfy the equation `reverse (reverse xs) == xs`. In addition, QuickCheck can also *shrink* such inputs in order to provide the programmer with useful counterexamples if a property fails. The core of this general principle is provided by the `Arbitrary` type class of QuickCheck:

```
class Arbitrary a where
  arbitrary :: Gen a
  shrink    :: a -> [a]
```

Given an instance of `Arbitrary [Int]`, QuickCheck can test properties that quantify over lists of integers such as `prop_rev` above: First `arbitrary` generates random values of type `[Int]`. Then it supplies these random values to the function `prop_rev` one by one. Finally, if the property fails for one of the generated inputs, say `xs`, then `shrink xs` will produce smaller lists with which to test `prop_rev` in order to obtain a smaller counterexample.

In the context of reactive systems, PBT can offer the same benefits: It can generate arbitrary input signals to explore the space of behaviours and shrink such signals to simpler counterexamples to help locate the source of errors. However, equational specifications alone are not sufficiently expressive to capture the complex behaviours expressible by asynchronous FRP programs.

3   Specification Language

3.1   Untyped Specification Language

PropRatt introduces a DSL for writing declarative specifications at a high level of abstraction, enabling property-based testing of FRP programs written in Async

Rattus. Such programs manipulate signals of different types, e.g. `zip` from Sect. 1 combines an `Int` and a `Char` signal. Therefore, the design of the specification language must be able to account for multiple, heterogeneously typed signals. But before turning to the concrete syntax of the typed specification language as implemented in PropRatt, we consider an idealized syntax of an untyped version of the language in Fig. 2 in order to discuss the essential ideas of the language.

$$Predicate\ \varphi ::= T \mid F \mid e \mid \neg\phi \mid \phi \wedge \psi \mid \phi \vee \psi \mid \phi \Rightarrow \psi$$
$$\mid \mathbf{X}\,\phi \mid \mathbf{F}\,\phi \mid \mathbf{G}\,\phi \mid \phi\,\mathbf{U}\,\psi \mid \phi\,\mathbf{R}\,\psi$$
$$Expression\ e ::= c \mid e_1\ e_2 \mid l \mid \checkmark l$$
$$Lookup\ l ::= \mathbf{prev}\ l \mid \mathbf{sig}_n$$

Fig. 2. Syntax of PropRatt's specification language.

The specification language consists of three components: a logical language of predicates ϕ, a language of expressions e, and a notation l for looking up signals at a specific (relative) time. The predicate language is exactly LTL with atoms of the form e written in the expression language. For example, we write $\mathbf{G}(\mathbf{sig}_1 > 0)$ to express that the signal identified by $\mathbf{sig}_1$ always has a positive value, and we write $\mathbf{sig}_1 > 0\ \mathbf{U}\ \mathbf{sig}_1 = \mathbf{sig}_2$ to express that the signal $\mathbf{sig}_1$ is positive until both $\mathbf{sig}_1$ and another signal $\mathbf{sig}_2$ have the same value.

In these examples, $\mathbf{sig}_1 > 0$ and $\mathbf{sig}_1 = \mathbf{sig}_2$ are Boolean-valued expressions, which can act as atoms in an LTL formula. Expressions combine constants (denoted c in Fig. 2), such as 0 and $>$, and signal lookups, such as $\mathbf{sig}_1$, using function application (denoted $e_1\ e_2$ in Fig. 2). In the case of operator constants such as $>$, we allow the infix notation $\mathbf{sig}_1 > 0$ instead of the prefix notation $> \mathbf{sig}_1\ 0$. In general, an LTL formula is a predicate over n signals whose current value can be referenced using $\mathbf{sig}_1, \ldots, \mathbf{sig}_n$. We can also reference a previous value of a signal by using $\mathbf{prev}$. For example, $\mathbf{G}(\mathbf{X}(\mathbf{prev}\ \mathbf{sig}_1 < \mathbf{sig}_1))$ stipulates that signal $\mathbf{sig}_1$ is strictly monotonically increasing.

Traditionally, LTL works only on a *single* execution trace, whereas PropRatt allows multiple parallel signals, which may produce new values independently of one another according to their own clocks. However, given such parallel, asynchronous signals, we can construct a single execution trace that maintains the relative timing information. We have seen an example of that in the execution trace for `zip`, shown in Fig. 1. It involves three signals, which, if combined, produce a trace where at each time step t_i at least one of the three signals ticks, i.e. produces a new value.

In the expression language, we have access to the timing information of such a combined trace via expressions of the form $\checkmark s$, which are true whenever the signal identified by s has ticked. Returning to the `zip` example from Fig. 1, we have that at time t_5, the expressions $\checkmark\mathbf{sig}_1$ and $\checkmark\mathbf{sig}_3$ are true, since both s_1 and `zip` $s_1\ s_2$ produced a new value, whereas $\checkmark\mathbf{sig}_2$ is false as s_2 did not produce a new value. Using this more formal notation for the specification language, specification (1) is written more precisely as $\mathbf{G}(\checkmark\mathbf{sig}_1 \Rightarrow \mathbf{sig}_1 = \mathtt{fst'}\ \mathbf{sig}_3)$, where `fst' :: a :* b -> a` is the first projection of the strict pair type.

To further illustrate the specification language, suppose we have a GUI with the following signals:

```
timer :: Sig Int        -- time to display
reset :: Sig ()         -- reset button
```

The `timer` signal is meant to increment by one every second and `reset` produces a unit value () every time the 'reset' button in the GUI is pressed. Assuming that the signals we wish to test are supplied in the order they appear above, i.e. $\mathbf{sig}_1 = \mathtt{timer}$ and $\mathbf{sig}_2 = \mathtt{reset}$, we can specify that `timer` increments whenever the clock of `timer` ticks and the reset button is not pressed:

$$\mathbf{G}(\checkmark\mathbf{sig}_1 \wedge \neg\checkmark\mathbf{sig}_2 \Rightarrow \mathbf{X}(\mathbf{prev}\ \mathbf{sig}_1 < \mathbf{sig}_1)) \tag{2}$$

$\mathbf{G}$ and $\mathbf{X}$ are standard LTL temporal operators. The *expression* $\checkmark\mathbf{sig}_1$ checks whether the first signal has updated in the current time step, while $\mathbf{sig}_1$ retrieves the value of that signal. The *lookup* $\mathbf{prev}\ \mathbf{sig}_1$ accesses the value of the timer from the previous time step. The property asserts that at any time ($\mathbf{G}$), whenever the timer signal ticks ($\checkmark\mathbf{sig}_1$) but 'reset' has not been pressed ($\neg\checkmark\mathbf{sig}_2$), then in the next step ($\mathbf{X}$) the timer ($\mathbf{sig}_1$) must have increased relative to its previous value ($\mathbf{prev}\ \mathbf{sig}_1$).

Note that the specification language features the LTL connective $\mathbf{F}$, which expresses a *liveness* property. Since liveness properties do not have finite counterexamples, testing them will always succeed. However, when liveness properties occur in a negative position in a larger specification, i.e. in negated form or to the left of $\Rightarrow$, they become safety properties (e.g. $\neg(\mathbf{F}\phi)$ is equivalent to $\mathbf{G}(\neg\phi)$). Thus, such connectives are still useful for writing compositional specification.

3.2   Typed Specification Language

The syntax in Fig. 2 is untyped and to ensure well-typedness we have to give a type system so that only Boolean-valued expressions are used as atoms, and expressions themselves are also well-typed, e.g. $e_1\ e_2$ is only well-typed if e_1 is of type $\tau_1 \rightarrow \tau_2$ and e_2 is of type τ_1. Instead of presenting such a type system, we give the encoding of this type system in Haskell.

The concrete syntax of PropRatt's specification language is intrinsically well-typed and uses generalized algebraic data types (GADTs) to represent the typing information. The full definition of the syntax is given in Fig. 3. The type of predicates `Pred` is indexed by a list of type `ts :: [Type]` , which represents the types of the signals over which we want to specify a property. For example, for the property involving the `timer :: Sig Int` and `reset :: Sig ()` signals, this list of types is `'[Int,()]`.[2]

---

[2] The quote notation ' distinguishes a type-level list `'[Int]` from the list type `[Int]`. Similarly, `':` denotes the type-level list cons operation in Fig. 3.

```
data Pred (ts :: [Type]) where
  TT, FF                 :: Pred ts
  Now                    :: Expr ts Bool -> Pred ts
  Not, X, G, F           :: Pred ts -> Pred ts
  And, Or, (:=>), U, R :: Pred ts -> Pred ts -> Pred ts

data Expr (ts :: [Type]) (t :: Type) where
  Pure  :: t -> Expr ts t
  App   :: Expr ts (t -> r) -> Expr ts t -> Expr ts r
  Val   :: Lookup ts t -> Expr ts t
  Tick  :: Lookup ts t -> Expr ts Bool

data Lookup (ts :: [Type]) (t :: Type) where
  Prev  :: Lookup ts t -> Lookup ts t
  Sig1  :: Lookup (Value t ': x) t
  Sig2  :: Lookup (x1 ': Value t ': x2) t
         :
         :
```

Fig. 3. Well-typed syntax of PropRatt.

Similarly, expressions are indexed by such a list of types $ts :: [Type]$ as well. But they also have an additional type index $t :: Type$ that indicates the type of values produced when evaluating such expressions. Using the Now constructor, predicates over signal types ts may include expressions of type Bool over signal types ts. In turn, expressions have access to the values and timing information of the signals via Val and Tick, respectively. In addition, they also have an applicative functor structure provided by Pure and Apply. These two constructors correspond directly to the two operations pure and <*> of the applicative functor interface. For example the expression $\mathbf{prev\,sig}_1 < \mathbf{sig}_1$ from the timer specification (2) above, is written

$$(<) \; <\$> \; Val \; (Prev \; Sig1) \; <*> \; Val \; Sig1$$

where <\$> is the map operator of applicative functors, defined by $f <\$> x = pure \; f <*> x$. The above expression is of type Expr '[Int,()] Bool| and thus can be used in a predicate using Now. The type of the Sig1 constructor ensures that the type of the expression Val Sig1 matches exactly the first signal, and likewise for the remaining constructors Sig2, Sig3, etc.

Putting all of this together, specification (2) can be expressed as follows:

```
prop :: Pred '[Int,()]
prop = G ((Now (Tick Sig1) `And` Not (Now (Tick Sig2)))
      :=> X (Now ((<) <$> Val (Prev Sig1) <*> Val Sig1)))
```

To make properties more readable, the specification language also provides shorthands, defined in Fig. 4. This includes shorthands for looking up the current

```haskell
prop :: Pred '[Int,()]
prop = G ((tick1 'And' Not tick2) :=> X (prev sig1 |<| sig1))
sig1 :: Expr (Value t ': ts) t
sig1 = Val Sig1

tick1 :: Pred (Value t ': ts)
tick1 = Now (Tick Sig1)


-- sig2, tick2, etc. are defined similarly

prev :: Expr ts t -> Expr ts t
prev (Pure x)   = Pure x
prev (App f x)  = App (prev f) (prev x)
prev (Val lu)   = Val (Prev lu)
prev (Tick lu)  = Tick (Prev lu)

instance Num t => Num (Expr ts t) where
  (+) x y = (+) <$> x <*> y
  -- similar definitions for (-), (*), etc.

(|<|) :: Ord t => Expr ts t -> Expr ts t -> Pred ts
x |<| y = Now ((<) <$> x <*> y)
-- similar definitions for comparison operators (==), (<=), etc.
```

Fig. 4. Shorthand notations for the specification language.

value of a signal (`sig1`, `sig2`, etc.), checking whether a signal has ticked (`tick1`, `tick2`, etc.), `Prev` generalized to the expression language (`prev`), common arithmetic operators for the expression language, and common comparison operators for the predicate language ($|<|, |==|$, etc.). With these shorthands the above property `prop` can be written more concisely:

```haskell
prop :: Pred '[Int,()]
prop = G ((tick1 'And' Not tick2) :=> X (prev sig1 |<| sig1))
```

4   Case Study

To evaluate the expressiveness of the specification language, we have compiled two sets of example specifications: A set of specifications for the signal combinators provided by the Async Rattus library and a set of specifications for a simple timer GUI. Here we give a selection of these specifications, but the complete set can be found in the accompanying Haskell package [12].

Signal Combinators. The first set of examples comprises specifications for signal combinators like `zip` and `map`. We have seen one such specification in the form of the LTL formula $\mathbf{G}(\checkmark\mathbf{sig}_1 \Rightarrow \mathbf{sig}_1 = \mathtt{fst'}\,\mathbf{sig}_3)$ for the `zip` combinator. This can be written in the typed specification language as follows:

```
-- sig3 = zip sig1 sig2
prop_zip :: Pred '[Int, Char, (Int :* Char)]
prop_zip = G (tick1 :=> (sig1 |==| (fst' <$> sig3)))
```

This property is able to catch the following wrong implementation of `zip`:

```
zipWrong :: (Stable a, Stable b) => Sig a -> Sig b -> Sig (a :* b)
zipWrong (a ::: as) (b ::: bs) = (a :* b) ::: delay (
  case select as bs of
    Fst (a' ::: as') bs'  -> zipWrong (a' ::: as') (b ::: bs')
    Snd as' (b' ::: bs')  -> zipWrong (a  ::: as') (b ::: bs')
    Both as' bs'          -> zipWrong as' bs')
```

In the `Snd` case, this definition uses the value `b` (rather than `b'`) in the recursive call to `zipWrong`. This is incorrect according to the specification, given that the value is now stale in the presence of the newly produced value `b'`. Upon evaluating the property using QuickCheck the test indeed fails:

```
*** Failed! Falsified (after 2 tests and 14 shrinks):
[!(0 :* 0); !0; !0;
,!(0 :* 0); _0; !1;]
```

Each row of the above counterexample represents a time step, and each column represents a signal with its current value and whether it ticked (!) or not (_).

Async Rattus can express dynamic dataflows using the `switch` combinator, which takes a signal `s1` and a delayed signal `s2` and produces a new signal that first behaves like `s1` and behaves like `s2` as soon as that delayed signal `s2` arrives. We can express this property as follows:

```
-- sig3 = switch sig1 sig2
prop_switch :: Pred '[Int, Int, Int]
prop_switch = (sig3 |==| sig1) `U` (tick2 `And` G(sig3 |==| sig2))
```

Note that PropRatt's until operator U has the semantics of the 'weak until' operator (often denoted $\mathbf{W}$). In an LTL formula $\phi\,\mathbf{U}\,\psi$, the 'strict until' operator requires ψ to become true at some point in the future (and ϕ to be true at all times before that). However, this requirement of ψ becoming true at some point is a liveness property, which cannot be tested using PBT since such properties have only infinite counterexamples. Therefore, by necessity, PropRatt adopts the weak form which does not require ψ to become true. This 'weak until' semantics of U matches the semantics of `switch` because the second (delayed) signal passed to `switch` may never arrive.

GUI Application. For the second set of example specifications, we consider a GUI application that extends the timer example from Sect. 3.1 to include additional signals. This GUI application is taken from Disch et al. [6] and implements the timer of Kiss's 7GUIs benchmark [11].

The timer application displays a value of elapsed time, a reset button, and a slider for adjusting a maximum duration. Users may interact with the timer in two ways: pressing the reset button and adjusting the slider which changes the maximum value the timer may reach. Once the timer reaches this maximum, it stops incrementing until the slider is moved again or the reset button is pressed. The GUI processes three inputs: a reset button (`reset :: Sig ()`), a slider to adjust the maximum of the timer (`max :: Sig Int`), and a signal that ticks every second (`sec :: Sig ()`). These three signals are combined to form the signal of type `state :: Sig (Int :* Int)`, which captures the state of the GUI. Its first component holds the current timer value and its second component is the maximum value currently chosen by the user.

Kiss [11] provides a specification of the timer application consisting of several informal properties, which we can now formally express in the PropRatt specification language. First, the timer must stop whenever it reaches its maximum. That is, the timer value never exceeds the maximum value supplied by the user:

```
-- sig1: state; sig2: reset; sig3: max; sig4: sec
prop1 :: Pred '[(Int :* Int), (), Int, ()]
prop1 = G ((snd' <$> sig1) |<=| sig3)
```

Second, if the timer has not yet reached its maximum, then it must increase every second:

```
prop2 :: Pred '[(Int :* Int), (), Int, ()]
prop2 = G ( ((snd' <$> sig1) |<| sig3 `And` X tick4)
      :=> X ((snd' <$> sig1) |==| ((+1) . snd' <$> prev sig1)))
```

Third, whenever the user presses the reset button, then in that same time step the timer value must be 0:

```
prop3 :: Pred '[(Int :* Int), (), Int, ()]
prop3 = G (tick2 :=> (pure 0 |==| (fst' <$> sig1)))
```

Finally, implicit in the specification is the property that the timer remains constant unless a second has passed or the reset button was pressed:

```
prop4 :: Pred '[(Int :* Int), (), Int, ()]
prop4 = G (X ((Not tick2 `And` Not tick4)
          :=> ((fst' <$> prev sig1) |==| (fst' <$> sig1))))
```

Testing these properties confirms that the implementation of the timer GUI by Disch et al. [6] does indeed satisfy the specification.

5   Implementation

In Sect. 3, we introduced the key type `Pred`, which defines well-typed temporal specifications. We now turn to the implementation details that connect these specifications to property-based testing with QuickCheck [3].

A specification is tested using the following function:

```
evaluate :: Pred ts -> Sig (HList ts) -> Bool
```

The type `Sig (HList ts)` represents a flattened trace of a program containing data from all signals under test such as the example trace for `zip` in Fig. 1. Understanding this type requires a short detour into how asynchronous signal behaviour is represented. A naive approach might model a trace as a list of independent signals `[Sig a]`. This representation is insufficient as it does not allow us to inspect the timing relationships between signals directly. Instead, we want a *single* signal of lists, where the nth value in a list corresponds to the value produced by the nth signal of the property we are testing. In order to also represent cases where some of the signals do not produce a new value, we can represent such a single signal with the type `Sig [Maybe a]`. This representation is essentially the idea of the type `Sig (HList ts)` used by `evaluate` above, but instead of a list it uses a heterogeneous list type (`HList`) that allows different signals to have different types:

```
data HList :: [Type] -> Type where
  HNil :: HList '[]
  (:%) :: !x -> !(HList xs) -> HList (x ': xs)
```

Users can construct a heterogeneous list of signals to test:

```
-- assuming s1 :: Sig Int, s2 :: Sig Char
sigsOfZip :: HList '[Sig Int, Sig Char, Sig (Int :* Char)]
sigsOfZip = s1 :% s2 :% zip s1 s2 :% HNil
```

Such a heterogeneous list of signals is then flattened into a single signal that can then be passed to `evaluate`:

```
traceOfZip :: Sig (HList '[Value Int,Value Char,Value (Int:*Char)])
traceOfZip = flatten sigsOfZip
```

Before looking more closely at flattening, we take a look at the `Value` type.

To support operators such as ✓ and **prev**, the trace must maintain past values and indicate whether a signal has emitted a fresh value at the current time step. We collect this data in the `Value` type:

```
newtype HasTicked = HasTicked Bool deriving Show
data     Value a  = Current !HasTicked !(List a)
```

Recall the definition of the `Lookup` type in Fig. 3 that represents lookups of signal values. The type of each `Sign` constructor enforces that the nth type in the list of types `ts` is of the form `Value t` in the type signature of `evaluate`.

To illustrate this representation, we show the trace from Fig. 1 as a value of type `Sig (HList '[Value Int, Value Char, Value (Int :* Char)])`:

	s_1	s_2	zip s_1 s_2
t_0	(T,[1])	:% (T,['a'])	:% (T,[(1,'a')]) :% HNil
t_1	(F,[1])	:% (T,['b','a'])	:% (T,[(1,'b'),(1,'a')]) :% HNil
t_2	(T,[2, 1])	:% (T,['c','b','a'])	:% (T,[(2,'c'),(1,'b'),(1,'a')]) :% HNil
$\vdots$	$\vdots$		

At t_0, both signals produce a new value, whereas at t_1, only the second signal emits a new value while the first carries over its previous one, which is also indicated by the false Boolean flag at t_1.

Flattening of Signals to Traces. To construct traces from individual signals, we define the function `prepend`, which merges a signal `Sig t` with an already-flattened signal of heterogeneous list `Sig (HList ts)`:

```
prepend :: (Stable t, Stable (HList ts), Falsify ts)
   => Sig t -> Sig (HList ts) -> Sig (HList (Value t ': ts))
```

The key idea is that `prepend` *unions* the clocks of the delayed computations from both arguments, which means the resulting signal updates whenever either of the input signals would update. This enables us to explore traces systematically. The `Stable` constraints ensures that the values produced by either signal argument are temporally-independent and safe to move to the future according to the type system of Async Rattus, and `Falsify` is a type class that implements a single method for a `Value` to negate the `HasTicked` flag. To flatten a heterogeneous list of signals to a trace, we recursively apply `prepend` through the `flatten` method defined in the multi-parameter type class `Flatten`:

```
class Stable (HList vals) =>
  Flatten sigs vals | sigs -> vals, vals -> sigs where
    flatten :: HList sigs -> Sig (HList vals)

instance Flatten '[] '[] where
  flatten HNil = emptySig

instance (Stable a, Stable (Value a), Flatten as bs, Falsify bs)
   => Flatten (Sig a ': as) (Value a ': bs) where
    flatten (HCons h t) = prepend h (flatten t)
```

We use a type class to implement `flatten` so that we can express the relation between the argument type `HList sigs` and return type `Sig (HList vals)`. Namely, `sigs` is a list of types of the form `Sig t`, whereas `vals` is the corresponding list of types of the form `Value t`. The type class declaration uses functional dependency annotations to make explicit that `sigs` and `vals` are in a one-to-one correspondence, which helps the type checker to infer types.

Generating Signals. Recall from Sect. 2 that the clock of a delayed computation is represented by a set of channels. For example, the clock $\{\kappa_1, \kappa_2\}$ indicates that it will tick if data arrives on channel κ_1 or channel κ_2. Clocks such as $\{\kappa_1, \kappa_2\}$ and $\{\kappa_2, \kappa_3\}$ may tick simultaneously if data has arrived on a channel that both clocks share, in this case κ_2. Concretely, channels are simply addresses that are represented as integers in Async Rattus, so that clocks are represented using the type `IntSet` of finite sets of integers.

At each step, a signal consists of a current value and a delayed computation that produces the future state of that signal. Hence, in order to generate a signal, PropRatt must generate the clocks of these delayed computations. In turn, the generated clocks need to adequately reflect the asynchronous interaction of multiple signals. To this end, we randomly assign each delayed computation of a generated signal a clock drawn from the non-empty subsets of $\{\kappa_1, \kappa_2, \kappa_3\}$:

```
genClock :: Gen Clock
genClock = do
  n <- chooseInt (1, 3)
  case n of
    1 -> do x <- chooseInt (1,3)
            return (IntSet.fromList [x])
    2 -> elements $ map IntSet.fromList [[1,2], [2,3], [1,3]]
    3 -> return (IntSet.fromList [1,2,3])
```

After each step, a signal has a new delayed computation, and thus the clock of a signal may dynamically change over time. Moreover, by drawing from a set of three channels, we are able to represent complex asynchronous behaviour where different signals may have identical, disjoint, or overlapping clocks.

To simulate the behaviour of signals producing values asynchronously, we must apply a strategy that at each time step choses a channel κ on which the program has received input and which therefore causes the relevant clocks to tick (namely all clocks θ with $\kappa \in \theta$). This strategy can be deterministic, because the clocks themselves have been randomly generated. Moreover, since PropRatt flattens all signals to a single *trace* signal, we only have to pick a channel from the clock of that single signal. We make use of the fact that channels are represented as integers and simply pick the channel with the smallest integer representation.

In short, this approach allows us to generate random input signals that mimic asynchronous external interaction, combine them with user-supplied signals if desired, and integrate the resulting outputs into a single trace of our program. This single trace is then deterministically traversed by choosing the smallest channel for each step. As a consequence, tests are able to explore different values of the randomly generated inputs as well as different timings of these inputs.

Shrinking. We supply implementations of the `shrink` method given by the `Arbitrary` type class from QuickCheck. We implemented a shrinker for signals by converting signals into a list that preserves the clocks of delayed computations:

```
type TSig a = [(a, Clock)]
```

This representation allows us to shrink signals using a strategy similar to that for lists implemented in QuickCheck: Shrink the signal by iteratively dropping contiguous chunks of values and shrink the remaining values contained in the signal themselves as well. After producing new shrink candidates, we rebuild them as signals and reapply the saved clocks so the delayed-computation strategy is preserved. QuickCheck evaluates shrink candidates iteratively until the property no longer fails. This yields compact failing inputs and correspondingly short traces that help pinpointing errors in the implementation or the specification.

6 Related Work

LTL has long been recognized as a suitable specification language for reactive programs. Jeffrey [9] and Jeltsch [10] independently discovered that LTL can be seen as a type system for functional reactive programs. Later, Perez and Nilsson [14,15] used LTL as a specification language for property-based testing of functional reactive programs. LTL-based specification languages have also been used for property-based testing of web applications [13]. The work most closely related to PropRatt is the property-based testing library developed for Rattus [5], a synchronous version of Async Rattus.

In all previous work mentioned above, the LTL-based specification language always targets *single, synchronous* executions of programs. By contrast, PropRatt specifications are *hyperproperties*, i.e. properties over several parallel execution traces of signals. Variants of LTL for hyperproperties have been suggested [4], but we are not aware of any property-based testing framework that uses these ideas, apart from the thesis of Nielsen and Kristiansen [2] which this paper summarizes. However, we are not the first to devise a specification language for PBT of asynchronous reactive systems. Hughes et al. [8] have proposed *temporal relations* as a specification language for testing the asynchronous behaviour of a communication protocol. A temporal relation is a relation between time intervals and values. Such relations provide a compositional way to specify properties of asynchronous computations.

Sculthorpe and Nilsson [17] embedded an FRP language in the dependently-typed language Agda, which allows safety properties to be formally *proved*. In later work, Sculthorpe and Nilsson [18] devised an LTL-like, shallowly embedded logic in Agda to express and *prove* temporal specifications of FRP programs.

7 Conclusion and Future Work

The focus of the present work is to explore the expressiveness of asynchronous LTL specifications and to demonstrate it with case studies. This leaves considerations of ergonomics of the specification language for future work. Such considerations are important, because the ease with witch specifications can be written, read, and modified do significantly contribute to the utility of a PBT framework. The design of PropRatt as a hybrid DSL with a deeply embedded core allows for further improvements to the specification language. For example, by inspecting the AST of specifications, we can produce a warning when the user tries to test liveness properties, which by their nature do not have finite counterexamples and thus cannot be tested.

In addition, we could extend the language with further connectives. For example, the predicate fragment of the specification language has combinators that move forward in time (such as **X** and **U**), whereas the expression fragment has a combinator that moves backwards in time (namely **prev**). While this design decision simplifies the implementation of an efficient checking procedure for specifications, it can lead to unnatural or inelegant specifications. However, it is possible to extend the specification language with combinators that allow e.g. the expression fragment to also move forward in time. Specifications written in this richer specification language can then be translated into an equivalent specification in the simpler specification language presented in this paper.

References

1. Bahr, P., Houlborg, E., Rørdam, G.T.S.: Asynchronous reactive programming with modal types in Haskell. In: Gebser, M., Sergey, I. (eds.) PADL 2024. LNCS, vol. 14512, pp. 18–36. Springer, Cham (2024). https://doi.org/10.1007/978-3-031-52038-9_2
2. Nielsen, C.E., Kristiansen, M.F.: Property-based testing for functional reactive programming in Async Rattus using linear temporal logic. Master's thesis, IT University of Copenhagen (2025)
3. Claessen, K., Hughes, J.: QuickCheck: a lightweight tool for random testing of Haskell programs. In: ICFP 2000: Proceedings of the Fifth ACM SIGPLAN International Conference on Functional Programming, pp. 268–279. ACM (2000). https://doi.org/10.1145/351240.351266
4. Clarkson, M.R., Finkbeiner, B., Koleini, M., Micinski, K.K., Rabe, M.N., Sánchez, C.: Temporal logics for hyperproperties. In: Abadi, M., Kremer, S. (eds.) POST 2014. LNCS, vol. 8414, pp. 265–284. Springer, Heidelberg (2014). https://doi.org/10.1007/978-3-642-54792-8_15
5. Dannebrog Jensen, L.: Property based testing of functional reactive programs using linear temporal logic. Master's thesis, IT University of Copenhagen (2023)
6. Disch, J.C., Heegaard, A., Bahr, P.: Functional reactive GUI programming with modal types. In: Gibbons, J. (ed.) TFP 2025. LNCS, vol. 15652, pp. 93–114. Springer, Cham (2026). https://doi.org/10.1007/978-3-031-99751-8_5
7. Elliott, C., Hudak, P.: Functional reactive animation. In: Proceedings of the second ACM SIGPLAN international conference on Functional programming, ICFP 1997, pp. 263–273. Association for Computing Machinery (1997). https://doi.org/10.1145/258948.258973
8. Hughes, J., Norell, U., Sautret, J.: Using temporal relations to specify and test an instant messaging server. In: Proceedings of the 5th Workshop on Automation of Software Test, AST 2010, pp. 95–102. Association for Computing Machinery (2010). https://doi.org/10.1145/1808266.1808281

9. Jeffrey, A.: LTL types FRP: linear-time temporal logic propositions as types, proofs as functional reactive programs. In: Proceedings of the Sixth Workshop on Programming Languages Meets Program Verification, PLPV 2912, pp. 49–60. ACM (2012). https://doi.org/10.1145/2103776.2103783
10. Jeltsch, W.: Towards a common categorical semantics for linear-time temporal logic and functional reactive programming. Electron. Notes Theor. Comput. Sci. **286**, 229–242 (2012). https://doi.org/10.1016/j.entcs.2012.08.015
11. Kiss, E.: 7GUIs: A GUI programming benchmark (2014). https://eugenkiss.github.io/7guis/
12. Nielsen, C.E., Kristiansen, M.F., Bahr, P.: `PropRatt` Haskell library package (2025). https://hackage.haskell.org/package/PropRatt
13. O'Connor, L., Wickström, O.: Quickstrom: property-based acceptance testing with LTL specifications. In: Proceedings of the 43rd ACM SIGPLAN International Conference on Programming Language Design and Implementation, PLDI 2022, pp. 1025–1038. Association for Computing Machinery (2022). https://doi.org/10.1145/3519939.3523728
14. Perez, I., Nilsson, H.: Testing and debugging functional reactive programming. Proc. ACM Program. Lang. **1**(ICFP), 1–27 (2017). https://doi.org/10.1145/3110246
15. Perez, I., Nilsson, H.: Runtime verification and validation of functional reactive systems. J. Funct. Program. **30** (2020). https://doi.org/10.1017/S0956796820000210
16. Pnueli, A.: The Temporal logic of programs. In: Proceedings of the 18th Annual Symposium on Foundations of Computer Science, SFCS 1977, pp. 46–57. IEEE Computer Society (1977). https://doi.org/10.1109/SFCS.1977.32
17. Sculthorpe, N., Nilsson, H.: Safe functional reactive programming through dependent types. In: Proceedings of the 14th ACM SIGPLAN International Conference on Functional Programming, ICFP 2009, pp. 23–34. ACM (2009). https://doi.org/10.1145/1596550.1596558
18. Sculthorpe, N., Nilsson, H.: Keeping calm in the face of change. High.-Order Symb. Comput. **23**(2), 227–271 (2010). https://doi.org/10.1007/s10990-011-9068-x

Graph Rewriting Language as a Platform for Quantum Diagrammatic Calculi

Kayo Tei[(✉)] [iD], Haruto Mishina[iD], Naoki Yamamoto[iD], and Kazunori Ueda[iD]

Department of Computer Science and Engineering, Waseda University,
Tokyo, Japan
`{tei,mishina,yamamoto,ueda}@ueda.info.waseda.ac.jp`

Abstract. Systematic discovery of optimization paths in quantum circuit simplification remains a challenge. Today, ZX-calculus, a computing model for quantum circuit transformation, is attracting attention for its highly abstract graph-based approach. Whereas existing tools such as PyZX and Quantomatic offer domain-specific support for quantum circuit optimization, visualization and theorem-proving, we present a complementary approach using LMNtal, a general-purpose hierarchical graph rewriting language, to establish a diagrammatic transformation and verification platform with model checking. Our methodology shows three advantages: (1) a direct and concise encoding of the ZX-calculus, where quantifiers simplify complex rule specification; (2) a verification framework using state-space exploration and model checking to analyze rewrite strategies; and (3) an open platform for strategic experimentation combining programmable syntax with interactive visualization. Through case studies, we demonstrate how our framework helps understand optimization paths and design new algorithms and strategies. This suggests that the declarative language LMNtal and its toolchain could serve as a new platform to investigate quantum circuit transformation from a different perspective.

Keywords: Graph Rewriting Language · Circuit Optimization · Visualization · Model Checking · ZX-Calculus

1 Introduction

The drive towards practical quantum computing is heightening the need for effective methodologies for circuit representation and optimization. The ZX-calculus [10] has emerged as a powerful graphical language for this purpose. It allows us to handle quantum circuits as equational theories over diagrams, which provides both a higher-level of abstraction (compared to standard, matrix-based formulation) and expressiveness coming from the ability to handle diagrams with an arbitrary number of wires [12,23,24]. State-of-the-art dedicated tools have addressed this new formalism from different angles. Performance-oriented libraries like PyZX [25] introduce sophisticated, built-in heuristics to simplify

© The Author(s), under exclusive license to Springer Nature Switzerland AG 2026
N. Amin and J. Arias (Eds.): PADL 2026, LNCS 16401, pp. 57–76, 2026.
https://doi.org/10.1007/978-3-032-15981-6_4

large-scale circuits efficiently. Interactive proof assistants like Quantomatic [27] provide a formal environment for verifying the correctness of specific proof steps.

On the other hand, the connection between the dedicated graphical calculus and other computing and programming paradigms including general-purpose declarative languages remains largely unexplored. This paper addresses this gap by proposing a new method using a general-purpose graph rewriting language, LMNtal [34], and its extension QLMNtal [29]. This is inspired by the affinity of the data structures the ZX-calculus and (Q)LMNtal handle. The goal of the present work is not a competitor of dedicated tools for circuit optimization but a laboratory for exploring and validating strategies for quantum computing.

LMNtal was born as an attempt to unify constraint-based concurrency (a.k.a. concurrent constraint programming) [35] and Constraint Handling Rules [17]. It later turned out to serve as a "unifying" formalism of diverse computational formalisms including process calculi, the λ-calculus and Proof Nets [31,33]. The publicly available implementation of LMNtal [28] supports state-space search and model checking of graph rewriting that scales up to 10^9 states [18] and comes with a state space visualizer for non-large problems [3]. Along with the toolchain, our approach utilizes QLMNtal's support for *quantified* pattern matching. This feature allows us to directly and declaratively express ZX-rules over an arbitrary number of components (n links, m nodes) within a single, formal rewrite rule.

The above-mentioned affinity between the two paradigms overcomes the procedural complexity inherent in other approaches based on general-purpose languages and tools. It makes it easier and practical to model, execute, and formally analyze the behavior of user-defined rewrite strategies. By leveraging LMNtal's built-in support for state-space search and LTL model checking, we can formally answer questions about the properties of a rule set, such as termination and confluence, before building it into high-performance tools.

This research makes three foundational contributions:

1. *Bridging Declarative Programming and the ZX-Calculus*—We show direct encoding of the ZX-diagrams and rules in LMNtal and demonstrate that QLMNtal's quantifiers provide a direct and concise encoding for ZX-rules involving an arbitrary number of nodes and links.

2. *Rewrite Strategy Verification Framework*—We show how state-space exploration and model checking can be applied to the design and analysis of rewrite strategies. Our case studies show how this approach can be used to verify optimization paths, validate the execution trace of intricate proof procedures, and explore the behavior of non-confluent rule sets to gain practical insights.

3. *Open Platform for Strategic Experimentation*—We provide an extensible infrastructure that combines a programmable, quantified syntax with interactive state-space visualization, establishing a platform for the analysis of quantum optimization strategies.

The paper proceeds as follows: Sect. 2 introduces LMNtal, a graph rewriting language, and QLMNtal, a recent extension of LMNtal with quantified rules. Section 3 is a brief introduction of the ZX-calculus. Section 4 details our basic

Process	$P ::= \mathbf{0} \mid p(X_1, \ldots, X_n) \mid P, P \mid m\{P\} \mid T :\text{-} T$
Process template	$T ::= \mathbf{0} \mid p(X_1, \ldots, X_n) \mid T, T \mid m\{T\} \mid T :\text{-} T \mid \$p$

Fig. 1. Syntax of LMNtal.

LMNtal implementation of the ZX-calculus along with quantified rule examples. Section 5 presents the state space exploration framework with several case studies. Sections 6 and 7 present related and future work and conclusion.

2   LMNtal: A Hierarchical Graph Rewriting Language

We briefly explain the hierarchical graph rewriting language LMNtal [34]. Unlike many other formalisms of graph rewriting, LMNtal consists of (i) term-based syntax, (ii) structural congruence on terms that provides interpretation of terms as graphs, and (iii) small-step reduction relation, in the style of standard programming language definitions. For lack of space, we omit detailed syntactic conditions of (i) and introduce (ii) and (iii) informally, adapting from the description of [31], and leaving details to [32, Appendix A]. We also leave related work on hierarchical graph rewriting ([13] and many others) to [31]. A tutorial introduction to LMNtal can be found in [36] and the full formal definition in [34].

2.1   Overview of LMNtal

The syntax of LMNtal is given in Fig. 1, where three syntactic categories, link names (denoted by X), atom names (denoted by p), and possibly empty membrane names (denoted by m), are presupposed.

Since LMNtal was originally developed as a model of concurrency, the hierarchical graphs of LMNtal are also called *processes*. $\mathbf{0}$ is an inert process; $p(X_1, \ldots, X_n)\,(n \geq 0)$ is an n-ary *atom* (a.k.a. node) with *ordered links* (a.k.a. edges) $X_1, \ldots, X_n$; P, P is parallel composition; $\{P\}$ is a *cell* formed by wrapping P with an optionally named *membrane* $\{\ \}$; and $T :\text{-} T$ is a *rewrite rule*.

Occurrences of a link name represent endpoints of a one-to-one link between atoms (or more precisely, atom arguments). For this purpose, each link name in a process P is allowed to occur at most twice (Link Condition). A link whose name occurs only once in P is called a *free link* of P. Links may cross membranes and connect atoms located at different "places" of the membrane hierarchy. A graph in which each node has its own arity and totally ordered links, like an LMNtal graph, is often called a *port graph* [16].

Process templates on both sides of a rewrite rule allow *process contexts* [34, 37]. A process context, denoted $\$p$, works as a *wildcard* that matches "the rest of the processes" within the membrane in which it occurs. Whereas LMNtal allows us to specify what free links must occur in $\$p$, here we go without this feature, and $\$p$ matches a process with any number of free links.

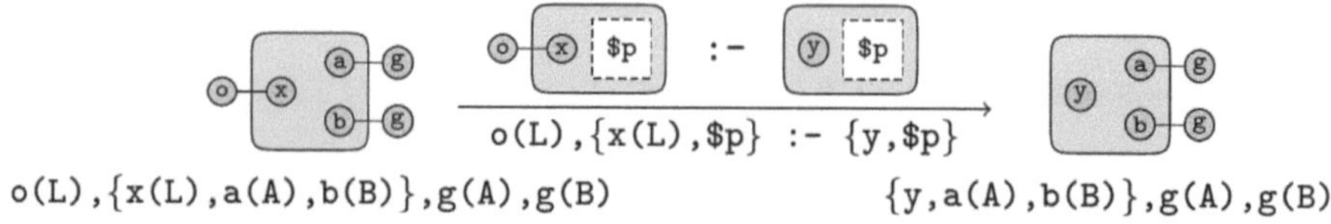

Fig. 2. Rewriting with (o(L),{x(L),$p}) :- {y,$p} .

Rewrite rules must observe several syntactic conditions [34] so that Link Condition is preserved in the course of program execution. Most importantly, link names in a rule must occur exactly twice, and each process context must occur exactly once at the top level of distinct cells in the left-hand side of a rule.

Figure 2 shows a simple example of an LMNtal process containing a membrane, in both textual and visual forms, and a rewriting step using a rule containing a process context.

The application of rules in LMNtal is nondeterministic because (i) a rule may be able to rewrite different subgraphs of a given graph, and (ii) different rules may be able to rewrite the same graph. The LMNtal runtime SLIM provides a *nondeterministic execution mode* that constructs the whole state space of rewriting, which can also be visualized using StateViewer [3]. Furthermore, SLIM provides an LTL model checker of the state space [18], and LaViT (LMNtal Visual Tools), which is a graphical IDE for LMNtal, provides visualizers of LMNtal graphs as well as a visualizer of state space called StateViewer.

LMNtal supports *guarded* rewrite rules of the form "T :- *Guard* | T." Guards restrict rule applications based on data types, comparison operators, and arithmetic operations. In addition, we allow some abbreviations including:

- unary atoms '+' and '-' can be written without parenthesis as +X and -X;
- atoms in arguments are regarded as connected via 'fresh' local links, e.g., a(b,c) ≡ a(B,C),b(B),c(C);
- a reserved binary atom '=', called a *connector*, fuses two links;
- a rule can be prefixed with a rule name followed by "@@".

2.2   QLMNtal: LMNtal with Quantification

QLMNtal[1] [29] is an extension of LMNtal that introduces *quantification* to both pattern matching and rewriting. The main features of QLMNtal are as follows: (i) it introduces three kinds of quantifiers, *cardinality*, *non-existence*, and *universal quantification* in a unified setting; (ii) it allows mixed and nested use of multiple quantifiers, enabling complicated quantification in a single rewrite rule; and (iii) it introduces *labelled* quantifiers to control the (in)dependency between different quantifiers occurring within a rewrite rule.

Cardinality quantification allows us to specify any number of processes within a specified range and rewrite them in a single step.

---

[1] The LMNtal runtime SLIM already fully supports intermediate code for QLMNtal, though some of the quantified rules are currently hand-compiled.

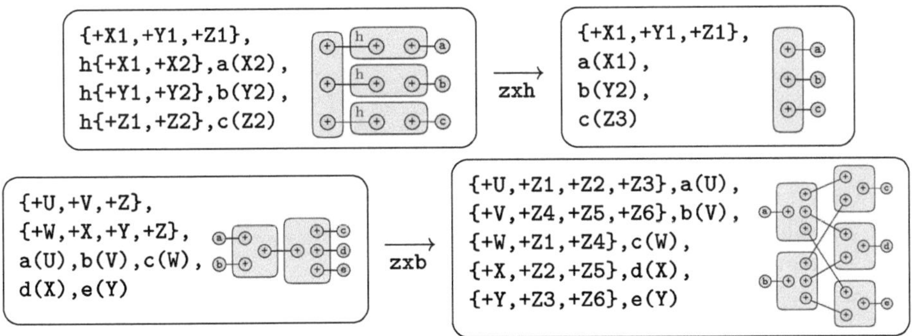

Fig. 3. Rewriting with Rules `zxh` (upper) and `zxb` (lower).

For example,

```
zxh@@ {<*>+L1}, <*>h{+L1,+L2} :- {<*>+L2}
```

is a QLMNtal rule that expresses the simplified Color Change rule of the ZX-calculus (Sect. 4.3), and Fig. 3 shows an example of rewriting. Here, `<*>` is a *cardinality quantifier* that represents "zero or more", and the three cardinality quantifiers in this rule, related to each other by empty labels, stand for the same number of processes.

QLMNtal also allows us to control the (in)dependency of quantifiers by labeling. For example,

```
zxb@@ {M<*>+L1,+L2},{+L2,N<*>+L3} :- M<*>{+L1,N<*>+L2},N<*>{M<*>+L2,+L3}
```

is a QLMNtal rule that expresses the essense of the (generalized) bialgebra rule (Sect. 4.3). Figure 3 shows an example of rewriting. M and N are quantifier labels; quantifiers with different labels are independent of each other. In this way, QLMNtal allows mixed and nested use of multiple quantifiers. For details including the syntax and formal semantics, the readers are referred to [29].

3 ZX-Calculus

Quantum programming frameworks such as Qiskit [22] and Cirq [8] use circuit-based descriptions where programs are expressed as temporally ordered sequences of operations on qubits. They use basic operations called *quantum gates* to implement arbitrary quantum computations. However, circuit representations alone often pose challenges for optimization [2,30] and verification [21].

The ZX-calculus [9,10] provides a diagrammatic rewriting system using simple structures built from two types of nodes connected by wires, serving as a computational model that describes both quantum circuits and their transformations. This visual and intuitive framework for representing quantum computations has a rigorous mathematical foundation from *string diagrams* [1,7,10].

3.1 ZX-Diagrams

The core component of the ZX-calculus, the ZX-diagram, consists of two types of nodes: green (Z-spiders) and red (X-spiders), as in Fig. 4. Z-spiders correspond to the computational basis $\{|0\rangle, |1\rangle\}$, whereas X-spiders correspond to the Hadamard basis $\{|+\rangle, |-\rangle\}$. Each node possesses a phase parameter $\alpha \in [0, 2\pi)$ and any number of input/output terminals. Hadamard gates can be constructed from these spiders, also shown in Fig. 4. The "$\ldots$" denotes arbitrarily many wires.

ZX-diagrams follow the principle of *only connectivity matters*, meaning that wires can be arbitrarily bent or stretched as long as the connectivity is preserved. Additionally, a single-input/output Hadamard gate can be formed using Z- and X-spiders as in Fig. 4. By connecting these components with wires, the framework provides a unified representation of quantum gates, states, and protocols. Further details of the foundations and the use of the ZX-calculus can be found in [9,10,38].

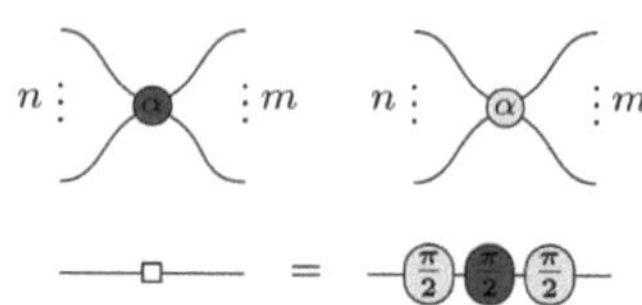

Fig. 4. ZX-spiders (upper), Hadamard gate (lower) [38]. (Color figure online)

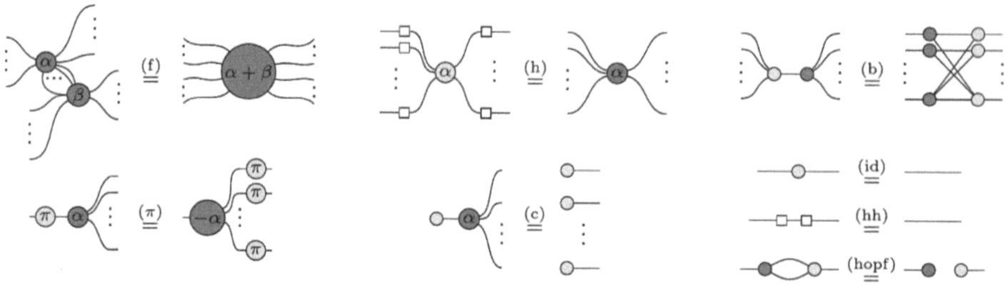

Fig. 5. Key Rewrite Rules in ZX-Calculus [38]. (f): spider fusion, (h): color change (b): (generalized) bialgebra rule, (π): π commutation, (c): copy, (id): identity, (hh): Hadamard cancellation, (hopf): Hopf. (Color figure online)

3.2 Basic Rewrite Rules

The ZX-calculus consists of rewrite rules of ZX-diagrams. Figure 5 shows the key rules, which allow the *color swapping* [39] symmetry (Z $\leftrightarrow$ X) and enable visual verification of complex quantum protocols. For details, see [9,10,38].

3.3 Circuit Extraction Problem

The conversion from quantum circuits to ZX-diagrams is straightforward by replacing each gate with its corresponding ZX-diagram. However, the reverse problem is known to be challenging. As mentioned in [38], there are two approaches to address this issue.

The first approach is to extend the definition of quantum circuits to allow arbitrary linear maps between qubits, which requires extending the definition of

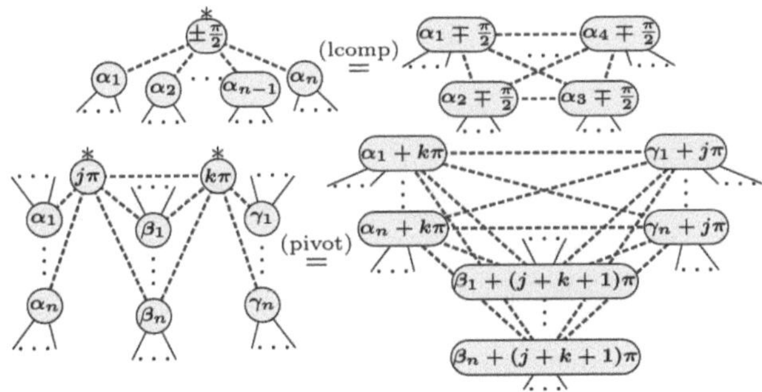

Fig. 6. ZX-rules based on local complementation and pivoting. Blue dotted wires are wires with a Hadamard gate [38] (Color figure online).

a circuit to include a broader class of quantum operations. In LMNtal, this can be achieved by defining a rule that translates each spider into a series of CNOT gates, which can then be applied to obtain the circuit.

The second approach is to restrict ZX-diagrams to represent only unitary computations. Since unitarity is a global property of a diagram, it is challenging to construct circuits efficiently by examining their local structure only. Recently, methods have been proposed that focus on a structural property of the diagram known as gflow [5,14]. These methods utilize specific graph transformation rules, such as local complementation and pivoting (Fig. 6), to systematically reshape the diagram into a circuit-like structure.

3.4 !-Boxes

The (informal) "..." notation is used to represent an arbitrary number of wires in ZX-diagrams, but a formal expression that avoids possible confusion has been proposed. The !-box [12,23,24] is represented as a square enclosing a part of the ZX-diagram, indicating that the enclosed part can be copied an arbitrary number (≥ 0) of times. Multiple !-boxes can exist within a single diagram, and they can overlap or be nested. The LMNtal counterpart of the !-boxes is the quantifiers of QLMNtal, which allow nested, labelled quantifiers and allow one to express rules like (generalized) bialgebra, as was shown in Sect. 2.2. However, translating these powerful !-box diagrams into executable rewrite rules can be complex in many programming environments, often requiring procedural workarounds.

There appears to be a direct correspondence between the structure of !-boxes and QLMNtal's quantifiers. An !-box enclosing a part of a diagram can be systematically translated into a cardinality quantifier `<*>` (zero or more) acting on the corresponding LMNtal atoms. Furthermore, in more complex scenarios, nested or overlapping !-boxes correspond to the nested, labeled quantifiers in QLMNtal. The generalized bialgebra rule in Fig. 7 serves as a prime example. The two !-boxes map directly to the two quantifiers (`M<*>` and `N<*>`) in the QLMNtal rule **zxb** (Sect. 2.2), where the nested quantifier on the right-hand slide stands for multiplicative copies of the link L2. This suggests the potential for a direct, systematic encoding from !-graph rules to QLMNtal rules.

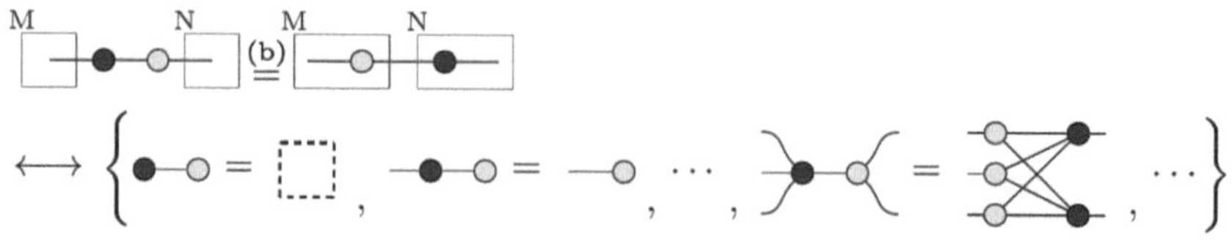

Fig. 7. !-graph for the generalized bialgebra rule (b) (Fig. 5). Each blue box is a !-box [38, p.47]. (Color figure online)

Although !-boxes are powerful, not all repetitive structures can be expressed. For example, they cannot represent complete graphs or local complementation [38], which is the case with QLMNtal also. However, we have confirmed that QLMNtal allows one to express pivoting (a.k.a. edge-local complementation) as a single rewrite rule. The idea is that, unlike complete graphs, it is sufficient to be able to express *complete bipartite graphs* to express pivoting. Furthermore, as illustrated in Sect. 4, LMNtal allows one to express rewriting strategies or procedures within the language, i.e., by using additional or modified rules.

4   ZX-Calculus Implementation in QLMNtal

This section describes the implementation strategy for the ZX-Calculus in LMNtal and QLMNtal.[2]

4.1   ZX-Diagram

The two basic components of the ZX-diagram, spiders and wires, can be directly represented using LMNtal membranes and links, respectively. Whereas each LMNtal atom has a fixed arity and its links are totally ordered, a membrane may hold outgoing links that are unordered. Thus, any ZX-diagram can be represented in LMNtal, since both frameworks do not care about diagram rotation or input/output. LMNtal's undirected links, which disregard length or orientation, ideally model the "only connectivity matters" principle of ZX-diagrams.

Spiders. Although each membrane can be given a name, we represent the two types of spiders with *unnamed* membranes as in Fig. 8. This is to treat the two types of spiders in a unified manner, since in the ZX-calculus, inverting the color of each spider in a rule gives us another valid rule. A membrane representing a spider holds input/output wires, a c atom holding the spider color, and an e^i atom holding the phase $\alpha \in [0, 360)$.

Hadamard gates. Although Hadamard gates can be constructed from basic components, we give them a dedicated LMNtal representation (Fig. 8) for simplicity. A Hadamard gate is represented using a membrane named h, which holds spider wires and a phase equals to π in the membrane, but no atoms representing colors. For the reason why the h membranes hold the constant phase π, see [32, Appendix C].

---

[2] All the implementations shown in Sect. 4 and Sect. 5 are available at https://github.com/lmntal/ZX-calculus.

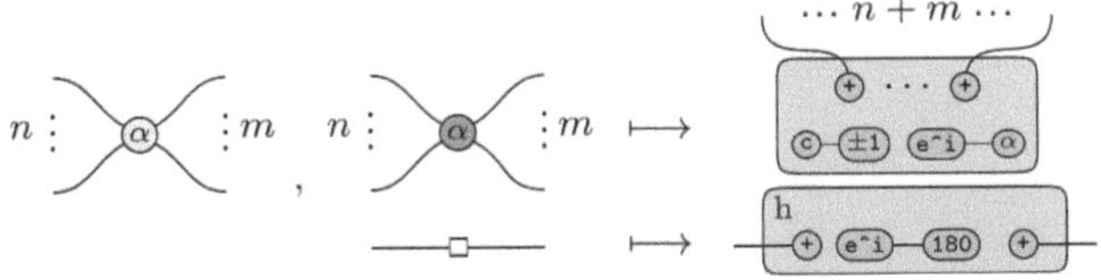

Fig. 8. Representation of Spiders (upper) and and a Hadamard gate (lower). (Color figure online)

4.2 The Challenge of Rule Implementation in Plain LMNtal

Plain LMNtal has sufficient expressiveness to implement the rewrite rules of the ZX-calculus. However, representing certain rules that handle an arbitrary number of wires, such as (π), (c), (h) and (b), is not straightforward in plain LMNtal. These rules require a *procedural* description consisting of multiple intermediate steps, rather than a single pattern-matching of diagrams.

The complexity is most evident in the generalized bialgebra rule (b). This rule defines a operation that duplicates spiders according to the number of wires (m and n, respectively) that are *not* connected between two spiders of different colors, and connects them to form a complete bipartite graph. Implementing this in plain LMNtal requires a multi-step procedure combining several rules: (i) counting the number of wires m and n, (ii) duplicating the spiders according to that number, and (iii) correctly connecting the duplicated spiders. An overview of this procedure is shown in Fig. 9. Specifically, this implementation consists of 10 LMNtal rules and requires $O(mn)$ rewriting steps in total. See [32, Appendix B] for details of how this approach works for all the ZX-rules including (b).

While this procedural implementation translates the declarative nature of a single ZX-rule into an executable workflow, it introduces intermediate states that do not directly correspond to valid ZX-diagrams. However, this is a manageable trade-off. Our framework offers control mechanisms to treat a series of rules as an atomic transaction. Furthermore, the abstraction techniques in our toolchain allow these intermediate states to be omitted from the state space, enabling analysis to focus solely on valid ZX-diagrams.

Note that implementing rules for a fixed, constant number of wires is straightforward and can still be done in a single LMNtal rule. To streamline this process, we have developed a converter that automatically generates LMNtal code from a ZX-diagram and rule representation, available at https://github.com/lmntal/zx-lmn-converter.

4.3 Simplifying the Encoding with QLMNtal

As shown in Sect. 4.2, the implementation of ZX-rules requires multiple LMNtal rules and thus multiple execution steps to represent (π), (c), (h), and (b). However, the cardinality construct introduced into QLMNtal turns out to be powerful enough to express each ZX-rule with a single QLMNtal rule as in Table 1. In particular, (b) is implemented using nested quantifiers, as explained in Sect. 2.2.

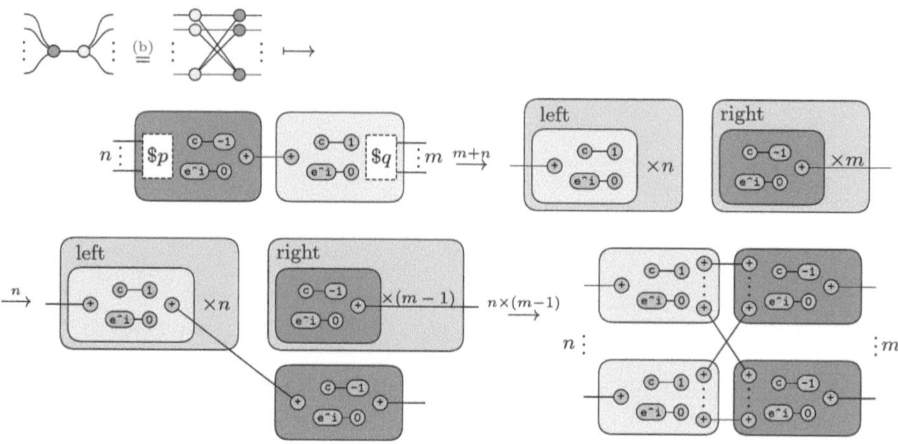

Fig. 9. Generalized bialgebra rule (b) represented in plain LMNtal. (Color figure online)

The LMNtal implementations shown in Table 1 are left-to-right transformations of the original ZX-rule equalities. This is because right-to-left applications of the rules may lead to an explosion of the state space in the non-deterministic execution of LMNtal. A right-to-left application of (c) and (f) would generate arbitrary phases, and that of (id) and (hh) would generate an identity spider from an empty wire.

While the right-to-left (b) rule can be expressed in a single QLMNtal rule and works, the inherent combinatorial complexity of the matching process at runtime remains. However, if the user knows the number of wires needed for the rules, it is easy to add special cases of the right-to-left rules. Also, we can easily control how many times they should be applied by adding any strategy. Our framework is thus positioned as a platform for formalizing and verifying human-designed rewrite strategies. Users can define a set of directed rules and use our platform to exhaustively analyze its consequences, such as reachability, termination, and confluence for certain classes of diagrams.

We would like to emphasize that in QLMNtal, all right-to-left transformation rules in Table 1 can also be implemented with a single rule by *simply swapping its left- and right-hand sides* and adjusting guard conditions.

5   Running the Examples

This section demonstrates our implementation using three example problems. All descriptions in this section are based on the ZX-calculus implementation in QLMNtal, showcasing how the platform can be used to model and verify different classes of rewrite strategies. Details on the example problems can be found in [38, Section 5]. Figures 11, 12, 14, 15 and 18 are state transition diagrams output using StateViewer (Sect. 2.1), which shows the final states in red so they can be easily identified from the state space. LMNtal's runtime SLIM reports the number of final states and their corresponding graphs. Additionally, LaViT allow us to visualize the graph associated with each state.

5.1 Analyzing Optimization Paths

Table 1. Left-to-Right QLMNtal implementation of ZX-rules.

ZX-rule	QLMNtal implementation

(π)	`{+L1,+L2,e^i(180),c(C1)}, {+L2,<*>+L3,e^i(A),c(C2)} :-`
	`  AA=-A, C1*C2=:=-1 |`
	`  {+L1,<*>+L2,e^i(AA),c(C2)}, <*>{+L2,+L3,e^i(180),c(C1)}`

(c)	`{+L1,e^i(0),c(C1)}, {+L1,<*>+L2,e^i(A),c(C2)} :-` `  int(A), C1*C2=:=-1 | <*>{+L2,e^i(0),c(C1)}`
(h)	`{<*>+L1,e^i(A),c(C)}, <*>h{+L1,+L2,e^i(180)} :-` `  int(A), CC=-C | {<*>+L2,e^i(A),c(CC)}`
(b)	`{M<*>+L1,+L2,e^i(0),c(1)}, {+L2,N<*>+L3,e^i(0),c(-1)} :-` `  M<*>{+L1,N<*>+L2,e^i(0),c(-1)}, N<*>{M<*>+L2,+L3,e^i(0),c(1)}`

The first case study demonstrates how our platform can be used to analyze optimization paths by introducing a simple, non-confluent rule and checking its impact on the state space. The goal is to answer a common question in optimization: *is it ever beneficial to temporarily increase a diagram's complexity to find a better solution?*

To model this, we introduce a right-to-left version of the (id) rule, `idgen_g`, which adds a Z-spider to an arbitrary wire. While potentially useful in some contexts, such a rule can also create inefficient pathways and dramatically expand the state space. We applied a basic set of simplification rules, (f), (id), and (h), to two typical circuits, (i) the quantum teleportation circuit [6,9] and (ii) the GHZ preparation circuit, which generates the Greenberger-Horne-Zeilinger state [19,26]. We then compared the resulting state space to the one where the `idgen_g` rule was permitted to be applied at most once:

```
idgen_g@@ {+L1,$p1}, {+L2,$p2}, idgen_g(N)
   :- int(N), N>0, NN=N-1 |
   {+L1,+LL1,$p1}, {+L2,+LL2,$p2}, {+LL1,+LL2,e^i(0),c(1)}, idgen_g(NN).
```

In order to perform LTL model checking, we defined the proposition p as "`idgen_g` is never applied and the simplification has been completed," and by refuting the claim that p is never satisfied (`!<>`p), we showed that the path where Z-spiders are not generated is the most efficient.

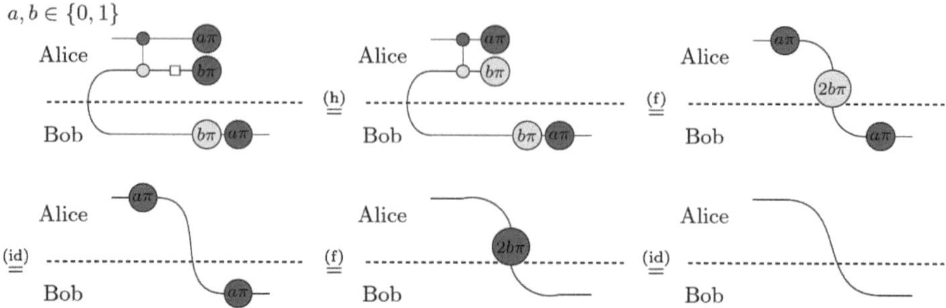

Fig. 10. Simplification of the quantum teleportation circuit in ZX-calculus [38]. (Color figure online)

Quantum Teleportation Circuit: An example of simplifying a quantum teleportation circuit is shown in Fig. 10. In this paper, we choose fixed values for a and b. The results for the quantum teleportation circuit are shown in Fig. 11 (without `idgen_g`) and Fig. 12 (with `idgen_g`).

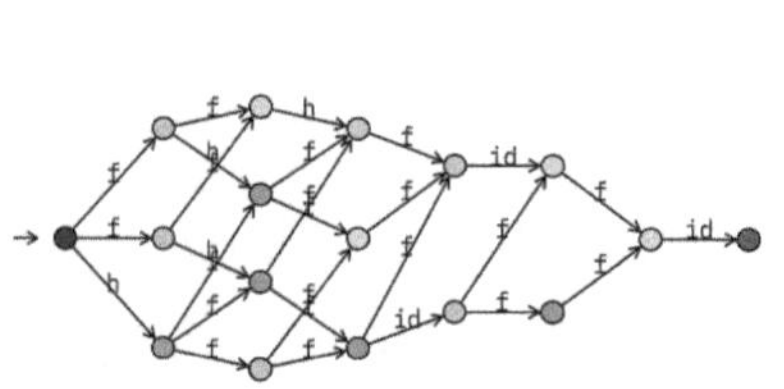

Fig. 11. State space of the quantum teleportation circuit (17 states).

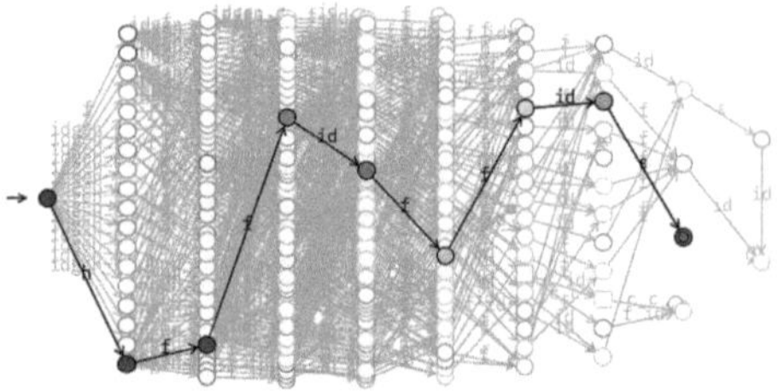

Fig. 12. Application result of `idgen_g` in the quantum teleportation circuit (313 states).

We used LTL model checking to formally verify the property that "the simplified final state can be reached without ever applying the `idgen_g` rule." The successful refutation of the claim `!<> p` (where p represents completion without using `idgen_g`) proves that all shortest paths avoid this rule. This confirms that, for this rule set, adding an identity spider only creates suboptimal solution paths.

GHZ Preparation Circuit: The experiments on GHZ preparation circuits yielded the same conclusion. The 3-bit circuit can be simplified as in Fig. 13, and in Figs. 14 and 15, we show examples of the experiment results on this circuit. This demonstrates the platform's ability to exhaustively analyze and validate the efficiency of a given optimization strategy.

We extended this analysis to GHZ preparation circuits from 4 to 10 bits. The results, shown in Table 2, reveal an exponential growth pattern, where the number of states quadrupled for each additional qubit. For the 10-bit circuit, which

Table 2. State space of GHZ preparation circuits.

Bit	# of states
3	39
4	156
5	606
6	2424
7	9624
8	38596
9	153696
10	614784

starts from an initial graph of 28 spiders and one Hadamard gate, our system successfully explored all 614,784 states. Although the size of intermediate state graphs varies, considering LMNtal's demonstrated ability to explore state spaces of up to 10^9 states, it is reasonable to assume that our framework can handle significantly larger problems.

5.2   Verifying an Inductive Proof Strategy

Beyond simple path analysis, our framework can formally verify complex, human-designed proof strategies for specific instances. We demonstrate this by encoding the inductive proof of a key lemma Fig. 16 from [10, Lemma 9.129], hereafter Lemma L, which is central to the local complementation rule.

While the proof can be done inductively from ZX-rules as shown in [10, Section 9.4], a model checker cannot handle mathematical induction over n, which is the domain of proof assistants. However, its strength is to be able to make sure that the logic of a proof holds for a concrete, non-trivial case, as an invaluable step towards validating a complex algorithm. Here, we check Lemma L for the $n = 4$ case by checking the inductive step from $n = 3$ to $n = 4$.

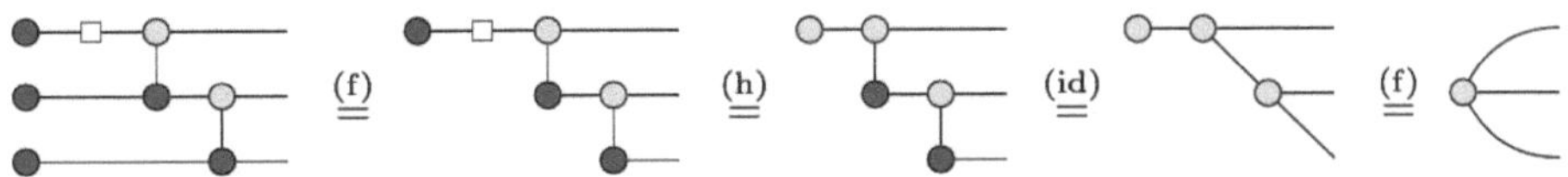

Fig. 13. Simplification of the 3-bit GHZ preparation circuit [38]. (Color figure online)

Lemma L is about a structure with a complete graph K_n connected by Hadamard edges (Fig. 16). In this procedure, first we check that Lemma L holds for $n = 0$. Then, we show that Lemma L also holds for $n = 1, 2, \ldots, N$ for some N using LMNtal rules representing the inductive definition.

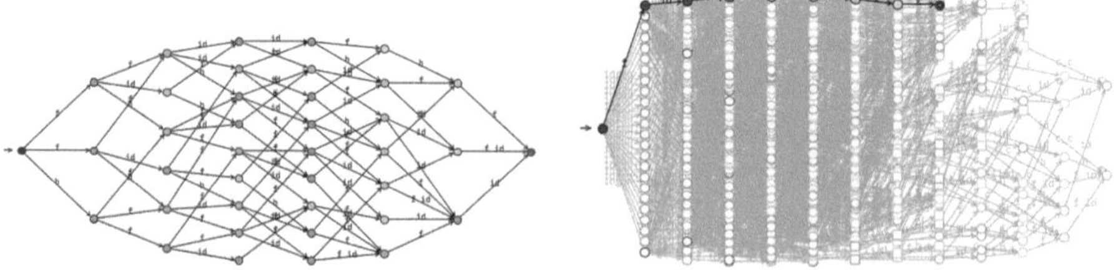

Fig. 14. State space of the 3-bit GHZ preparation circuit (39 states).

Fig. 15. Application result of `idgen_g` in the 3-bit GHZ preparation circuit (800 states).

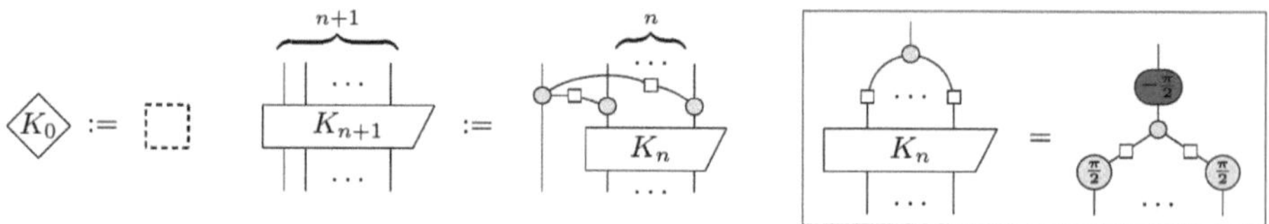

Fig. 16. Definition of K_n and Lemma L (blue box) to be proved. (Color figure online)

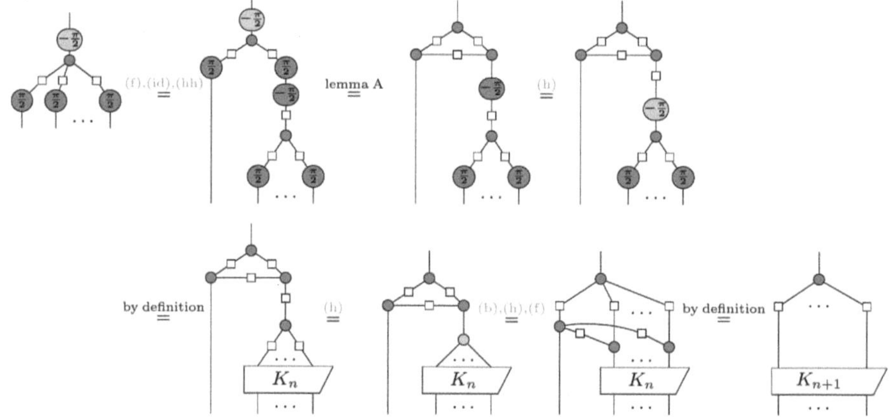

Fig. 17. Proof Flow of Lemma L. (Color figure online)

The overall flow is shown in Fig. 17. When the rewriting procedure is clear, we can avoid state space explosion by assigning a *rule token* to each rule and preparing a *linked list of the rule tokens*. This technique imposes procedural control onto the declarative rule set. A linked list of tokens, each corresponding to a specific rule in the proof sequence, is added to the graph. A rule is only permitted to fire if its corresponding token is at the head of the list. Upon firing, the rule consumes the token, activating the next rule in the sequence. In addition, for right-to-left rules, we can restrict the redexes by modifying the naively implemented ones. The state space generated by the $n = 4$ case is shown in

Fig. 18. The graph visualizes the proof trace itself. The initial branching shows the four possible choices for selecting the $n = 3$ subgraph required by the inductive hypothesis. Each path then follows the encoded proof steps, all converging on the single final state on the far right, which is the expected conclusion of the lemma. This demonstrates how our platform can serve as a useful tool for the mechanical verification of intricate, human-devised proof procedures.

5.3   Exploring Non-confluent Strategies

This case study demonstrates the platform's utility in exploring non-confluent state space. By analyzing the complete state space, we can gain insights into the rule set's behavior, identify "dead ends" (undesirable final states), and discover heuristics for guiding rewriting towards simplified forms.

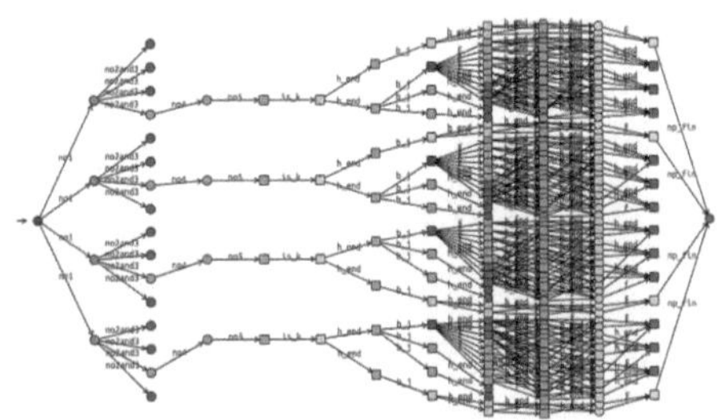

Fig. 18. State Space of Lemma L ($n = 4$, 266 states).

Our toolchain is well-suited for this analysis. The StateViewer visualizer allows for interactive exploration of the paths leading to each terminal state, including tracing transitions backward and filtering them by rule names. This enables a detailed inspection of which rule sequences lead to desirable or undesirable outcomes. Furthermore, specific hypotheses about path efficiency can be formally specified and verified using LTL model checking.

The (π) and (b) rules are recursive, in the sense that their right-hand sides can match their left-hand sides, causing infinite loops. To manage this, we constrained their number of applications to a constant sufficient for simplification in these experiments. As shown in Table 3, we see that the choice of the rule set impacts the scale of the strategic challenge. The Pauli pushing

Table 3. State space of non-confluent examples

Example (Rules)	# of states	# of final states
Pauli pushing ((π)×4, (f), (id))	533	7
2-qubit QFT ((π)×2, (f), (id), (c), (h))	1186	8
Detecting Entanglement ((c), (f), (h), (hopf), (id))	436711	60

example, with a relatively simple set of rules, generates a manageable but non-trivial state space with seven final states. The Detecting Entanglement problem results in a larger state space, caused by an interplay between specific rules. The application of (hopf) can delete wires between spiders and create new graph structures that become valid targets for the (c) rule. Each application of (c) then increases the number of spiders, thereby unlocking diverse rewrite paths.

From the state space by 2-qubit QFT, we observed that applying the (id) rule early in the rewriting process often led to "dead ends", and applying the (π)

rule in the middle stage tended to lead to more successful simplifications. This suggests a testable heuristic for optimization: rather than reducing the number of spiders in early stage, applying certain rules to temporarily increase complexity may open up more effective simplification paths later on. Analyzing the conditions under which such heuristics hold in different contexts is a promising direction for future research using our platform. For more details about the 2-qubit QFT example, see [32, Appendix E].

6   Related Work

PyZX [25] is a mature Python library optimized for large-scale quantum circuit simplification using built-in and learned heuristics. Our framework is not intended to be a competitor for optimization performance. Instead, it serves as a modeling platform to design and verify the underlying rewrite strategies themselves. For instance, a new simplification heuristic could be modeled in QLMNtal and its properties (e.g., confluence or termination for certain inputs) be analyzed in our system before being implemented in a performance-oriented tool like PyZX.

Quantomatic [27] is a graphical proof assistant for string diagrams, focusing on interactive, step-by-step theorem proving using *directed* equations. Our approach is complementary, centered on the automatic, exhaustive state-space exploration of rewrite strategies using model checking. Whereas Quantomatic has graphical syntax for string diagrams, LMNtal is a general-purpose language with programming language-style text syntax and semantics supporting hierarchical port graphs [36], which offers familiarity and more control (Sect. 5) for developers wishing to script and manage rule sets. Furthermore, the notation of hierarchy and wildcards in QLMNtal is expressive enough to capture the structures of string diagrams in symmetric monoidal categories.

Comparison between LMNtal and other graph transformation languages and tools, including Groove and GP 2, can be found in [29] and [31].

7   Conclusion and Future Work

This paper introduced an approach and a tool for modeling and analyzing complex rewriting strategies for quantum graphical calculi. We demonstrated that QLMNtal's quantified pattern matching can directly and declaratively express ZX-rules involving arbitrary numbers of wires, which can be non-intuitive and verbose in conventional procedural encodings. Using this representation, we presented a method based on state-space exploration and model checking to formally verify properties of human-designed rewrite strategies.

By combining quantified hierarchical graph rewriting with interactive state visualization, our framework serves as a laboratory for exploring new ideas in quantum computing. As shown in our case studies, this allows us to analyze optimization paths, validate the execution trace of intricate proof procedures, and explore the behavior of non-confluent rule sets to gain practical insights.

This approach bridges the gap between the informal notation of diagrammatic reasoning and its executable, verifiable application.

For future work, we plan to extend our platform to other calculi like the ZW-calculus [20] to build a comprehensive library of verified strategies. (We already implemented another variation, ZH-calculus [4]; see [32, Appendix C].) We also plan to systematically analyze existing optimization techniques to uncover new findings and utilize LMNtal's capabilities for novel global rewriting methods.

On the practical side, extending our current translator to support input from standard formats like OpenQASM [11] would further enhance the platform's utility for the quantum computing community. Our team is also currently working on introducing probabilities into the LMNtal language and system, which we hope can lead to the modeling of measurement-based quantum computing [15].

Acknowledgments. This work is partially supported by Grant-In-Aid for Scientific Research (23K11057), JSPS, Japan, and Waseda University Grant for Special Research Projects (2025C-427).

Disclosure of Interests. The authors have no competing interests to declare that are relevant to the content of this article.

References

1. Abramsky, S., Coecke, B.: Categorical quantum mechanics. In: Engesser, K., Gabbay, D.M., Lehmann, D. (eds.) Handbook of Quantum Logic and Quantum Structures, pp. 261–323. Elsevier, Amsterdam (2009). https://doi.org/10.1016/B978-0-444-52869-8.50010-4
2. Amy, M.: Towards large-scale functional verification of universal quantum circuits. In: 15th International Conference on Quantum Physics and Logic (QPL 2018). EPTCS, vol. 287, pp. 1–21. Open Publishing Association (2019). https://doi.org/10.4204/EPTCS.287.1
3. Ayano, T., Hori, T., Iwasawa, H., Ogawa, S., Ueda, K.: LMNtal model checking using an integrated development environment. Comput. Softw. **27**(4), 4_197–4_214 (2010). https://doi.org/10.11309/jssst.27.4_197
4. Backens, M., Kissinger, A.: ZH: a complete graphical calculus for quantum computations involving classical non-linearity. In: 15th International Conference on Quantum Physics and Logic (QPL 2018). EPTCS, vol. 287, pp. 23–42. Open Publishing Association (2019). https://doi.org/10.4204/eptcs.287.2
5. Backens, M., Miller-Bakewell, H., de Felice, G., Lobski, L., van de Wetering, J.: There and back again: a circuit extraction tale. Quantum **5**, 421 (2021). https://doi.org/10.22331/q-2021-03-25-421
6. Bennett, C.H., Brassard, G., Crépeau, C., Jozsa, R., Peres, A., Wootters, W.K.: Teleporting an unknown quantum state via dual classical and Einstein-Podolsky-Rosen channels. Phys. Rev. Lett. **70**, 1895–1899 (1993). https://doi.org/10.1103/PhysRevLett.70.1895
7. Biamonte, J., Bergholm, V.: Tensor networks in a nutshell (2017). https://doi.org/10.48550/arXiv.1708.00006
8. Developers, C.: Cirq. Zenodo (2024). https://doi.org/10.5281/zenodo.4062499

9. Coecke, B., Duncan, R.: Interacting quantum observables: categorical algebra and diagrammatics. New J. Phys. **13**(4), 043016 (2011). https://doi.org/10.1088/1367-2630/13/4/043016

10. Coecke, B., Kissinger, A.: Picturing Quantum Processes: A First Course in Quantum Theory and Diagrammatic Reasoning. Cambridge University Press (2017). https://doi.org/10.1017/9781316219317

11. Cross, A.W., Bishop, L.S., Smolin, J.A., Gambetta, J.M.: Open quantum assembly language (2017). https://doi.org/10.48550/arXiv.1707.03429

12. Dixon, L., Duncan, R.: Graphical reasoning in compact closed categories for quantum computation. Ann. Math. Artif. Intell. **56**, 23–42 (2009). https://doi.org/10.1007/s10472-009-9141-x

13. Drewes, F., Hoffmann, B., Plump, D.: Hierarchical graph transformation. J. Comput. Syst. Sci. **64**(2), 249–283 (2002). https://doi.org/10.1006/jcss.2001.1790

14. Duncan, R., Kissinger, A., Perdrix, S., van de Wetering, J.: Graph-theoretic simplification of quantum circuits with the ZX-calculus. Quantum **4**, 279 (2020). https://doi.org/10.22331/q-2020-06-04-279

15. Duncan, R., Perdrix, S.: Rewriting measurement-based quantum computations with generalised flow. In: Abramsky, S., Gavoille, C., Kirchner, C., Meyer auf der Heide, F., Spirakis, P.G. (eds.) ICALP 2010. LNCS, vol. 6199, pp. 285–296. Springer, Heidelberg (2010). https://doi.org/10.1007/978-3-642-14162-1_24

16. Ene, N.C., Fernández, M., Pinaud, B.: Attributed hierarchical port graphs and applications. In: Fourth International Workshop on Rewriting Techniques for Program Transformations and Evaluation (WPTE 2017). EPTCS, vol. 265, pp. 2–19. Open Publishing Association (2018). https://doi.org/10.4204/eptcs.265.2

17. Früwirth, T.: Theory and practice of Constraint Handling Rules. J. Logic Program. **37**(1), 95–138 (1998). https://doi.org/10.1016/S0743-1066(98)10005-5 Handling Rules. J. Logic Program. **37**(1), 95–138 (1998). https://doi.org/10.1016/S0743-1066(98)10005-5

18. Gocho, M., Hori, T., Ueda, K.: Evolution of the LMNtal runtime to a parallel model checker. Comput. Softw. **28**(4), 137–157 (2011). https://doi.org/10.11309/jssst.28.4_137

19. Greenberger, D.M., Horne, M.A., Zeilenger, A.: Going beyond bell's theorem. In: Kafatos, M. (ed.) Bell's Theorem, Quantum Theory and Conceptions of the Universe, pp. 69–72. Springer, Cham (1989). https://doi.org/10.1007/978-94-017-0849-4_10

20. Hadzihasanovic, A.: A diagrammatic axiomatisation for qubit entanglement. In: 30th Annual ACM/IEEE Symposium on Logic in Computer Science (LICS 2015), pp. 573–584. IEEE Computer Society (2015). https://doi.org/10.1109/LICS.2015.59

21. Hietala, K., Rand, R., Hung, S.H., Li, L., Hicks, M.: Proving quantum programs correct. In: 12th International Conference on Interactive Theorem Proving (ITP 2021). Leibniz International Proceedings in Informatics (LIPIcs), vol. 193, pp. 21:1–21:19 (2021). https://doi.org/10.4230/LIPIcs.ITP.2021.21

22. Javadi-Abhari, A., et al.: Quantum computing with Qiskit (2024). https://doi.org/10.48550/arXiv.2405.08810

23. Kissinger, A., Quick, D.: Tensors, !-graphs, and non-commutative quantum structures. New Gener. Comput. **34**, 87–123 (2016). https://doi.org/10.1007/s00354-016-0203-4

24. Kissinger, A., Merry, A., Soloviev, M.: Pattern graph rewrite systems. In: Developments in Computational Models 2012 (DCM 2012). EPTCS, vol. 143, pp. 54–66. Open Publishing Association (2014). https://doi.org/10.4204/eptcs.143.5

25. Kissinger, A., van de Wetering, J.: PyZX: large scale automated diagrammatic reasoning. In: 16th International Conference on Quantum Physics and Logic (QPL 2019). EPTCS, vol. 318, pp. 229–241. Open Publishing Association (2020). https://doi.org/10.4204/EPTCS.318.14
26. Kissinger, A., van de Wetering, J.: Reducing the number of non-Clifford gates in quantum circuits. Phys. Rev. A **102**(2) (2020). https://doi.org/10.1103/physreva.102.022406
27. Kissinger, A., Zamdzhiev, V.: Quantomatic: a proof assistant for diagrammatic reasoning. In: Felty, A.P., Middeldorp, A. (eds.) CADE 2015. LNCS (LNAI), vol. 9195, pp. 326–336. Springer, Cham (2015). https://doi.org/10.1007/978-3-319-21401-6_22
28. LMNtal Developers: LMNtal, a unifying language and model checking tools (2024). https://github.com/lmntal
29. Mishina, H., Ueda, K.: Introducing quantification into a hierarchical graph rewriting language. In: 34th International Symposium on Logic-Based Program Synthesis and Transformation (LOPSTR 2024). LNCS, vol. 14919, pp. 220–239. Springer Cham (2024). https://doi.org/10.1007/978-3-031-71294-4_13, extended version available at https://arxiv.org/abs/2411.14802
30. Nam, Y., Ross, N.J., Su, Y., Childs, A.M., Maslov, D.: Automated optimization of large quantum circuits with continuous parameters. NPJ Quantum Inf. **4**(1), 1–12 (2018). https://doi.org/10.1038/s41534-018-0072-4
31. Takyu, K., Ueda, K.: Enhancing a hierarchical graph rewriting language based on MELL Cut Elimination. In: 27th International Symposium on Practical Aspects of Declarative Languages (PADL 2025). LNCS, vol. 15537, pp. 196–214. Springer Cham (2025). https://doi.org/10.1007/978-3-031-84924-4_13, extended version available at https://arxiv.org/abs/2409.11015
32. Tei, K., Mishina, H., Yamamoto, N., Ueda, K.: Graph rewriting language as a platform for quantum diagrammatic calculi (2025). https://arxiv.org/abs/2511.15581
33. Ueda, K.: Encoding the pure lambda calculus into hierarchical graph rewriting. In: Voronkov, A. (ed.) RTA 2008. LNCS, vol. 5117, pp. 392–408. Springer, Heidelberg (2008). https://doi.org/10.1007/978-3-540-70590-1_27
34. Ueda, K.: LMNtal as a hierarchical logic programming language. Theoret. Comput. Sci. **410**(46), 4784–4800 (2009). https://doi.org/10.1016/j.tcs.2009.07.043
35. Ueda, K.: Logic/constraint programming and concurrency: the hard-won lessons of the Fifth Generation Computer Project. Sci. Comput. Program. **164**, 3–17 (2018). https://doi.org/10.1016/j.scico.2017.06.002
36. Ueda, K.: Gentle introduction to LMNtal: language design and implementation. Tutorial given at the 17th International Conference on Graph Transformation (ICGT 2024) (2024). https://conf.researchr.org/details/icgt-2024/icgt-2024-research-papers/17/Gentle-Introduction-to-LMNtal-Language-Design-and-Implementation
37. Ueda, K., Kato, N.: LMNtal: a language model with links and membranes. In: Mauri, G., Păun, G., Pérez-Jiménez, M.J., Rozenberg, G., Salomaa, A. (eds.) WMC 2004. LNCS, vol. 3365, pp. 110–125. Springer, Heidelberg (2005). https://doi.org/10.1007/978-3-540-31837-8_6

38. van de Wetering, J.: ZX-calculus for the working quantum computer scientist (2020). https://doi.org/10.48550/arXiv.2012.13966
39. de Witt, C.S., Zamdzhiev, V.: The ZX-calculus is incomplete for quantum mechanics. In: 11th Workshop on Quantum Physics and Logic (QPL 2014). EPTCS, vol. 172, pp. 285–292. Open Publishing Association (2014). https://doi.org/10.4204/EPTCS.172.20

Determinacy Checking for Elpi:
an Higher-Order Logic Programming
Language with Cut

Davide Fissore[(✉)] [ID] and Enrico Tassi [ID]

Université Côte d'Azur, Inria, Nice, France
`davide.fissore@inria.fr`

Abstract. Elpi is a higher-order logic programming language derived from λProlog and widely used to extend the Rocq interactive theorem prover. Typical users are familiar with types and functional programming but often lack experience with backtracking.

We introduce a language of signatures to declare that a predicate is operationally deterministic, meaning that calling the predicate does not leave any choice points. The signature language handles higher-order programs and dynamic programs.

We present a static analyzer that verifies these signatures and report its application to the majority of public Elpi code in the Rocq ecosystem.

Keywords: Determinacy Analysis · Higher Order · Logic Programming · Cut

1   Introduction

Elpi is a higher-order logic programming language, a dialect of λProlog, particularly well suited for manipulating syntax trees with binders (see [6,14,22,23]). It is used as an extension language for the Rocq Prover (formerly the Coq proof assistant) and has become an important piece of infrastructure: several projects and libraries depend on Elpi [1,3,8,9,17,20]. Examples include the Hierarchy-Builder library-structuring tool [4], which supports the Mathematical Components ecosystem [21] and mechanizations such as the Odd Order and Four Color theorems [11,12], and Derive [13,29,30], a program-and-proof synthesis framework with industrial applications at SkyLabs AI.

Over the years Elpi was put in the hands of quite a number of Rocq users and the most widely cited barrier to entry has been the paradigm shift to a logic programming one. Rocq users are comfortable with typed and functional programming but often lack experience with backtracking and its control. Uncontrolled backtracking can produce slower programs and complicate debugging.

This work has been supported by the French government, through the France 2030 investment plan managed by the Agence Nationale de la Recherche, as part of the "UCA DS4H" project, reference ANR-17-EURE-0004.

To lower this barrier we design a system of determinacy signatures that allows programmers to declare when a predicate behaves like a function: at most one result is produced and the runtime will not consider alternative results. This notion of determinism is called *semidet* by Henderson et al. [16] and named *operationally deterministic* by Nakamura [25]. Alternative notions exist, for example Warren [5] considers predicates *observably deterministic* when they produce the same result multiple times or diverge. We chose operational determinacy since it matches the behavior of functions in mainstream functional languages.

Our determinacy checker covers Elpi's higher-order features, including higher-order predicates (for example map and fold, see Sect. 2.1) and dynamic predicates that extend themselves at runtime (see Sect. 2.2).

We apply these signatures to a large portion of publicly available Elpi code in the Rocq ecosystem and report our experience. Our findings indicate that most Elpi programs are intended to be backtracking-free and require only minimal signatures for the static analyzer we implemented to verify determinacy.

Contributions. 1) we design a language of signatures to assert the determinacy of predicates that covers higher-order logic programming constructs such as first-class predicates and dynamic predicates; 2) we implement a static analyzer for that language; 3) we apply the static analyzer to most of the Elpi code available in the Rocq ecosystem.

2   Elpi and Determinacy Signatures by Examples

As in most logic programming languages, Elpi programs are organized in rules. When rules are not *mutually exclusive*, i.e. multiple rules apply on the same query, the runtime continues the computation using the rule with highest priority. Moreover it stores the other rules as a *choice point* and can backtrack to that point to continue the computation. What makes backtracking tricky to Elpi users is that it is an opt-out feature of logic programming: it is left to the programmer to tell the runtime to commit to one rule and discard the choice point, rather than the other way around. If the user forgets to commit to a rule, his program still works but becomes much harder to debug and typically slower to run in case of failures.

The simplest example is the list-membership *relation* that can succeed more than once if the element we are looking for occurs multiple times in the list:

```
1    mem X [Y|_ ]  :- X = Y.     % the head is the X we are looking for, or
2    mem X [_|YS]  :- mem X YS.  % recurse on the tail
```

In the code above each line represents a rule. By convention, unification variables are capitalized, and following the λ-calculus tradition application is written without parentheses, i.e. $f\ x$ rather than $f(x)$. Square brackets are used for lists with pipe separating the head from the tail. The :- symbol separates the head of a rule from its premises. Rules are tried in the order of their declaration by unifying their head with the current query.

The first rule for `mem` is the base case: it succeeds if the head of the list is equal to the `X` we are looking for. The second one discards the list's head and continues looking for `X` in the tail. A query such as `mem` 2 [2,3,2] can be solved in two different ways: either using rule 1 immediately, or using rule 2 twice to discard the first two items, and then conclude with rule 1.

Elpi users often have a background in functional programming and simply do expect `mem` to be a *function* testing membership, and not a relation. Moreover one needs to look, carefully, at how `mem` is implemented in order to see the peril. This misconception becomes a problem when they use `mem` in a larger piece of code and observe its execution.

```
main L :- code_before L, mem 1 L, code_after L.
```

For example, in the code above, one may see `code_after` being executed multiple times: each choice point left by `mem` enables the runtime to backtrack to that point in time and continue from there. Even worse, if `code_after` is expensive and fails, one pays its cost multiple times.

It must be said that backtracking can be very useful in some situations and that a programmer with experience in logic programming can take advantage of that. We want the Elpi casual user to be able to write code without mastering all that, and simply declare that they expect *their code* to compute functions.

```
func main list int -> . % the signature for main
```

The signature starts by a keyword declaring the determinacy of the predicate: `func` for deterministic predicates, that we also call functions, and `pred` for any predicate, including both functions and relations. Inputs are separated from outputs by the arrow symbol, and in the case of `main` there is no output.

```
main L :- code_before L, mem 1 L, code_after L.
%                         ^^^^^^ error: non-deterministic atom
```

Since `main` was declared as a function, our static analysis invites the user to discard the choice points left by `mem`, for example by inserting a ! (a *cut* directive) after it. Assuming `code_after` is a functions, this code is accepted, since the cut discards all choice points generated by `mem` and `code_before L`.

```
main L :- code_before L, mem 1 L, !, code_after L. % OK
```

Note that the programmer may also write a functional membership test as follows, and use it in functional code with no additional safeguard. In this case the cut discards the second rule as soon as `X = Y` succeeds.

```
func in int, list int -> .
in X [Y|_ ] :- X = Y, !. % commit to this rule, discard the next one
in X [_|YS] :- in X YS.

main L :- code_before L, in 1 L, code_after L. % OK
```

Tracking the use of backtracking code statically is a well known technique in logic programming called determinacy analysis [5,28]. What the literature lacks is a treatment of Elpi features not available in plain Prolog, see Sects. 2.1 and 2.2.

2.1 Higher-Order Programs

A notable higher-order program is the one turning relations into functions.[1]

```
func once (pred) -> .  % a function taking a fully applied predicate
once P :- P, !.        % the ! commits to the first success
```

We say that the signature of the **once** predicate marks it as *unconditionally* a function: **once** leaves no choice points, no matter what it receives as the higher-order argument P.

An example of a *conditional* function is the predicate to map over a list:

```
func map (func A -> B), list A -> list B.
map _ [] [].
map F [X|XS] [Y|YS] :- F X Y, map F XS YS.
```

We say that the signature of **map** has a *precondition*, namely that F is a function, and a *postcondition*, namely that **map** is a function, i.e., the call **map F L L'** leaves no choice points. If the precondition is not met the postcondition is not guaranteed to hold and we say that **map** is *miscalled*. In this case we weaken its signature to[2]:

```
pred map (func A -> B), list A -> list B.
```

Our static analysis tracks miscalled functions and considers them as relations for the analysis of the surrounding code. This is important to avoid code duplication, i.e., we can just have one copy of **map** in our library. We give an example of four scenarios involving calls and miscalls to **map**.

```
% a function                        % a relation
func incr int -> int.               pred get_pdiv int -> int.
incr 1 2.                           get_pdiv 6 3. get_pdiv 6 2.

          % four predicates calling map or miscalling map
func p list int -> list int.        pred q list int -> list int.
p L R :- map incr L R. % OK          q L R :- map get_pdiv L R. % OK

func r list int -> list int.        func r1 list int -> list int.
r L R :- map get_pdiv L R.          r1 L R :- map get_pdiv L R, !. % OK
         % ^^^^^^^^^ error: non-deterministic atom
```

---

[1] The syntax (pred), equivalent to (pred ->), is for fully applied predicates, i.e. for terms with neither inputs nor outputs.

[2] We explain in detail this weakining operation in Sect. 5.

Here p is a function because the precondition of map is respected (incr is a function). The body of q contains a miscall to map; as a consequence q may leave choice points. This is not an error because q is declared to be a relation. The body of q and r are identical, but r should be a function and hence the static analyzer complains. The predicate r1 has the same signature of r but it compensates the miscall to map by discarding choice points via a cut. The static analyzer accepts this last declaration. We point out that, partial applications, like, (map incr), are accepted in our system, see Sect. 5.

2.2   Dynamic Programs

The domain where Elpi really shines is the manipulation of higher-order data represented via the so-called λ-tree syntax [24] also called HOAS [26]. Such data is pervasive in interactive provers based on Type Theory such as Rocq. In the paradigmatic example below tm is the data type for λ-terms.

```
kind tm type.                    % datatype of λ-terms in HOAS form
type app tm -> tm -> tm.         %  - binary application
type lam (tm -> tm) -> tm.       %  - λ-abstraction
```

In the HOAS encoding of syntax with binders we do not find a node for variables: we re-use the notion of bound variable of the programming language to encode the one of the syntax tree. At the level of types we see that the lam node carries an Elpi function over terms. It is by applying this function that one can recover the body of the λ-abstraction. A simple program manipulating higher-order data is the function performing a deep copy of a term:

```
func copy tm -> tm.
copy (app A B) (app C D)  :- copy A C, copy B D.
copy (lam F) (lam G)      :- pi x\ copy x x => copy (F x) (G x).
```

The copy of an application is built from the copies of the subterms. What is more interesting is how one copies under a binder. The "pi x\ copy x x =>" instruction generates a fresh constant x and adds to the program the rule copy x x for the rest of the execution of copy. That rule explains how to copy the new constant x. Intuitively "pi x\.. => .." amounts to a well-bracketed use of Prolog's assert/1 and retract/1. Finally the code performs a recursive call over F x: by applying the Elpi function F to the fresh symbol x one obtains the body of the λ-abstraction where the bound variable is replaced by the new symbol x.

In Elpi, all predicates are *dynamic*, or open, hence the code of copy can be augmented with rules at runtime. Even so copy is a function because no two rules can apply to the same input: lam and app are different constants, and each constant x generated dynamically is guaranteed to be fresh by the pi operator, hence each copy x x rule is mutually exclusive with the other rules.

The copy predicate, as given, implements the identity and may seem rather useless, but it is not! Since the program is open, one can add new rules for copy and change its behavior. For example the code below computes the weak head normal form of a λ-term by contracting the application of a λ-abstraction to an argument and uses `copy` to perform the substitution:

```
func whd tm -> tm.
whd (app H A) R :- whd H (lam F), !,        % we fire the redex
  pi x\ copy x A => copy (F x) S, whd S R.  %   and we continue
whd X X.                                     % or we stop
```

The argument `A` is put in place of the (previously) bound variable in `F` by replacing that variable with `x` and by running `copy` with the addition of a special rule copying `x` to `A`. Our static analysis understands this programming pattern and is able to recognize that `whd` is also a function. In particular the first rule, if taken, discard the second rule (due to the cut) and only calls functions.

3   Elpi's Abstract Syntax and Rule Selection

Any static analysis to rule out non-determinism must depend on the operational semantics of the language. In particular the order in which rules are applied and the order in which rule premises are executed directly impact the scope of the cut directive.

Here we specify the relevant aspects of Elpi. Its abstract syntax is given below.

$$
\begin{array}{llll}
\mathbb{K}\mathrm{p} ::= p, q, \ldots & \text{predicate} & \mathbb{C} ::= \mathbb{K}\mathrm{p} \mid \mathbb{V} \mid \mathbb{C}\,\mathbb{T}\mathrm{m} & \text{callable} \\
\mathbb{K}\mathrm{d} ::= f, g \ldots x, y, \ldots & \text{constant} & \mathbb{H} ::= \mathbb{K}\mathrm{p} \mid \mathbb{H}\,\mathbb{T}\mathrm{m} & \text{head} \\
\mathbb{V} ::= X, Y \ldots & \text{variable} & \mathbb{A} ::= \mathbb{C} \mid \mathrm{cut} \mid \mathrm{pi}\mathbb{K}\mathrm{d}\,\mathbb{R}\,\mathbb{A} & \text{atom} \\
\mathbb{T}\mathrm{m} ::= \mathbb{K}\mathrm{p} \mid \mathbb{K}\mathrm{d} \mid \mathbb{V} \mid \mathbb{T}\mathrm{m}\,\mathbb{T}\mathrm{m} & \text{term} & \mathbb{R} ::= \mathbb{H} :\text{-} \mathbb{A}^* & \text{rule}
\end{array}
$$

We assume a set $\mathbb{K}\mathrm{p}$ of predicate names, a set $\mathbb{K}\mathrm{d}$ of term constructors, and a set $\mathbb{V}$ of unification variables. We call the union of these three syntactic categories *symbols*. In the syntax of atoms $\mathbb{A}$ we find predicate calls ($\mathbb{C}$), the `cut` operator (explained in Sect. 4) and the `pi` operator.[3] The arguments of predicate calls are in the $\mathbb{T}\mathrm{m}$ nonterminal, for terms, that includes predicate calls along with first order data construction. Because of space constraint we omit from the syntax the construction of data with binders since it plays no interesting role in the static analysis of determinacy. We reserve s for symbols ($\mathbb{K}\mathrm{p} \cup \mathbb{K}\mathrm{d} \cup \mathbb{V}$), v for variables, k for terms in $\mathbb{K}\mathrm{p} \cup \mathbb{K}\mathrm{d}$, a and b for atoms, c for callables and r for rules. Given a rule $h :\text{-} b_1 \ldots b_n$ we call h the *head*, $b_1 \ldots b_n$ the *body* and each b_i a *body atom*. We use non-terminals to represent the class of objects they identify; for example, $\mathbb{T}\mathrm{m}$ identifies (or is the type of) terms. We use $\mathbb{P}$ for the type of programs, being lists of rules in $\mathbb{R}$, and we reserve t for terms and $\mathcal{P}$ for programs.

---

[3]   In reality, in Elpi, `pi` and `=>` are two separate operators, generating a fresh symbol and loading a rule respectively, but for simplicity we only consider their combination.

Rule Priority. Each rule in a program has a unique identifier called priority; this priority stems from the order in which the rule should be applied at runtime. There exists a unique total order for rules following their priority. When a rule is applied, its body atoms are executed in order.

This selection strategy is called SLD and is the standard one for logic programs. In this strategy non-determinism arises when: 1) at least two rules can be used (successfully) to the *same query* (i.e., lack of mutual exclusion between rules, see Sect. 4); 2) the call to a non-deterministic predicate, or the miscall of a deterministic one, is not followed by a cut (see Sect. 5).

4   Hard Cut and Mutual Exclusion

We focus on how to address the first source of non-determinism.

In order to precisely describe `cut`, we need to introduce the notion of choice points, or alternatives. The type of an alternative $\mathbb{L}$ is equal to $\Sigma \times \overrightarrow{\mathbb{G}}$, that is a substitution and a list of goals. The type of a goal $\mathbb{G}$ is equal to $\mathbb{P} \times \mathbb{A}$, that is a program and a query (an atom). Since the program can dynamically change due to `pi`, each (sub)goal must contain the program in which it should be solved. A substitution σ is a partial mapping from unification variables $\mathbb{V}$ to terms $\mathbb{Tm}$. We call this function space Σ and we write ε for the empty substitution. We write $\sigma \cdot t$ for the application of a substitution σ to a term t.

Definition 1 (Hard cut). *Given a rule for predicate k with priority p and body $b_1 \ldots b_i$ cut $\ldots$, the effect of reaching* cut *is that the runtime discards all alternatives generated by $b_1 \ldots b_i$ and all rules for k with lower priority than p.*

Elpi applies rules by matching the input arguments, like B-Prolog's "matching clauses" [31], and by unifying the output ones using Miller's algorithm [22].

Definition 2 (Unification/Matching). *Two terms t and u unify if there exists a substitution σ such that $\sigma \cdot t = \sigma \cdot u$. We say that a term t matches (the pattern) u if there exists a substitution σ such that $\sigma \cdot u = t$ and the domain of σ is the free variables of u*

Finally, in the next definition we distinguish between global rules, i.e., rules that are part of the program $\mathcal{P}$, and local rules that are loaded via the `pi` operator. For example, the `copy` predicate from Sect. 2.2 has two global rules and one local rule.

Definition 3 (Mutual exclusion (mut_excl $\mathbb{P}$ $\mathbb{R}$**).** *Given a program $\mathcal{P}$ and a rule r, such that $r \notin \mathcal{P}$, we say that r is mutually exclusive with the rules in $\mathcal{P}$ if it has the highest priority and one of the following additional conditions holds:*

(a) there is a cut *in the body of r, or*
(b) r is a gloabl rule and all rules r' in $\mathcal{P}$ have an input argument not unifying with the corresponding input in r, or

(c) r is a local rule introduced via `pi x r b`*, x is an input of r and for all rules r′ in the program, the corresponding input is not a variable*

For example, the rules for predicate p below are not mutually exclusive, so choice points may remain after a query resolution, hence introducing non-determinism. For instance, `p 1 X` has two solutions, namely `X = 3` and `X = 2`.

```
pred p int -> int.        func q int -> int.        func r int -> int.
p 1 3.                    q 1 3.                    r X R :- p X R, !.
p 1 2.                    q 2 4.                    r X R :- q X R.
```

Conversely, q satisfies mutual exclusion: no query can trigger both rules. Note that, since inputs are matched, a query like `q X Y` has no solution in Elpi. Standard Prolog implementation would reject the query as not well moded since the input X is not ground. Both rules for r match any input. If the first rule succeeds, the cut removes the alternatives created by the call to p and also discards the other rule `r X R :- q X R`. If the first rule fails, the cut is not reached hence the second rule is not discarded. Thus, at most one rule can succeed for q.

The predicates s and s1 below illustrate the role of pi

```
func s int -> int.                    func s1 int -> int.
s X R :- pi y\ q y 3 => q X R.        s1 X R :- pi y\ q 1 5 => q X R.
                 % error: mutxecl violated      ^^^^^
```

The local rule `q y 3` is mutually exclusive with the rules for q above since y is fresh: each time the rule is loaded y is different from 1 and 2 and any other fresh constants generated before. On the contrary the local rule `q 1 5` is not mutually exclusive: the query `s1 1 R` has two results, namely `R = 5` and `R = 3`.

Note that condition *(c)* also rules out the following example, since the pi -quantified symbol y is not used in input position.

```
func s2 int -> int.
s2 1 R :- pi y\ q 3 5 => s2 2 R.
s2 2 R :- pi y\ q 3 6 => q 3 R.
%                 ^^^^^ error: mutxecl violated
```

Both rules for s2 load a local rule for q. All these local rules are mutually exclusive with the global rules in the program, but the query `s2 1 R` has two results namely `R = 5` and `R = 6`.

5   Static Analysis of Determinacy Signatures

The abstract syntax of signatures is given below. Predicate signatures $\mathbb{Ty}$ start with input arguments from the $\mathbb{S}_i$ non-terminal, continue with output arguments from the $\mathbb{S}_o$ non-terminal and end with a determinacy marker $\mathbb{D}$: Fun for functions and Rel for relations (respectively **func** and **pred** in the concrete syntax).

$$\mathbb{S}_i ::= \mathbb{S}_o \mid \mathbb{S}_i \xrightarrow{i} \mathbb{S}_i \mid \bigstar \xrightarrow{i} \mathbb{S}_i \quad \text{sign. start} \qquad \mathbb{D} ::= \texttt{Fun} \mid \texttt{Rel} \quad \text{determinacy}$$
$$\mathbb{S}_o ::= \mathbb{D} \mid \mathbb{S}_i \xrightarrow{o} \mathbb{S}_o \mid \bigstar \xrightarrow{o} \mathbb{S}_o \quad \text{sign. stop} \qquad \bigstar ::= \star \qquad\qquad \text{all data}$$
$$\mathbb{T}\!y ::= \mathbb{S}_i \qquad\qquad\qquad\qquad\qquad \text{signature}$$

We collapse all data types into a single type $\bigstar$ and we disallow to store predicates into data, i.e., one cannot form a list of predicates. Note that the grammar of $\mathbb{T}\!y$ forces all input arguments to come first. We reserve d for instances of type $\bigstar$, ρ and τ for signatures and $\mathcal{D}$ for instances of $\mathbb{D}$. For example the signature `func map (func A -> B), list A -> list B` corresponds to $(\star \xrightarrow{i} \star \xrightarrow{o} \texttt{Fun}) \xrightarrow{i} \star \xrightarrow{i} \star \xrightarrow{o} \texttt{Fun}$.

We denote booleans $\mathbb{B} = \{\top, \bot\}$; contexts Γ being partial maps from symbols to signatures. We use $\varnothing$ for the empty list and $x :: xs$ for prepending the element x to a list xs. We reserve Γ for contexts.

Operations on Signatures. We compare signatures using the standard subtyping relation of functional languages. In particular, we compare inputs contravariantly and outputs covariantly. It is similar to [15], except for the absence of the **Any** terminal. `Fun` is smaller than `Rel` since functions generate a "smaller number of results" than relations.

$$\star \subseteq \star \qquad \mathcal{D} \subseteq \mathcal{D} \qquad \textsc{Fun} \subseteq \textsc{Rel}$$
$$\rho \xrightarrow{i} \tau \subseteq \rho' \xrightarrow{i} \tau' \quad \text{iff} \quad \rho' \subseteq \rho \wedge \tau \subseteq \tau'$$
$$\rho \xrightarrow{o} \tau \subseteq \rho' \xrightarrow{o} \tau' \quad \text{iff} \quad \rho \subseteq \rho' \wedge \tau \subseteq \tau'$$

The static analysis needs often to keep the stronger or weaker signature among two. We hence derive from $\subseteq$ a min and max operators defined below.

$$\text{min } \star \ \star = \star \qquad \text{min } \mathcal{D} \ \mathcal{D} = \mathcal{D}$$
$$\text{min } \textsc{Fun } \textsc{Rel} = \text{min } \textsc{Rel } \textsc{Fun} = \textsc{Fun}$$
$$\text{min } (\rho \xrightarrow{i} \tau) \ (\rho' \xrightarrow{i} \tau') = \text{max } \rho \ \rho' \xrightarrow{i} \text{min } \tau \ \tau'$$
$$\text{min } (\rho \xrightarrow{o} \tau) \ (\rho' \xrightarrow{o} \tau') = \text{min } \rho \ \rho' \xrightarrow{o} \text{min } \tau \ \tau'$$

$$\text{max } \star \ \star = \star \qquad \text{max } \mathcal{D} \ \mathcal{D} = \mathcal{D}$$
$$\text{max } \textsc{Fun } \textsc{Rel} = \text{max } \textsc{Rel } \textsc{Fun} = \textsc{Rel}$$
$$\text{max } (\rho \xrightarrow{i} \tau) \ (\rho' \xrightarrow{i} \tau') = \text{min } \rho \ \rho' \xrightarrow{i} \text{max } \tau \ \tau'$$
$$\text{max } (\rho \xrightarrow{o} \tau) \ (\rho' \xrightarrow{o} \tau') = \text{max } \rho \ \rho' \xrightarrow{o} \text{max } \tau \ \tau'$$

When a predicate is miscalled we need to weaken its signature.

We define strong and weak as follows:

$$\text{strong } \star = \star$$
$$\text{strong } \textsc{Rel} = \textsc{Fun} \qquad \text{strong } \textsc{Fun} = \textsc{Fun}$$
$$\text{strong } (\rho \xrightarrow{i} \tau) = \text{weak } \rho \xrightarrow{i} \text{strong } \tau$$
$$\text{strong } (\rho \xrightarrow{o} \tau) = \text{strong } \rho \xrightarrow{o} \text{strong } \tau$$

$$\text{weak } \star = \star$$
$$\text{weak } \textsc{Fun} = \textsc{Rel} \qquad \text{weak } \textsc{Rel} = \textsc{Rel}$$
$$\text{weak } (\rho \xrightarrow{i} \tau) = \text{strong } \rho \xrightarrow{i} \text{weak } \tau$$
$$\text{weak } (\rho \xrightarrow{o} \tau) = \text{weak } \rho \xrightarrow{o} \text{weak } \tau$$

The set of signatures that only differ by a leaf in $\mathcal{D}$ form a lattice w.r.t. the order relation $\subseteq$, the join operator max and meet operator min. The infimum of the lattice is computed by strong and the supremum is computed by weak.

In Sect. 2.1 we have weakened the signature of `map` from $\tau = (\star \xrightarrow{i} \star \xrightarrow{o} \texttt{Fun}) \xrightarrow{i} \star \xrightarrow{i} \star \xrightarrow{o} \texttt{Fun}$ to $(\star \xrightarrow{i} \star \xrightarrow{o} \texttt{Fun}) \xrightarrow{i} \star \xrightarrow{i} \star \xrightarrow{o} \texttt{Rel}$.

One could define the supremum of τ as $\tau' = (\star \xrightarrow{i} \star \xrightarrow{o} \texttt{Rel}) \xrightarrow{i} \star \xrightarrow{i} \star \xrightarrow{o} \texttt{Rel}$, which intuitively amounts to considering all `Fun` as `Rel`, i.e., dropping all `Fun` in case of error. However, this would contradict the lattice property: $\max \tau\ (\mathsf{weak}\ \tau) = \mathsf{weak}\ \tau$, since we would have $\max \tau\ \tau' = \tau'$, but $\tau \not\subseteq \tau'$. Moreover, since we compare input signatures using $\subseteq$, this alternative definition of weak (resp. strong) would not make the checker accept more programs.

The Idea. The static analyzer accumulates knowledge on variables in a context Γ initially only containing the signature of predicates. The checking algorithm considers one rule at a time. It begins by updating Γ using the preconditions on the *inputs* of the head, then it scans all body atoms and finally checks the postconditions: the determinacy of the body and the determinacy of the *outputs* of the head.

For example, consider the predicates `comp` and `compose` below: `comp` is a function that takes as input two functions `F` and `G`, and calls them in sequence, whereas `compose` builds a new function from the two received in input.

```
func comp (func int -> int), (func int -> int), int -> int.
comp F G X Z :- F X Y, G Y Z.
```

```
func compose (func int -> int), (func int -> int) -> (func int -> int).
compose F G (comp F G).
```

After updating Γ w.r.t. the preconditions of `comp`, Γ flags `F` and `G` as functions. Then the algoritms scans all body atoms computing the $\max$ of their determinacies: since both `F X Y` and `G Y Z` are `Fun`, also their $\max$ is. Finally the analyzer checks that the determinacy of the body matches the declared one. The analysis for `compose` needs to check two postconditions: 1) the *output* term `comp F G` is a function, since the two arguments of `comp` match its signature; 2) the body of `compose` is deterministic since empty.

We now move to an example that involes a non-deterministic body atom.

```
func r (func int -> int), (pred int -> int), int -> int.
r F G X Y :- map G [X] [Z], !, compose F F H, H Z Y.
```

After analyzing the head the context asserts that `F` (resp. `G`) is a function (resp. a relation). In the body of `r`, the first atom is non-deterministic, since `G` violates the preconditions of `map`. The signature of `map G [X] [Z]` is hence weakened to `Rel`. Even if this atom could generate multiple alternatives, the `cut` commits to the first one restoring the determinism of the body of `r` up to that point. The call to `compose` satisfies its preconditions, so its postconditions apply: the entire atom `compose F F H` is considered deterministic *and* `H` is marked as a function in Γ. The final atom `H Z Y` is also deterministic because of the knowledge about `H` accumulated so far in Γ.

$$\frac{\begin{array}{cc} x \text{ fresh in } \Gamma & P,\ \Gamma + \{x \mapsto \star\} \vdash_r r \\ \mathsf{mut\_excl}\ P\ \Gamma\ x\ r & (r :: P),\ \Gamma + \{x \mapsto \star\},\ \mathcal{D} \vdash_a a = \mathcal{D}',\ \Gamma' \end{array}}{P,\ \Gamma,\ \mathcal{D} \vdash_a \mathsf{pi}\ x\ r\ a = \mathcal{D}',\ \Gamma'} \quad (a_\forall)$$

$$\frac{}{P,\ \Gamma,\ \_ \vdash_a \mathsf{cut} = \mathsf{Fun},\ \Gamma} \ (a_!) \qquad \frac{\Gamma \vdash^i_{tm} c = \mathsf{Rel},\ \bot}{P,\ \Gamma,\ \_ \vdash_a c = \mathsf{Rel},\ \Gamma} \ (a_\bot)$$

$$\frac{\Gamma \vdash^i_{tm} c = \mathcal{D}',\ \top \qquad \Gamma \vdash^o_{ca} c : \mathcal{D}' = \Gamma'}{P,\ \Gamma,\ \mathcal{D} \vdash_a c = \mathsf{max}\ \mathcal{D}\ \mathcal{D}',\ \Gamma'} \ (a_c)$$

Fig. 1. Rules for **check atom**: its type is $\mathbb{P},\ \Gamma,\ \mathbb{D} \vdash_a \mathbb{A} = \mathbb{D},\ \Gamma$

The Algorithm. We present the static analyzer using derivation rules. Each procedure has an associated entails-like symbol, e.g., context $\vdash^{\text{flag}}_{\text{name}}$ intake = result. We use the equal sign to "mode" the rule, i.e., separate what is given to the rule from what is generated by it. The static analyzer is composed of seven procedures for a total of 24 rules. Here we list only the interesting ones, leaving the rest to the appendix in Fissore and Tassi [10].

The main entry point is **check rule** ($\mathbb{P},\ \Gamma \vdash_r \mathbb{R}$), that verifies if a rule validates the signature ascribed to its predicate. The procedure stores in Γ all the knowledge available on variables in $\mathbb{V}$ and it verifies that the precondition made by the signature entails the postcondition.

$$\frac{\Gamma \vdash^i_{hd} c = \mathcal{D}_1,\ \Gamma_1 \quad \forall i \in 1 \ldots n\ \mathrm{do}\ P,\ \Gamma_i,\ \mathcal{D}_i \vdash_a b_i = \mathcal{D}_{i+1},\ \Gamma_{i+1} \quad \Gamma_{n+1} \vdash^o_{hd} c : \mathcal{D}_{n+1}}{P,\ \Gamma \vdash_r c \text{ :- } b_1 \ldots b_n} \ (r)$$

In particular the **assume head input** ($\Gamma \vdash^i_{hd} \mathbb{Tm} = \mathbb{Ty},\ \Gamma$) procedures loads in Γ_1 the information assumed from the head inputs while **check head output** ($\Gamma \vdash^o_{hd} \mathbb{Tm} : \mathbb{Ty}$) verifies that Γ_{n+1} entails the postcondition. Each of the n body atoms b_i is processed by **check atom** (Fig. 1, $\mathbb{P},\ \Gamma,\ \mathbb{D} \vdash_a \mathbb{A} = \mathbb{D},\ \Gamma$) that updates the context and computes the determinacy of the entire body $\mathcal{D}_{n+1}$.

We now focus on the analysis of an atom. The **check atom** procedure has two rules to handle cut ($a_!$) and $\mathsf{pi}(a_\forall)$, and two more rules to handle predicate calls (a_c) and predicate miscalls ($a_\bot$). The cut operator resets the current determinacy to Fun, while pi introduces a fresh symbol, checks the hypothetical rule and proceeds after adding r to $\mathcal{P}$. Rule (a_c) verifies that the preconditions for c are met, and assumes its postcondition generating an updated Γ'. The determinacy is set to the maximum of current determinacy and the one of the predicate. When the preconditions are not met the context is left untouched and the current determinacy is set to Rel.

The most interesting procedure is the one to check if the preconditions of a predicate call are met, that is **check input** (Fig. 2, $\Gamma \vdash^i_{tm} \mathbb{Tm} = \mathbb{Ty},\ \mathbb{B}$). The procedure ignores data arguments and output arguments and simply fetches from the context the signature of constants and variables (tm^i_k). Rule ($\mathsf{tm}^i_\top$)

$$\frac{\Gamma \vdash s = \tau}{\Gamma \vdash^{i}_{tm} s = \tau,\ \top}\ (tm^{i}_{k}) \qquad \frac{\Gamma \vdash^{i}_{tm} f = \rho \xrightarrow{i} \tau,\ \top \qquad \Gamma \vdash^{i}_{tm} t = \rho',\ \top \qquad \rho' \subseteq \rho}{\Gamma \vdash^{i}_{tm} f\ t = \tau,\ \top}\ (tm^{i}_{\top})$$

$$\frac{\Gamma \vdash^{i}_{tm} f = \rho \xrightarrow{i} \tau,\ b_1 \qquad \Gamma \vdash^{i}_{tm} t = \rho',\ b_2 \qquad b_1 = \bot \vee b_2 = \bot \vee \rho' \not\subseteq \rho}{\Gamma \vdash^{i}_{tm} f\ t = \text{weak } \tau,\ \bot}\ (tm^{i}_{\bot})$$

Fig. 2. Rules for **check input**: its type is $\Gamma \vdash^{i}_{tm} \mathbb{T}m = \mathbb{T}y,\ \mathbb{B}$

$$\frac{\tau' = \text{if } X \in \Gamma \text{ then } \Gamma\ X \text{ else } \tau}{\Gamma \vdash^{o}_{tm} X : \tau = \Gamma + \{X \mapsto \text{min } \tau\ \tau'\}}\ (tm^{o}_{X}) \qquad \frac{\Gamma\ k = \tau' \quad \tau' \subseteq \tau}{\Gamma \vdash^{o}_{tm} k : \tau = \Gamma}\ (tm^{o}_{k})$$

$$\frac{\Gamma \vdash^{o}_{tm} f : \rho \xrightarrow{i} \tau = \Gamma' \qquad \Gamma' \vdash^{o}_{tm} t : \rho = \Gamma''}{\Gamma \vdash^{o}_{tm} f\ t : \tau = \Gamma''}\ (tm^{o}_{i})$$

Fig. 3. Rules for **assume output**: its type is $\Gamma \vdash^{o}_{tm} \mathbb{T}m : \mathbb{T}y = \Gamma$

is the standard typing rule for application: if the input argument matches the expected signature it computes the return type, signaling no miscalls (i.e. $\top$). When the head or the argument contain a miscall, or when the argument does not match the expected signature, the rule $(tm^{i}_{\bot})$ signals a miscall and computes the return type by weakening the one obtained from the head, i.e., the predicate call is considered as a relation, and the signature of the output arguments is also recursively weakened.

The procedure to update the context when an atom is found to be a good call is **assume call output** ($\Gamma \vdash^{o}_{ca} \mathbb{T}m : \mathbb{T}y = \Gamma$). Other than ignoring input arguments it calls **assume output** on output arguments.

$$\frac{\Gamma \vdash^{o}_{ca} f : \rho \xrightarrow{o} \tau = \Gamma' \qquad \Gamma' \vdash^{o}_{tm} t : \rho = \Gamma''}{\Gamma \vdash^{o}_{ca} f\ t : \tau = \Gamma''}\ (a^{o}_{o})$$

The **assume output** procedure (Fig. 3, $\Gamma \vdash^{o}_{tm} \mathbb{T}m : \mathbb{T}y = \Gamma$) updates the context when it encounters variables (tm^{o}_{X}). When variable is already ascribed a signature in the context, we keep the stronger signature. Data and output arguments are skipped, while input arguments are recursively traversed: the signature of variables in their input positions are also updated in the context.

The processing of the head of a rule is akin to the one of body atoms, but symmetric in which arguments are used to strengthen the context and which are checked for conformance. The **assume head input** procedure ($\Gamma \vdash^{i}_{hd} \mathbb{T}m = \mathbb{T}y,\ \Gamma$) called at the very beginning of (r), ignores outputs and calls **assume output** on inputs.

The **check head output** ($\Gamma \vdash^{o}_{hd} \mathbb{T}m : \mathbb{T}y$) procedure is called at the very end.

$$\frac{\Gamma \vdash^{o}_{hd} f : \rho \xrightarrow{o} \tau \qquad \Gamma \vdash^{i}_{tm} t = \rho',\ \top \qquad \rho' \subseteq \rho}{\Gamma \vdash^{o}_{hd} f\ t : \tau}\ (hd^{o}_{o})$$

It ignores input arguments but checks that the output ones satisfy the ascribed signature in the current context, that is the result of assuming the rule preconditions and all the postconditions of well called body atoms.

6   Determinism Guarantees

In order to express *operational determinacy* we need to use an operational semantics for Elpi. That semantics, for its higher-order logic-programming part, is essentially the one given by Qi [27] using a last-in-first-out goal selection. However it must be complemented with a treatment of choice points to describe the behavior of the cut operator following de Bruin and de Vink [2]. Moreover Elpi has a peculiar runtime threatment of input arguments, that are matched rather than unified (see Definition 2).

For space constraints we omit the rules defining run, they can be found in the appendix of Fissore and Tassi [10].

Definition 4 (Operational semantics *(run : $\mathbb{L} \times \overrightarrow{\mathbb{L}} \to \Sigma \times \overrightarrow{\mathbb{L}}$)). Run is a partial function from a non-empty list of alternatives to a solution consisting in a substitution and a list of yet-to-be-explored alternatives.*
The properties of run relevant to the current paper are:

1. cut *behaves as per Definition 1*
2. pi$x$ r b *generates a fresh constant for x available in r and b*
3. pi$x$ r b *loads r in the program giving it the highest priority*
4. *input arguments are matched against the query as per Definition 2*

Definition 5 (Operationally deterministic execution (deterministic$_a$ $\mathbb{P}$ $\mathbb{A}$).
We say that a query atom b is operationally deterministic in a program $\mathcal{P}$ iff

$$\forall \sigma, \mathsf{run}\ (\sigma,\ (\mathcal{P},b) :: \varnothing)\ \varnothing = (\_, a)\ \Rightarrow\ a = \varnothing$$

In other words a deterministic query leaves no alternatives when it succeeds. We now link the static check to the deterministic execution of a query.

Definition 6 (Checked program (checked$_p$ Γ $\mathbb{P}$)). *A program $\mathcal{P}$ is checked against a context of signatures Γ iff it validates these rules:*

$$\frac{}{\mathsf{checked_p}\ \Gamma\ \varnothing} \qquad \frac{\mathsf{checked_p}\ \Gamma\ \mathcal{P} \qquad \mathsf{mut\_excl}\ \mathcal{P}\ r \qquad \mathcal{P},\ \Gamma \vdash_r r}{\mathsf{checked_p}\ \Gamma\ (r :: \mathcal{P})}$$

The intuition is that we build the program from the end, always adding new rules with highest priority.

Definition 7 (Checked query atom ($\mathsf{checked_a}\ \Gamma\ \mathbb{A}$)**).** *An atom b is checked against a context of signatures Γ iff*

$$\varnothing,\ \Gamma,\ \mathsf{Fun} \vdash_a b = \mathsf{Fun},\ \_$$

We can now state the main theorem linking the static analsysis of a program and query with its execution.

Theorem 1 (Static analysis). *Given program $\mathcal{P}$, a context of signatures Γ and a query atom b, $\mathsf{checked_p}\ \Gamma\ \mathcal{P} \wedge \mathsf{checked_a}\ \Gamma\ b \Rightarrow \mathsf{deterministic_a}\ \mathcal{P}\ b$.*

The proof of Theorem 1 has been mechanized in the Rocq proof assistant, formerly known as Coq, for the first-order part [7]. The mechanization for the higher-order part is ongoing.

7   Experience Report

The static analyzer we describe was integrated in the Elpi language version 3.0. It consists of about 200 lines of OCaml code for the implementation of mut_excl and about 800 lines of code for the implementation of **check rule**, along with all the related auxiliary functions. We have ported some Rocq libraries written using Elpi: Rocq-Elpi, Hierarchy Builder, Algebra Tactics, Trocq, and BRiCk.

We can divide the porting of these libraries into two categories: libraries in which we have traversed all the predicates and carefully changed **pred** markers to `func` (Elpi, Rocq-Elpi, and Hierarchy Builder), and libraries that have been ported to just pass the static analyzer. In particular, the latter class of libraries measures the minimal cost for adapting code to the changes we made to the Elpi and Rocq-Elpi standard libraries. The typical example of code requiring a fix is code that loads a local rule containing no cut, typically `copy`.

We summarize these results in Table 1. In the Elpi standard library, we annotated 272 predicates out of 281 as functions, with 37 occurrences of higher-order arguments, as in `map, filter, fold`, etc. We identified 1 error, i.e., a missing cut. In Rocq-Elpi, we have 928 functions out of 1181, with 62 higher-order predicates. We added 91 cuts to please the static analyzer, 78 of which were clearly bugs in the code. The remaining 13 cuts are due to mut_excl, which is not powerful enough to discriminate among rules. The algorithm could be improved to better distinguish mutual exclusion by extending Definition 3, as in López-García et al. [19], but the problem is, in general, undecidable. An example of this issue is given below:

```
func fact int -> int.
fact 0 1.
fact N R :- N > 0, N' is N - 1, fact N' R', R is N * R'.
```

The two rules for `fact` are in mutual exclusion: the input cannot be *0* and *greater than 0* at the same time. But a complete algorithm identifying all of these scenarios does not exists, and we require an explicit `cut` in the first rule.

Table 1. Experience report

Software	LOC	% Fun	cut added	cut needed (bugs)
Elpi	1448	97%	1	1 (100%)
Rocq-Elpi	13164	79%	91	78 (85%)
Hierarchy Builder	5326	94%	33	30 (90%)
Algebra Tactics	1799	–	1	1 (100%)
Trocq	2918	–	4	4 (100%)
BRiCk (public)	2500	–	11	11 (100%)
BRiCk (private)	7500	–	6	6 (100%)
Total	34655	85%	147	131 (89%)

In Hierarchy Builder, we have 460 functions out of 488, with 33 higher-order arguments, and we have corrected 30 bugs in the code.

Overall, we can conclude that 85% of the predicates were functions.

In Algebra Tactics, we added 1 cut over 1799 lines of codes; in Trocq, we added 4 cuts over 2918 lines of code. None of these libraries were using `copy` as a relation, i.e. to generate all possible copies of a term. The BRiCk application has some public code we ported ourselves and some closed source code ported by the SkyLabs AI company, that we thank for sharing these numebrs. In the public code we added 11 cuts over 2500 lines of code, while in the private one they added 11 cuts over 7500 lines.

8   Related Work and Concluding Remarks

We summarize several related works in Table 2. One key difference between our work and Debray and Warren [5,15,18,19,28] is that they focus on *closed* predicates, that do not evolve during execution, while λProlog, hence Elpi, allows rules to be dynamically loaded. For closed predicates, programs can be transformed into *super-homogeneous* form by merging all rules into one with disjunctions. This simplifies determinacy inference and may allow to compile the code to a faster binary. However, this transformation is not feasible in our dynamic setting (Sect. 2.2).

Regarding modes, Elpi's matching procedure over input arguments allows us to dispense with explicit mode analysis – an essential component in Debray and Warren [5], Kriener and King [18], López-García et al. [19], Somogyi et al. [28].

We differ from Red Alert [18] in that we pick an operational semantics that explicitly represents choice points as a list of alternatives, and that hence is very close to the actual behavior of Elpi's runtime. They pick a denotational semantics over the super-homogeneous form that in turn lets them formulate the static analyzer as an abstract interpreter. It is unclear if a denotational semantics can be written without transforming the program in super-homogeneous form.

Some of the higher-order features of the Elpi language are available in Mercury [28], although in a more constrained way ( ). For example `once` from Sect. 2.1 is considerably more useful if the input relation is allowed to be non-ground, e.g., `once (map get_pdiv [6] L)`. We allow higher-order predicates to be miscalled, while Mercury does not. Instead, it requires higher-order functions to be annotated with explicit mode and determinacy signatures for each possible behavior. As a result, Mercury ascribes 11 signatures to the `foldr` predicate and any call that does not match exactly one of these signatures results in a compilation failure ( ). Elpi targets less technically inclined users, more familiar with functional programming languages than logic ones, hence we strive for simplicity, defining only one determinacy class and immediately classifying wrong calls as non-deterministic. As a result the signature for `foldr` is just `func foldr (func L, A -> A), list L, A -> A`, familiar to our audience.

Table 2. Comparison with related work

Authors	System	Mode analysis	Dynamic	H.O.	Miscalls
Debray and Warren [5]	SB-Prolog	required	✗	✗	✗
López-García et al. [19]	Ciao	required	✗	✗	✗
Kriener and King [18]	Red Alert	required	✗	✗	✗
Somogyi et al. [28]	Mercury	required	✗	✓‡	✗†
Hanus and Prott [15]	Curry	no need	✗	✓	✓
Fissore and Tassi	Elpi	no need	✓	✓	✓

The "determinism types" of Curry [15] are much more similar to our signatures, and Curry supports miscalled functions as well. In the work of Hanus and Prott the `Any` type stands for non-determinism and like a black hole it absorbs the determinism of the surrounding sub-terms. This is a convenient way to capture all miscalls and treat them uniformly. In our presentation, we have no equivalent; instead, we use weak to change the signature of a term when a miscall is detected ($\mathbf{tm}_{\perp}^{i}$) (or atom calls ($\mathbf{a}_{\perp}$)). The advantage is that weak only changes the leaves ($\mathbb{D}$) of the signature while leaving its structure intact. Although we do not analyze data in this paper, our set of rules can be complemented to perform full type checking (in addition to determinacy checking) in one pass.

In Curry the `allValues` builtin can be used to turn a relation into a function. Prolog, and also Elpi, provide a similar `findall` builtin, but in addition to that they also let one commit to the first result by either using `once`, or by placing a cut after the non-deterministic call. It is this "after the fact" commitment that make the analysis a bit more complex. In fact, in the body of a deterministic predicate we can have calls to relations (or miscalled functions) and still consider the rules valid with respect to determinacy (see ($a_!$)). The notion of *functional context* in [5] is closely related to this difficulty.

Our experience report confirms most of the Elpi code out there is made of functional predicates and that the static analyzer accepts the vast majority of it requiring no changes. The main improvement we will consider is about *mode subtyping* for higher-order arguments. In the definition of $\subseteq$ we currently accept only arrows that have the same input/output mode. However, it seems possible to relax this condition. For example we could allow passing to `map` a function of type $\star \xrightarrow{o} \star \xrightarrow{o} \mathrm{Fun}$, since the modes of higher-order arguments seem to play no role in the determinacy of code that receives and calls them.

Acknowledgments. We are grateful to Laurent Théry for his help in redacting this paper, and SkyLabs AI for running the static analyzer on the private BRiCk code and sharing the results. We also want to thank the anonymous reviewers for their very valuable feedback.

References

1. Blot, V., et al.: Compositional pre-processing for automated reasoning in dependent type theory. In: Krebbers, R., Traytel, D., Pientka, B., Zdancewic, S. (eds.) Proceedings of the 12th ACM SIGPLAN International Conference on Certified Programs and Proofs, CPP 2023, Boston, MA, USA, 16–17 January 2023, pp. 63–77. ACM (2023). https://doi.org/10.1145/3573105.3575676
2. de Bruin, A., de Vink, E.P.: Continuation semantics for prolog with cut. In: Díaz, J., Orejas, F. (eds.) TAPSOFT '89, pp. 178–192. Springer, Heidelberg (1989). ISBN 978-3-540-46116-6
3. Cohen, C., Crance, E., Mahboubi, A.: Trocq: proof transfer for free, with or without univalence. In: Weirich, S. (ed.) Programming Languages and Systems, pp. 239–268. Springer, Cham (2024). ISBN 978-3-031-57262-3
4. Cohen, C., Sakaguchi, K., Tassi, E.: Hierarchy builder: algebraic hierarchies made easy in coq with elpi. In: Proceedings of FSCD, LIPIcs, vol. 167, pp. 34:1–34:21 (2020), ISBN 978-3-95977-155-9. ISSN 1868-8969. https://doi.org/10.4230/LIPIcs.FSCD.2020.34. https://drops.dagstuhl.de/entities/document/10.4230/LIPIcs.FSCD.2020.34
5. Debray, S.K., Warren, D.S.: Functional computations in logic programs, vol. 11, p. 451–481. Association for Computing Machinery (1989). ISSN 0164-0925. https://doi.org/10.1145/65979.65984
6. Dunchev, C., Guidi, F., Coen, C.S., Tassi, E.: ELPI: fast, embeddable, λProlog interpreter. In: Proceedings of LPAR, LNCS, vol. 9450, pp. 460–468. Springer, Heidelberg (2015). https://doi.org/10.1007/978-3-662-48899-7_32. https://inria.hal.science/hal-01176856v1
7. Fissore, D.: Elpi formalization (2025). https://github.com/gares/elpi-formalization
8. Fissore, D., Tassi, E.: A new type-class solver for coq in elpi. In: The Coq Workshop (2023). https://inria.hal.science/hal-04467855
9. Fissore, D., Tassi, E.: Higher-order unification for free!: reusing the meta-language unification for the object language. In: Proceedings of PPDP, pp. 1–13. ACM (2024). ISBN 9798400709692. https://doi.org/10.1145/3678232.3678233

10. Fissore, D., Tassi, E.: Determinacy Checking for Elpi: an Higher-Order Logic Programming language with Cut (2025). https://inria.hal.science/hal-05026472
11. Gonthier, G.: A computer-checked proof of the Four Color Theorem. Technical report, Inria (2023). https://inria.hal.science/hal-04034866
12. Gonthier, G., et al.: A machine-checked proof of the odd order theorem. In: Blazy, S., Paulin-Mohring, C., Pichardie, D. (eds.) Interactive Theorem Proving - 4th International Conference, ITP 2013, Rennes, France, 22–26 July 2013. Proceedings, Lecture Notes in Computer Science, vol. 7998, pp. 163–179. Springer, Heidelberg (2013), https://doi.org/10.1007/978-3-642-39634-2_14. https://inria.hal.science/hal-00816699v1
13. Grégoire, B., Léchenet, J.C., Tassi, E.: Practical and sound equality tests, automatically. In: Proceedings of CPP, pp. 167–181. Association for Computing Machinery (2023). ISBN 9798400700262. https://doi.org/10.1145/3573105.3575683
14. Guidi, F., Coen, C.S., Tassi, E.: Implementing type theory in higher order constraint logic programming. In: Mathematical Structures in Computer Science, vol. 29, pp. 1125–1150. Cambridge University Press (2019). https://doi.org/10.1017/S0960129518000427
15. Hanus, M., Prott, K.O.: Determinism Types for Functional Logic Programming. In: Proceedings of PPDP, pp. 47–59 (2025)
16. Henderson, F., Somogyi, Z., Conway, T.: Determinism analysis in the mercury compiler. In: Proceedings of Australian Computer Science Conference, pp. 337–346 (1996)
17. Krebbers, R., van der Maas, L., Tassi, E.: Inductive predicates via least fixpoints in higher-order separation logic. In: Forster, Y., Keller, C. (eds.) 16th International Conference on Interactive Theorem Proving (ITP 2025), Leibniz International Proceedings in Informatics (LIPIcs), vol. 352, pp. 27:1–27:21. Schloss Dagstuhl – Leibniz-Zentrum für Informatik, Dagstuhl (2025). ISBN 978-3-95977-396-6. ISSN 1868-8969. https://doi.org/10.4230/LIPIcs.ITP.2025.27. https://drops.dagstuhl.de/entities/document/10.4230/LIPIcs.ITP.2025.27
18. Kriener, J., King, A.: Redalert: Determinacy Inference for Prolog, vol. 11, pp. 537–553. Cambridge University Press, Cambridge (2011)
19. López-García, P., Bueno, F., Hermenegildo, M.: Determinacy analysis for logic programs using mode and type information. In: Etalle, S. (ed.) Logic Based Program Synthesis and Transformation, pp. 19–35. Springer, Heidelberg (2005). ISBN 978-3-540-31683-1
20. van der Maas, L.: Extending the Iris Proof Mode with Inductive Predicates using Elpi. Master's thesis, Radboud University Nijmegen (2024). https://doi.org/10.5281/zenodo.12568604
21. Mahboubi, A., Tassi, E.: Mathematical Components. Zenodo (2022). https://doi.org/10.5281/zenodo.7118596
22. Miller, D.: A logic programming language with lambda-abstraction, function variables, and simple unification. In: Extensions of Logic Programming, pp. 253–281. Springer, Heidelberg (1991). ISBN 978-3-540-46879-0
23. Miller, D., Nadathur, G.: Programming with Higher-Order Logic. Cambridge University Press, Cambridge (2012)
24. Miller, D.A.: Mechanized metatheory revisited. J. Autom. Reason. **63**, 625–665 (2018)
25. Nakamura, K.: Control of logic program execution based on the functional relations. In: Proceedings of ICLP, pp. 505–512. Springer, Heidelberg (1986). ISBN 3540164928

26. Pfenning, F., Elliott, C.: Higher-order abstract syntax. In: Proceedings of PLDI, pp. 199–208. Association for Computing Machinery (1988). ISBN 0897912691. https://doi.org/10.1145/53990.54010
27. Qi, X.: An Implementation of the Language Lambda Prolog Organized around Higher-Order Pattern Unification. Ph.D. thesis, Graduate School of the University of Minnesota (2009). https://arxiv.org/abs/0911.5203
28. Somogyi, Z., Henderson, F., Conway, T.: The execution algorithm of mercury, an efficient purely declarative logic programming language, vol. 29, pp. 17–64 (1996). ISSN 0743-1066. https://doi.org/10.1016/S0743-1066(96)00068-4. https://www.sciencedirect.com/science/inproceedings/pii/S0743106696000684
29. Tassi, E.: Elpi: an extension language for Coq (Metaprogramming Coq in the Elpi λProlog dialect). In: The Fourth International Workshop on Coq for Programming Languages (2018). https://inria.hal.science/hal-01637063
30. Tassi, E.: Deriving proved equality tests in Coq-Elpi. In: Proceedings of ITP, LIPIcs, vol. 141, pp. 29:1–29:18 (2019). https://doi.org/10.4230/LIPIcs.CVIT.2016.23. https://inria.hal.science/hal-01897468
31. Zhou, N.f.: The language features and architecture of b-prolog. Theory Pract. Log. Program. **12**(1–2), 189–218 (2012), ISSN 1471-0684. https://doi.org/10.1017/S1471068411000445

Multi-configurable Search Rules in Prolog and Application to Testing

Daniela Ferreiro[1,2]([✉]) [ID], Jose F. Morales[1,2] [ID], Pedro López-García[1,3] [ID], and Manuel V. Hermenegildo[1,2] [ID]

[1] Universidad Politécnica de Madrid (UPM), Madrid, Spain
[2] IMDEA Software Institute, Madrid, Spain
{daniela.ferreiro,josef.morales,manuel.hermenegildo}@imdea.org
[3] Spanish Council for Scientific Research, Madrid, Spain
pedro.lopez@imdea.org

Abstract. Prolog systems traditionally employ leftmost, depth-first search as their execution strategy. This choice is well-justified for efficiency reasons, generally accepted, and useful in practice. However, it is also well-known that it can lead to incompleteness when evaluating programs over infinite search spaces and may not be ideal for complex search spaces. We revisit the role of search strategies in Prolog programs, and present a new approach, that enables programmable and composable control of search. While advanced search strategies can always be *programmed* in Prolog, we opt instead for an approach that separates the search strategy used from the actual code, so that different strategies can be used on the same set of clauses. We provide constructs for controlling the search strategies that allow adapting the search dynamically. We also illustrate the usefulness of the proposed approach by applying it in the context of testing (constraint) logic programs, showing how composable search parameters enable more controlled and targeted exploration of program behavior.

Keywords: Prolog · Search Rules · Assertion-based Testing · Property-based Testing · (Constraint) Logic Programming

1 Introduction

Ever since Kowalski's well-known equation *Algorithm = Logic + Control* [22], the advantages of separating the logic and control components of a program have been well established. In Prolog, the *Logic* component is expressed through Horn clauses, while *Control* is handled by the engine, primarily via the search strategy. Standard systems rely on SLD resolution, typically using a fixed top-down, left-to-right strategy that corresponds to depth-first search. While this

Partially funded by MICIU projects CEX2024-001471-M María de Maeztu and TED2021-132464B-I00 PRODIGY, as well as by the Tezos foundation. We would also like to thank the reviewers for their very useful and constructive feedback.

choice is efficient in terms of memory, requiring storage only for the active branch, it is incomplete in general (i.e., for infinite search spaces). Moreover, it forces programmers to handle control issues such as cycles or left recursion indirectly, typically by rewriting rules or adding operational details, which can compromise the declarative character of the language.

Alternative search strategies, such as breadth-first, iterative deepening, or random search, offer different trade-offs among efficiency, completeness, and memory consumption. However, mainstream Prolog implementations provide little support for selecting or customizing these strategies. Consequently, programmers have limited influence over how the search space is explored, and control decisions remain implicit in the engine rather than expressible by the programmer.

This paper revisits the role of search strategies in the execution of logic programs and explores how to make the control component *configurable in flexible ways* while still supporting the full language and preserving the separation between *logic* and *control* in the spirit of declarative programming. Writing Prolog code from scratch that implements some search in a state space with a particular strategy is not especially difficult, nor is running Prolog predicates with other search rules by using variations of the standard meta-interpreter. However, our goal is to be able to provide the programmer with a mechanism that allows running the predicates of a standard Prolog program with different search strategies with a high degree of flexibility. Moreover, straightforward implementation approaches of alternative search strategies typically limit the use to a subset of Prolog and thus do not support the full expressiveness of the language. Our second goal is thus to maintain compatibility with modules, built-ins, and other libraries and features to a high degree.

We refine the meaning of a *search strategy* by defining it as the composition of: i) A *search engine*, which determines how the SLD-tree is traversed, e.g., depth-first, breadth-first, iterative deepening, random search; and ii) *control parameters*, which decide if/when to switch strategies, how far or how much to explore (e.g., depth, number of solutions, time limit), etc.

Our interest in alternative search rules comes from different angles. First, when teaching (C)LP and Prolog, the ability to switch between depth-first and fair search rules can help students visualize the true potential of the (C)LP paradigm and Prolog to gain a hands-on understanding of concepts such as *termination, decidability,* or *the halting problem* (see, e.g., [16]).

Also, Prolog programmers, for example when implementing Artificial Intelligence (AI) applications, can define and experiment with different search strategies to trade off efficiency against completeness. As mentioned before, the standard Prolog depth-first search can, in some cases, become trapped in an infinite branch and fail to produce a solution, even when solutions exist. As just an example, a strategy that begins with breadth-first search and switches to depth-first search once a certain resource-consumption threshold is reached may yield some, though possibly not all, solutions, yet these can still be useful.

Our final motivation, that we will use as running example throughout the paper, is *test case generation*. Some previous work in this area within LP leverages *assertion preconditions* as *test case generators* [23]. Since these preconditions are conjunctions of literals, the corresponding predicates can be used to systematically produce valid inputs. The key innovation lies in executing standard predicates under non-standard search rules, enabling either fully automatic or user-guided generation. By adapting the search strategy, we can control how the input space is explored, improving coverage and avoiding redundant or non-terminating test cases. Purely random generation may be sufficient for some programs, but for others, it can be inefficient or fail to reach deeper regions of the search space. For instance, when predicates involve multiple recursive clauses, random exploration may become trapped in certain branches, spending excessive time generating similar test cases. Taking into account alternative search strategies or combining different ones can provide useful alternatives.

Thus, the multi-configurable search rule framework presented in this paper can be used for various purposes. As already mentioned, we focus here on its application to testing.

The rest of the paper proceeds as follows: Sect. 2 provides the background on the test framework that we base our work on. Section 3 presents the proposed language of directives for specifying search strategies and explains its interaction with the assertion language of the test framework. It also provides examples that demonstrate how the framework can be extended using our multi-configurable search rules. Section 4 presents a case study on binary trees, including some experimental results. We close by discussing related work in Sect. 5 and conclusions in Sect. 6.

2   Some Background on the Testing Framework Used

In this section, we start by providing some background on concepts needed to understand how our multi-configurable search-rule framework is used to perform improved program testing. To this end, we introduce the assertion framework of Ciao Prolog [15,17,18], which already has many useful components for our purposes.

2.1   Checking Predicates Against Specifications

We begin by presenting how to determine whether a given predicate satisfies the preconditions and postconditions declared in program assertions in the Ciao model.[1] In the Ciao model, predicates are checked against their specifications through a combination of static and dynamic techniques. *Static checking* of these assertions is performed at compile time by the CiaoPP tool using abstract interpretation [12,19,24]. This allows many properties, such as types, modes, determinacy, and non-failure, to be verified automatically before execution. However,

---

[1] This model was a precursor of *gradual typing*, *hybrid-typing*, and similar approaches [10,26,29], sharing many general principles.

because static analysis is undecidable, some properties or parts of assertions may remain unproven. In such cases, these unverified assertions are annotated in the output program with **check** status. The resulting program can then be *instrumented* with run-time checks [30,31], to ensure safety during execution. This *run-time checking* process proceeds as follows: Given a set of queries Q and a set of assertions A, the run-time checking process executes the program on the queries in Q and determines whether the resulting derivations belong to the error set defined by the assertions. It is not expected that this process can prove an assertion to be *fully checked*, since that would require exploring all possible derivations from all valid queries, often an infinite set. Instead, the goal is to test a representative subset of queries, which, although incomplete, allows detecting many violations of the specification. An enabler here is the fact that properties are written in Prolog, and are thus *runnable*, meaning they can be verified at run-time. For instance, consider the following property:

```
:- prop sorted_int_list/1.
sorted_int_list([]).
sorted_int_list([X]) :- int(X).
sorted_int_list([X,Y|T]) :- int(X), int(Y), X >= Y, sorted_int_list([Y|T]).
```

The query `sorted_int_list(X)` succeeds for `X = []`, `X = [1]`, and `X = [2, 1]`; fails for `X = a` and `X = f(a)`; and instantiates variables for `X = [A,B]` and `X = A`. A predicate `check/1` exists that captures failure or further instantiation (the latter meaning that the argument is not as instantiated as the property requires), and raises an error in any of those cases.[2] This mechanism enables the dynamic verification of a wide range of properties, providing a smooth integration of static and dynamic checking. If the definition of these properties is provided directly in the source language, then such properties are typically already runnable and thus available for run-time checking. However, it is also possible to provide a specialized implementation for run-time checking if desired. For properties that are declared native but are not written in the source language, a run-time test version must be provided.

2.2   Generating Test Cases from Properties in Assertions

An important complement to static and dynamic checking is the ability to *test* a program automatically by generating input data that satisfies its preconditions. This idea builds on earlier work on random testing [14], later adapted to the Ciao assertion model [3,23]. Given an assertion for a predicate, the objective is to automatically generate goals whose arguments satisfy the assertion's precondition and then execute them to determine whether the corresponding postconditions (and global properties) hold or whether violations can be detected. In this setting, the notion of generating random test values from assertion preconditions arises naturally: since preconditions are typically expressed as conjunctions of property literals, these same property predicates can serve as *generators* of

---

[2] More precisely, these are *instantiation* checks. *Compatibility* checks are also supported, but the discussion is beyond the scope of this paper. See the previously cited bibliography on the Ciao assertion model for details.

Table 1. Syntax of the search strategy language.

$\langle sr\_decl \rangle$	::= :- **search_rule**($\langle sr\_name \rangle$, $\langle pred \rangle$)
$\langle sr\_definition \rangle$	::= :- **def_sr**($\langle sr\_name \rangle$, [$\langle options \rangle$])
$\langle pred \rangle$	::= $\langle pred\_name \rangle$ | ϵ
$\langle pred\_name \rangle$	::= Pred/$\langle arity \rangle$
$\langle arity \rangle$	::= Integer
$\langle options \rangle$	::= $\langle sr\_engine\_decls \rangle$, $\langle control\_parameter \rangle$, $\langle apply\_sr \rangle$
$\langle sr\_engine\_decls \rangle$	::= **extends**($\langle sr\_name \rangle$), $\langle sr\_engine\_decl \rangle$
$\langle sr\_engine\_decl \rangle$	::= $\langle sr\_engine\_pred \rangle$ | $\langle sr\_engine\_pred \rangle$, $\langle sr\_engine\_decl \rangle$
$\langle sr\_engine\_pred \rangle$	::= **set_sr**($\langle pred\_name \rangle$) = $\langle sr\_name \rangle$ | ϵ
$\langle sr\_name \rangle$	::= Sr | $\langle sr\_engine \rangle$ | [$\langle sr\_rules \rangle$]
$\langle sr\_engine \rangle$	::= **df** | **bf** | **rnd** | **id** | **af**
$\langle sr\_rules \rangle$	::= $\langle sr\_rule \rangle$ | $\langle sr\_rule \rangle$, $\langle sr\_rules \rangle$
$\langle sr\_rule \rangle$	::= _($\langle args \rangle$, $\langle sr\_name \rangle$) :- $\langle condition \rangle$
$\langle args \rangle$	::= Var | Var, $\langle args \rangle$
$\langle control\_parameter \rangle$	::= $\langle sr\_limit \rangle$, $\langle sr\_selector \rangle$, $\langle delay \rangle$
$\langle sr\_limit \rangle$	::= **time** = Integer | **depth** = Integer | **steps** = Integer | ϵ
$\langle sr\_selector \rangle$	::= **first_solution** | **all_solutions** | **num_solutions** = Integer | ϵ
$\langle delay \rangle$	::= **delay** = $\langle pred\_name \rangle$ | ϵ
$\langle apply\_sr \rangle$	::= **apply_to_pre** = [$\langle asserts \rangle$] | ϵ
$\langle asserts \rangle$	::= $\langle assert \rangle$ | $\langle assert \rangle$ $\langle asserts \rangle$
$\langle assert \rangle$	::= Id | $\langle pred\_name \rangle$ | ϵ

test inputs. The generation process is based on executing the property predicates in generation mode using a random search rule in order to produce a set of valid test cases. Once the test inputs are generated, the existing run-time check instrumentation provided is reused to perform the actual verification of assertions during execution. This combination allows a wide range of properties to be tested automatically, including those specific to (Constraint) Logic Programming, such as shape-based (regular) types, variable sharing, and instantiation patterns. By interpreting assertions both as specifications and as generators of input data, the Ciao model provides a smooth connection between specification, verification, and testing.

3   Strategy Specification and Assertion Languages

In this section, we describe the language for defining search strategies. Since program testing is the primary application in this paper, we also present the assertion language and explain how the two languages interact during assertion-based testing.

3.1 The Search Strategy Language

Table 1 presents the main grammar rules for the search strategy language. Such language enables assigning search strategies to a modular program through *search strategy declarations* ($\langle sr\_decl \rangle$) and search strategy definitions ($\langle sr\_definition \rangle$). The latter allow the definition of new strategies as compositions of existing ones. Each strategy defines the search engine ($\langle sr\_engine\_decls \rangle$) to be used for a specific predicate ($\langle pred\_name \rangle$) or for all the predicates of a whole module. The only mandatory element for defining a search strategy is the use of the extends(Sr) declaration, which specifies the search rule being extended and defines the *default* search rule. This declaration ensures that the new strategy inherits the complete behavior of search rule Sr. The search engine determines the order in which nodes of the SLD-tree are expanded, such as depth-first (df), breadth-first (bf), random (rnd), etc., user-defined ($\langle sr\_name \rangle$), or conditional composition of different searches. At each node, the control parameters ($\langle control\_parameters \rangle$) impose quantitative constraints on the exploration, such as depth, time, or solution selectors (first_solution, all_solutions, num_solutions), and determine the conditions under which goals and clauses are delayed.[3] These parameters compose the set of options ($\langle options \rangle$) in a search strategy definition, together with $\langle apply\_sr \rangle$, which is used as an interface between the assertion language and the search strategy language, and will be described in detail in Sect. 3.2. The grammar includes the following constants: "Pred" (any valid predicate name in the underlying language, normally non-empty strings starting with a lower-case letter or enclosed in quotes); "Var" (which corresponds to variable names, normally non-empty strings of characters that start with a capital letter or an underscore); "Integer" (which denotes any valid integer); and "Sr" and "Id" (which can be non-empty strings starting with a lower-case letter).

3.2 Assertion Language Used

So far, we have presented constructs for dynamic search rule selection, with the objective of using them for generating test cases, but without relating them directly to assertions. As mentioned before, we will use Ciao Prolog's assertion language for our purposes. We now briefly describe it. The general specification of a predicate p/n consists of declarations that provide partial specifications of its behavior. They have the following syntax:

:- [*Status*] pred *Head* [: *Calls*] [=> *Success*] [+ *Comp*] [# *Comm*].

which expresses that a) calls to predicate *Head* that satisfy precondition *Calls* are admissible and b) for such calls, if they succeed, the predicate must satisfy post-condition *Success* and global computational properties *Comp*. *Calls* and *Success* are conjunctions of property literals. *Comm* is a string that contains a textual description or encapsulates an identifier of the assertion. If there are several pred assertions, the disjunction of the *Calls* fields defines the admissible calls to the predicate.

---

[3] Any predicate can be delayed, but delaying is particularly useful for labeling.

The following code fragment provides two `pred` assertions defining two particular ways in which predicate `app/3` is expected to be called:

```
:- check pred app(X,Y,Z) : (list(X),list(Y),var(X)) => list(Z) + det # "[id0]".
:- check pred app(X,Y,Z) : (var(X),var(Y),list(Z)) => (list(X),list(Y)) + multi # "[id1]".

app([],X,X).
app([X|Xs],Ys,[X|Zs]) :-
   app(Xs,Ys,Zs).
```

The first pred assertion states that if `app/3` is called with the first two arguments instantiated to lists and the third a variable, and such call succeeds, then the third argument must be bound to a list. This first assertion also states that when called with such call pattern, predicate `app/3` must be deterministic (`det`, a global computational property). The second `pred` assertion states that `app/3` may also be called with the third argument instantiated to a list and the first two as variables, and that, if such a call succeeds, then the first and second arguments should be bound to lists. It also states that, if called that way, the predicate will produce one or more solutions, but not fail (`multi`, also a global computational property). Each of the two assertions is labeled with an (optional) identifier. The `check` status indicates that these are desired properties that need to be checked, statically or dynamically, but have not been proven true or false yet.

What links the generation properties of assertion preconditions with their corresponding search strategies is the identifier of each assertion, specified through the ⟨*apply_sr*⟩ option in the search rule declaration. This option defines the list of assertions to which the search rule applies. The list can include specific assertion identifiers or predicates, indicating that the search rule applies to all assertions associated with those predicates. For instance, the declaration on the left:

```
:- def_sr(sr1, [                  :- def_sr(sr2, [
     apply_to_pre = [id1],             apply_to_pre = [app/3],
     extends(bf)                       extends(bf)
]).                               ]).
```

states that breadth-first should be used as search rule for generating the properties that appear in the precondition of the assertion with identifier `id1`. In turn, the declaration on the right states that the search rule should be applied to the preconditions of all assertions for predicate `app/3`. If no explicit search rule declaration is provided, the default is that all properties are generated using a random strategy.

3.3   Illustrative Examples

We now illustrate the use of the strategy specification language through examples that show how to use it to generalize the test generation mechanism. This extension enables finer control over the generation of test inputs compared to previous work [3] in the Ciao system.

Dynamic Strategy Switching. Consider verifying a predicate `sumlist(L, S)` that computes the sum `S` of all elements in list `L`:

```
sumlist([], 0).
sumlist([H|T], Sum) :-
  sumlist(T, Rest),
  Sum is H + Rest.
```

A fundamental property is that the sum should be invariant under permutation, i.e., reordering the elements should not change the total sum. We can express this property formally as:

$$\forall L.\forall L'.\forall S.(sumlist(L, S) \land permutation(L, L')) \rightarrow sumlist(L', S)$$

which can be encoded as follows:

```
:- pred sum_perm(L) : list(int,L) + multi.
sum_perm(L) :- sumlist(L, S), permutation(L, L1), sumlist(L1, S).
```

where **permutation/2** is defined as:

```
permutation([], []).
permutation([X|Xs], [R|Rs]) :-
  select(R, [X|Xs], Y),
  permutation(Y, Rs).

select(X, [X|Xs], Xs).
select(X, [Y|Ys], [Y|Zs]) :-
  select(X, Ys, Zs).
```

During testing of our `sumlist` implementation, test lists `L` are generated, and then their sum `S` is computed, all `L'` permutations are generated for each test list, and it is then verified that `sumlist(L',S)` holds for each permutation.

For list generation, we would like to produce lists incrementally by length: `[]`, `[_]`, `[_,_]`, and so on. Native properties, such as `list/2` or `int/1`, rely on a specific implementation for generation, which requires dynamically switching to that internal code. The internal generators for these native properties can be executed under different search strategies. For instance, we apply a depth-first strategy to construct the list structure, and then fill the elements with randomly generated values.

Since we subsequently apply permutations, it is not worthwhile to generate very large lists, as simpler cases already provide good coverage for testing. We can define this search strategy and name it `sr_list` as follows:

```
:- def_sr(sr_list, [              :- def_sr(sr_int, [
   extends(df),                      extends(rnd),
   set_sr(int/1) = sr_int            first_solution
]).                               ]).
```

which extends the depth-first search rule by adding the declaration `set_sr(int/1) = sr_int`, which in turn sets the generation of numbers to be random.

This customized search strategy gives us the following output:

```
?- list(int, L).
L = [] ;
L = [-3] ;
L = [-51,-37] ;
```

```
L = [94,-73,-59] ;
L = [-69,-75,-86,-64] ;
L = [-63,-34,37,-83,-82] ;
...
```

Dependent Strategy Selection. Search strategy selection can be made dependent on the input. This enables, for instance, predicates to use two different search strategies depending on whether the input is ground or contains variables.

The following search rule declaration for the predicate `permutation/2` specifies different search strategies depending on the length of the input list:

```
:- def_sr(sr_perm, [
     extends(df),
     set_sr(permutation/2) = [
         (_(L,P,bf)  :- var(P), length(L,N), N =< 7),
         (_(L,P,rnd) :- var(P), length(L,N), N > 7),
         (_(L,P,bf)  :- var(L), ground(P))
     ],
     num_solutions = 500
]).
```

It expresses that for any call `perm(L,P)`, if the condition `var(P)`, `length(L,N)`, `N =< 7` holds (i.e., `P` is unbound and `L` is a list whose length is less than or equal to 7), then breadth-first search is used; otherwise, random search is applied. The declaration also states that if `L` is unbound and `P` ground, then breadth-first search must be used.

Finally, the parameter `num_solutions = 500` indicates that at most 500 solutions should be generated. This last parameter is one of many termination criteria supported by our framework, including: *depth-based* termination, which halts exploration upon reaching a specified depth; *solution-based* termination, which stops after discovering a target number of solutions; *step-based* termination, which bounds the number of transitions performed before a valid solution is produced; and *time-based termination*, which enforces a maximum time budget. The resulting search strategy definition for `perm/2`, including these search rules is shown in Fig. 1.

3.4   Some Implementation Details

As mentioned earlier, our goal is to maintain compatibility with modules, built-ins, and other libraries and features to a high degree. For example, supporting modules means that generators are not limited to local predicates. A predicate defined in one module can freely invoke predicates from other modules, inheriting or overriding their corresponding search strategies as needed.

The implementation of the search strategy language is built around a collection of module-aware meta-interpreters and orchestrated around a single predicate: `call_with_sr(Sr, Goal)`, which executes a given goal `Goal` under a search strategy `Sr`. When a module specifies a default search rule, predicates called from a context where no other `call_with_sr/2` is active are executed implicitly as if called through `call_with_sr/2` (using the default search rule specified

```
:- search_rule(prop_sr).

:- def_sr(prop_sr, [
     apply_to_pre = [id2],
     extends(df),
     set_sr(list/2) = sr_list,
     set_sr(permutation/2) = [
       (_(L,P,bf)   :- length(L,N), N =< 7),
       (_(L,P,rnd)  :- length(L,N), N > 7),
       (_(L,P,bf)   :- var(L), ground(P))
   ],
     num_solutions = 500
]).

:- def_sr(sr_list, [
     extends(df),
     set_sr(int/1) = sr_int
]).

:- def_sr(sr_int, [
     extends(rnd),
     first_solution
]).

:- pred prop_sum_perm(X) : list(int,X) + multi # "[id2]".
prop_sum_perm(L) :- sumlist(L, S), permutation(L, L1), sumlist(L1, S).
```

Fig. 1. Search strategy definition for `perm/2`.

for the module or for each of its predicates). That `call_with_sr/2` can also be invoked directly in the program to execute any subgoal under an explicitly specified search rule. To determine which search strategy engine or meta-interpreter needs to be used at each call, the system maintains a global stack that is updated whenever `call_with_sr/2` is invoked. The top of the stack records the current search rule, and when execution of that particular call ends, restores the previous most recently active `call_with_sr/2` invocation. Thus, the search rule applied to a predicate P is determined by looking up the definitions in the current search rule according to the following decreasing priority order: i) search rule declarations for the predicate; ii) declarations from inherited search rules; iii) the primitive search rule.

Once the search rule is determined, execution proceeds with the particular engine or meta-interpreter. For that, a dual representation is maintained for each predicate: the compiled version, for efficient execution under standard depth-first semantics, and the source-level version for metaprogramming. The dual representation allows access to the rules of the program at run-time through the built-in predicate `clause/2`. The implementation design relies on these two key aspects that preserve Prolog's module system semantics, while providing control over which predicates are affected by a given search rule.

Let us use Fig. 2 to illustrate this idea.

The module `main` defines the predicate `gen/2`, which uses the predicate `prop/2` defined in module `prop_def` and declares the search rule `sr0`. Within `sr0`, the search rule declares a specific search strategy for predicate `gen_/2` and extends the search rule `srA`. `srA` can refer either to the identifier of another search rule

```
:- module(main, [gen/2], [sr]).
:- use_module(prop_def).

:- search_rule(sr0).
:- def_sr(sr0, [
     extends(srA),
     set_sr(gen_/2) = srB
   ]).

:- def_sr(sr1, [...]).

gen(X,Y) :-
     call_with_sr([sr(sr1)],prop(X,Y)),
     gen_(Y).

gen_(X) :- ...
```

```
:- module(prop_def, [prop/2], [sr]).
:- use_module(lists).

:- search_rule(sr3).
:- def_sr(sr3, [...]).

:- search_rule(prop/2,sr4).
:- def_sr(sr4, [...]).
prop(L,M) :-
     length(L,N),
     prop_(N,M).

prop_(X,Y) :- ...
```

```
:- module(lists, [length/2,...], [sr]).

:- search_rule(length/2,sr2).
:- def_sr(sr2, [...]).
length(X,Y) :- ...
```

Fig. 2. Example of three modules with different search strategies defined.

declaration or to a primitive search rule (e.g., breadth-first, depth-first, random, etc.). In the case where `srA` refers to another search rule, the system recursively traces it until a primitive search rule is reached and establishes it as the *general* search rule for `sr0`.

For instance, if the goal `?- gen(X,Y)` is executed, it starts under the search strategy `srA`. Then `prop/2` is called; note that it is inside an explicit `call_with_sr/2`. Therefore, the search rule inside `call_with_sr/2` takes precedence over the search rule defined in module `prop_def` and the call to `prop/2` is executed using search rule `sr1`. Note that if the query executed is `?- prop(X,Y)`, it will be executed using `sr4`, the module default `sr3` is ignored because predicate level declarations take priority. Continuing the example, `prop/2` calls `length/2` from the `lists` module. The search rule applied is the one defined in the `lists` module, which is `sr2`. `prop/2` also calls the auxiliary predicate `prop_/2`. In this case, it inherits the strategy of `prop/2`, since the most recent active `call_with_sr/2` is that of `prop/2`. Once the execution of `prop/2` ends, `gen/2` calls `gen_/2`. In this case, the current search rule is `srA`. Since `srA` extends another search rule, the system looks up the extends chain to check whether a specific search rule is defined for the predicate `gen_/2`. In this example, it first looks up in the search declaration of `sr0` whether such a rule exists, and it is applied. Thus, `gen_/2` is executed using `srB`. Once the search finishes, the current search rule reverts to `srA`, and the call under the search rule `srA` terminates, completing the execution of goal `gen(X, Y)`.

As can be seen, even some system-defined predicates, such as `length/2` in the above example, can be executed using non-standard search rules, in particular those used as properties in assertions, such as `int/1`. To this end, we have developed alternative *generating* implementations of these built-ins, and these alternative implementations are selected dynamically based on the search strategy.

An important open question is the applicability of our mechanism in the presence of extra-logical constructs. While the approach works for pure programs, including those with constraints, predicates such as `assert/1`, `retract/1`, or other side-effects introduce dependencies on sequentiality that may interact non-trivially with some search rules. It is the programmer's responsibility to ensure that the behavior is as intended if these built-ins are used. Moreover, infinite or unbounded search spaces can be mitigated by imposing explicit limits, such as bounding the number of solutions, execution time, or search depth, but a more general mechanism for controlling such behavior remains as future work.

```
:- prop complex_property/2 # "A predicate generator".
complex_property(X,S) :-
    tree(X),
    sorted_tree(X),
    tsum(X,S).

:- regtype tree/1 # "Simple binary tree with integer nodes".
tree(empty).
tree(tree(LC,X,RC)) :-
    X #> 0, X #=< 100,
    tree(LC),
    tree(RC).

% Check if tree T is sorted
sorted_tree(T) :- ...

% tsum(T,N) : Constrains the sum of all node values in tree T to N
tsum(T,N) :- ...

% insert(X,T0,T1) : The result of inserting the node X into the tree T0 is T1
:- pred insert(X,T0,T1) : (nnegint(X), tree(T0), sorted_tree(T0))
                        => (sorted_tree(T1), non_empty_tree(T1))
                        + det # "[id2]".

insert(X,empty,tree(empty,X,empty)).
insert(X,tree(LC,X,RC),tree(LC,X,RC)).
insert(X,tree(LC,Y,RC),tree(LC_p,Y,RC)) :-
    X #=< Y, % <-- There is a bug!
    insert(X,LC,LC_p).
insert(X,tree(LC,Y,RC),tree(LC,Y,RC_p)) :-
    X #> Y,
    insert(X,RC,RC_p).

... % rest of the implementation of module predicates
```

Fig. 3. Binary tree library.

4   A Case Study: Generation of Binary Trees

Consider the excerpt in Fig. 3 from a library using binary trees. The `tree/1` property describes the shape of trees, which can be an empty tree (a terminal node) or a compound term (a non-terminal node) with a value, and left and right subtrees as arguments. The node values are integers between 1 and 100.

Generating a More Complex Property. Our intention is to generate values for `complex_property/2`, which is composed of several sub-properties: the tree structure, the ordering constraint (`sorted_tree/1`), and the total sum of node values (`tsum/2`). Such ordering constraint states that every node's left subtree contains only values less than the node's value, and every node's right subtree contains only values greater than the node's value. This ensures that an in-order traversal of the tree yields a sorted sequence.

To study the behavior of different search strategies, we conducted an experiment based on the property `complex_property(T,S)`, varying S. Each generation was executed with a limit of 100 solutions and a maximum time of 180 s per run. Figure 4 shows the execution time for several strategies: breadth-first (`bf`), breadth-first AND-fair (`af`), iterative deepening (`id`), and random (`rnd`), which is the default one. For small sums, $S \leq 500$, breadth-first yields the best performance, as it explores shallow trees first and quickly finds valid configurations. However, as S increases, the number of possible combinations grows exponentially, and breadth-first becomes less efficient. Iterative deepening (`id`) incurs moderate overhead due to repeated traversals but remains complete and scales reasonably well. In contrast, the random strategy (`rnd`) exhibits higher variance and slower convergence, particularly for larger values of S, as it lacks structural guidance and may repeatedly explore redundant branches. Finally, depth-first (`df`) proved the least effective. Because the number of required solutions was capped at 100, it frequently descended down deep branches and spent substantial time exploring a single path before backtracking, often resulting in timeouts.

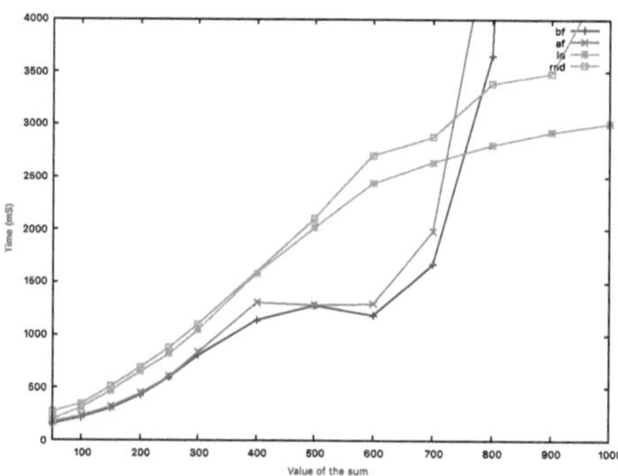

Fig. 4. Comparing search rules executing `complex_property(T,S)`.

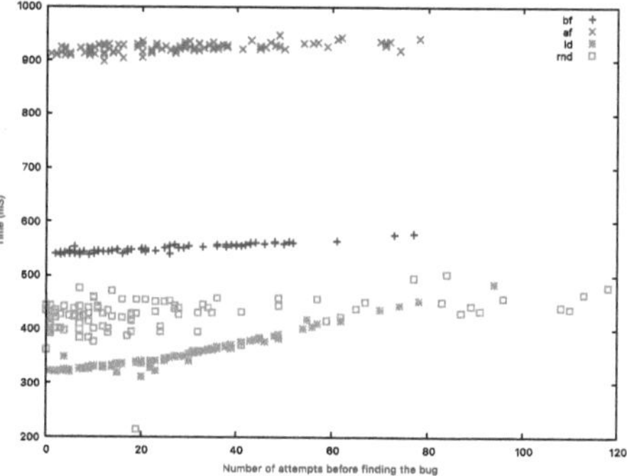

Fig. 5. Execution time and number of attempts until the bug is found.

The experimental results suggest that an effective search strategy for generating values for `complex_property/2` is the following:

```
:- def_sr(complex_prop_sr, [
      extends(df),
      set_sr(complex_property/2) = [
          (_(X,Y,bf) :- Y =< 500),
          (_(X,Y,id) :- Y > 500)
```

```
    ],
    delay = labeling/2,
    num_solutions = 100,
    time = 180
  ]).
```

This definition specifies that the `complex_property/2` predicate dynamically adapts its search strategy based on the metric value S. As suggested by the plot, if $S \leq 500$, breadth-first (`bf`) search is used; if $S > 500$, iterative deepening (`id`) is used. The remaining predicates that compose the generator are executed using depth-first search for efficiency. Additionally, labeling (via `labeling/2`) is delayed until the end of the computation, adopting a *constrain-and-generate* approach, common in constraint logic programming: constraints are accumulated during structure generation, and numeric variables are instantiated later.

Assertion Checking. We now turn to testing the predicate `insert/3`, also implemented in Fig. 3, which returns the tree resulting from adding a node to an existing tree. We have intentionally introduced a bug in the third clause: instead of using the correct constraint `#<`, the clause uses `#=<`. As a result, when the tree contains a node with the same number of input nodes, two clauses succeed, i.e., the clauses are not mutually exclusive, which violates the intended ordering property of the tree and the computational property `det` (deterministic). In this case, we evaluate which search rule for generating trees requires less time and fewer attempts to detect the bug. For `nnegint/1`, which generates non-negative integers, random search is used.

Figure 5 shows a scatter plot comparing the search rules in terms of execution time and the number of tests required to find the bug. We conducted the experiments using the same search rules as before, performing 100 runs for each. We observe that, regarding execution time, the iterative-deepening strategy is the fastest in finding bugs, typically requiring a relatively small number of attempts (mostly between 0 and 80). Breadth-first and breadth-first AND-fair strategies are more consistent in the number of attempts needed: most `bf` runs find the bug in fewer than 50 attempts, while `af` usually requires fewer than 65 attempts. However, both `bf` and `af` tend to take more time overall, especially `af`. The random strategy exhibits the highest variability, with some runs finding the bug quickly, while others require substantially more attempts. This strategy performs reasonably well in this example. However, it does not guarantee that the bug will be found within a limited number of attempts. If another search rule can provide such a guarantee, such as iterative deepening in this example, it is preferable to use it, as it offers more predictable and controllable search behavior.

Improving Fairness in Random Search. Let us now illustrate an extension of our search algorithm, useful to improve fairness when using random search strategies. As an example, consider the problem of generating random linear constraints:

```prolog
constraint(=(L1, L2))  :- lin_expr(L1, L2).
constraint(=<(L1, L2)) :- lin_expr(L1, L2).
constraint(>=(L1, L2)) :- lin_expr(L1, L2).
constraint(<(L1, L2))  :- lin_expr(L1, L2).
constraint(>(L1, L2))  :- lin_expr(L1, L2).

lin_expr(L1, L2) :- lin_expr(L1), lin_expr(L2).

lin_expr(C)          :- coefficient(C).
lin_expr(V)          :- var(V).
lin_expr(+(E))       :- lin_expr(E).
lin_expr(-(E))       :- lin_expr(E).
lin_expr(+(E1, E2))  :- lin_expr(E1), lin_expr(E2).
lin_expr(-(E1, E2))  :- lin_expr(E1), lin_expr(E2).
lin_expr(*(C, E))    :- coefficient(C), lin_expr(E).
lin_expr(*(E, C))    :- coefficient(C), lin_expr(E).

coefficient(C) :- C in 0..500, labeling([rnd],C).
% $VAR used as ground representation of variables
var(A)               :- uppercase_char(Arg), A = '$VAR'(Arg).
```

The previous rules define arithmetic constraints recursively, using relational operators (=, =<, >, etc.) and linear expressions that combine coefficients, variables and subexpressions through addition, subtraction, and multiplication. Each coefficient is an integer variable constrained to lay within a given range (here, 0 to 500). The final call to `labeling/2` enumerates concrete integer values for these coefficients.

These constraints are employed to synthesize programs that can serve as benchmarks for evaluating the polyhedra abstract domain [9]:

```prolog
p(C,F,G) :-
    5*A-67+F<100,
    A*(142*4)=G,
    3< -(47*M*78)*291,
    88* -(311*F)>=C,
    X*215=<O,
    - -H>(90+(C*(178*J)))*67.
```

Naive random exploration in this example may lead to non-termination when execution is trapped in the creation of more recursive clauses than base cases. To make search generation fair, our work proposes a method based on identifying recursive predicates within a given program, using the implementation of Tarjan's algorithm [32,33] used in CiaoPP to classify recursive and non-recursive predicates. Using this information, we alternate between base and recursive cases during generation, ensuring that the search process avoids infinite recursion. As future work, we plan to explore this idea further by leveraging static analysis to further enhance search strategies.

5   Related Work

Property-based testing [5] frameworks have become a widely used approach for validating program properties by generating and executing test cases. Originally developed for **Haskell** and functional programming [5], these frameworks allow developers to automatically generate random input data from some given properties. It has since been adapted to additional languages, including **Erlang** [25],

Curry with EasyCheck [4], and Prolog [1,7,9,23]. In the context of Constraint Logic Programming (CLP) and Constrained Horn Clauses (CHC), using predicates as property-based generators is particularly natural, since calling a predicate with free variables can automatically instantiate them. PrologCheck [1] provides a language for specifying properties and custom generators for Prolog programs. For complex data structures, such as sorted lists or AVL trees, naive random generation is often insufficient, and developers must provide specialized generators. The tool supports writing such generators, including properties that consider the modes of the arguments. As mentioned before, Ciao Prolog's LPcheck [9,23] introduced the concept of *assertion-based testing*, based on using the properties in its assertion language directly as generators. ProSyT [7] generates data structures for Erlang programs by combining symbolic data structure generation, constraint solving, and randomized variable instantiation via coroutining. Thus, it reduces the programmer's effort in writing custom generators.

The integration of search strategies into declarative languages has long also been explored. CLP systems [21,27] and most Prolog systems include Constraint Logic Programming (CLP) libraries [2,6,13,15,20,34] that provide predefined search strategies. These search rules are often embedded in labeling predicates for solving different classes of problems. In [8], search control was investigated by proposing a flexible framework for CHR∨ (Constraint Handling Rules with disjunction), extended with rule and search branch priorities. Schrijvers proposed Tor [28] as a mechanism for supporting the execution of predicates using alternative search rules. Tor represents a device that could certainly be useful as an implementation technique for our approach, although we currently use other mechanisms available in the Ciao Prolog system instead, which we have used as the basis for our experiments. In this work, however, we concentrate instead on providing a higher-level way for users to specify search strategies.

The idea of exploiting search strategies within property-based testing unifies these two lines of research. By viewing the testing process itself as a search problem, alternative search rules can guide how candidate test cases are generated and explored. Unlike earlier work where search and test generation were orthogonal, our approach treats the search strategy as a component of the testing process, providing a framework for exploring properties under different execution rules.

6   Conclusions

In this work, we have presented a framework for controlling the execution of Prolog programs through flexible search strategies. By separating the logic of predicates from their exploration order, our approach allows the same standard Prolog predicate to be executed under different search rules without modifying the program itself. This capability mitigates several common limitations of random property-based testing, such as infinite exploration, non-termination, or inefficient traversal of the search space. We introduced a search strategy specification language that combines search engines with control parameters such as clause selection, delayed evaluation, and termination criteria. The framework fully supports Prolog's expressive features, including constraints, DCGs, and modules, ensuring that predicates can call other predicates across modules while respecting or overriding their search strategies. Through several examples, we demonstrated how the proposed search strategy language improves exploration efficiency. Future work includes refining metric-based strategy selection, extending search strategies with static analysis guidance, and exploring richer scheduling policies, as well as, in the testing context, studying combinations with other orthogonal techniques such as those based on program coverage or concolic testing [11]. Overall, we argue that our framework provides a flexible, declarative, and practical approach to controlling the execution of logic programs, bridging the gap between declarative specifications and operational behavior.

References

1. Amaral, C., Florido, M., Costa, V.S.: PrologCheck - property-based testing in prolog. In: Functional and Logic Programming - 12th International Symposium, FLOPS. LNCS, vol. 8475, pp. 1–17. Springer, Cham (2014)
2. Carlsson, M., Ottosson, G., Carlson, B.: An open-ended finite domain constraint solver. In: Proceedings of the 9th International Symposium on Programming Languages: Implementations, Logics, and Programs: Including a Special Trach on Declarative Programming Languages in Education, PLILP 1997, pp. 191–206. Springer, London (1997). http://dl.acm.org/citation.cfm?id=646452.692956
3. Casso, I., Morales, J.F., Lopez-Garcia, P., Hermenegildo, M.: An integrated approach to assertion-based random testing in prolog. In: Gabbrielli, M. (ed.) Post-Proceedings of the 29th International Symposium on Logic-based Program Synthesis and Transformation (LOPSTR 2019). LNCS, vol. 12042, pp. 159–176. Springer, Cham (2020). https://doi.org/10.1007/978-3-030-45260-5_10
4. Christiansen, J., Fischer, S.: EasyCheck - test data for free. In: Functional and Logic Programming, 9th International Symposium, FLOPS. pp. 322–336 (2008)
5. Claessen, K., Hughes, J.: QuickCheck: a lightweight tool for random testing of haskell programs. In: Fifth ACM SIGPLAN International Conference on Functional Programming, ICFP 2000, , pp. 268–279. ACM (2000)
6. Diaz, D., Abreu, S., Codognet, P.: On the implementation of GNU Prolog. Theory Pract. Logic Program. **12**(1–2), 253–282 (2012)
7. De Angelis, E., Fioravanti, F., Palacios, A., Pettorossi, A., Proietti, M.: Property-based test case generators for free. In: International Conference on Tests and Proofs, pp. 186–206. Springer, Cham (2019)
8. De Koninck, L., Schrijvers, T., Demoen, B.: A flexible search framework for CHR, pp. 16–47. Springer, Heidelberg (2008)
9. Ferreiro, D., Casso, I., Lopez-Garcia, P., Morales, J.F., Hermenegildo, M.V.: Checkification: A Practical Approach for Testing Static Analysis Truths. Theory and Practice of Logic Programming (2025). https://arxiv.org/abs/2501.12093
10. Flanagan, C.: Hybrid type checking. In: 33rd ACM SIGPLAN-SIGACT Symposium on Principles of Programming Languages, POPL 2006, pp. 245–256 (2006)
11. Fortz, S., Mesnard, F., Payet, É., Perrouin, G., Vanhoof, W., Vidal, G.: An SMT-based concolic testing tool for logic programs. In: Functional and Logic Programming - 15th International Symposium, FLOPS. LNCS, vol. 12073, pp. 215–219. Springer, Cham (2020). https://doi.org/10.1007/978-3-030-59025-3_13

12. Garcia-Contreras, I., Morales, J.F., Hermenegildo, M.V.: Incremental analysis of logic programs with assertions and open predicates. In: Gabbrielli, M. (ed.) LOPSTR 2019. LNCS, vol. 12042, pp. 36–56. Springer, Cham (2020). https://doi.org/10.1007/978-3-030-45260-5_3
13. García de la Banda, M.J., Jeffery, D., Marriott, K., Nethercote, N., Stuckey, P.J., Holzbaur, C.: Building constraint solvers with hal. In: ICLP 2004, pp. 90–104 (2001)
14. Hamlet, D.: Random testing. In: Marciniak, J. (ed.) Encyclopedia of Software Engineering, pp. 970–978. Wiley (1994)
15. Hermenegildo, M.V., et al.: An overview of ciao and its design philosophy. Theory Pract. Logic Program. **12**(1–2), 219–252 (2012). https://doi.org/10.1017/S1471068411000457. https://arxiv.org/abs/1102.5497
16. Hermenegildo, M.V., Morales, J.F., Lopez-Garcia, P.: Teaching pure LP with prolog and a fair search rule. In: Proceedings of the 40th ICLP Workshops, vol. 3799. CEUR-WS.org (2024). https://ceur-ws.org/Vol-3799/paper2PEG2.0.pdf
17. Hermenegildo, M., Puebla, G., Bueno, F.: Using global analysis, partial specifications, and an extensible assertion language for program validation and debugging. In: Apt, K.R., Marek, V., Truszczynski, M., Warren, D.S. (eds.) The Logic Programming Paradigm: A 25–Year Perspective, pp. 161–192. Springer, Cham (1999)
18. Hermenegildo, M., Puebla, G., Bueno, F., Lopez-Garcia, P.: Program development using abstract interpretation (and the ciao system preprocessor). In: 10th International Static Analysis Symposium (SAS 2003). LNCS, vol. 2694, pp. 127–152. Springer, Cham (2003)
19. Hermenegildo, M., Puebla, G., Marriott, K., Stuckey, P.: Incremental analysis of constraint logic programs. ACM Trans. Program. Lang. Syst. **22**(2), 187–223 (2000)
20. Holzbaur, C.: OFAI CLP(Q,R) Manual, Edition 1.3.3. Technical report. TR-95-09, Austrian Research Institute for Artificial Intelligence, Vienna (1995)
21. Jaffar, J., Michaylov, S.: Methodology and implementation of a CLP system. In: Fourth International Conference on Logic Programming, pp. 196–219. University of Melbourne, MIT Press (1987)
22. Kowalski, R.: Algorithm = logic + control. Commun. ACM **22**(7), 424–436 (1979)
23. Mera, E., Lopez-García, P., Hermenegildo, M.: Integrating software testing and run-time checking in an assertion verification framework. In: Hill, P.M., Warren, D.S. (eds.) ICLP 2009. LNCS, vol. 5649, pp. 281–295. Springer, Heidelberg (2009). https://doi.org/10.1007/978-3-642-02846-5_25
24. Muthukumar, K., Hermenegildo, M.: Compile-time derivation of variable dependency using abstract interpretation. J. Log. Program. **13**(2/3), 315–347 (1992)
25. Papadakis, M., Sagonas, K.: A PropEr integration of types and function specifications with property-based testing. In: 10th ACM SIGPLAN workshop on Erlang, pp. 39–50 (2011)
26. Rastogi, A., Swamy, N., Fournet, C., Bierman, G., Vekris, P.: Safe & efficient gradual typing for typescript. In: 42nd POPL, pp. 167–180. ACM (2015)
27. Schimpf, J., Shen, K.: ECLiPSe – from LP to CLP. Theory Pract. Logic Program. **12**(1-2), 127–156 (2012). https://doi.org/10.1017/S1471068411000469
28. Schrijvers, T., Demoen, B., Triska, M., Desouter, B.: Tor: modular search with hookable disjunction. Sci. Comput. Program. **84**, 101–120 (2014)
29. Siek, J.G., Taha, W.: Gradual Typing for Functional Languages. In: Scheme and Functional Programming Workshop, pp. 81–92. University of Chicago Department of Computer Science (2006)

30. Stulova, N., Morales, J.F., Hermenegildo, M.: Practical run-time checking via unobtrusive property caching. In: Theory and Practice of Logic Programming, 31st International Conference on Logic Programming (ICLP 2015) Special Issue, vol. 15 (04-05), pp. 726–741 (2015). https://doi.org/10.1017/S1471068415000344. https://arxiv.org/abs/1507.05986
31. Stulova, N., Morales, J.F., Hermenegildo, M.: Reducing the overhead of assertion run-time checks via static analysis. In: 18th International ACM SIGPLAN Symposium on Principles and Practice of Declarative Programming (PPDP 2016), pp. 90–103. ACM Press (2016)
32. Tarjan, R.: Depth-first search and linear graph algorithms. SIAM J. Comput. **1**, 140–160 (1972)
33. Tarjan, R.E.: Fast algorithms for solving path problems. J. ACM **28**(3), 594–614 (1981). https://doi.org/10.1145/322261.322273
34. Wielemaker, J., Schrijvers, T., Triska, M., Lager, T.: SWI-prolog. Theory Pract. Logic Program. **12**(1–2), 67–96 (2012). https://doi.org/10.1017/S1471068411000494

An Efficient Compiler for the IDP-Z3 Knowledge Base System

Wout Piessens[1(✉)] , Simon Vandevelde[1] , Joost Vennekens[2] ,
and Tom Schrijvers[1]

[1] KU Leuven, Leuven, Belgium
{wout.piessens,s.vandevelde,tom.schrijvers}@kuleuven.be
[2] Vrije Universiteit Brussel, Ixelles, Belgium
joost.vennekens@vub.be

Abstract. Knowledge base systems (KBS) store declarative knowledge, on which they can execute different inference tasks, such as "propagation", which is the derivation of consequences of some given information with respect to the knowledge base. When building larger applications that make use of such a KBS, specific inference tasks are typically invoked through an imperative API. For instance, both the Clasp system for Answer Set Solving and the IDP-Z3 reasoning engine for the FO($\cdot$) language offer a Python API for this. However, when the application should be deployed, e.g., in the cloud or on embedded hardware, it is not always convenient or even possible to include the entire KBS as a separate component. For this reason, we investigate the compilation of a knowledge base into a Python program that can perform propagation inference without needing access to an external solver. We investigate this approach for the FO($\cdot$) language, presenting and comparing two compilation methods. Experimental results on these two methods demonstrate that high-level propagators achieve better performance than grounded propagators.

Keywords: Knowledge base systems $\cdot$ Compiler $\cdot$ Constraint propagation $\cdot$ IDP $\cdot$ Python

1 Introduction

Knowledge base systems (KBS) are used to represent declarative knowledge. One way that such systems can be designed is by using the Knowledge Base Paradigm (KBP) [10]. The central idea of this paradigm is to store knowledge in a declarative way, such that different inference tasks can be performed on the same knowledge base. In this paper, we focus on the IDP-Z3 KBS [5] for the FO($\cdot$) language [8], a rich extension of classical first-order logic (FO).

It has been shown [18] that the IDP-Z3 system is quite similar to Answer Set Programming (ASP) systems, such as clasp [13]. As a consequence, the KBP is also suitable as a paradigm for declarative problem solving in practical applications.

N. Amin and J. Arias (Eds.): PADL 2026, LNCS 16401, pp. 115–132, 2026.
https://doi.org/10.1007/978-3-032-15981-6_7

As evidence, IDP-Z3 has already been successfully used for developing interactive configuration tools in various application domains, such as law [11], manufacturing [1,20], and the financial field [4]. Here, a central piece of technology is the Interactive Consultant (IC) [6], a graphical user interface which allows a user to interactively navigate through the solution space of the configuration problem as expressed in their Knowledge Base (KB). The IC is essentially a front-end which communicates with the IDP-Z3 reasoning engine through a Python API in the background. Again, this is similar to how interactive GUIs are developed for ASP systems through libraries such as clinguin [3]. Central to the workflow of the IC is the inference task of "propagation": whenever the user makes a choice in the GUI, the consequences of this choice with respect to the knowledge base are derived, and this information is used to further update the GUI.

While the approach has been successful in the past, deploying such a system in a real-life setting introduces some technical challenges, as it requires the entire IDP-Z3 reasoning engine (which in turn requires the Z3 SMT solver [16]). For instance, previous work considered the application of IDP-Z3 to home automation [2] and to system interoperability on public transportation vehicles [14], both of which would require running IDP-Z3 on some form of embedded device (i.e., at home or in a vehicle). In practice, the imposed hardware constraints prevent us from running the entire reasoning engine on the device.

To address this type of issue, and obtain more flexibility in the use of IDP-Z3, we wish to obtain imperative code (e.g., in Python) that executes the propagation inference tasks on this knowledge base, without requiring the external reasoning engine. Writing such code to perform a logical reasoning task by hand is obviously too cumbersome, and verifying whether the code's behavior is consistent with the original KB is difficult. Moreover, such hand-written code is not easily adaptable if the original knowledge base were to change [22, p. 3].

In this paper, we therefore propose a compiler to transform FO($\cdot$) KBs into Python programs that specifically perform the propagation inference task. First some background information from the existing literature will be summarized in Sect. 2. Afterwards, the approach in developing the compiler will be explained in Sect. 3. Experimental results regarding the efficiency of the compiler will be shown next in Sect. 4. Lastly the research will be summarized in Sect. 5 and possible future research will be motivated.

The repository containing the compiler's code with detailed comments is available online[1].

The work presented in this paper was done in the context of the first author's master thesis [17].

2   Background

As we wish to specifically compile IDP-Z3 KBs, the language that will be used as input for our system is the FO($\cdot$) language, which is a rich extension of classical

---

[1] https://anonymous.4open.science/r/compiler-for-kbs-88C7.

first-order logic. In the context of this paper, however, we restrict ourselves to a core part of this language, namely typed first-order logic with comparison operators $(=, \neq, >, \geq, <, \leq)$.

As mentioned, this work is concerned with the inference task of "propagation" for this logic. This is formally defined as follows: Given a theory T in vocabulary V, and a structure S_0 which interprets some but not necessarily all of the symbols in V, the goal is to compute the set of all literals (i.e., atoms or negated atoms) L for which it is the case that $S \models L$ for all structures $S \supseteq S_0$ such that $S \models T$. Here, it is important that S_0 interprets at least all of the type symbols in V, so that the domain of the structures that need to be considered is fixed. As an example, consider the following FO($\cdot$) specification:

```
1  vocabulary V{
2      type Foo ≜ {1, 2, 3}.
3      p: Foo → 𝔹
4      q: Foo → 𝔹
5  }
```

```
1  structure S_0:V{
2      p ≜ {1, 3}.
3  }
4  theory T:V{
5      ∀x in Foo: p(x) ⇒ q(x)
        .
6  }
```

Here, the vocabulary declares a type Foo with domain {1, 2, 3}, together with two unary predicates over this type. In the structure S_0, we interpret the value of p. Lastly, theory T states that (at least) each value which satisfies p must also satisfy q. In other words, propagation will derive that all possible structures S that model T while extending S_0 must contain at least $q(1) = true$ and $q(3) = true$.

Because propagation requires considering *all* models $S \models T$ that extend the given S_0, it is computationally expensive. Therefore, in practice, it may be useful to perform *approximate* propagation, in which only some of the literals that can be propagated are computed.

In what follows we discuss propagation on four-valued structures S as defined in Wittocx et al. [23, p.6], and interpret all atoms following from V by assigning them a truth value from the set {*true, false, unknown, inconsistent*}. The value *inconsistent* indicates that there is no truth assignment to this atom that can lead to a model of T extending S_0. Since this type of structure can express partial information by means of the *unknown* value, it will be referred to as a partial structure throughout the paper.

The choice to focus on propagation inference is motivated by its benefits in an interactive setting, such as the Interactive Consultant (IC) user interface. This setting is suitable for solving problems where user interaction is important.

Lastly, functions that can take a partial structure, and extend the structure by performing propagation inference as previously defined, are called propagators. In our case, we wish to automatically derive such propagators based on an initial FO($\cdot$) KB, and convert them into Python code.

3   Approach

We present two methods for deriving and converting propagators, which we have named *grounded propagators* and *high-level propagators*. In the following subsections, we elaborate on both types.

3.1   Grounded Propagators

In this method, we begin by transforming an FO($\cdot$) specification into Equivalence Normal Form (ENF), as described by Wittocx et al. [23]. The reason for transforming to ENF rules, is that ENF rules allow for an analogous straightforward transformation into propagators, regardless of the specific literals in the rule. ENF has two main requirements. Firstly, ENF formulas no longer contain function symbols F/n of arity n; but instead replace them by a predicate $P_F/n+1$ together with a set of formulas to ensure the preservation of injectivity:

$$\forall \bar{x} \exists y : P_F(\bar{x}, y)$$
$$\forall \bar{x} \forall y_1 \forall y_2 : P_F(\bar{x}, y_1) \wedge P_F(\bar{x}, y_2) \Rightarrow y_1 = y_2$$

Secondly, ENF rules must either consist of a single literal L (referred to as a rule of type *Assert*) or be an equivalence of the form $\forall \boldsymbol{x} : L[\boldsymbol{x}] \Leftrightarrow \phi[\boldsymbol{x}]$, where L is an atom and ϕ is either a conjunction or disjunction of literals, or a universally or existentially quantified single literal. Essentially, ENF rules can therefore be obtained by introducing a new predicate symbol for each internal node of the parse tree of a complex formula. From here on, we refer to the 5 types of ENF rules by their names as given in Table 1.

Table 1. ENF rules

Name	ENF rule
Assert	L
ENFConjunctive	$\forall \bar{x}(L \Leftrightarrow L_1 \wedge L_2 \wedge ... \wedge L_n)$
ENFDisjunctive	$\forall \bar{x}(L \Leftrightarrow L_1 \vee L_2 \vee ... \vee L_n)$
ENFUniversal	$\forall \bar{x}(L[\bar{x}] \Leftrightarrow \forall \bar{y} L'[\bar{x}, \bar{y}])$
ENFExistential	$\forall \bar{x}(L[\bar{x}] \Leftrightarrow \exists y L'[\bar{x}, \bar{y}])$

To derive grounded propagators, we first ground the entire theory, i.e., we replace each universal (or existential) quantifier by a conjunction (or disjunction, respectively) over its domain. Quantifiers in the beginning of an ENF rule lead to multiple rules being derived (one for every possible assignment). After this step no more ENF rules of type *ENFUniversal* and *ENFExistential* remain.

Based on these grounded rules, we can now define so-called UNSAT sets. For each UNSAT set, at least one of the literals in the set must evaluate to *false*. The sets can be derived by converting the grounded ENF rules to a formula in

Conjunctive Normal Form (CNF). For every clause (disjunction of literals), the negation of all literals in the clause can be added to one UNSAT set, since they cannot all be true. Table 2 shows a mapping of the three remaining ENF types to their UNSAT sets.

Based on these sets, we can straightforwardly derive grounded propagators: intuitively, if all elements of an UNSAT set $L_1, ..., L_n$ evaluate to *true* except for one (L_i), that one must necessarily evaluate to *false*. Therefore the propagator takes a partial structure (as defined in Sect. 2) as input and extends the structure with $L_i = $ *false* in case that $L_1 = $ *true*, ..., $L_n = $ *true*. It can be shown by enumeration that all possible logical consequences of a grounded ENF rule can be derived in this way. However, although the propagation method is complete with respect to the grounded ENF rules in isolation, it is not complete with respect to the initial rules: information will inevitably be lost during the transformation. In other words, we are performing *approximate* propagation.

More specifically, the reason information is lost is because a "shallow" propagation is performed. Consider the following example:

$$A = true, \; A \Rightarrow (B \vee C), \; (B \vee C) \Rightarrow D$$

Here, an exhaustive form of propagation should be able to derive that $D = true$, regardless of the values of B and C. However, due to our conversion to ENF rules and corresponding propagators, our method can no longer derive this. Indeed, the relationship between the last two rules is effectively lost due to substitution. The new predicate symbols that are introduced during the conversion to ENF are agnostic to a possible correspondence between the subexpressions for which they were substituted. However, our decision to use shallow propagation is motivated by the fact that we prefer easy-to-use and fast code without the need for a separate solver. Moreover, all propagation steps that occur during execution of the generated propagation algorithm are correct, so the only problem is that sometimes not enough propagation steps occur, allowing the user to make a configuration choice that leads to an inconsistency.

Transforming the grounded propagators into Python code is trivial: they correspond to `if` statements in an imperative programming language. The generated Python program using these `if` statements can be used to perform propagation inference on the provided FO($\cdot$) specification.

Table 2. Corresponding UNSAT sets for each grounded ENF rule

ENF	UNSAT set(s)
L	$\{\neg L\}$
$L \Leftrightarrow L_1 \wedge L_2 \wedge ... \wedge L_n$	$\{L, \neg L_1\}, \{L, \neg L_2\}, ..., \{L, \neg L_n\}, \{\neg L, L_1, L_2, ..., L_n\}$
$L \Leftrightarrow L_1 \vee L_2 \vee ... \vee L_n$	$\{\neg L, L_1\}, \{\neg L, L_2\}, ..., \{\neg L, L_n\}, \{L, \neg L_1, \neg L_2, ..., \neg L_n\}$

3.2 Propagation with High-Level Propagators

One possible downside of the previous method is that the number of grounded propagators is dependent on the domain size of types in the vocabulary of the FO($\cdot$) specification. In our second method, we therefore work with high-level propagators to avoid the grounding step during compilation.

To avoid grounding, we keep information about the given predicates in a data structure that represents the interpretation of the predicates in a four-valued partial structure. More specifically, for every n-ary predicate P (with $n \in \mathbb{N}$), we store an n-dimensional matrix containing the truth values {*true, false, unknown, inconsistent*}.

By using this partial structure to look up information, we can define high-level propagators as a function that takes a partial structure as input and outputs an extended partial structure containing the logical consequences that follow from the input and from a high-level data structure. This high-level data structure is derived from the ENF rules.

In total, we distinguish between four types of high-level propagators depending on this high-level data structure. However, their general idea is largely the same, so we will first focus on explaining one type called "*normal* propagators". The high-level data structure that helps define a normal propagator is a *general* UNSAT set, which we derive from (quantified) *ENFConjunctive* and *ENFDisjunctive* rules.

The normal propagator is defined to be *activated* by any change to the elements of the UNSAT set that can lead to more logical consequences being derived. When activated, logical consequences are derived according to this definition. Both the available knowledge in the four-valued partial structure, and the constraint equivalent with the general UNSAT set, are taken into account in the definition. To illustrate this, we study the following example, where a normal propagator P is defined by means of the following general UNSAT set:

$$\forall x \in \{1, 2\} : \{A(x), \neg B(x, 3)\}$$

In other words, for any assignment to x, it is impossible for both elements in the set to evaluate to *true*. Some possible conditions and consequences are as follows:

- condition: $A(1)$, consequence: $B(1, 3)$
- condition: $\neg B(2, 3)$, consequence: $\neg A(2)$
- condition: $\neg B(2, 2)$, consequence: none (propagator not activated)
- condition: $\neg A(1)$, consequence: none (propagator not activated)

Although the derived consequences will be equivalent to those of grounded propagators, the crucial difference is that the grounded approach determines all conditions-consequences pairs during compilation time. By contrast, high-level propagators maintain a higher level of abstraction until execution time.

Two of the other types of propagators are also derived from ENF rules: *specifying propagators*, which are activated by a change to the predicate to the left of the equivalence ($\Leftrightarrow$) in an *ENFUniversal* or *ENFExistential* rule, and *generalizing propagators*, which are activated by a change to the predicate to the right of the equivalence in an *ENFUniversal* or *ENFExistential* rule.

The fourth and last type of propagator are *function propagators*. These are not derived from ENF rules directly, but instead originate from our earlier transformation of function symbols F into predicates P_F. Recall that for this transformation to be consistent, we needed to add two additional formulas to the KB for each function symbol to ensure that the $n + 1$-ary predicate behaves like the original n-ary function. By instead defining our function propagators to mimic this behavior and to be activated whenever a change is made to a predicate P_F, we can avoid these formulas and reduce the size of our KB. In essence, this leads to one function propagator doing the work otherwise done by multiple propagators, again achieving a higher level of abstraction.

Important to note is that these high-level propagators are all defined in such a way that they are complete with respect to the high-level data structure (e.g. general UNSAT set) that they are associated with. However, as discussed earlier, this does not mean that they are complete with regards to the original FO($\cdot$) rules, due to the transformation steps that have taken place. This is analogous to the case of grounded propagators.

Caching. An additional feature that can be added to the compiler is caching. To prevent the need for looking up truth values in the partial structure each time, we introduce two lists that can be consulted to learn specific truth values more quickly:

True List. The *true list* contains all auxiliary predicates that evaluate to true for all parameter values. The algorithm that converts FO($\cdot$) rules to ENF rules employs auxiliary predicates to substitute and represent certain logical subexpressions. It is clear that an auxiliary predicate P (with arity 0) that represents an entire logical rule must always evaluate to *true*. If P is related to another auxiliary predicate P' by a rule of type *ENFUniversal* ($P \Leftrightarrow \forall \bar{x} : P'[\bar{x}]$) or *ENFConjunctive* ($P \Leftrightarrow P' \wedge ...$), predicate P' must be true for all its arguments. This process repeats for predicates related to P'. This way the truth list can be constructed by the compiler in advance.

Unknown List. The *unknown list* initially contains all predicates. A predicate's truth value will only be immediately overridden if it also appears in the true list. Moreover, when a change in a predicate is detected for a certain argument (during execution of the generated propagation algorithm, so not during compilation, unlike the *true list*), the predicate is removed from the *unknown list*.

Implementation in Python. The way that the generated Python code performs propagation inference has so far only been discussed at an abstract level. However, in the code a distinction is made between three 'types' of propagation inference. The types are characterized by the number of conditions that need to be checked before consequences can be derived.

122   W. Piessens et al.

Unconditional Propagation: apart from the condition that activates the propagator, no other condition needs to be checked and the propagator can immediately derive consequences. This is used by specifying, generalizing and function propagators in certain scenarios, and since the number of derived consequences can be very large (it scales with the domain size of a certain type), the Python code is optimized to write the consequences to the partial structure quickly. For example, a specifying propagator related to $P \Leftrightarrow \forall x \in \{1, ..., 1000\} : Q(x)$ is activated by $P = true$.

Conditional Propagation: this is the propagation method always used in normal propagation, but never in the other three propagation types. The number of conditions that need to be checked varies, but is not dependent on domain size, only on the number of elements in the general UNSAT set that helps define the normal propagator.

Incremental Propagation: this is the propagation method used when the number of conditions that need to be checked can scale with the domain size of a certain type. If this is the case, we can apply a trick to avoid doing unnecessary calculations. The way it works is comparable to the two-watched literal strategy for SAT solving [15]. Consider for example the rule $P \Leftrightarrow \forall x \in \{1, ..., 1000\} : Q(x)$, and suppose a corresponding specifying propagator is activated by $P = false$. We then know that for at least one $x \in \{1, ..., 1000\}$, $Q(x)$ must be false. We can go over all possible values for x, but we know that we can stop in two cases.

- If we find one $x \in \{1, ..., 1000\}$ so that $Q(x) = false$.
- If we find two $x \in \{1, ..., 1000\}$ so that $Q(x) = unknown$. In that case both of them (or possibly $Q(x')$ for another x') could still evaluate to *false*, so we cannot derive anything with certainty yet.

Incremental propagation can be used by specifying, generalizing and function propagators.

4   Experiments

To validate our compiler, we perform multiple experiments. First, grounded and high-level propagators will be compared on compilation time and propagation time. Next, the usefulness of caching, function propagators and incremental propagation will be investigated. Lastly, the generated propagation algorithm will be compared to IDP-Z3's propagation method.

All experiments have a time limit of 5 min. They were executed with Python 3.11.9 on a device with 8 GB of main memory and an Intel(R) Core(TM) i5-1035G1 CPU, with 4 cores and a clock speed of 1.00 GHz. All our benchmark files are available online[2]. In this repository, numbers in the name of an `.idp` file refer to the domain size of a certain type, and in the case of `domain_rules`,

---

[2] https://anonymous.4open.science/r/compiler-benchmarks-87CC.

they also refer to the number of rules in the theory. These are subject to change in other experiments. The main goal of the smaller benchmarks is to examine the difference in scaling behaviour for increasing domain sizes of both methods. Larger benchmarks are used to simulate realistic use cases. To be complete, we now briefly describe each file:

- `equivalence`: contains only the formula "$\forall x \in T : A(x) \Leftrightarrow \neg B(x)$" with a partial interpretation for A and B.
- `edges` [21]: describes rules for the edges of a graph, using for instance "$\forall x, y \in Node : x \neq y \Rightarrow (edge(x,y) \vee edge(y,x))$". Only the domain of $Node$ is interpreted here.
- `function`: contains the formula "$\forall y \in Type2 : \forall x \in Type1 : \neg predicate(x) \Rightarrow function2(y) \neq x$" together with an interpretation for $Type1$, $Type2$ and $predicate$. Moreover, $function1$ does not appear in the theory but is interpreted in the structure.
- `complex_rules` [4]: the anonymised and shortened version of a real-life KB running in production at an industry partner, which contains an assortment of rules over predicates and functions.
- `laptop_benchmark` [9]: contains knowledge on laptop configurations, which is used for interactive configuration. Consists of 16 formulas over 100 laptops with about 30 configurable components.
- `triangle_graph` [19]: contains a formula defining when nodes in a graph form a triangle (i.e., "$edge(x,y) \wedge edge(y,z) \wedge edge(x,z)$"), where the edges are interpreted.
- `domain_rules`: contains n rules of the form $\forall x \in Type1 : a_n(x) \Rightarrow a_{n+1}(x)$, together with an interpretation for a_1.

4.1   Comparison of Grounded and High-Level Propagators

To test if compilation and propagation with a single rule work well, we use the `equivalence` benchmark. Figure 1 shows the compilation time for both grounded and high-level propagators with an increasing domain size for type T. As expected, this demonstrates that compilation time takes significantly longer if grounded propagators are used, especially for larger domains. This is explained by the fact that the number of grounded propagators scales with the domain, whereas the number of high-level propagators is independent of domain size.

While compilation is typically faster for high-level propagators, the propagation time tells a different story. Figure 2 shows the propagation time for grounded and high-level propagators (with and without caching). It is clear that the propagation time for high-level propagators without caching is worse than that of grounded propagators, as executing the former's propagation algorithm comes with higher overhead. This is mainly due to the maintenance of the data structure that represents the four-valued partial structure. Moreover, the correct arguments for a predicate may have to be calculated during runtime by filling in variables: for instance if $A(x) = true$ implies $B(x, 3, x) = true$, it must be

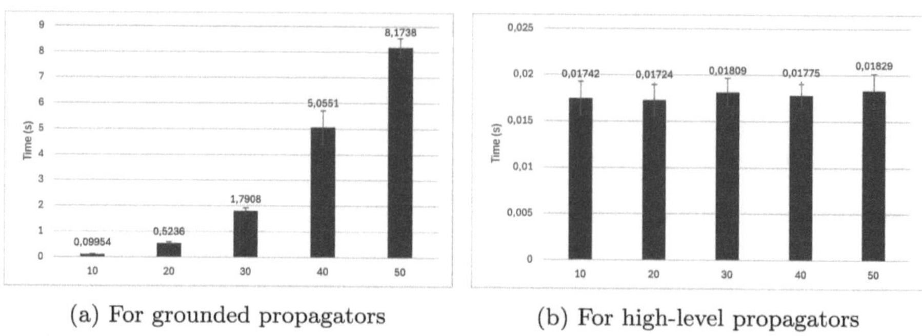

(a) For grounded propagators   (b) For high-level propagators

Fig. 1. Mean compilation time and standard deviation for benchmark `equivalence` with increasing domain size (x-axis), sample size = 10

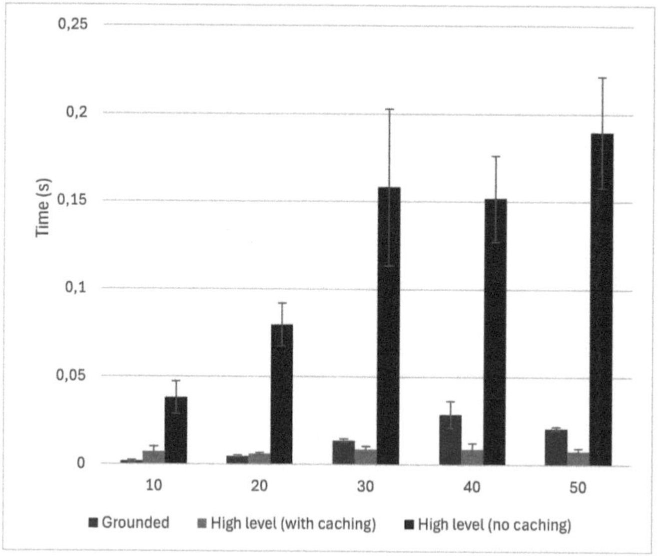

Fig. 2. Mean propagation time and standard deviation for benchmark `equivalence`, sample size = 10

calculated that if $A(2) = true$, then $B(2, 3, 2) = true$. By contrast, the grounded propagators effectively pre-calculate these operations during compilation.

However, through the caching mechanism, the high-level propagators are able to outperform the grounded propagators once the domain size is sufficiently large. These experiments show that using grounded propagators is not feasible for larger domain sizes due to the long compilation time, whereas the propagation time for high-level propagators is made manageable by our compiler's additional functionalities such as caching.

4.2   Improvements to High-Level Propagators

The three improvements to the compiler (caching, function propagators and incremental propagation) try to minimize the overhead associated with high-level propagators, while still keeping its main advantage: a manageable (domain-independent) number of propagators. To quantify the benefits of these improvements, we have performed some additional experiments.

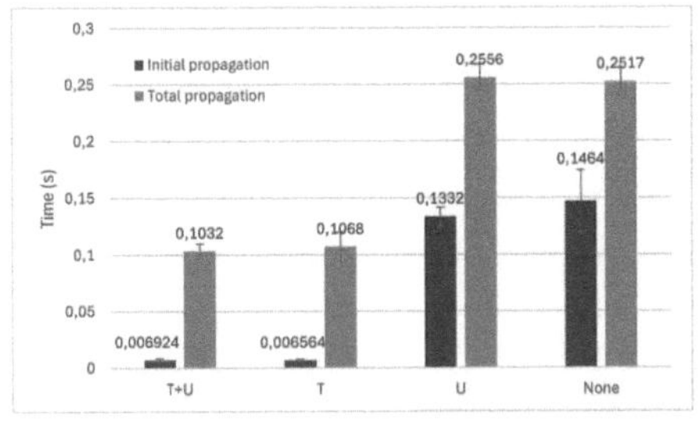

(a) Benchmark `equivalence`

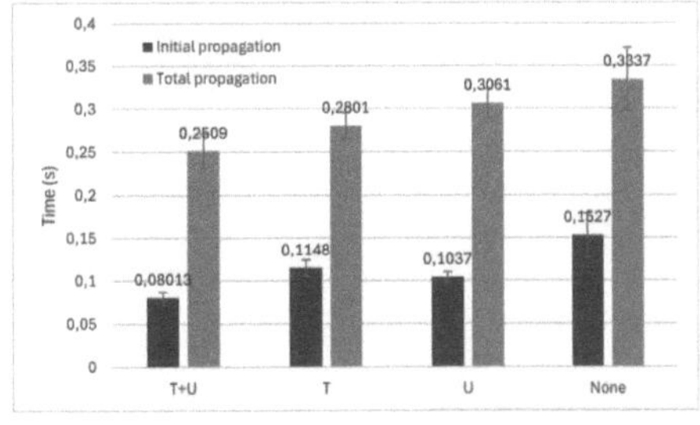

(b) Benchmark `edges`

Fig. 3. Mean propagation time and standard deviation with specific caches, T = true list, U = unknown list, sample size = 10

As was already shown in Fig. 2, caching can improve on the propagation speed by preventing large queries to the partial structure. Figure 3 gives a more detailed look on how emptying the *true list*, *unknown list*, or both affects propagation time on different benchmarks. One of them is the previously discussed benchmark `equivalence` (with domain size 50), the other one is benchmark `edges` (with domain size 5). Tables 3 and 4 show more detailed information on the number of requests that were found in the true list ("true hits"), unknown list ("unknown hits"), or had to be searched in the partial structure ("misses"). The key observation is that propagation time in Fig. 3 is proportional to the number of misses, thereby proving the usefulness of caching.

We also distinguish between "initial propagation" and "total propagation". Initial propagation time refers to the propagation time needed to derive the logical consequences from the initial knowledge. Total propagation refers to the time needed for deriving logical consequences until no more atoms are assigned *unknown*: when propagation is finished and there are still unknowns, a random assignment is made and propagation starts again. This random assignment is used to simulate interactive choices by users, e.g., through the Interactive Consultant. The graphs show that both cache mechanisms have a significant effect, and caching tends to have a greater effect on initial propagation. The latter is also illustrated by the experiment in Fig. 4 that illustrates which propagation steps are influenced the most by caching during total propagation.

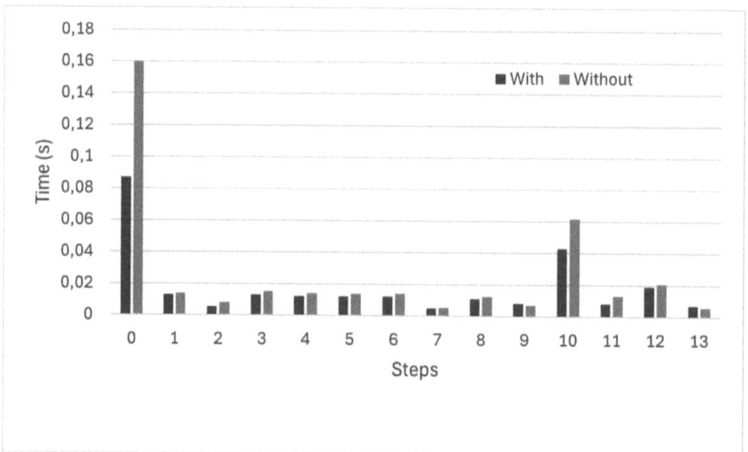

Fig. 4. Illustration of the influence of caching on different propagation steps during total propagation on benchmark **edges** (with domain size 5). Step 0 is the initial propagation step.

Table 3. Benchmark **equivalence**

	IT	IU	IM	TT	TU	TM
T + U	12	0	13	204	0	301
T	12	0	13	204	0	301
U	0	4	46	0	4	526
None	0	0	50	0	0	530

Table 4. Benchmark **edges**

	IT	IU	IM	TT	TU	TM
T + U	7	16	26	127	18	586
T	7	0	42	127	0	608
U	0	19	33	0	21	715
None	0	0	52	0	0	738

Detailed caching information regarding the number of hits to the true list (T), hits to the unknown list (U) and misses (M) (second letter) during initial propagation (I) and during total propagation (T) (first letter). A distinction is made between the cases where both the true list and unknown list are present (T+U), either one of them separately, or none.

To understand this, we focus on the (dis)advantages of both the *true list* and the *unknown list* in more detail.

– *true list*: The *true list* is mainly useful during initial propagation because it saves time on some time-intensive requests that often happen at the start of propagation. In particular, for universal rules $\forall \bar{x} : \phi(\bar{x})$, the truth of ϕ (and some of its subformulas) must be asserted for all tuples $\bar{x}$. We avoid having to set the corresponding predicates to true for all possible arguments by already determining during compilation time that they will evaluate to true for all arguments. Therefore, we save propagation time during initial propagation by avoiding these possibly very large queries. For benchmark **equivalence**, a larger proportion of the auxiliary predicates is *true* for all tuples $\bar{x}$ compared to **edges**, explaining the difference in time gain during initial propagation. After initial propagation, the *true list* is still occasionally useful for saving time on queries.

– *unknown list*: The *unknown list* is also mainly useful during initial propagation, because at that time, there are more predicates which have unknown truth values for all arguments. As more information is propagated, more and more predicates will be removed from the list. This is unlike the *true list*, which stays the same size during all propagation steps.

Moreover, it is important to note that caching never has a noticeable negative effect on propagation time because the cache is calculated during compilation time. Only the removal of predicates from the *unknown list* occurs during propagation time, and this operation is negligible in duration. In general, it is a good idea to do as many calculations as possible during compilation, since this only needs to happen once. Possibly interesting future research could be to do all initial propagation during compilation.

We also investigate the effect of function propagators, compared to adding extra rules to the FO($\cdot$) specification, and the effect of incremental propagation, compared to using conditional propagation in its place. Tests are run on the benchmark `function` with increasing domain sizes. Figure 5 indicates that these additions are beneficial to propagation efficiency. In the case of function propagators, this is due to one propagator being able to do the work of many. In the case of incremental propagation, this is due to calculations being stopped early. Both improvements have stronger effects as the domain size increases.

4.3   Comparison with IDP-Z3

Lastly, we compare the performance of the propagation algorithm generated by the compiler (high-level propagators, with all improvements) to IDP-Z3's `propagate()` method as a baseline. We use more complex benchmarks for this comparison to assess if our propagation method scales to larger use cases. Though comparing the propagation time to that of IDP-Z3 does not give the full picture, since compilation time should be accounted for, the actual compilation time when using high-level propagators is negligible: no compilation time longer than half a second was observed. Moreover, compiling only needs to happen once. Therefore it is ignored in the subsequent experiments.

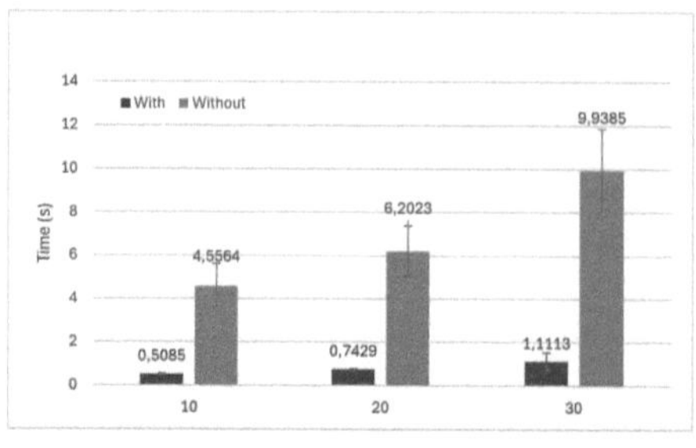

(a) Function propagators

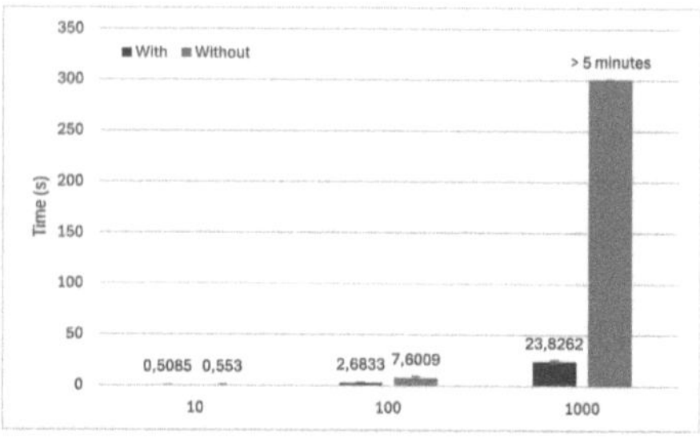

(b) Incremental propagation

Fig. 5. Mean propagation time and standard deviation with/without specific improvements. X-axis shows increase in domain size. Sample size = 10.

Figure 6 shows some comparative results on several benchmarks, which demonstrate a high variability between benchmarks. In the three `triangle_graph` benchmarks (with 10, 20 and 30 vertices in the graph), we see that IDP-Z3 is initially faster, but that our propagation method seems to scale better w.r.t. domain size. On the `complex_rules` benchmark, IDP-Z3 seems to outperform our propagators by just under a factor of two. Lastly, the `laptop_benchmark` benchmark, which is based on a realistic use case where a user wants to buy a laptop, shows a result in which our propagators are 8.5 times slower than the original. The poor performance on this last benchmark shows that there is still work to be done if this compiler is to be used in a realistic use case with many constraints.

Moreover, we notice a certain trend based on our benchmarks: FO($\cdot$) specifications with larger domains and/or a greater arity of predicates (such as `triangle_graph`) tend to perform better with our method, whereas FO($\cdot$) specifications with more complex rules and/or a greater number of rules (such as `complex_rules`) tend to perform better with IDP-Z3. To investigate this assumption, we test on benchmark `domain_rules`, which can grow both in the number of formulas and in the domain size of the type.

Table 5 shows how our propagation method and IDP-Z3's method are influenced by changes in these two variables. Some of the results in Table 5 will likely be caused by implementation differences. However, if we fix the number of rules, and if we calculate the ratio between IDP-Z3's propagation time and our propagation time, we see that our method always performs relatively better for *domain_size = 1000* than for *domain_size = 100*. If we fix the domain size, we see that IDP-Z3 always performs relatively better for *rules = 50* than for *rules = 10*.

This illustrates that our propagation method tends to be more efficient on larger domains, whereas IDP-Z3 is more equipped to handle a large number of logical rules. This is related to the fact that high-level propagators are domain independent, but not rule independent. To improve efficiency on a large number of rules, the compiler could be made to detect redundant rules, or complex rules

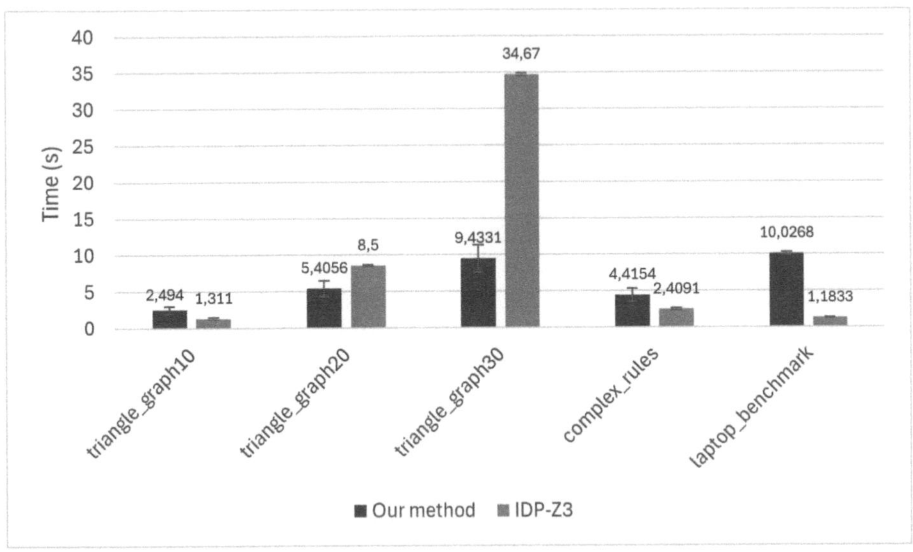

Fig. 6. Propagation time on several benchmarks, sample size = 10, error bars = standard deviation

Table 5. Average propagation time of our compiler vs IDP-Z3 on `domain_rules` benchmark, sample size = 10.

Nb. Rules	domain_size = 10			domain_size = 100			domain_size = 1000		
	IDP-Z3	Ours	*Ratio*	IDP-Z3	Ours	*Ratio*	IDP-Z3	Ours	*Ratio*
2	0, 0645	0, 0124	*5.2*	0, 119	0, 0873	*1,36*	0, 821	0, 354	*2,32*
10	0, 141	0, 0915	*1,54*	0, 691	0, 849	*0,81*	6, 275	1, 584	*3,96*
50	0, 577	1, 867	*0,31*	3, 472	18, 320	*0,19*	41, 418	46, 135	*0,9*

could be associated with a certain precondition (potentially given by the user) and the propagators associated with the rule could only be activated when that precondition is fulfilled.

Lastly, it is important to remark that the lack of completeness caused by shallow propagation often has consequences on larger benchmarks. In our experiments, the propagation was complete with respect to all benchmarks except for `complex_rules`, where some truth values of a specific predicate (`predicate5`) cannot be derived. In contrast, IDP-Z3 is able to derive these truth values.

In the context of the `laptop_benchmark` benchmark, a logical consequence that our propagation method cannot derive is illustrated with the following example: suppose that certain laptop specifications have already been chosen, leading to only a small number of laptops fulfilling all requirements. The propagation algorithm can correctly derive which ones. However, if none of these laptops uses Windows 10 Pro as an operating system, then the propagation algorithm (due to its incompleteness) cannot eliminate Windows 10 Pro as a possible operating system until the user selects it: only then will an inconsistency be derived.

5 Conclusion

A compiler that generates Python code executing propagation inference on the knowledge given as input, has many advantages. The generated code is easy to integrate in a software project, but the user still has the option of specifying knowledge in a flexible and easily extensible way using IDP-Z3.

Comparing grounded propagators and high-level propagators leads to the conclusion that high-level propagators are the preferred choice, at least if they are paired with other optimizations such as function propagators, incremental propagation and caching. Using high-level propagators avoids unnecessary code and saves space in memory. This makes the compiled code especially useful in systems where memory efficiency is crucial, such as embedded devices.

Whether the propagation algorithm generated by the compiler can perform propagation inference faster than IDP-Z3 depends on the use case: typically our method is better equipped to handle larger domains, whereas IDP-Z3 can handle a large number of rules better.

A lot of future research is possible in this research domain. New compilers could be developed for other inference tasks. The current compiler could be extended to support more FO($\cdot$) syntax (e.g. aggregates), to facilitate this new types of high-level propagators could be developed. Moreover, the compilation method could be reconsidered, and better methods could be designed to transform the initial knowledge to propagators, with a trade-off between the simplicity of the propagators and the completeness. For instance, A. Darwiche et al. [7] propose different methods to compile NNF (Negation Normal Form) rules, accounting for succinctness and the number of possible queries and transformations on the knowledge. Other ways of eliminating the grounding bottleneck could be explored, inspired by methods in ASP [12]. A hybrid approach could be chosen, where some rules are grounded and others are converted to high-level propagators. This way, the advantages of both methods are combined: we obtain fast propagation for grounded propagators and fast compilation for high-level propagators.

References

1. Aerts, B., Deryck, M., Vennekens, J.: Knowledge-based decision support for machine component design: a case study. Expert Syst. Appl. **187**, 115869 (2022). https://doi.org/10.1016/j.eswa.2021.115869, https://linkinghub.elsevier.com/retrieve/pii/S0957417421012288
2. Alens, T., Vandevelde, S., Van Laer, L.: User-friendly home automation using IDP (2025)

3. Beiser, A., Hahn, S., Schaub, T.: ASP-driven user-interaction with clinguin. Electron. Proc. Theor. Comput. Sci. **416**, 215–228 (2025). https://doi.org/10.4204/eptcs.416.19

4. Callewaert, B., Decleyre, N., Vandevelde, S., Comenda, N., Coppens, B., Vennekens, J.: Facilitating investment strategy negotiations through logic. In: 2023 IEEE Symposium Series on Computational Intelligence (SSCI), pp. 103–108 (2023). https://doi.org/10.1109/SSCI52147.2023.10372044

5. Carbonnelle, P., Vandevelde, S., Vennekens, J., Denecker, M.: IDP-Z3: a reasoning engine for FO(.) (2022). https://doi.org/10.48550/arXiv.2202.00343

6. Carbonnelle, P., Vandevelde, S., Vennekens, J., Denecker, M.: Interactive configurator with FO(.) and IDP-Z3 (2023). https://arxiv.org/abs/2202.00343

7. Darwiche, A., Marquis, P.: A knowledge compilation map. J. Artif. Intell. Res. **17**, 229–264 (2002). https://doi.org/10.1613/jair.989, https://jair.org/index.php/jair/article/view/10311

8. De Cat, B., Bogaerts, B., Bruynooghe, M., Janssens, G., Denecker, M.: Predicate logic as a modeling language: the IDP system. In: Kifer, M., Liu, Y.A. (eds.) Declarative Logic Programming: Theory, Systems, and Applications, pp. 279–323. ACM (2018). https://doi.org/10.1145/3191315.3191321

9. De Vogelaere, R., Van Dessel, K., Vennekens, J.: A practical approach to handling tabular data in logic. In: Erdem, E., Vidal, G. (eds.) PADL 2025. LNCS, vol. 15537, pp. 88–103. Springer, Cham (2025). https://doi.org/10.1007/978-3-031-84924-4_6

10. Denecker, M., Vennekens, J.: Building a knowledge base system for an integration of logic programming and classical logic. In: Garcia de la Banda, M., Pontelli, E. (eds.) ICLP 2008. LNCS, vol. 5366, pp. 71–76. Springer, Heidelberg (2008). https://doi.org/10.1007/978-3-540-89982-2_12

11. Deryck, M., Vennekens, J., Devriendt, J., Marynissen, S.: Legislation in the knowledge base paradigm: interactive decision enactment for registration duties. In: 2019 IEEE 13th International Conference on Semantic Computing (ICSC), pp. 174–177. IEEE, Newport Beach (2019). https://doi.org/10.1109/ICOSC.2019.8665543, https://ieeexplore.ieee.org/document/8665543/

12. Dodaro, C., Mazzotta, G., Ricca, F.: Blending grounding and compilation for efficient ASP solving. In: Proceedings of the 21st International Conference on Principles of Knowledge Representation and Reasoning, pp. 317–328 (2024). https://doi.org/10.24963/kr.2024/30

13. Gebser, M.: Conflict-driven answer set solving (2007)

14. Lameyse, G.: Solving data exchange challenges at De Lijn with the knowledge-base paradigm (2023)

15. Moskewicz, M.W., Madigan, C.F., Zhao, Y., Zhang, L., Malik, S.: Chaff: engineering an efficient SAT solver (2001)

16. de Moura, L., Bjørner, N.: Z3: an efficient SMT solver. In: Ramakrishnan, C.R., Rehof, J. (eds.) TACAS 2008. LNCS, vol. 4963, pp. 337–340. Springer, Heidelberg (2008). https://doi.org/10.1007/978-3-540-78800-3_24

17. Piessens, W.: Een efficiënte compiler voor een kennisbanksysteem (2025)

18. Van Dessel, K., Devriendt, J., Vennekens, J.: FOLASP: FO(.) as input language for answer set solvers. Theory Pract. Log. Program. **21**(6), 785–801 (2021). https://doi.org/10.1017/S1471068421000351

19. Van Laer, L., Vandevelde, S., Vennekens, J.: DIRT: a literature-based benchmark suite for grounders. In: Casini, G., Dundua, B., Kutsia, T. (eds.) JELIA 2025. LNCS, vol. 16093, pp. 343–356. Springer, Cham (2026). https://doi.org/10.1007/978-3-032-04587-4_21

20. Vandevelde, S., Vennekens, J., Jordens, J., Van Doninck, B., Witters, M.: Knowledge-based support for adhesive selection: will it stick? Theory Pract. Logic Program. **24**(3), 560–580 (2024). https://doi.org/10.1017/S1471068424000024
21. Vandevelde, S., et al.: Benchmark (2025). https://gitlab.com/Vadevesi/benchmark. Accessed 22 May 2025
22. Vlaeminck, H., Vennekens, J., Denecker, M.: A logical framework for configuration software. In: Proceedings of the 11th ACM SIGPLAN Conference on Principles and Practice of Declarative Programming, pp. 141–148. ACM, Coimbra (2009). https://doi.org/10.1145/1599410.1599428
23. Wittocx, J., Denecker, M., Bruynooghe, M.: Constraint propagation for first-order logic and inductive definitions. ACM Trans. Comput. Log. (2013)

A Functional Logic Perspective on Indentation-Sensitive Parsing

Steven Libby[(✉)] [ID]

University of Portland, Portland, OR, USA
`libbys@up.edu`

Abstract. Parsing is one of the foundational problems in the field of programming languages. While the theory of parsing with context free grammars is well understood, parsing more complex languages remains a hard problem. Indentation-sensitive languages are an important subset of languages that have been studied extensively. We build on both Adams' work of indentation-sensitive parsing and Caballero et al.'s work on functional logic parsing to show how functional logic languages can elegantly solve the problem of indentation-sensitive parsing.

1 Introduction

The theory of Context Free Languages and parsing is one of the most studied and well understood topics in Computer Science [5]. Numerous tools and libraries support parsing with Context-Free Grammars (CFGs). However, many programming languages do not fit this model. One common example is indentation-sensitive languages such as Haskell [25], Python [1], and Markdown [14] where the structure of the program is determined by the indentation of the first non-whitespace character of a line.

One early example of an indentation-sensitive language is Landin's ISWIM [22] which introduced the "offsides rule" that says "The southeast quadrant that just contains the phrase's first symbol must contain the entire phrase, except possibly for bracketed subsegments." In modern terms, this means that every token in an expression must be at an indentation greater than the token at the start of the expression. We can see an example using an expression in a Haskell like language.

```
case x of
  Left _  → id
 Right
```

This expression could be parsed in one of two ways: either as

```
case x of Left _  →  (id Right)
```

or as

```
(case x of Left _  →  id) Right.
```

According to the offsides rule, since `Right` is less indented than the `id` token, but more indented than the `case` token, the second parse is correct.

© The Author(s), under exclusive license to Springer Nature Switzerland AG 2026
N. Amin and J. Arias (Eds.): PADL 2026, LNCS 16401, pp. 133–142, 2026.
https://doi.org/10.1007/978-3-032-15981-6_8

Although the offsides rule gives an idea of how indentation can be used to define language structure, most parsers for indentation-sensitive languages use ad-hoc solutions. Adams' formalization of indentation-sensitive CFGs [2] allows us to define indentation-sensitive grammars, however the implementations [2,3] tend to be complicated and involve trade-offs.

Functional logic programming offers an alternative perspective. Caballero et al. [9] defined a parser using the functional logic language $\mathcal{TOY}$ by taking advantage of non-determinism and logic variables. This led to a simple implementation of a parser combinator library, which was conceptually simpler than monadic parser combinator libraries like Parsec [23]. In their approach, a parser is just a function from tokens to tokens. If the author wants to build a representation such as an AST, then the representation is passed in as a free variable which is bound while the parser is running.

We extend the work of Adams and Caballero et al. in order to create a functional logic parser for the language Curry [17] that can parse using indentation-sensitive grammars. Our main contribution is the library and an analysis of its design trade-offs and optimizations. In the next section we give an overview of functional logic programming, and Curry in particular. Then we review the concepts of indentation-sensitive parsing. Next we review functional logic parsing. After that we discuss our main contribution by combining the two libraries, and discussing design trade-offs. Finally, we review other approaches and conclude.

2   Background

In this section, we give a brief overview of functional logic programming in Curry in particular and then review indentation-sensitive parsing and functional logic parsing. This is by no means a comprehensive review of functional logic programming or Curry. For more details on Curry, see the surveys in [6,16].

2.1   Functional Logic Programming

Curry [17] is a demand-driven functional logic language which aims to incorporate both of the ideas of functional and logic languages. Syntactically, Curry is similar to Haskell and supports many of the same features including pattern matching, higher order functions, lazy evaluation, and algebraic data types. Curry also supports features from logic programming including free (logic) variables, non-determinism, unification, and constraints. See [16] for more details.

The syntax for Curry is largely the same as Haskell98 [25]. Functions are defined using equations and pattern matching. New data types are defined as algebraic data types with the `data` keyword. Functions can contain guards, case expressions, function applications, let bound variables, and where bound variables. Curry supports strong typing with polymorphic types, and Hindly-Milner type inference, as well as type classes.

While the syntax is largely similar, Curry has three notable differences. First we allow for overlapping patterns of the left-hand side of a function definition. Semantically, Curry will evaluate this non-deterministically and eventually return all possible evaluations. We can see this with the choice operator (?) defined in Fig. 1. The expression `1 ? 2` will return both 1 and 2 as different non-deterministic results. The second difference is that Curry allows free variables to be introduced on the right hand side of a function. Free variables are not given a value, but their value may later be constrained. The `isTwo` function in Fig. 1 demonstrates this. The variable x is free, but is constrained to have the value of 2. The `=:=` operator is the unification operator in Curry.

The final difference is that Curry supports functional patterns [7]. These are similar in idea to Wadler's view patterns [26] or Erwig's active patterns [12], but they have a more general mechanism. A typical use of free variables in Curry is to constrain an argument with an equation and "fill in" the free variables in that equation. Consider the example of `pick` defined in Fig. 1. We constrain xs so that x is an element in the middle. Functional patterns allow us to put the right hand side of the constraint as the pattern itself, as in `pick2`.[1]

Curry provides the `oneValue` function to control the non-determinism inherent in functional logic programs. This function takes a non-deterministic expression and will fully evaluate it. If the operation fails, then the value `Nothing` is returned; otherwise it will return `Just v` where v is a single value.

```
(?) :: a  →  a  →  a            isTwo :: Int
x ? y = x                       isTwo | x =:= 2 = x
x ? y = y                           where x free

pick :: [a]  →  a               pick2 :: [a]  →  a
pick xs                         pick2 (_ ++ [x] ++ _) = x
  | xs =:= as ++ [x] ++ bs = x
  where as,x,bs free
```

Fig. 1. Examples of Curry functions showing overlapping rules, free variables, and functional patterns

2.2   Functional Logic Parsing

Functional logic parsing incorporates the strengths of both logic parsers and functional parsers. Logic parsers are typically written using Definite Clause Grammars (DCG) [21]. These are grammars written in the style of a context free grammar that are desugared into logic programs. They handle the inherently non-deterministic nature of context free grammars well, and logic variables can be used to construct an output representation.

---

[1] For efficiency reasons the semantics of functional patterns are more complicated. The constrained unification approach must fully evaluate the argument in order to solve the constraint. However, the functional pattern can lazily evaluate its arguments.

Functional parsers like Parsec [23] closely resemble Parsing Expression Grammars (PEGs) [13]. Non-terminal parsing functions have a single definition, but they are built up using higher order combinators.

While DCGs are easy to implement because they translate directly to logic programs, they are inherently first order, so they are not as expressive. Similarly PEGs are more expressive, but they come at the cost of a much more complicated implementation requiring monads to hide the underlying machinery.

Caballero and López-Fragaus proposed an elegant solution by combining the strengths of functional and logic parsers [9]. They defined a parser as simply a function from tokens to tokens. Parsers supported (`<*>`) for concatenation, (`<|>`) for alternation, `empty` for the empty parser, and `terminal` for a parser that only matched a single token. They further defined the `ParserRep` type which attaches a representation to the parser. This came with five new operations: (`<||>`) is an alternative for a `ParserRep`, (`>>>`) attaches a representation to a `Parser` transforming it into a `ParserRep`, `satisfy` which determined if a token satisfied a boolean condition, and `star` and `some` for repetition.

Remarkably, the implementation of this parser was very simple. The Curry implementation [15] requires only 13 lines of code not counting white space, comments, or type notions. This is largely built on the composability of the parser. A `ParserRep` applied to a representation is a `Parser`. Because of this, almost any operation that works with a `Parser` will automatically work with a `ParserRep`. The only exception to this is the (`<||>`) operation, which is because the same representation needs to be passed to both parsers.

In order to use a `ParserRep`, we pass in the representation as a free variable. When the parser runs, it will attach the representation using the (`>>>`) operator and fill in the free variable.

2.3 Indentation Sensitive Parsing

Adams' solution to the problem of parsing indentation-sensitive languages is to use an Indentation-Sensitive Context Free Grammar (IS-CFG). This is similar to a standard CFG except that each terminal and non-terminal on the right hand side of the grammar is augmented with a relation. The operations are typically one of $=, >, \geq, \circledast$ for equal, greater than, greater than or equal, and no relation respectively. The relation adds a constraint to the parse tree. When parsing we assign a non-negative integer to each node in the parse tree representing the indentation of that particular node. If an assignment of integers to parse nodes satisfying the parse tree relations cannot be found, then the grammar does not parse our string.

For an example, consider the grammar in Fig. 2. This grammar matches all strings of balanced parentheses and brackets, but nested pairs must be indented and opening curly braces have the same indentation as the closing curly braces. If we have the token string $\{^1 \ (^7 \ )^6 \ \{^4 \ \}^4 \ \}^1$, where the superscript is the indentation of the token, we would generate the parse tree in Fig. 2.

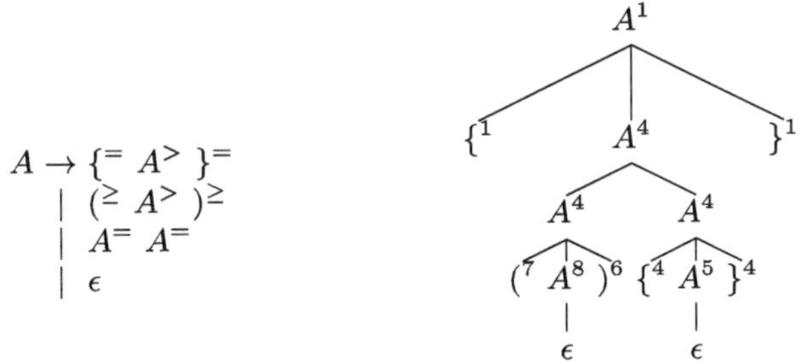

$$A \rightarrow \{^= A^> \}^=$$
$$\mid (^\geq A^>)^\geq$$
$$\mid A^= A^=$$
$$\mid \epsilon$$

Fig. 2. A parser and parse tree for matching parentheses and curly braces.

IS-CFGs are very versatile and can be used to parse many indentation-sensitive languages. They also come with some nice composition properties. Any assignment of indentations to a parse tree is a valid assignment of indentations to any subtree. This is a relatively trivial property, but it is important because it means we can validate the indentation while in the middle of parsing.

While IS-CFGs are a powerful tool, their implementation into real parsers is rather complex. There are two implementations of this idea in Haskell. One translates the grammar over several steps into an $LR(k)$ grammar [2]. Aside from being a complex translation, this requires a parser generator, so it cannot just be a library in the language. The other approach integrates these ideas with the Parsec library [23]. This implementation is less intrusive to the parser writer, but comes with some caveats. The implementation must thread the indentation state throughout the parser, which results in a tricky interaction between the underlying monad and the token stream. Both of these approaches work well, but are difficult to implement. In the next section, we show how to combine the ideas of indentation-sensitive parsing with functional logic parsing.

3   Combining Strategies

Adding indentation-sensitivity to our parsers is surprisingly simple in a functional logic language.[2] In fact, it is the same mechanism that we used to attach representations to parsers. We pass in a free variable to represent our layout, then that argument is bound to our layout representation and checked for validity.

We start with the changes to the underlying types and add a new type we call `LayoutParser` . This is simply a parser that checks the indentation. For simplicity we have chosen to represent the tokens as a pair (`token`, `Int`) for the token and indentation respectively, but this could be a more general type using a typeclass. One unfortunate but necessary side effect is that our `Parser` type is incompatible with the `Parser` from the `fl-parser` library. This is because we need the indentation information in our tokens. The `LayoutParser` simply adds a layout relation, which is one of `Eq`, `Gt`, `Ge`, `Any`, and a `Layout` parameter

---

[2] link to implementation at https://github.com/libbys-up/layout-parsing.

that is filled in later. The `Layout` parameter is just a skeleton of the parse tree, where a symbol is either a terminal or non-terminal that contains a relation. A terminal symbol contains the indentation where the terminal was seen, and a non-terminal symbol contains a list of children. Finally a `LayoutParserRep` adds a representation, similar to the original idea in functional logic parsing.

The parser combinators are almost identical to Caballero et al.'s original implementation. We add a new (`<|||>`) combinator, because we have a new level of parser, but this has the obvious implementation. The (`<*>`) and (`>>>`) combinators are completely unchanged except for the type and some light parameter juggling. A major addition to our parser is the layout binding operator (`<<<`) shown below. This operator is the equivalent of the representation binding operator. It turns a `Parser t` into a `LayoutParser t` by running the underlying parser and constructing the `Layout` tree from the layout expression passed in.

```
(<<<) :: Parser t  →  [Layout]  →  LayoutParser t
p <<< layExp = attach layExp
  where attach le rel (NT rel le) sentence = p sentence
```

The `empty`, `terminal`, `satisfy`, `star`, and `some` combinators are largely the same. The only difference with `terminal` and `satisfy` is that they set the layout parameter. Operationally, narrowing is used to set the parameter efficiently. The `star` and `some` combinators show how we can use the layout parameters in practice. Layouts are declared as free variables, then bound to the parser. For these parsers, we always pass the relation `Eq` to be consistent with the Adams layout semantics [3]. We also flatten the layout tree so that the `star` makes a single node where each child is a layout from running the `p` parser. This isn't necessary, but it simplifies using the parser and is more efficient.

While we are parsing the input, we need to check that the tokens satisfy our layout rules at each step. We could solve this with generate and test by running the parser, generating every possible parse and filtering out the invalid layouts at the end, but this would result in a lot of invalid parses. Instead we check layout in the (`<<<`) function with `check`. To check a `Layout` for validity, we simply need to assign a non-negative integer to each node in the tree such that all rules are satisfied. In fact, this is very easy to do in Curry. For each node, we generate an integer and check that it satisfies all of the constraints. Because there can be many valid ways to satisfy a layout tree, the `check` function is inherently non-deterministic. However, we can use `oneValue` to force a deterministic value.

We can see these combinators in action in Fig. 3, which shows a parser for a small Haskell like language. The `idp` parser matches a single `TID` token and binds the result to a string, and the `expr` parser matches a sequence of variables or case expressions, and the `alt` parser matches a single branch of the case expression. We can see the effect of the layout by considering the function `f` below. Without considering indentation, this definition would be ambiguous; but because `Right` is less indented than the first branch of the case expression, it is not considered as part of the expression. Therefore there is only a single, unambiguous parse of this definition.

```
case x of
  Left _  →  id
 Right
```

```
    expr = star atom Eq l es <<< [l] >>> foldr1 App es
      where l, es free

    atom r = (terminal TCase Ge l1 <*> expr Ge l2 e
                <*> terminal TOf Ge l3 <*> star alt Ge l4 bs
                  <<< [l1,l2,l3,l4] >>> Case e bs
                  <|||> idp Ge l1 x <<< [l1] >>> ID x) r
      where l1,l2,l3,l4, x, e, bs free
```

Fig. 3. A LayoutParser for a Haskell like language.

3.1   Design Space

Unsurprisingly, there are several alternative ways we could have designed our combinators. We discuss a few of them here and give reasons for choosing the design we settled on, as well as some of the limitations of our design.

One of the most fundamental decisions is the representation of the layout. Initially we wanted to represent the layout as a single integer, however this does not work in practice. The problem becomes apparent with the matching curly brace parser from Fig. 2. If we have the tokens $\{^1(^7)^9\{^4\}^4\}^1$, this should match our grammar, but when parsing $(^7)^9$ we must make a decision for the indentation of the entire non-terminal symbol. While parsing this substring, there are two choices that make sense for indentation. We could pick 7 because the first token has that indentation, or we could pick 2 because that is the lowest possible indentation we could use. Unfortunately, both of these options will fail when we try to parse $\{^4\}^4$, which requires that the indentation be exactly 4. Now we must re-parse the $(^7)^6$ string again and check that 4 is a valid indentation. This implementation failed to parse even small strings in a reasonable time.

A more practical option would be to represent all of the indentation relations as constraints and feed them into a constraint solver. While Curry has constraint solving libraries, we chose to focus on using narrowing to solve the problem.

One possible complaint with this library is that the user must keep track of the layout variables. This is possible, but it would require putting modifying the (<*>) operator to only work with LayoutParser s instead of Parser s. It would be possible to hide many of these details inside of a monad.

There is one problem that we were not able to solve. In the Haskell parser in Fig. 3 we defined atom to take the Rel parameter explicitly, and then we constructed our parser only to apply it to the supplied parameter. We should be able to use η-reduction to remove the r parameter.

Unfortunately, η-reduction does not hold in general in Curry. This is a consequence of call-time choice semantics [18]. If we η-reduce `atom`, then `atom` is no longer a function, but instead it is an unevaluated, fully-applied expression. If `atom` is used multiple times in the same expression, there is no problem. Each use of `atom` is allowed to evaluate to a different result. However, if `atom` is passed to another function such as `star`, then all occurrences of that argument must evaluate to the same value. Our solution to this problem is to simulate run-time choice semantics by making the `Rel` parameter in `atom` explicit. Another option would be to add a dummy () parameter to our parsers.

The final considerations are of efficiency. First, we can modify the (`<*>`), (`<<<`), and (`>>>`) to be lazy in their token stream argument. The current implementation unifies the output token stream with a free variable, which will fully evaluate the result. This is done to ensure that the parser executes, but we can accomplish the same thing by forcing the parser to evaluate to head normal form using the (`$!`) operator or a case expression. While this does improve efficiency on small test cases, we only found an improvement of about 8%.

There are two efficiency improvements that were much more significant. The first one is not very surprising. Using a deterministic function to check the validity of the layout tree improved sped up larger test cases by a factor of 17. This suggests that the non-deterministic check algorithm is asymptotically slower than the deterministic version. Finally, we can check the validity of the layout tree every time the (`<<<`) operator runs. This should fail on invalid parses sooner. Surprisingly, if we use a deterministic layout checking algorithm, this actually runs about 20% slower for larger test cases.

4   Related Work and Conclusion

While this work is heavily based on the work of Adams [2,3], there is still no agreement on the best way to handle indentation-sensitive languages.

Modern implementations of Haskell [25] and Python [1] use surprisingly old technology. The lexer inserts special layout tokens into the token stream for the parser to handle. This results in "some mildly complicated interactions between the lexer and parser" [20].

Erdweg et al. [11] proposed a scheme to embed constraints into the grammar at specific border points. This allows the parser to control the shape of the grammar without having to specify the indentation for every symbol. Their solution used an SLGR parser to generate all of the possible parsing results and filter out all parsers that failed their indentation rules. Amorim et al. [10] extend this idea by creating a higher level domain specific language for parsers and pretty printers. Liu et al. [24] use a similar specification to determine the ambiguity of indentation-sensitive parsers. Other approaches include building layout into a context dependent parser such as Iguana [4], where layout can be encoded as constraints for data dependent grammars [19]. One possible novel approach is parsing using derivatives [8]. However, it is not currently known if this can be extended to handle indentation-sensitive languages.

Indentation-sensitive languages are becoming more common, and these languages will require a theoretical foundation and tools to adequately support them. We have shown how we can combine formalism of indentation-sensitive CFGs with the tools of functional logic programming to create an indentation-sensitive functional logic parser.

References

1. Python. The python language reference. Technical report (2025)
2. Adams, M.: Principled parsing for indentation-sensitive languages: revisiting Landin's offside rule. In: Giacobazzi, R., Cousot, R. (eds.) The 40th Annual ACM SIGPLAN-SIGACT Symposium on Principles of Programming Languages, POPL 2013, Rome, Italy, 23–25 January 2013, pp. 511–522. ACM (2013)
3. Adams, M., Agacan, Ö.: Indentation-sensitive parsing for parsec. In: Swierstra, W. (ed.) Proceedings of the 2014 ACM SIGPLAN Symposium on Haskell, Gothenburg, Sweden, 4–5 September 2014, pp. 121–132. ACM (2014)
4. Afroozeh, A., Izmaylova, A.: One parser to rule them all. In: Murphy, G., Steele, Jr., G. (eds.) 2015 ACM International Symposium on New Ideas, New Paradigms, and Reflections on Programming and Software, Onward! 2015, Pittsburgh, PA, USA, 25–30 October 2015, pp. 151–170. ACM (2015)
5. Aho, A., Sethi, R., Ullman, J.: Compilers: Principles, Techniques, and Tools. Addison-Wesley Series in Computer Science/World Student Series Edition. Addison-Wesley (1986)
6. Antoy, S., Hanus, M.: Functional logic programming. Commun. ACM **53**(4), 74–85 (2010)
7. Antoy, S., Hanus, M.: Declarative programming with function patterns. In: Hill, P.M. (ed.) LOPSTR 2005. LNCS, vol. 3901, pp. 6–22. Springer, Heidelberg (2006). https://doi.org/10.1007/11680093_2
8. Brachthäuser, J., Rendel, T., Ostermann, K.: Parsing with first-class derivatives. In: Visser, E., Smaragdakis, Y. (eds.) Proceedings of the 2016 ACM SIGPLAN International Conference on Object-Oriented Programming, Systems, Languages, and Applications, OOPSLA 2016, Part of SPLASH 2016, Amsterdam, The Netherlands, 30 October–4 November 2016, pp. 588–606. ACM (2016)
9. Caballero, R., López-Fraguas, F.J.: A functional-logic perspective of parsing. In: Middeldorp, A., Sato, T. (eds.) FLOPS 1999. LNCS, vol. 1722, pp. 85–99. Springer, Heidelberg (1999). https://doi.org/10.1007/10705424_6
10. Eduardo, S., de Amorim, L., Steindorfer, M., Erdweg, S., Visser, E.: Declarative specification of indentation rules: a tooling perspective on parsing and pretty-printing layout-sensitive languages. In: Pearce, D.J., Mayerhofer, T., Steimann, F. (eds.) Proceedings of the 11th ACM SIGPLAN International Conference on Software Language Engineering, SLE 2018, Boston, MA, USA, 05–06 November 2018, pp. 3–15. ACM (2018)
11. Erdweg, S., Rendel, T., Kästner, C., Ostermann, K.: Layout-sensitive generalized parsing. In: Czarnecki, K., Hedin, G. (eds.) SLE 2012. LNCS, vol. 7745, pp. 244–263. Springer, Heidelberg (2013). https://doi.org/10.1007/978-3-642-36089-3_14
12. Erwig, M.: Active patterns. In: Kluge, W. (ed.) IFL 1996. LNCS, vol. 1268, pp. 21–40. Springer, Heidelberg (1997). https://doi.org/10.1007/3-540-63237-9_17

13. Ford, B.: Parsing expression grammars: a recognition-based syntactic foundation. In: Jones, N., Leroy, X. (eds.) Proceedings of the 31st ACM SIGPLAN-SIGACT Symposium on Principles of Programming Languages, POPL 2004, Venice, Italy, 14–16 January 2004, pp. 111–122. ACM (2004)
14. Gruber, J.: Markdown: syntax. Technical report, Accessed on Oct 2025
15. Hanus, M.: FL-parser. https://cpm.curry-lang.org/pkgs/fl-parser.html, version 3.0.0. Accessed on Oct 2025
16. Hanus, M.: Functional logic programming: from theory to curry. In: Voronkov, A., Weidenbach, C. (eds.) Programming Logics. LNCS, vol. 7797, pp. 123–168. Springer, Heidelberg (2013). https://doi.org/10.1007/978-3-642-37651-1_6
17. Hanus, M. (ed.): Curry: an integrated functional logic language (vers. 0.9.0) (2016). http://www.curry-lang.org
18. Hußmann, H.: Nondeterministic algebraic specifications and nonconfluent term rewriting. J. Log. Program. **12**(3&4), 237–255 (1992)
19. Jim, T., Mandelbaum, Y., Walker, D.: Semantics and algorithms for data-dependent grammars. In: Hermenegildo, M., Palsberg, J. (eds.) Proceedings of the 37th ACM SIGPLAN-SIGACT Symposium on Principles of Programming Languages, POPL 2010, Madrid, Spain, 17–23 January 2010, pp. 417–430. ACM (2010)
20. Jones, M.: The implementation of the gofer functional programming system. Technical report, Yale University (1994)
21. Krause, P.: The Art of Prolog, 2nd edn. by Leon Sterling and Ehud Shapiro, p. 509. MIT Press, Cambridge (1994). £19.95 (paperback), £44.94 (hardback), ISBN 0-262-19338-8. Knowl. Eng. Rev. **10**(4), 411 (1995)
22. Landin, P.: The next 700 programming languages. Commun. ACM **9**(3), 157–166 (1966)
23. Leijen, D., Meijer, E.: Parsec: direct style monadic parser combinators for the real world. Technical Report UU-CS-2001-27, July 2001. User Modeling 2007, 11th International Conference, UM 2007, Corfu, Greece, 25–29 June 2007
24. Liu, J., Zhu, F., He, F.: Automated ambiguity detection in layout-sensitive grammars. Proc. ACM Program. Lang. **7**(OOPSLA2), 1150–1175 (2023)
25. Peyton Jones, S. (ed.) Haskell 98 Language and Libraries—The Revised Report. Cambridge University Press (2003)
26. Wadler, P.: Views: a way for pattern matching to cohabit with data abstraction. In: Conference Record of the Fourteenth Annual ACM Symposium on Principles of Programming Languages, Munich, Germany, 21–23 January 1987, pp. 307–313. ACM Press (1987)

Using Prolog to Translate Set Theory and B to SAT

Michael Leuschel[(✉)] [iD]

Heinrich Heine University Düsseldorf, Universitätsstr. 1, 40225 Düsseldorf, Germany
`michael.leuschel@hhu.de`

Abstract. Various approaches to solving set theory constraints exist, for example within verification tools for the TLA+ and B formal methods. In this paper we present a way to solve set theory constraints in general and B formulas in particular using SAT solvers, by using Prolog technology. First, a preliminary analysis uses CLP(FD) constraint solving to infer finite bounds for decision variables. Second, Prolog translation rules map constraints to answer set programming (ASP), by encoding logical and set-theoretic operators as Horn clauses. Finally, the Clingo tool translates the ASP encoding to SAT to produce ASP models, which we translate back to set theory and B using Prolog DCG rules. The scheme of the paper has been implemented in SICStus Prolog, as an alternate backend for the PROB validation tool. We evaluate the new backend on a series of benchmarks. Our paper highlights the usefulness of Prolog, for analysis, inference and transformation rules and ASP as a high-level interface to SAT solving.

1   Introduction

The formal B method [1,2] is rooted in set theory, predicate logic and arithmetic. Particularly when using Unicode syntax, B formulas look like typical mathematic formulas. While the B method originally targets code generation and systems modelling for safety critical systems, it also provides a convenient way to express complex constraint solving and optimisation tasks, ranging from University time tabling to biological applications and data generation for railway systems.

The PROB [23] validation tool for B and uses Prolog to bring the underlying mathematics of B to life [21]. At its core is a constraint solver for predicate logic, arithmetic and set theory and supporting higher-order sets, relations and functions. The solver is implemented in SICStus Prolog [7] and is built on top of CLP(FD) [8]. The solver is well adapted for validation tasks like animation and data validation. Still, for some applications, other solving approaches are more appropriate. E.g., some constraint solving and optimisation tasks are easy to express in B (or set theory), but too difficult [22] to solve or optimise with the default CLP(FD) solver, or other solving backends based on Z3 [27] or Kodkod [26]. [22] proposed a bare metal translation to SAT, called B2SAT, which can tackle those tasks very efficiently. However, the B2SAT approach currently only

N. Amin and J. Arias (Eds.): PADL 2026, LNCS 16401, pp. 143–160, 2026.
https://doi.org/10.1007/978-3-032-15981-6_9

supports a small subset of data types and B constructs, and more work is required to encode arithmetic and more data types and aggregates. Here comes the idea of this paper: we want to employ answer set programming [25] as a high-level, logic programming road to SAT solving and optimisation. This would provide the encodings of arithmetic operators, data types and aggregates for free. In particular, we use the CLINGO tool [13,14] to translate ASP logic programs to SAT. The translation rules from B to ASP themselves can be expressed in Prolog itself. Also, before doing the translation, we need to determine finite base types for all unbounded variables of the original formula. This analysis is also written in Prolog, making use of CLP(FD) to infer finite bounds for sets and scalars.

In summary, this paper presents a purely logic programming approach to solving B formulas (aka set theory, predicate logic and arithmetic), via

- a CLP(FD) based bounds analysis,
- a principled translation of set theory and B to ASP programs (aka Horn clauses) encoded as Prolog rules,
- using CLINGO to translate and solve ASP programs via SAT solving,
- a Prolog back-translation of ASP models to B values.

We also report on experiences, pitfalls and successes of the translation and solving approach. The approach in this paper can be adapted for other formalisms rooted in set theory and logic. Out of the box, our backend implemented in PROB can target TLA+ [19], Z [28] and Alloy [16] in addition to B.

2   Overview of the Translation and Solving Process

Let us take the very simple B formula $pq = 1 \mathinner{.\,.} 2 \cap \{2, 4\}$, where pq is implicitly existentially quantified. To solve this constraint with our new B2ASP translation we can issue the following command into the PROB console. Note that $/\backslash$ is the ASCII version of the set intersection $\cap$.[1]

```
>>> :clingo  pq = 1..2 /\ {2,4}
PREDICATE is TRUE
Solution:
        pq = {2}
```

While the formula is simple to solve, it is sufficient to exhibit relevant aspects of the B2ASP solving process, as shown in Fig. 1. The B formula is transformed by our technique into a Horn clause (ASP) encoding, which is then translated by CLINGO [13,14] to a SAT formula. CLINGO sends this formula to a SAT solver, whose models are back-translated to models of the Horn clause ASP program. Our tool then translates this ASP model back to a solution in terms of the original B representation. Let us now get a first look at these phases.

---

[1] One can also use the Unicode symbol in the console.

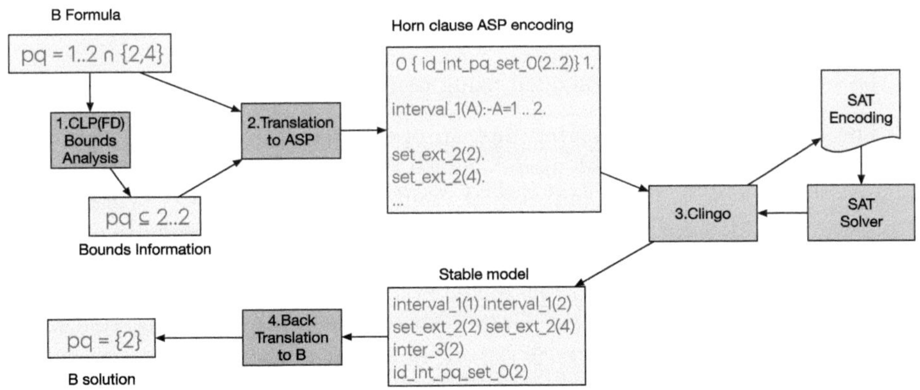

Fig. 1. Overview of the B2ASP Solving process

1. Bounds Analysis. In order to translate B to ASP, we first need to infer finite bounds for all identifiers. The identifier pq in the formula above is of type $\mathbb{P}(\mathbb{Z})$, i.e., it is unbounded and we need to restrict its possible values to a finite subtype. We do this by inferring intervals of possible values and processing the formula bottom-up:

1. We set up an unconstrained interval $low..up$ for the identifier pq. Initially, the bounds have no constraints, and the interval could also be empty.
2. We process the set expression $1 .. 2$, returning as bounds for its possible elements the interval $1 .. 2$.
3. We process $\{2,4\}$, returning as bounds for its elements the interval $2 .. 4$.
4. We process the intersection $\cap$, returning the interval $2 .. 2$.
5. We unify the unconstrained interval for pq from step 1 with $2 .. 2$, inferring that pq is a set with all its values in the interval $2 .. 2$.

Our analysis ensures that $\forall pq.(pq = 1 .. 2 \cap \{2,4\} \Rightarrow pq \subseteq 2 .. 2)$. Concretely, this means that to encode the possible values of pq in SAT one proposition is sufficient (namely to encode whether $2 \in pq$ or $2 \notin pq$ holds). Note that for this simple formula, the bounds analysis has almost solved the problem, but not entirely: we do not know whether a solution exists and if it does, whether $pq = \{2\}$ or $pq = \emptyset$. In Sect. 3 we show how this preliminary bounds analysis is implemented in constraint logic programming over finite domains.

2. Conversion to ASP. To translate $pq = 1 .. 2 \cap \{2,4\}$ to ASP, we translate each sub-expression to its own ASP predicate. The full translation of the formula is shown below. A set S expression in B is thereby translated into an ASP predicate $p/1$, where $p(x)$ is true for each member $x \in S$. The constant sub-expressions of our formula are translated as follows:

– the interval $1 .. 2$ is translated into `interval_1`, using CLINGO syntax to generate one fact per element of the interval,

- the set extension $\{2, 4\}$ is translated into `set_ext_2`, with one fact per element of the set,
- the set intersection $\cap$ is encoded using conjunction within `inter_3` below.

The identifier pq is translated into an open predicate `id_int_pq_set_0`, for which CLINGO will later find model values. We use the result of the bounds analysis to provide a finite universe of candidates. The CLINGO syntax below expresses that all solutions must lie in the interval 2..2, and there are at least 0 and at most 1 facts (i.e., elements in pq). The result of the bounds analysis is used to restrict the possible values of pq in the first line below. Observe that our top-level formula must be encoded as an integrity constraint for CLINGO. Hence, our translator cannot assert $pq = 1..2 \cap \{2, 4\}$, but must assert $\neg(pq \neq 1..2 \cap \{2, 4\})$. The set inequality $\neq$ is encoded in the predicate `not_set_equal_4` with two clauses, stating that the two sets are not equal if either there is an element of pq not in the intersection, or an element in the intersection not in pq. Also observe the use of ASP negation (which must be to the right of calls instantiating its arguments to be safe).

```
0 { id_int_pq_set_0(2..2)} 1.
interval_1(A)  :- A=1 .. 2.
set_ext_2(2).
set_ext_2(4).
inter_3(A)  :- interval_1(A),set_ext_2(A).
not_set_equal_4 :- id_int_pq_set_0(A), not inter_3(A).
not_set_equal_4 :- inter_3(A), not id_int_pq_set_0(A).
:- not_set_equal_4.
```

3. Solving and Backtranslation. Running the above ASP file using CLINGO generates a model consisting of the following atoms (which are true in the model):

```
interval_1(1) interval_1(2)    set_ext_2(2) set_ext_2(4)    inter_3(2)
id_int_pq_set_0(2)
```

We now need to translate the model atoms for `id_int_pq_set_0` back to a B value for pq, namely the set $\{2\}$. This is done using a small DCG parser written in Prolog.

3   Bounds Analysis of B Formulas via CLP(FD)

Remember that our overall goal is to translate a B formula to ASP, where existential quantifiers are encoded as "open" predicates. We thus need a bounds analysis to determine a finite set of possible for those identifiers. More precisely, given a quantified formula $\exists x_1, \ldots, x_k, s_{k+1}, \ldots, s_l.P$, where each x_i is a scalar and each s_j is a set, we want to find bounding sets B_i such that $\forall x_1, \ldots, x_k.(P \Rightarrow x_i \in B_i)$ and $\forall s_{k+1}, \ldots, s_l.(P \Rightarrow s_i \subseteq B_i)$. We also require the bounding sets to have a special form, namely to be either intervals or cartesian product of intervals. We also accept the full type for finite types like boolean.

After running the bounds analysis on the full formula, we also apply the above analysis for inner quantifiers, passing information about the bounds found for the outer identifiers. To process universal quantifiers $\forall y_1, \ldots, y_k.P \Rightarrow Q$ and comprehension sets $\{y_1, \ldots, y_k \mid P\}$, we simply run the analysis on $\exists y_1, \ldots, y_k.P$.

Our analysis has been implemented using the CLP(FD) [8] library of SICStus Prolog, using finite domain variables to represent possible integer values. The goal was to re-use the CLP(FD) implementation for intervals of possible values, for an efficient and easy to develop analysis. For example, given the constraint $x > 1 \wedge x < y \wedge y < 10$, we can use the finite domain variables X and Y for x and y, post constraints about the possible values, and then obtain the interval of possible values using the `fd_min` and `fd_max` predicates of CLP(FD):

```
| ?- X #> 1, X #<Y, Y #< 10,
     fd_min(X,MinX), fd_max(X,MaxX), fd_min(Y,MinY), fd_max(Y,MaxY).
MinX = 2, MaxX = 8,
MinY = 3, MaxY = 9,
X in 2 .. 8, Y in 3 .. 9 ?
yes
```

Above, we have not applied CLP(FD) labeling, as we want a (finite) "safe approximation" of the possible solutions of x and y in the form of an interval and not an enumeration of all possible values.[2]

The above approach works well for scalars, but for sets the analysis is more tricky. In principle, one could also use a single FD value to represent possible values of a set, but a set can be empty without the entire formula being inconsistent. For example, the formula $x \subseteq 1..2 \wedge x \subseteq 3..4$ is satisfiable and has the solution $x = \emptyset$, while the CLP(FD) constraint X in 1..2, X in 3..4 is inconsistent and would lead to failure of our bounds analysis.

Our solution is to use *two* finite domain variables to represent the possible values of a set. The first variable is a lower bound for all elements of the set, while the second one is an upper bound. If the two bounds cross, the set is empty. This solves the inconsistency problem for empty sets, but the propagation rules are still more tricky than one would hope. Quite often we need to know whether intervals are empty or not. For example, when processing the constraint $S_1 = S_2$ for two sets, we cannot simply unify the respective upper and lower bounds. Indeed, suppose both S_1 and S_2 are empty and we have detected the interval 4..3 for S_1 and 5..1 for S_2, unifying 4..3 = 5..1 would lead to failure of the analysis, even though the B constraint is satisfiable.

Our final solution was to use *three* finite domain variables for a set, encoded internally using the term `binterval(Low,Up,NonEmpty)`, where `NonEmpty` is 0 or 1 and is defined via reification: `NonEmpty #<=> (Low #=< Up)`. At the end of the analysis, to extract the bounds of such an interval, we tentatively ground NonEmpty flag to get bounds.

---

[2] Our implementation has the option of performing a labeling step to find one solution and ensure consistency of the constraints. If the bounds constraints are inconsistent, the entire predicate can be optimized into falsity ($\perp$). We have, however, not used that option in the experiments below.

Other data structures used in the analysis are `bint(FDVal)` for scalar values `bcart(Dom,Range,NonEmpty)` for cartesian products (aka relations and functions in B). Note that B strings are registered and translated to numbers (and the back translation needs to remember the type of the identifier). Similarly, enumerated set elements are also translated to numbers. However, we currently to do not try to find bounds for them, as enumerated sets are finite by definition in B.

The following shows the implementation of the set intersection and operators. Observe how we use the CLP(FD) operators to encode interval propagation rules:

```
intersect_bounds(binterval(Low1,Up1,NE1),
                 binterval(Low2,Up2,NE2),Bounds) :-
   init_binterval(Low,Up,Bounds),
   NE #=< NE1, % if set1 is empty then the intersection is empty
   NE #=< NE2, % ditto for set 2
   Low #= max(Low1,Low2), Up #= min(Up1,Up2).
union_bounds(binterval(Low1,Up1,NE1),binterval(Low2,Up2,NE2),Bounds) :-
   init_binterval(Low,Up,Bounds,NE),
   NE1 #=< NE, % if union empty then set1 empty
   NE2 #=< NE, % ditto for set 2
   NE #=< NE1+NE2, % if set1 & set2 empty then union is empty
   (NE1 #= 0) #=> (Low #= Low2 #/\ Up #= Up2), % if set1 empty copy set2
   (NE1 #= 1 #/\ NE2 #= 1)
       #=> (Low #= min(Low1,Low2) #/\ Up #= max(Up1,Up2)).


init_binterval(Low,Up,binterval(Low,Up,NonEmpty),NonEmpty) :-
   NonEmpty #<=> (Low #=< Up).
```

Another tricky aspect of our analysis is well-definedness [3,5,20]. I.e., we do not want our analysis to fail if at some point we perform a problematic operator like dividing by 0 or applying a function outside of its domain. In this case our analysis returns a dummy value. Note that this is a sound result: the analysis can provide a strict superset of the possible solutions for the identifiers. The processing of how to process well-definedness issues is left to the main solver.

The full source code contains around 530 lines of code.[3] As we see later in Sect. 5, the analysis turned out to be efficient (with a maximum runtime of 6 ms for the considered benchmarks).

4   Translation from B to ASP in Prolog

In this section we describe the translation of B formulas and set theory constraint to answer set programs, which can then be solved by CLINGO [13,14]. Set theoretic operators will be encoded in Horn clause logic and an ASP model will provide values for all existentially quantified formulas of the original B formula (see Sect. 2).

---

[3] Which can be found in the bounds_analysis.pl module of the PROB source code available at https://prob.hhu.de/w/index.php?title=Download.

The syntax of B [1,2,9] distinguishes between predicates like $x + 1 > 0$ and expressions like $x + 1$. B also has statements (aka substitutions in B), but our translation only focusses on translating predicates and expressions to B. This is similar to all other back-ends of PROB [22,26,27]; there are symbolic verification algorithms which can unwind statements into predicates [17], e.g., for bounded model checking.

Our translation traverses the abstract syntax tree and translates B predicates and expressions ϕ into ASP predicates P_ϕ. The meaning of the ASP predicate depends on the type of the (sub-)formula and is summarised in the following table:

Type of ϕ	Arity of P_ϕ	Semantics of ASP predicate P_ϕ
Scalar Expression	Unary predicate	Exactly one solution with value of scalar
Set Expression	Unary predicate	Multiple solutions, one per element of set
Predicate	Proposition	True if ϕ false

An interesting observation is that scalars and sets are both translated into unary ASP predicates. For scalars, the predicate will have exactly one solution, while for sets there can be more solutions or even none (for the empty set).

Below we show some of the translation rules. Each translation rule is actually realised as a Prolog clause. Full Prolog code for this translation (in the b2asp module in https://prob.hhu.de/w/index.php?title=Download) has about 1300 lines of code and covers more B operators and data types (couples, booleans, enumerated set elements and strings). The following tables describe the high-level gist of the translation for each type (set expression, scalar expression and predicate). In Prolog code it is realised as the `trans_set` predicate. Later, we will see that the translation rules will require an additional environment to deal with universally quantified variables, and that some improvements (such as inlining of literals) are required for performance.

Set Expression ϕ	Clauses for P_ϕ	Side Condition (comment)
$\emptyset$	`P`$_\phi$`(X) :- 1=2.`	
x	`0{`P_ϕ`(Low..Up)}n.`	$x \subseteq Low..Up$ (bounds analysis) $n = Up + 1 - Low$
$A \ldots B$	P_ϕ`(Z) :- `P_A`(X), `P_B`(Y), Z = X..Y.`	
$A \cup B$	P_ϕ`(X) :- `P_A`(X).` P_ϕ`(X) :- `P_B`(X).`	
$A \cap B$	P_ϕ`(X) :- `P_A`(X), `P_B`(X).`	
$A \setminus B$	P_ϕ`(X) :- `P_A`(X), not `P_B`(X).`	
$dom(A)$	P_ϕ`(X) :- `P_A`((X,_)).`	
$ran(A)$	P_ϕ`(X) :- `P_A`((_,X)).`	
A^{-1}	P_ϕ`((X,Y)) :- `P_A`((Y,X)).`	(inverse)
$A; B$	P_ϕ`((X,Z)) :- `P_A`((X,Y)), `P_B`((Y,Z)).`	(composition)
$closure1(A)$	P_ϕ`((X,Y)) :- `P_A`((X,Y)).` P_ϕ`((X,Z)) :- `P_A`((X,Y)), `P_ϕ`((Y,Z)).`	(transitive closure)

In the last five entries of the table you can see that CLINGO does support more than pure Datalog as input: we can use pairs as predicate arguments. This means that we can use the same encoding of the basic set operations like $\cup$ an $\cap$ for sets of scalars and for binary or n-ary relations. This greatly simplifies our translation scheme.

The following table shows some rules for translating B scalar expressions (realised in Prolog as `trans_scalar` predicate):

Scalar Expression ϕ	Clauses for P_ϕ	Side Condition (comment)
x	`1{`P_ϕ`(`$Low..Up$`)}1.`	$x \in Low..Up$ (bounds analysis)
n	P_ϕ`(`n`).`	n is an integer literal
$A + B$	P_ϕ`(Z) :- `P_A`(X), `P_B`(Y), Z=X+Y.`	
$A * B$	P_ϕ`(Z) :- `P_A`(X), `P_B`(Y), Z=X*Y.`	(similar for -,...)
$f(A)$	P_ϕ`(Y) :- `P_A`(X), `P_f`((X,Y)).`	A is scalar
$prj1(A)$	P_ϕ`(X) :- `P_A`((X,_)).`	(projection)
$prj2(A)$	P_ϕ`(X) :- `P_A`((_,X)).`	(projection)
IF A THEN B ELSE C END	P_ϕ`(X) :- `P_A`, `P_B`(X).` P_ϕ`(X) :- `P_C`(X), not `P_A`.`	
card(A)	P_ϕ`(X) :- X=#count{Y : `P_A`(Y)}.`	
$\Sigma(x).(x \in A\|x)$	P_ϕ`(X) :- X=#sum{Y : `P_A`(Y)}.`	x identifier

Finally, this table describes how some B predicates get translated into ASP integrity constraints (the full Prolog code is realised in `trans_not_pred` predicate):

Predicate ϕ	Clauses for P_ϕ	Side Condition
$\top$ (truth)	P_ϕ` :- 1=2.`	
$\bot$ (falsity)	P_ϕ`.`	
$A \wedge B$	P_ϕ` :- `P_A`.` P_ϕ` :- `P_B`.`	
$A \vee B$	P_ϕ` :- `P_A`, `P_B`.`	
$A \subseteq B$	P_ϕ` :- `P_A`(X), not `P_B`(X).`	
$A \in B$	P_ϕ` :- `P_A`(X), not `P_B`(X).`	
$A = B$	P_ϕ` :- `P_A`(X), not `P_B`(X).` P_ϕ` :- `P_B`(X), not `P_A`(X).`	A,B are sets
$A = B$	P_ϕ` :- `P_A`(X), `P_B`(Y), X`$\neq$`Y.`	A,B are scalars
$A > B$	P_ϕ` :- `P_A`(X), `P_B`(Y), X`$\leq$`Y.`	

Scalars vs Sets. Above we see that, surprisingly, the translation of $A \subseteq B$ and $A \in B$ is identical. We already observed, that scalars and sets are both translated into unary ASP predicates. This actually means that a scalar A has the same internal representation as a singleton set $\{A\}$. In other words, a scalar can simply be seen as a singleton set. As we have that $A \in B \Leftrightarrow \{A\} \subseteq B$, the "mystery" can be explained logically. This idea also appears in the Alloy language [16], where scalars are treated as singleton sets. We can see here that this idea also arises naturally in our SAT translation.

Universal Quantification. The above translation scheme deals with existentially quantified variables. Indeed, every variable has its own "open" ASP predicate with a declaration of its possible solutions. For universal quantifiers the approach is different: there are *no* separate ASP predicates encoding the quantified variables. Indeed, here we do not want to find a single valuation (as part of the model), we need to check *all* valuations. This requires a different translation scheme. We generate those valuations using an auxiliary generator predicate, and represent the local variable as extra arguments to predicates in the scope. More precisely, the translation of $\forall x.(A \Rightarrow B)$ will have the form:

$$P_\phi \text{ :- } P_x(\texttt{X}), \, P_A(\texttt{X}), \, \text{not } P_B(\texttt{X}).$$

where P_x generates all possible values for x, and these values are passed to other ASP predicates as an *additional* argument X (and not in the form of a named predicate). Take for example the formula $x \subseteq 1..10 \land \forall y.(y \in x \Rightarrow y < 3)$, and examine the translation:

```
0 { id_int_x_set_0(1..10)} 10.
interval_1(A):-A=1 .. 10.
not_subset_2:-id_int_x_set_0(A), not interval_1(A).
member_3(A) :- A=1 .. 10, id_int_x_set_0(A).
arith_4(A) :- A=1 .. 10, A>=3.
not_forall_5 :- A=1 .. 10, member_3(A), arith_4(A).
not_conjunct_6 :- not_subset_2.
not_conjunct_6 :- not_forall_5.
:- not_conjunct_6.
#show id_int_x_set_0/1.
```

Here `not_forall_5` encodes the universal quantifier. Observe, how `member_3` and `arith_4` have received an additional argument for the universally quantified variable x. Also observe, that the translation of x and y differ: in `arith_4` the value of y is simply "extracted" from its argument list, while x is translated in `not_subset_2` by calling the ASP predicate `id_int_x_set_0`.

This means the above translation rules become more complicated and require an extra environment argument, storing information about the quantified variables, which influence the code generation.

For illustration purposes, here is the Prolog rule for the translation of a subset predicate $A \subseteq B$ to the ASP clause P_ϕ :- $P_A(\texttt{X})$, not $P_B(\texttt{X})$. You can see the additional `Env` argument, an auxiliary predicate to insert comments into the generated ASP code, and an auxiliary predicate to generate ASP clauses.

```
trans_not_pred(subset(A,B),Env,Prop) :- !,
   trans_set(A,Env,P1), trans_set(B,Env,P2),
   clingo_format_comment('% subset (negative)~n',[]),
   gen_clingo_pred_clause(not_subset,Prop,[], Env,
                   (ecall(P1,[X],Env), not(ecall(P2,[X],Env)) )).
                   % :- P1(X), not P2(X).
```

For the formula $x \subseteq 1..10$, this code will generate the first three clauses of the output above (with comments). The calls to `trans_set` generate the clauses for `id_int_x_set_0` (the translation of x) and `interval_1` (the translation of 1..10).

Other Optimisations. Sometimes the CLINGO model can be very large and we are actually only interested to obtain model for top-level identifiers. Luckily, we can use the show directive of CLINGO to only transmit back relevant model atoms.

CLINGO is sometimes very sensitive to the way constraints are expressed. In particular for cardinality constraints, there is a big difference between these two encodings:

```
arith_1 :- 2 != #count{Var:id_int_x_set_0(Var)}.
```

```
p(2).
arith_1 :- p(X), X != #count{Var:id_int_x_set_0(Var)}.
```

The first encoding, where bounds are given directly, is much more efficient. For the crowded chessboard benchmark later in Sect. 5, this results in an order of magnitude difference between 2 min and 40 s for the former encoding, and 31 min runtime for the latter. As such, our translation rules also have special cases for expressions, trying to generate inlined literals if possible, and using auxiliary ASP predicates only if necessary.

In our work, we also observed that sometimes CLINGO is not fully generic; i.e., some aggregates seem to be allowed in arbitrary context. E.g., we were not able to add the maximum of two sets inside a single expression, and our translation has to decompose those special cases. But unfortunately, there are still some cases where CLINGO produces errors we do not understand.

Current Restrictions. The translation still has a few limitations which we plan to address in the future. One is that, while one can nest existential quantifiers, name clashes are not yet allowed. Also, existential quantifiers cannot be nested inside universal quantifiers and set comprehensions. This limitation is purely technical, and requires adapting the source code on how environment information is passed to inner quantifiers. It turns out that the treatment of quantified universal quantifiers can be expensive for large domains. In future we plan to find out which variables are actually used in a sub-expression and only pass (and ground) relevant quantified variables. Also, only certain patterns of the summation operator Σ are supported (those accepted directly by CLINGO). There are also limitations that are inherent to our approach and shared by all SAT-based approaches:

- higher-order values (sets of sets, ...) are not supported,
- only scalar values can be quantified inside $\exists$, $\forall$ and set comprehensions.

B2ASP will emit error messages when attempting to translate unsupported constructs. By interleaving B2ASP with PROB's default solver (as done for B2SAT in [22]), we would be able to provide some support for high-order values and quantification over sets.

5   Tooling and Experiments

We have added several ways in ProB to interact with the new solver backend. First, in the REPL (Read-Eval-Print-Loop) you have the commands `:clingo` and `:clingo-double-check` commands. We have seen the first command in Sect. 2. The second command double-checks the solution with ProB's default solver. The latter command is also used in ProB's integration tests.

One can use the command `:clingo #file=FILE` to load the predicate from a file. The new backend can also be used to solve the PROPERTIES (aka axioms) of B and Event-B models by setting the `SOLVER_FOR_PROPERTIES` preference. This preference can take the new value CLINGO as well as the old values: prob, sat, sat-z3, z3, cdclt.

5.1   Positive Examples: N-Bishops and Crowded Chessboard

Let us look at two interesting puzzles from [12]. First, the N-Bishops puzzle[4] requires to to place as many bishops as possible on a chess board so that they do not attack each other. For an 8 by 8 chessboard, ProB's default solver can find a solution with more than 13 bishops in roughly 1.6 s. However, confirming that there is no solution with more than 14 bishops takes about 5 min. ProB's Kodkod backend [26] cannot be used due to issues related to integer overflows (see discussion below in Sect. 6).

The puzzle can be solved in 0.155 secs with the new B2ASP CLINGO backend, and it takes 13.5 s to confirm there is no better solution. The translation time is just 0.003 s and the back translation time of the CLINGO model to B just 0.009 s. The B2SAT [22] backend requires rewriting the B specification to use total functions mapping to booleans, as it currently does not support more complex datatypes in the SAT translation part (as discussed as motivation for the present article in Sect. 1).

Now let us look at a more challenging puzzle, namely the crowded chessboard puzzle 306 from [12]. The task is to place 8 queens, 8 rooks, 14 bishops and 21 knights on a 8 by 8 chessboard, so that each class of pieces do not attack each other. The puzzle was was set out as a challenge in [18]. The puzzle can be solved by our backend in 2 min and 42 s (before inlining and constant propagation this was over 31 min; see Sect. 4). Neither ProB's default backend, nor the Kodkod, Z3, or the CDCLT backend can solve this puzzle. It can, however, be solved in 0.5 s by the bare metal translation produced by B2SAT. So, in this case our backend is considerably slower than going directly to SAT, but is still able to solve the problem within reasonable time.

Note, after solving, solutions can be double-checked very efficiently by ProB's default solver. Indeed, that is what happens automatically, when one opens the state view in the UI (as shown in the top-left of Fig. 2).

---

[4] Number 297 BISHOPS—UNGUARDED in [12]; see also http://mathworld.wolfram. com/BishopsProblem.html.

5.2 Experiments

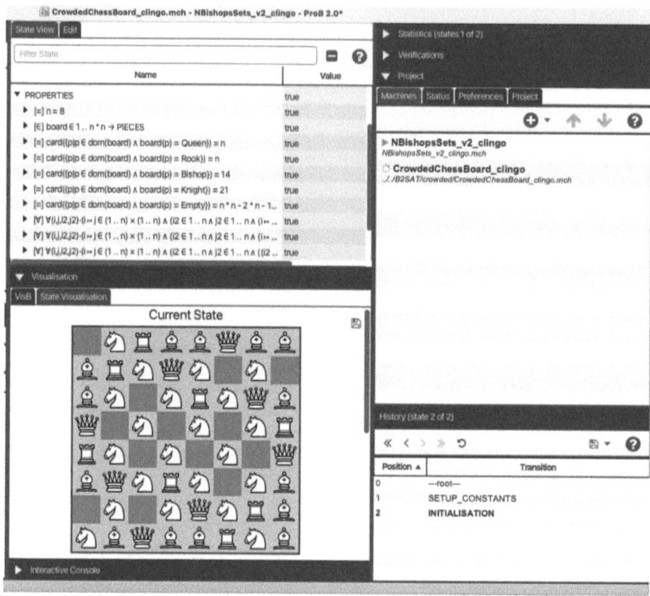

Fig. 2. Partial Screenshot of ProB2-UI after Crowded Chessboard example and solving it with B2ASP backend

In this subsection we evaluate the backend on a set of benchmarks and compare it against the default CLP(FD) backend, as well as against other backends. The benchmark are biased, in the sense that they target tasks for which B2ASP and B2SAT were developed for. E.g., we do not include problems using higher-order values, infinite sets or typical animation and model checking tasks for which PROB already works very well. All benchmarks were run on a Macbook Air with M2 processor, 24 GB RAM and with version 1.15.1-nightly[5] of PROB compiled with SICStus Prolog 4.9.0. For the Kodkod backend we have changed the SAT solver to Glucose (from the default Sat4j). All times are walltimes in milliseconds (ms) and the timeout was set at 15 s.

The benchmark files are available as an archive https://doi.org/10.5281/zenodo.17660150 and at https://stups.hhu-hosting.de//models/b2asp/. Some examples were taken directly from B2SAT [22]. We included three pure SAT problems (blocksworld and uuf) in B, to detect if there is an overhead when writing SAT problems in B rather than in CNF format. We have also translated some benchmarks to B from the IDP-Z3 [6]: transitive closure, and pigeon hole. The dominating set benchmarks stem from biological applications, and had to be re-written from [22]. B2SAT expects booleans and total functions to booleans.

---

[5] Version from 19/11/2025 (cd4e68c2cb668818b67010ac3bfe0a13cbe676a3).

B2ASP can deal with those, but works better with sets rather than a total function to BOOL. Also, B2SAT can deal with higher-order aspects, as long as PROB can expand them before conversion to SAT. B2ASP is not yet interleaved in this way with the PROB solver; it is a completely stand-alone process with a fully static compilation to ASP. For the N-bishops example above we thus have two versions: one natural version using sets (NBishopsSet) and one (NBishopsBV) for B2SAT using total functions. We could not run the crowded chessboard puzzle with our benchmarking script for technical reasons.[6] JustQueens is another constraint programming benchmark, requiring to place two armies of queens (black and white) which do not attack each other [15]. HardGraph_Nr5 is a hard graph isomorphism problem and IceCream_Generic a smaller dominating set problem, while Loop is a small compiler optimisation example.

Table 1. B2ASP Backend: $\star_1$ B to ASP translation time (including bounds analysis which is at most 6 ms), $\star_2$ ASP model to B conversion time and $\star_3$ total walltime for solving formula with clingo (including columns $\star_1$ and $\star_2$). Model size is expressed as the number of atoms.

Benchmark	B → ASP $\star_1$ (ms)	ASP → B $\star_2$ (ms)	Model size	Result	Total $\star_3$ (ms)
pigeon_30	3	1	91	sat	103
transitive_closure_50_bv	4	10	2707	sat	1232
blocksworld_medium	96	1	116	sat	303
blocksworld_medium_unsat	77	0	-	unsat	284
uuf-250-016	132	0	-	unsat	3684
NBishopsSet	3	1	16	sat	432
NBishopsBV	5	2	65	sat	62
WhoKilledAgatha	5	2	12	sat	39
JustQueens_8_9	9	0	38	sat	341
Loop	3	1	26	sat	95
NQueensBig	2	1	25	sat	189
HardGraph_Nr5	4	2	240	sat	1724
IceCream_Generic	5	1	175	sat	160
DominatingSet_BV_Middle_lt13	8	2	752	sat	376
DominatingSet_BV_Middle_lt12	6	0	-	unsat	404
SendMoreMoney	3	0	-	unknown	15069

---

[6] The benchmark script currently runs on stand-alone files, containing one big formula. The crowded chessboard example makes heavy use of auxiliary definitions for movements of the pieces.

Table 2. B2ASP compared to other backends of PROB. All runtimes are relative to B2ASP. ✠ stands for unknown (either due to time out or unsupported constructs), ✓ for the correct result.

Benchmark	B2ASP SAT	Kodkod SAT	Default CLP(FD)	B2SAT SAT	Z3 SMT
pigeon_30	sat 1	✓ 11.04	✓ 1.75	✓ 0.17	✠ 146.35
transitive_closure_50_bv	sat 1	✠ 0.01	✓ 5.06	✓ 1.26	✠ 12.93
blocksworld_medium	sat 1	✓ 1.14	✓ 0.61	✓ 0.53	✓ 8.55
blocksworld_medium_unsat	unsat 1	✓ 1.00	✓ 0.60	✓ 0.51	✓ 8.15
uuf-250-016	unsat 1	✓ 1.13	✠ 4.14	✓ 0.51	✓ 1.51
NBishopsSet	sat 1	✠ 0.01	✠ 34.88	✠ 173.96	✠ 34.78
NBishopsBV	sat 1	✠ 0.10	✠ 243.26	✓ 0.48	✠ 244.10
WhoKilledAgatha	sat 1	✠ 0.18	✓ 0.36	✓ 0.44	✠ 12.77
JustQueens_8_9	sat 1	✓ 201.13	✠ 44.35	✓ 221.20	✠ 56.16
Loop	sat 1	✠ 0.05	✓ 0.20	✓ 0.14	✠ 0.34
NQueensBig	sat 1	✓ 97.81	✓ 0.60	✓ 0.11	✠ 79.83
HardGraph_Nr5	sat 1	✓ 2.06	✓ 0.04	✓ 0.02	✓ 1.61
IceCream_Generic	sat 1	✓ 0.25	✓ 0.21	✓ 0.11	✠ 100.94
DominatingSet_BV_Middle_lt13	sat 1	✓ 1.39	✠ 40.15	✓ 0.07	✠ 43.40
DominatingSet_BV_Middle_lt12	unsat 1	✓ 1.61	✠ 37.28	✓ 0.07	✠ 40.47
SendMoreMoney	✠ 1	✓ 0.02	✓ 0.00	✓ 0.00	✓ 0.00

Analysis. The three SAT problems (blocksworld and uuf) show that B2ASP is capable of solving pure SAT problem encoded in B, with less overhead than the Kodkod or Z3 backends, but not as effectively as the direct translation of B2SAT.

The most disappointing benchmark is the SendMoreMoney puzzle. B2ASP can actually solve it in 172 min, but this is disappointingly slow. This is despite the fact that the bounds analysis is very precise. We found anecdotal evidence, that even encoding the puzzle efficiently by hand for CLINGO is not easy.[7] The performance problem seems to stem from grounding. We have also noted this with other experiments for relations with large base types.

On the positive side, we can see that there are six benchmarks solved by B2ASP which cannot be solved by PROB's default CLP(FD) backend. For the JustQueens benchmark it is even considerably faster than B2SAT.

In summary, the results show that our new backend is very useful for some applications, but there is scope for improvement. Also, it is not designed to be a replacement of the existing default solver; it is meant to be an additional backend for dedicated tasks like optimisation or symbolic verification.

---

[7] https://www.hakank.org/constraint_programming_blog/2010/12/
a_first_look_at_answer_set_programming.html.

Validation of the Implementation. One question is how to validate the correctness of the B2ASP implementation. Luckily there are other solvers in PROB to double-check its results. Note that while PROB's default CLP(FD) solver cannot efficiently solve some of the examples above (Fig. 1), it can efficiently check that a solution is correct (see top-left of Fig. 2). For integration tests we use the `:clingo_double_check` command on a large number of formulas (currently 154 tests). Also, when using the new backend to solve a problem in practice, we can double check its solution.

6   Related Work

SAT-Based Backends for B. There are now three SAT based backends for PROB: B2ASP, B2SAT and the Kodkod backend. The Kodkod backend [26] uses the Kodkod library [29] to perform an indirect translation of B to SAT (via the relational logic API of [29]). B2SAT [22] can translate a subset of B directly to SAT, and uses PROB's default solver to expand quantifiers. PROB's default solver is based on constraint logic programming.

- B2ASP and Kodkod use a ahead-of-time translation to SAT, while B2SAT interleaves PROB's default CLP(FD) solver with SAT translation. The default solver can deal with infinite sets, relations and functions, and can expand higher-order aspects before doing the SAT translation. We hope to enable this interleaving also for B2ASP.
- the three backends cannot process the entire B language (no sets of sets, no higher-order relations or functions). B2SAT can deal with those, provided the default solver can eliminate them before the SAT translation.
  The Kodkod backend is currently restricted to binary relations, while B2ASP can deal with arbitrary n-ary relations.
- B2ASP and Kodkod support aggregates such as cardinality and sum. B2SAT only supports certain cardinality constraints at the moment.
- There is an issue with integer overflows in the current Kodkod backend. This means that the current backend is not sound for cardinality constraints or integer membership constraints. Thus far it was not possible to fix these issues, and the backend should only be used if the solution can be double checked by another solver. CLINGO does not require the user to provide bit width annotations for integers and does not produce erroneous results.

Other SAT-Based Tools. The Alloy analyzer [16] uses the Kodkod library [29], and is again a static ahead-of-time translation to SAT. A related approach is IDP-Z3 [24], based on inductive definitions rather than logic programs. IDP-Z3 is a re-implementation of an earlier IDP version [31]. We have used some IDP-Z3 benchmarks above. There were also research [11] to translate first order logic to ASP as backend. The authors noted that "artifacts introduced by the translation" (like auxiliary predicates) led to poor performance. We also noted this here, see earlier discussions about the importance of inlining literals for aggregates. Maybe in future one could apply more powerful optimisations, like partial evaluation [10] to the generated ASP programs. Other related work is Picat [32], making good use of SAT solvers for constraint satisfaction.

7   Conclusion and Future Work

There are parts of the B2ASP translation that can be improved, such as allowing arbitrary nesting of quantifiers, adding further optimisations for special features of CLINGO, and interleaving B2ASP with PROB's default solver. One can extend the precision of the bounds analysis in Sect. 3 to cover more B operators more precisely (the current analysis safely ignores unknown conjuncts for the bounds analysis). Still, the bounds analysis is generic and can be used for other solving backends. This might be particularly interesting for the Z3 translation (whose results in Table 2 are not very good), e.g., to be able to use the bit-vector theory. The principles of the bounds analysis and of the encoding of set theory can also be re-used for processing other languages or tasks.

For arithmetic the B2ASP performance is still quite disappointing. One solution could be the switch to clingcon [4]. Indeed, SAT versus constraint programming is a long-running debate [30].

In summary, we have developed a new approach to solve B formulas with set theoretic constraints. We have used Prolog and logic programming technology all throughout the tool chain, by translating B to ASP and then to SAT and back. For some applications we still have issues with arithmetic constraints and grounding performance of CLINGO, but we have obtained some very good results for some experiments and case studies. While not as fast as B2SAT, it is already more widely applicable to a larger class of formulas.

Acknowledgements. Maxime Zielinger developed first hand-translations of B to ASP, that laid the foundation for the later systematic translation using Prolog rules. He also provided various tips and tricks to improve the translation. We also thank Jan Gruteser, attendees of the Scryer Prolog meetup 2025 and anonymous reviewers for their useful feedback.

References

1. Abrial, J.-R.: The B-Book. Cambridge University Press (1996)
2. Abrial, J.-R.: Modeling in Event-B: System and Software Engineering. Cambridge University Press (2010)
3. Abrial, J.-R., Mussat, L.: On using conditional definitions in formal theories. In: Bert, D., Bowen, J.P., Henson, M.C., Robinson, K. (eds.) ZB 2002. LNCS, vol. 2272, pp. 242–269. Springer, Heidelberg (2002). https://doi.org/10.1007/3-540-45648-1_13
4. Banbara, M., Kaufmann, B., Ostrowski, M., Schaub, T.: Clingcon: the next generation. Theory Pract. Log. Program. **17**(4), 408–461 (2017)

5. Behm, P., Burdy, L., Meynadier, J.: Well defined B. In: Bert, D. (ed.) Proceedings B 1998. LNCS, vol. 1393, pp. 29–45. Springer (1998)

6. Carbonnelle, P., Vandevelde, S., Vennekens, J., Denecker, M.: IDP-Z3: a reasoning engine for FO(.). CoRR, abs/2202.00343 (2022)

7. Carlsson, M., Mildner, P.: SICStus prolog - the first 25 years. Theory Pract. Log. Program. $12(1\text{--}2)$, 35–66 (2012)

8. Carlsson, M., Ottosson, G., Carlson, B.: An open-ended finite domain constraint solver. In: Glaser, H.G., Hartel, P.H., Kuchen, H. (eds.) Proceedings PLILP 1997. LNCS, vol. 1292, pp. 191–206. Springer (1997)

9. ClearSy. Atelier B, User and Reference Manuals. Aix-en-Provence, France (2009). http://www.atelierb.eu/

10. Cuteri, B., Dodaro, C., Ricca, F., Schüller, P.: Partial compilation of ASP programs. Theory Pract. Log. Program. $19(5\text{--}6)$, 857–873 (2019)

11. Dessel, K.V., Devriendt, J., Vennekens, J.: Folasp: Fo($\cdot$) as input language for answer set solvers. Theory Pract. Log. Program. $21(6)$, 785–801 (2021)

12. Dudeney, H.E.: Amusements in Mathematics (1917). https://www.gutenberg.org/ebooks/16713

13. Gebser, M., Kaminski, R., Kaufmann, B., Ostrowski, M., Schaub, T., Wanko, P.: Theory solving made easy with clingo 5. In: Carro, M., King, A., Saeedloei, N., Vos, M.D. (eds.) Technical Communications ICLP 2016. OASIcs, vol. 52, pp. 2:1–2:15. Schloss Dagstuhl - Leibniz-Zentrum für Informatik (2016)

14. Gebser, M., Kaminski, R., Kaufmann, B., Schaub, T.: Multi-shot ASP solving with clingo. Theory Pract. Log. Program. $19(1)$, 27–82 (2019)

15. Gent, I.P., Petrie, K.E., Puget, J.-F.: Symmetry in constraint programming. Found. Artif. Intell. $\mathbf{2}$, 329–376 (2006)

16. Jackson, D.: Alloy: a lightweight object modelling notation. ACM Trans. Softw. Eng. Methodol. $\mathbf{11}$, 256–290 (2002)

17. Krings, S., Leuschel, M.: Proof assisted bounded and unbounded symbolic model checking of software and system models. Sci. Comput. Program. $\mathbf{158}$, 41–63 (2018)

18. Krings, S., Leuschel, M., Körner, P., Hallerstede, S., Hasanagić, M.: Three is a crowd: SAT, SMT and CLP on a chessboard. In: Calimeri, F., Hamlen, K., Leone, N. (eds.) PADL 2018. LNCS, vol. 10702, pp. 63–79. Springer, Cham (2018). https://doi.org/10.1007/978-3-319-73305-0_5

19. Lamport, L.: Specifying Systems, The TLA+ Language and Tools for Hardware and Software Engineers. Addison-Wesley (2002)

20. Leuschel, M.: Fast and effective well-definedness checking. In: Dongol, B., Troubitsyna, E. (eds.) IFM 2020. LNCS, vol. 12546, pp. 63–81. Springer, Cham (2020). https://doi.org/10.1007/978-3-030-63461-2_4

21. Leuschel, M.: ProB: harnessing the power of Prolog to bring formal models and mathematics to life. In: Warren, D.S., Dahl, V., Eiter, T., Hermenegildo, M.V., Kowalski, R., Rossi, F. (eds.) Prolog: The Next 50 Years. LNCS, vol. 13900, pp. 239–247. Springer, Cham (2023)

22. Leuschel, M.: B2SAT: a bare-metal reduction of B to SAT. In: Proceedings FM 2024. LNCS, vol. 14934, pp. 122–139. Springer, Cham (2024)

23. Leuschel, M., Butler, M.J.: ProB: an automated analysis toolset for the B method. STTT $10(2)$, 185–203 (2008)

24. Mikhailov, L., Butler, M.: An approach to combining B and alloy. In: Bert, D., Bowen, J.P., Henson, M.C., Robinson, K. (eds.) ZB 2002. LNCS, vol. 2272, pp. 140–161. Springer, Heidelberg (2002). https://doi.org/10.1007/3-540-45648-1_8

25. Niemelä, I.: Logic programs with stable model semantics as a constraint programming paradigm. Ann. Math. Artif. Intell. $25(3\text{--}4)$, 241–273 (1999)

26. Plagge, D., Leuschel, M.: Validating B,Z and TLA$^+$ using PROB and kodkod. In: Giannakopoulou, D., Méry, D. (eds.) FM 2012. LNCS, vol. 7436, pp. 372–386. Springer, Heidelberg (2012). https://doi.org/10.1007/978-3-642-32759-9_31
27. Schmidt, J., Leuschel, M.: SMT solving for the validation of B and event-b models. Int. J. Softw. Tools Technol. Transf. **24**(6), 1043–1077 (2022)
28. Spivey, J.M.: The Z Notation: a reference manual. Prentice-Hall (1992). https://github.com/Spivoxity/zrm
29. Torlak, E., Jackson, D.: Kodkod: a relational model finder. In: Grumberg, O., Huth, M. (eds.) TACAS 2007. LNCS, vol. 4424, pp. 632–647. Springer, Heidelberg (2007). https://doi.org/10.1007/978-3-540-71209-1_49
30. Walsh, T.: SAT v CSP. In: Dechter, R. (ed.) CP 2000. LNCS, vol. 1894, pp. 441–456. Springer, Heidelberg (2000). https://doi.org/10.1007/3-540-45349-0_32
31. Wittocx, J., Mariën, M., Denecker, M.: Grounding fo and fo(id) with bounds. J. Artif. Intell. Res. (JAIR) **38**, 223–269 (2010)
32. Zhou, N.: Modeling and solving graph synthesis problems using sat-encoded reachability constraints in picat. In: Formisano, A., et al. (eds.) Proceedings ICLP 2021. EPTCS, vol. 345, pp. 165–178 (2021)

REGAL: Extracting Implicit Rules in Text Using LLMs with Logic Program Feedback

Abhiramon Rajasekharan$^{(\boxtimes)}$ and Gopal Gupta

Department of Computer Science, University of Texas at Dallas, Richardson, USA
{axr200004,gupta}@utdallas.edu

Abstract. Solving textual reasoning problems by translating them into logic has proven effective, as it reduces hallucinations and allows the logic solver to handle complex reasoning. However, there is one major challenge that makes this technique difficult to apply to many practical reasoning problems. Arguments presented in text often have implicit rules that are assumed to be part of commonsense knowledge and are therefore omitted. They need to be identified and explicitly added to a logic program for accurate reasoning. This process is typically called *argument reconstruction*. Discovering these implicit logic rules is a challenging problem that previous text-to-logic translation systems struggle with. In this paper, we present a novel system that reconstructs these implicit rules in 3 stages: (i) Translating the problem from text to First Order Logic (FOL), (ii) Translating FOL to an equivalent s(CASP) answer set program that can compute gap predicates (predicates whose derivation requires implicit rules), and (iii) Using an LLM to generate required implicit rules for these gap predicates. We show that our system generates implicit rules to effectively solve reasoning problems drawn from a popular benchmark designed to be challenging for LLMs.

Keywords: Argument Reconstruction · Large Language Models · Answer Set Programming

1 Introduction

Effectively automating logical reasoning can deliver significant benefits in the real world; medical treatment can be safely recommended in hospitals based on a patient's medical history, rulings delivered in courts can be verified to remain faithful to the law, and conversation agents can keep track of users' time conflicts or dietary requirements when scheduling restaurant reservations. Large Language Models (LLMs) are effective for a range of natural language tasks. Models released by companies such as o1 by OpenAI are designed to be better at reasoning benchmarks by producing long chains of thought during inference time [20]. However, reasoning doesn't always improve with scaling test-time compute [28], and the reasoning steps in the chain of thought might not correspond to the true reasoning the model uses [23,25].

N. Amin and J. Arias (Eds.): PADL 2026, LNCS 16401, pp. 161–180, 2026.
https://doi.org/10.1007/978-3-032-15981-6_10

Recent line of research instead relies on the coding proficiency of LLMs to first translate text into logic programs, which can then be executed to compute a solution to reasoning problems [18,22,24]. This method allows LLMs to be used for their strength in translating diverse and potentially ambiguous natural language into structured, human-readable logic programs, thereby leaving the task of logical reasoning to specialized provers that have been specifically developed for this purpose. While this method is effective in a range of reasoning problems, there is a fundamental challenge that limits its applicability in real-world settings. Natural language text often has implicit information in the form of facts or logical rules that need to be extracted and made explicit to obtain a complete logic program. Consider a simple example, let's say we have a rule 1) *every animal can move* and we are given that 2) *John is a fox*. To conclude that *John can move*, we need the implicit premise, 3) *every fox is an animal*.

The field of argument extraction tackles a similar problem. An argument typically has a claim and premises that offer support to the claim. Sometimes, the premise does not directly support the claim, but requires another *implicit premise* that logically connects the premise to the claim. Such an argument with implicit premises is called an enthymeme [5], and the task of identifying and making implicit premises explicit is called *enthymeme reconstruction* or *argument reconstruction*. Prior work in this field typically focus on generating a single implicit premise that connects a given premise-conclusion pair [5,12,32]. In typical reasoning problems, we usually have multiple premises and claims that can have an arbitrary number of implicit rules that connect them. Hence, a framework is needed that is not only able to generate correct implicit rules, but also can identify where these rules are needed.

To bridge this gap, we present our system called REGAL: Reconstructing Enthymemes using Goal-directed Answer Set Programming and Large Language Models. REGAL has three steps (see Fig. 1):

1. **Text to First Order Logic (FOL) translation**: A problem in text is first translated into FOL for two main reasons: (i) LLMs are better at generating FOL as an intermediate langauge for reasoning tasks, compared to other logic-based formalisms [3], (ii) Text-FOL pairs are available as datasets that can be used to train LLM models effective for the translation task [13].
2. **FOL to s(CASP) translation**: To identify where implicit rules are needed, we leverage the goal-directed Answer Set Programming system, s(CASP). Using s(CASP) code expressed in a certain format (see Sect. 3.2), we extract logic predicates that we call *reasoning gap predicates* (or *gap predicates* for short). These are the set of predicates that could not be derived using the premises given in the problem, indicating that implicit rules might be needed. We provide an algorithm to convert FOL code into s(CASP) in the explained format while preserving its models.
3. **Implicit rule generation**: Using the gap predicates, we use an LLM to generate implicit rules needed to complete the logic program.

We compare the implicit rules generated by REGAL against rules generated by a baseline LLM model that is prompted using a comparable prompt that

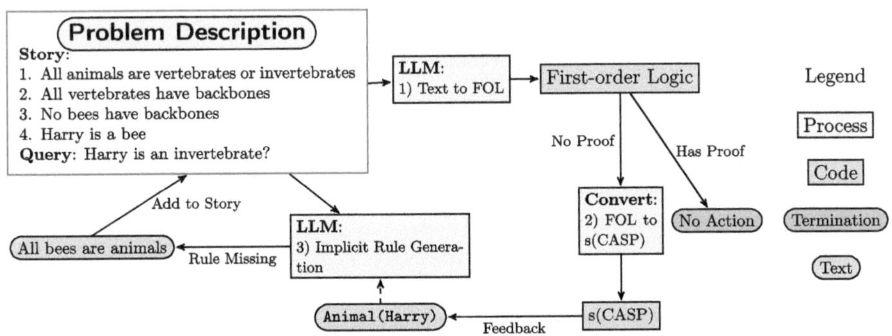

Fig. 1. This figure shows all three steps of the REGAL framework using an example adapted from the FOLIO dataset [13]. Step 1) Text is translated into FOL, Step 2) FOL is translated into s(CASP) and executed to find the gap predicate, `animal(harry)`. Step 3) The implicit rule 'All bees are animals' is generated and added to the story.

doesn't use gap predicates. We show that our method performs better on a reasoning benchmark, BoardgameQA [14], that is designed to test LLMs on their ability to reason with incomplete information.

2   Background

First Order Logic: First Order Logic (FOL) allows us to represent English text as logical expressions. An FOL formula comprises of predicates and logic symbols that connect them. For example, the predicate, `StudentAt(Mary, Stanford)` holds the value True if Mary is a student at Stanford and False if not. The arguments, `Mary` and `Stanford`, are called terms. We adopt the standard logic symbols $(\wedge, \vee, \neg, \exists, \forall, \rightarrow, \oplus)$. We use Prover9 [17] to execute FOL formulae in this paper for proving theorems in FOL (explained in more detail in Sect. 4.1).

s(CASP): The s(CASP) system, developed by Arias *et al.* [1], is an Answer Set Programming (ASP) framework [4] that extends the traditional ASP paradigm by supporting predicates, constraints over non-ground variables, and uninterpreted functions. A key feature of s(CASP) is its top-down, query-driven execution model. This design allows s(CASP) to produce answers containing non-ground variables, potentially subject to constraints, and to compute only the relevant portion of a stable model needed to justify the query result. Unlike Prolog's negation-as-failure or the default negation in traditional ASP, a query such as `not p(X)` in s(CASP) can return bindings for `X` that make `p(X)` fail.

Commonsense knowledge can be effectively represented and queried in ASP through the predicate-based, query-driven framework provided by s(CASP) [8, 11,29]. Such representations typically rely on (i) *default rules*, (ii) *integrity constraints*, and (iii) *multiple possible worlds* [8,11]. Default rules encode general assumptions along with their exceptions. This enables an elaboration-tolerant form of reasoning that accommodates exceptions naturally [8].

The s(CASP) system is a great candidate to extract gap predicates for the following reasons. (i) Since it can model multiple worlds, we can simulate all possible models in the original FOL program, and (ii) Being goal-directed, it allows us to execute a query and look at the trace to identify the predicates that could not be derived, leading to no models. Finding these predicates is fundamental to the REGAL framework (see Sect. 3).

3   Methodology

In this section, we describe the three main steps (components) of REGAL. The complete system is described in Fig. 1.

3.1   Step 1: Text to FOL Translation

In this step, we focus on the direct translation of text to logic programs, setting aside the challenge of identifying the implicit rules for later. LLMs have a difficult time generating code, especially for logic languages as they appear less frequently in their pre-training data [16,18,22]. Some common syntax errors we observe are mismatched brackets in the formulae, and characters and symbols in the formulae that are incompatible with the logic programming solver used.

Incorrect Symbol Use. While the program might be syntactically correct, symbols might be incorrectly replaced for each other, leading to semantic errors. For example, symbols $\vee$ (disjunction) and $\oplus$ (exclusive disjunction) tend to be incorrectly replaced for each other since they are close in meaning. Sometimes, brackets might be balanced but incorrectly placed, which changes the meaning of the sentence.

Predicate Mismatch: Another challenge for the model is coming up with the right set of predicates to use. The same concept can be written in many ways using different predicates. For example, the sentence 'john' went to the third Avengers movie' can be encoded using predicates as (i) `WentToThirdAvengersMovie(John)`, (ii) `WentToMovie(John, Avengers)`, or (iii) `WentTo(John, movie)`. The choice of which predicate representation the model uses depends on the structure of reasoning present in the story. For example, the story might be: 'John went either to the third Avengers movie or a mall yesterday. If John goes to a movie, he does not shop. Suppose the query is 'Did John shop yesterday?', the representation (iii) above is sufficient since the details of which movie he went to are irrelevant. Hence, depending on the story, the LLM learns what concepts to pay attention to and what to ignore. Since this is a tough task, the model sometimes omits useful information or uses different predicate names for the same concept (predicate mismatch).

The *predicate names and terms in the program must match*. If the story encoded the fact using `WentTo(John, movie)` and the rule uses `GoesTo(John, movie)`, the predicates will not match, and the program will not execute correctly. This error occurs frequently in LLM-generated logic programs.

Also, the *ordering of terms* changes the meaning of the predicate. For example, the sentence 'If a person has a pet, they care for that pet.' can be translated using the predicates, `Pet(y)`, `OwnedBy(x,y)`, and `Cares(x, y)`. If, instead, `OwnedBy(y,x)` is generated, then the order of terms in the arguments of predicate 'OwnedBy' changes the program's meaning.

Finetuning a Text to FOL Model (T2FOL): To mitigate these syntax and semantic errors, previous methods apply majority voting or correction based on the compiler's error message as feedback [18,22]. These methods are not very effective, especially in dealing with semantic errors. Instead, we **fine-tune** an LLM with text-FOL data to expose the model to a wide range of variations, thereby significantly reducing errors. The dataset we use for finetuning is the training set of FOLIO [13]. Folio has complex and diverse logical reasoning problems in English, which are paired with their FOL translations. Compared to datasets such as MALLS [30] that have FOL translations of individual sentences, FOLIO has FOL translations for complete problems. This makes it a better resource to train LLMs as it enables them to learn mapping similar concepts to the same predicates, which is a crucial requirement for correct FOL programs. We refer to the finetuned model as T2FOL. The prompt used to finetune this model is given in Appendix A.1.

3.2   Step 2: Extracting Gap Predicates Using s(CASP)

The first half of the challenge in generating an implicit rule is identifying where it might be needed. We use the goal-directed Answer Set Programming system, s(CASP), to aid with this task. The FOL code generated for the problem is transformed into a s(CASP) program. Executing the s(CASP) program, we obtain an interpretable execution trace. This trace is then used to identify a predicate for the reasoning gap. We explain these steps in further detail below:

FOL to s(CASP) Translation. We present a method to translate First Order Logic code to s(CASP) while preserving its models. The format of the s(CASP) program needs to be suitable for extracting gap predicates. This translation task is non-trivial as the semantics of ASP are quite different from those of FOL. Similar to prior work [2], we translate FOL expressions into s(CASP) code via Conjunctive Normal Form (CNF). Given each clause in the CNF, we first transform it into an ASP constraint combined with even loops for each predicate. The even loops simulate negation, similar to FOL, for each predicate. For example, suppose we have the literals L_1, L_2, and L_3. Let $-L_i$ be the negation of an arbitrary literal L_i. We can then represent the clause, $-L_1 \lor L_2 \lor -L_3$ as the constraint,

```
1   :- L₁, -L₂, L3.
```

Let P_1, P_2 and P_3 be the predicates corresponding to L_1, L_2 and L_3. Below are the even loops introduced to create the possible worlds for every predicate, simulating all possible models in FOL.

```
1   -P_1 :- not P_1.
2    P_1 :- not -P_1.
3
4   -P_2 :- not P_2.
5    P_2 :- not -P_2.
6
7   -P_3 :- not P_3.
8    P_3 :- not -P_3.
```

Using the even loops and constraints for each clause, we can effectively reproduce the same models that hold True for the initial FOL expression. Any existential quantifiers in FOL are translated into Skolem constants in the ASP formulation. We make a minor change to the constraint representation in order to allow s(CASP) to extract gap predicates. We transform each constraint into a set of rules where each literal is negated and placed as the head of the rule. For example, the previous constraint becomes the following set of rules,

```
1   -L_1 :- -L_2, L_3.
2    L_2 :-  L_1, L_3.
3   -L_3 :- -L_2, L_1.
```

Having rules in this form allows us to leverage s(CASP)'s goal-directed execution to identify predicates where the execution halts.

Gap Predicate Extraction. Part of a s(CASP) program after translation is given below as an example:

```
1    ...
2    % All animals with backbones reproduce by male-and-female mating.
3    reproduceby(X, maleandfemalemating) :- animal(X), backbone(X).
4    -backbone(X) :- animal(X), -reproduceby(X, maleandfemalemating).
5    -animal(X) :- backbone(X), -reproduceby(X, maleandfemalemating).
6    % All bees do not reproduce by male-and-female mating.
7    -reproduceby(X, maleandfemalemating) :- bee(X).
8    -bee(X) :- reproduceby(X, maleandfemalemating).
9    % All queen bees are bees.
10   bee(X) :- queenbee(X).
11   -queenbee(X) :- -bee(X).
12   % Harry is a bee.
13   bee(harry).
14   q :- -queenbee(harry).
15   ?- q.
```

Executing this query in s(CASP) gives us the program trace shown below:

```
1    % QUERY:?- q.
2    (0) q
3    (1) -queenbee(harry)
4    (2) -bee(harry)
5    (3) reproduceby(harry,maleandfemalemating)
```

```
6  (4) animal(harry)
7   FAIL
```

The code execution fails because the rules provide information that Harry is a bee, but it is not explicitly given anywhere that Harry is an animal. This predicate is hence unknown and is needed to apply the remaining rules. Thus, *animal(harry)* is correctly extracted as a reasoning gap predicate.

In practice, we can identify all gap predicates efficiently in one go instead of one at a time. This can be done by adding the gap predicate as a potential fact to the FOL and re-executing Step 2 to find new gap predicates. This process can be repeated until the s(CASP) code finds answer sets and no more gap predicates are found. All of these gap predicates can be provided as feedback to LLM to generate implicit rules, as explained in the next part (Sect. 3.3).

3.3   Step 3: Generating Implicit Rules

In this step, we provide an LLM with the original problem as well as the gap predicates identified in Step 2 to generate implicit rules. The implicit rules we aim to generate are English statements that fill the missing logical connections in the problem.

Not all gap predicates extracted are due to missing implicit rules. It is possible that the predicate identified is not a fact supported by the story. In that case, we do not need to identify implicit rules for the predicate. We leave the burden to distinguish between such cases to the LLM, which can utilize its general knowledge to identify when a gap predicate is relevant and can use an implicit rule that helps derive it from the story. The prompt used for this task is given in Appendix A.2. To predict an answer for a given problem, we can add the implicit English rules generated to the premises given in the problem and regenerate FOL (using the model T2FOL described in Step 1). The new FOL code can then be used to make a prediction. Further details are presented in Sect. 4.1.

4   Experiments

4.1   Implementation Details

In this section, we describe the implementation details of the experiments.

Large Language Models. We use a GPT-4.1 mini model [21] to generate implicit premises for both REGAL and its baseline. We fine-tune a GPT-4o model [19] to generate FOL code using sentence-FOL pairs for each problem. The hyperparameters we used are 3 epochs, batch size 1, LR multiplier 2, and seed 948603966. The number of training tokens used for fine-tuning is 104661.

FOL Solver. We use Prover9 [17] to execute the generated FOL code. Since the generated FOL code does not use the same notation as Prover9, we implemented a parser in Python that converts each FOL formula into a parse tree. The parse trees of all the formulae are then put together as a Prover9 program.

Each problem in BoardgameQA and Folio has a set of premises and a conclusion. We need to determine if the conclusion in the problem is True, False, or Uncertain, given the premises. We arrive at this answer using the following approach. We prepare two FOL programs, one for the positive query and one for the negative query (positive query, but the goal is negated). An example from the FOLIO dataset [13] is given below:

```
1   assign(max_given, 30).
2   formulas(assumptions).
3   bornin(Ailtonsilva, Yr1995).
4   (footballplayer(Ailtonsilva) &
5           loanedoutto(Ailtonsilva, Braga)).
6   (brazilian(Ailtonsilva) &
7           footballplayer(Ailtonsilva) &
8           playsfor(Ailtonsilva, Nautico)).
9   (footballclub(Nautico) & footballclub(Braga)).
10  footballclub(Fluminense).
11  end_of_list.
12
13  formulas(goals).
14  -((exists x ((footballclub(x) &
15          loanedoutto(Ailtonsilva, x)))))).
16  end_of_list.
```

We execute both queries: let PQ be the positive query and NQ be the negative query. Let the function $S(P)$ be True if program P has a proof and False if there is no proof. The following algorithm is used to determine if the prediction is True, False, or Uncertain:

Listing 1.1. Computing FOL program prediction

```
1   def get_logic_program_prediction(PQ, NQ, S):
2       if S(PQ) == True and S(NQ) == False:
3           return 'True'
4       elif S(PQ) == False and S(NQ) == True:
5           return 'False'
6       else:
7           return 'Uncertain'
```

4.2 Datasets

We use two datasets in this paper: FOLIO [13] and BoardgameQA [14]. FOLIO has complex logical reasoning problems, accompanied by the First Order Logic translations of each sentence. All the information required is typically given for each problem. However, we notice that a few problems have missing implicit rules. On the other hand, BoardgameQA is specifically designed for reasoning using commonsense knowledge, making it a challenging benchmark and a suitable test set for our framework.

FOLIO. The dataset has around 480 stories, each of which describes a certain World [13]. There are a total of 1001 problems in the training set and 203 problems in the test set written around these 480 stories. Each problem has a group of premises, a conclusion, and a label that holds a value of True, False, or Uncertain. The label is True if the conclusion follows from the premises, False if the conclusion can never be True given the premises, or Uncertain if the information is not sufficient to conclude whether or not the conclusion follows from the premises. Each premise and conclusion sentence is accompanied by its First-Order Logic (FOL) form that captures its meaning. The dataset is prepared such that multiple reasoning steps are required to solve each problem, making it a challenging test bed for LLMs. Numerous problems contain complex sentences and their FOL translations (often more complex than individual sentences in BoardgameQA). Hence, the training set of FOLIO is well-suited to fine-tune the T2FOL model.

BoardgameQA. This dataset is constructed to test LLM's ability to reason under implicit and potentially contradictory information [14]. Each problem has a given set of facts, rules, and preferences that describe the priority with which the rules should be applied. A goal is given in the problem, and the task is to answer whether the goal is 'Proved', 'Disproved', or 'Unknown' according to the information given in the problem. These labels are similar to 'True', 'False', and 'Uncertain' in FOLIO (we use 'True', 'False', and 'Uncertain' for both datasets in our experiments for uniformity). The problems are divided into categories based on their reasoning depth, general knowledge requirement (to identify implicit rules), and conflicts. Since our evaluation is based on implicit reasoning, we select only *zero-conflict* category problems, as handling rule conflicts is not the focus of our experiments. This gives us a test set of 100 logical reasoning problems.

4.3   Experimental Setup

Our goal is to evaluate REGAL for its ability to generate implicit premises. We choose to measure the quality of the implicit rules based on their ability to help solve the given problem. Hence, we compare the answer prediction accuracy for the problems in the test set with and without adding the implicit rules generated by our model.

In addition, we also want to establish the benefit of using gap predicates as feedback, compared to directly generating implicit rules without them. To do this in a fair setting, we compare REGAL against a baseline LLM model that is directly prompted to generate implicit rules for the problems. The prompt used by the baseline (given in Appendix A.3) is equivalent to the prompt used by REGAL to generate implicit rules, except, we do not provide gap predicates to this model. Our hypothesis is that REGAL provides a way to extract these crucial gap predicates that allow LLMs to generate implicit rules effectively.

Since the generated implicit rules are in English, we add the rules to the problem's premises and regenerate FOL code that can be executed to compute predictions for the problems (described in Sect. 4.1). The baselines and experiment steps are described below:

- We first generate FOL code for the problem using the T2FOL model (from Sect. 3.1) and compute a prediction *without* adding any implicit rules. We refer to this baseline method simply as **T2FOL-NoRules**.
- Next, we generate implicit rules using an LLM (without using gap predicates). We add these rules to the original set of premises and re-generate FOL code for the problem. The FOL code is then executed to obtain an answer prediction for the problem. We refer to this baseline, **T2FOL-Direct**, for 'direct prediction'.
- Finally, we generate implicit rules using REGAL and add it to the original premises and re-generate FOL code to compute answer predictions. We refer to this method **T2FOL-Regal**.

4.4   Results and Analysis

The answer prediction accuracy results for the three methods are presented in Table 1.

Table 1. Accuracy Metrics: Regal vs Direct (on BoardgameQA - ZeroConflicts). We compare the total accuracy, as well as the accuracy specific to individual class labels. A higher number indicates better predictions in all columns.

Method	Total Accuracy	Per-Class Accuracy		
		True	False	Uncertain
T2FOL-NoRules	0.511	0.355	0.290	0.900
T2FOL-Direct	0.480	0.387	0.065	0.633
T2FOL-Regal	0.576	0.677	0.258	0.800

Regal has an increased accuracy in answer prediction of around 9.6% on the test set compared to the Direct baseline and 6.5% compared to NoRules. This shows that the information gap predicates provide helps in improving the implicit rules generated. Below are examples of some implicit rules generated by REGAL that helped predict the correct answer, along with the corresponding gap predicates.

```
1  Problem 7/100
2  Fact given: The finch is watching a movie from 1993.
```

```
3  Rule given: Regarding the finch, if it is watching a movie that was
       released before Shaquille O'Neal retired, then we can conclude
       that it neglects the dolphin.
4
5  Gap predicate: releasedbefore(movie,yr2011)
6  Regal implicit rule: If a movie was released in 1993, then it was
       released before the year 2011
```

```
1  Problem 10/100
2  Fact given: The badger has 4 friends, and has a 20 × 14 inches notebook
       .
3  Rules given:
4      1) The badger will take over the emperor of the shark if it has a
       notebook that fits in a 10.9 × 10.9 inches box. And,
5      2) This is a basic rule: if the badger takes over the emperor of
       the shark, then the conclusion that "the shark hugs the flamingo"
       follows immediately and effectively.
6
7  Gap predicate: -hugs(shark,flamingo)
8  Regal implicit rule: A notebook that measures 20 × 14 inches does not
       fit into a box that measures 10.9 × 10.9 inches
```

Interestingly, we also see that Direct implicit rule generation actually drops below the performance of NoRules. This falls in line with research findings that direct feedback from LLMs cannot be fully relied on [9]. Instead, integrating useful feedback from tools such as REGAL can help LLMs bridge the reasoning gap.

5   Related Works

Chain-of-thought reasoning [27] showed that prompting LLM to generate a sequence of reasoning steps before generating the final answer helps it establish a higher accuracy on reasoning datasets. Inspired by this idea, researchers have developed methods to allow LLMs to explore different reasoning chains before trying to answer a question [26,31]. However, the reasoning steps do not always correspond to the final answer generated by the model [23,25]. This implies that a chain of thought doesn't necessarily expose the true reasoning process of the model.

In a different direction, recent research uses LLMs to generate domain-specific programs that are used to solve reasoning tasks. This is typically applied to tasks that require precision, such as mathematics, reasoning, or planning [7, 15]. This framework allows the LLMs to interpret the potentially ambiguous problem descriptions (which are typically at a higher level of abstraction) and generate human-readable code that can accurately solve the problem at hand. However, the generation of programs from text using an LLM tends to be an error-prone process. The errors that are present in the generated programs should be fixed. A related direction explored to solve this problem uses LLMs to debug the generated code. The debugging might either use prompting an LLM [6], or also incorporate feedback from an external source [9]. Such program generation and debugging have also been employed for logical reasoning tasks [16,18,22]. Instead, we observe that simply fine-tuning LLMs on Text-to-FOL data reduced these errors. Also, these methods are not designed to capture implicit rules in the logic programs generated [18,22]. In this paper, we propose an effective way to identify and generate these rules.

Previous work in the field of argumentation tackle a similar problem. An argument has premises and claims. Premises provide reasons that together support a given claim. Often arguments might have premises that are not given (*implicit*), which are needed to correctly entail a claim. Such arguments with implicit premises are called enthymemes. A similar argument structure that is seen in literature is according to Toulmin's theory, which introduces the terms: reason, claim, and *warrant*. Warrants in this theory are the implicit premises that connect reasons to a claim. Prior work mostly focuses on generating implicit premises that connect a given premise-claim pair [5,12,32]. Unlike these works, we focus on a more commonly seen setting of generating implicit premises for a complete argument that has multiple premises and claims. The challenge here is not only to generate the implicit premise that correctly connects given premises to claims, but also identifying where an implicit premise might be needed. Gupta *et al.* (2024) [10] tackle the task of argument explication, which is most similar to ours, but they rely purely on a prompt-based approach. Instead, we leverage logic programs' ability to handle reasoning to identify the gap predicates where an implicit premise might be needed.

6   Conclusion

In this paper, we present a novel method to generate implicit rules present in logical reasoning problems effectively. Our method has three steps: 1) Translating a problem in English text to First Order Logic (FOL), 2) Converting FOL to a s(CASP) program to extract missing predicates, which we call *reasoning gap predicates*, and 3) Generating implicit rules using the extracted gap predicates.

For Step 1, we explain the main problems in text-to-logic translation and how fine-tuning helps overcome this challenge. In Step 2, we present a way to translate FOL code into a s(CASP) program that preserves its models. We show how a logic constraint in the program can be rewritten into multiple rules, enabling the discovery of gap predicates. In Step 3, we explain the implementation of implicit rule generation using the discovered gap predicates.

We present the experimental setup, where we compare REGAL against two baseline methods. Using the logical reasoning dataset, BoardgameQA, we evaluate the quality of implicit rules generated using answer prediction accuracy as the metric. The baseline, *NoRules*, is used to compute the answer prediction quality without any implicit rules added. Another baseline *Direct* is added as an ablation to evaluate the impact of gap predicates for implicit rule generation. Comparing REGAL against NoRules and Direct, we show an improvement in answer prediction accuracy and how meaningful rules are discovered by REGAL .

Though our method is effective in finding implicit rules, there are some limitations. We rely on LLMs to distinguish between the cases where a gap predicate can and cannot be derived using information in the problem. But LLMs can sometimes still hallucinate and miss implicit rules or add incorrect ones. We only experiment with FOL as the intermediate language for answer prediction. Other logic programs, especially ASP, can be used instead, albeit with more prompt engineering or data collection for finetuning a text-to-logic translation model. Future work can aim to expand the set of logic programs used.

Acknowledgment. We are grateful to Joaquín Arias of Universidad Rey Juan Carlos, Madrid, Spain, for help with the s(CASP) system. Authors have been partially supported by NSF grant IIS 1910131 and industry grants through the Center for Applied AI and Machine Learning.

A   Prompt Details

A.1   Prompt for Text to FOL Translation

```
 1  # Instructions
 2  Given a story (group of sentences in English), translate each sentence
        to first order logic (FOL) that captures its meaning accurately.
 3  Allowed symbols for first order logic (FOL):
 4  ∧ (conjunction)
 5  ∨ (disjunction)
 6  ¬ (negation)
 7  ∀ (universal quantifier)
 8  ∃ (existential quantifier)
 9  ⇒ (implication)
10  ⟺ (bi-implication)
11  ⊕ (exclusive disjunction)
12  = (equal)
13  Output Format:
14  For each sentence, print out each English sentence followed by '% '.
        In the next line, print out its translation in First Order Logic
15
16  # Gudelines
17  Follow these translation guidelines strictly:
18  * Avoid nested predicates.
19  * Make sure that the a) predicate names, b) terms and c) predicate
        arity are the same across FOL rules for all sentences.
20  * Follow these translation ideas for relevant sentences:
21      * Sentences of the form 'A is B' can be written using ⇒ as
        ∀x(A(x) ⇒ B(x)).
22      * Different types of an object may be represented using ⊕, such
        as '∀x(Time(x) ⇒ Day(x) ⊕ Night(x))'
```

Below is an example input-output pair used for fine-tuning the LLM.

T2FOL Input Example

```
1 William Dickinson was a British politician who sat in the House of
      Commons
2 William Dickinson attended Westminster school for high school and then
      the University of Edinburgh.
3 The University of Edinburgh is a university located in the United
      Kingdom.
4 William Dickinson supported the Portland Whigs.
5 People who supported the Portland Whigs did not get a seat in the
      Parliament.
6 William Dickinson did not get a seat in Parliament.
```

T2FOL Output Example

```
1  % William Dickinson was a British politician who sat in the House of
       Commons
2  British(williamDickinson) ∧ Politician(williamDickinson) ∧ SatIn(
       williamDickinson, houseOfCommons)
3  % William Dickinson attended Westminster school for high school and
       then the University of Edinburgh.
4  Attended(williamDickinson, westminsterSchool) ∧ Highschool(
       westminsterSchool) ∧ Attended(williamDickinson,
       universityOfEdinburgh)
5  % The University of Edinburgh is a university located in the United
       Kingdom.
6  University(universityOfEdinburgh) ∧ LocatedIn(universityOfEdinburgh,
       unitedKingdom)
7  % William Dickinson supported the Portland Whigs.
8  Supported(williamDickinson, portlandWhigs)
9  % People who supported the Portland Whigs did not get a seat in the
       Parliament.
10 ∀x (Supported(x, portlandWhigs) ⇒ ¬SatIn(x, parliament))
11 % William Dickinson did not get a seat in Parliament.
12  ¬SatIn(williamDickinson, parliament)
```

A.2   Prompt for Regal Implicit Rule Generation

System Prompt

```
1 ***INSTRUCTIONS***
2 You are a logician and general knowledge expert. You are given a
      logical reasoning problem which has premises and a potential
      conclusion. You are also given logic predicates corresponding to
      the problem that could not be derived from the premises. We call
      them gap predicates.
3 A logic predicate is a statement that is either True or False. A
      predicate has a predicate name and a number of terms in the form '
      predicate_name(term1, term2, ...)'. The prefix {ASP_NEG} before
      any predicate name indicates that the predicate is NEGATED.
```

We were not able to derive the gap predicates since some world
knowledge is missing. Your task is to identify what general
knowledge statements (facts or rules) are missing that would be
needed to derive the given logic predicates.

CRITICAL REQUIREMENT: GENERAL KNOWLEDGE ONLY
You must ONLY generate general knowledge statements (facts or rules)
that require world knowledge, NOT problem-specific rules. The
statements should be:
- Commonsense knowledge or world knowledge that most people would know
- Helpful in deriving the given gap predicates from the premises

WHAT NOT TO GENERATE
DO NOT generate general knowledge statements (facts or rules) that:
- Something that can be derived from the given premises
- Only related to the premises and does not add new world knowledge to
the problem

OUTPUT FORMAT
Return a JSON with the following format:
- The JSON must have a top-level field called "missing_rules"
- Inside "missing_rules", provide an array of English logical rules
that express the missing essential general knowledge needed to
derive the given gap predicates and the potential conclusion.
- Each rule should be a clear, well-formed English logical statement
- Keep responses succinct and focused only on the essential logical
rules required.
- Only provide the missing general knowledge rules. Don't add any
additional rules that are not adding new information to the
problem.
- Make sure all the rules added are CORRECT according to commonsense.
- If no additional rules are needed, return an empty array

Examples:

Example 1 (GOOD - General Knowledge):
Input:
Logic Predicates:
[animal(tweety), fly(tweety)]
The problem's premises are given below:
All animals can breathe.
All birds can fly.
Tweety is a pigeon.
The problem's potential conclusion is given below:
Tweety can fly and breathe.

Output:
```json
```

```
43 {"missing_rules": ["All pigeons are birds", "All birds are animals"]}
44 ```
45
46 Example 2 (GOOD - General Knowledge):
47 Input:
48 Logic Predicates:
49 [is_metal(material)]
50 The problem's premises are given below:
51 All metals conduct electricity.
52 The wire is made of copper.
53 The problem's potential conclusion is given below:
54 The wire conducts electricity.
55
56 Output:
57 ```json
58 {"missing_rules": ["If something is made of copper, then it is a metal
       "]}
59 ```
```

User Prompt

```
1 The problem's premises are given below:
2 {premises}
3 The problem's potential conclusion is given below:
4 {conclusion}
5
6 Gap Predicates (logic predicates that could not be derived from the
       premises):
7 {logic_predicates}
```

A.3   Prompt for Direct Implicit Rule Generation

System Prompt

```
1 ***INSTRUCTIONS***
2 You are a logician and general knowledge expert. You are given a
       logical reasoning problem which has premises and a potential
       conclusion. Your task is to identify what general knowledge
       statements (facts or rules) are missing that would be needed to
       derive the potential conclusion from the premises.
3
4 We were not able to derive the potential conclusion since some world
       knowledge is missing. Your task is to identify what general
       knowledge statements (facts or rules) are missing that would be
       needed to derive the potential conclusion from the premises.
5
6 ***CRITICAL REQUIREMENT: GENERAL KNOWLEDGE ONLY***
```

7 You must ONLY generate general knowledge statements (facts or rules)
      that require world knowledge, NOT problem-specific rules. The
      statements should be:
8 - Commonsense knowledge or world knowledge that most people would know
9 - Helpful in deriving the potential conclusion from the premises
10
11 ***WHAT NOT TO GENERATE***
12 DO NOT generate general knowledge statements (facts or rules) that:
13 - Something that can be derived from the given premises
14 - Only related to the premises and does not add new world knowledge to
      the problem
15 - Create new problem-specific relationships
16
17 ***OUTPUT FORMAT***
18 Return a JSON with the following format:
19 - The JSON must have a top-level field called "missing_rules"
20 - Inside "missing_rules", provide an array of English logical rules
      that express the missing essential general knowledge needed to
      derive the potential conclusion from the premises.
21 - Each rule should be a clear, well-formed English logical statement
22 - Keep responses succinct and focused only on the essential logical
      rules required. Don't add rules that can be derived from other
      rules.
23 - Only provide the missing general knowledge rules. Don't add any
      additional rules that are not adding new information to the
      problem.
24 - Make sure all the rules added are CORRECT according to commonsense.
25 - If no additional rules are needed, return an empty array
26
27 ***Examples:***
28
29 Example 1 (GOOD - General Knowledge):
30 Input:
31 The problem's premises are given below:
32 All animals can breathe.
33 All birds can fly.
34 Tweety is a pigeon.
35 The problem's potential conclusion is given below:
36 Tweety can fly and breathe.
37
38 Output:
39 ```json
40 {"missing_rules": ["All pigeons are birds", "All birds are animals"]}
41 ```
42
43 Example 2 (GOOD - General Knowledge):
44 Input:
45 The problem's premises are given below:
46 All metals conduct electricity.
47 The wire is made of copper.

```
48 The problem's potential conclusion is given below:
49 The wire conducts electricity.
50
51 Output:
52 ```json
53 {"missing_rules": ["If something is made of copper, then it is a metal
      "]}
54 ```
```

User Prompt

```
1 The problem's premises are given below:
2 {premises}
3 The problem's potential conclusion is given below:
4 {conclusion}
5
6 Please identify what implicit rules (general knowledge) are missing
      that would be needed to derive the potential conclusion from the
      premises.
```

References

1. Arias, J., Carro, M., Salazar, E., Marple, K., Gupta, G.: Constraint answer set programming without grounding. TPLP **18**(3–4), 337–354 (2018). https://doi.org/10.1017/S1471068418000285
2. Baral, C.: Knowledge Representation, Reasoning and Declarative Problem Solving. Cambridge University Press (2003)
3. Beiser, A., Penz, D., Musliu, N.: Intermediate languages matter: formal choice drives neurosymbolic LLM reasoning (2025). https://arxiv.org/abs/2502.17216
4. Brewka, G., Eiter, T., Truszczynski, M.: Answer set programming at a glance. Commun. ACM **54**, 92–103 (2011). https://doi.org/10.1145/2043174.2043195
5. Chakrabarty, T., Trivedi, A., Muresan, S.: Implicit premise generation with discourse-aware commonsense knowledge models. In: Moens, M.F., Huang, X., Specia, L., Yih, S.W.T. (eds.) Proceedings of the 2021 Conference on Empirical Methods in Natural Language Processing, pp. 6247–6252. Association for Computational Linguistics, Online and Punta Cana, Dominican Republic (2021). https://doi.org/10.18653/v1/2021.emnlp-main.504. https://aclanthology.org/2021.emnlp-main.504/
6. Chen, X., Lin, M., Schärli, N., Zhou, D.: Teaching large language models to self-debug. arXiv abs/2304.05128 (2023). https://api.semanticscholar.org/CorpusID:258059885
7. Gao, L., et al.: PAL: program-aided language models. In: Krause, A., Brunskill, E., Cho, K., Engelhardt, B., Sabato, S., Scarlett, J. (eds.) Proceedings of the 40th International Conference on Machine Learning. Proceedings of Machine Learning Research, vol. 202, pp. 10764–10799. PMLR (2023). https://proceedings.mlr.press/v202/gao23f.html
8. Gelfond, M., Kahl, Y.: Knowledge Representation, Reasoning, and the Design of Intelligent Agents: Answer Set Programming Approach. Cambridge University Press (2014). https://doi.org/10.1017/CBO9781139342124

9. Gou, Z., et al.: Critic: large language models can self-correct with tool-interactive critiquing. arXiv abs/2305.11738 (2023). https://api.semanticscholar.org/CorpusID:258823123
10. Gupta, A., Zuckerman, E., O'Connor, B.: Harnessing toulmin's theory for zero-shot argument explication. In: Ku, L.W., Martins, A., Srikumar, V. (eds.) Proceedings of the 62nd Annual Meeting of the Association for Computational Linguistics (Volume 1: Long Papers), pp. 10259–10276. Association for Computational Linguistics, Bangkok, Thailand (2024). https://doi.org/10.18653/v1/2024.acl-long.552. https://aclanthology.org/2024.acl-long.552/
11. Gupta, G.: Automating common sense reasoning with ASP and s(CASP) (2022). Technical Report. https://utdallas.edu/~gupta/csr-scasp.pdf
12. Habernal, I., Wachsmuth, H., Gurevych, I., Stein, B.: The argument reasoning comprehension task: Identification and reconstruction of implicit warrants. In: Walker, M., Ji, H., Stent, A. (eds.) Proceedings of the 2018 Conference of the North American Chapter of the Association for Computational Linguistics: Human Language Technologies, Volume 1 (Long Papers), pp. 1930–1940. Association for Computational Linguistics, New Orleans, Louisiana (2018). https://doi.org/10.18653/v1/N18-1175. https://aclanthology.org/N18-1175/
13. Han, S., et al.: Folio: natural language reasoning with first-order logic (2024). https://arxiv.org/abs/2209.00840
14. Kazemi, M., et al.: Boardgameqa: a dataset for natural language reasoning with contradictory information (2023). https://arxiv.org/abs/2306.07934
15. Liu, B., et al.: LLM+P: empowering large language models with optimal planning proficiency. arXiv abs/2304.11477 (2023). https://api.semanticscholar.org/CorpusID:258298051
16. Lyu, Q., et al.: Faithful chain-of-thought reasoning. In: Park, J.C., et al. (eds.) Proceedings of the 13th International Joint Conference on Natural Language Processing and the 3rd Conference of the Asia-Pacific Chapter of the Association for Computational Linguistics (Volume 1: Long Papers), pp. 305–329. Association for Computational Linguistics, Nusa Dua, Bali (2023). https://doi.org/10.18653/v1/2023.ijcnlp-main.20. https://aclanthology.org/2023.ijcnlp-main.20/
17. McCune, W.: Prover9 and mace4 (2005–2010). http://www.cs.unm.edu/~mccune/prover9/
18. Olausson, T., et al.: LINC: a neurosymbolic approach for logical reasoning by combining language models with first-order logic provers. In: Bouamor, H., Pino, J., Bali, K. (eds.) Proceedings of the 2023 Conference on Empirical Methods in Natural Language Processing, pp. 5153–5176. Association for Computational Linguistics, Singapore (2023). https://doi.org/10.18653/v1/2023.emnlp-main.313. https://aclanthology.org/2023.emnlp-main.313/
19. OpenAI: Gpt-4o model (2024). https://platform.openai.com/docs/models/gpt-4o
20. OpenAI: Learning to reason with LLMs (2024). chrome-extension://efaidnbmnnnibpcajpcglclefindmkaj/https://cdn.openai.com/o1-system-card.pdf
21. OpenAI: Gpt-4.1 mini model (2025). https://platform.openai.com/docs/models/gpt-4.1
22. Pan, L., Albalak, A., Wang, X., Wang, W.: Logic-LM: empowering large language models with symbolic solvers for faithful logical reasoning. In: Bouamor, H., Pino, J., Bali, K. (eds.) Findings of the Association for Computational Linguistics: EMNLP 2023. Association for Computational Linguistics, Singapore (2023). https://doi.org/10.18653/v1/2023.findings-emnlp.248. https://aclanthology.org/2023.findings-emnlp.248/

23. Paul, D., West, R., Bosselut, A., Faltings, B.: Making reasoning matter: measuring and improving faithfulness of chain-of-thought reasoning. In: Al-Onaizan, Y., Bansal, M., Chen, Y.N. (eds.) Findings of the Association for Computational Linguistics: EMNLP 2024, pp. 15012–15032. Association for Computational Linguistics, Miami, Florida, USA (2024). https://doi.org/10.18653/v1/2024.findings-emnlp.882. https://aclanthology.org/2024.findings-emnlp.882/
24. Sun, H., et al.: Determlr: augmenting LLM-based logical reasoning from indeterminacy to determinacy, pp. 9828–9862 (2024). https://doi.org/10.18653/v1/2024.acl-long.531
25. Turpin, M., Michael, J., Perez, E., Bowman, S.R.: Language models don't always say what they think: unfaithful explanations in chain-of-thought prompting. In: Proceedings of the 37th International Conference on Neural Information Processing Systems, NIPS 2023. Curran Associates Inc., Red Hook (2023)
26. Wang, X., Wei, J., Schuurmans, D., Le, Q., Chi, E.H., Zhou, D.: Self-consistency improves chain of thought reasoning in language models. arXiv abs/2203.11171 (2022). https://api.semanticscholar.org/CorpusID:247595263
27. Wei, J., et al.: Chain of thought prompting elicits reasoning in large language models. arXiv abs/2201.11903 (2022). https://api.semanticscholar.org/CorpusID:246411621
28. Wu, G.: It's not that simple. An analysis of simple test-time scaling (2025). https://arxiv.org/abs/2507.14419
29. Xu, Z., Arias, J., et al: Jury-trial story construction and analysis using goal-directed answer set programming. In: Proceedings of PADL. LNCS, vol. 13880, pp. 261–278. Springer, Cham (2023). https://doi.org/10.1007/978-3-031-24841-2_17
30. Yang, Y., Xiong, S., Payani, A., Shareghi, E., Fekri, F.: Harnessing the power of large language models for natural language to first-order logic translation. In: Ku, L.W., Martins, A., Srikumar, V. (eds.) Proceedings of the 62nd Annual Meeting of the Association for Computational Linguistics (Volume 1: Long Papers), pp. 6942–6959. Association for Computational Linguistics, Bangkok, Thailand (2024). https://doi.org/10.18653/v1/2024.acl-long.375. https://aclanthology.org/2024.acl-long.375/
31. Yao, S., et al.: Tree of thoughts: deliberate problem solving with large language models. In: Proceedings of the 37th International Conference on Neural Information Processing Systems, NIPS 2023. Curran Associates Inc., Red Hook (2023)
32. Zhao, W., Chiu, J., Cardie, C., Rush, A.: Abductive commonsense reasoning exploiting mutually exclusive explanations. In: Rogers, A., Boyd-Graber, J., Okazaki, N. (eds.) Proceedings of the 61st Annual Meeting of the Association for Computational Linguistics (Volume 1: Long Papers), pp. 14883–14896. Association for Computational Linguistics, Toronto, Canada (2023). https://doi.org/10.18653/v1/2023.acl-long.831. https://aclanthology.org/2023.acl-long.831/

Declarative Debugging for Modern Networks

Anduo Wang[1(✉)] and Matthew Caesar[2]

[1] Temple University, Philadelphia, PA, USA
anduo.wang@gmail.com
[2] University of Illinois Urbana-Champaign, Champaign, IL, USA
caesar@illinois.edu
https://anduowang.github.io/

Abstract. Network troubleshooting today relies largely on ticket systems, which log, record, replay, and analyze live events, while overlooking recent advances in SDNs, programmable networks, and verified data centers, all of which have produced a rich body of models and control software. We argue instead that this modern network software—including abstract models and system code—provides a vantage point for troubleshooting, enabled by a debugger that, when things go bump in the night, allows someone who neither wrote the software nor is familiar with the DSL or verification tools to pinpoint the exact culprit line— a stepping stone for systematically diagnosing the underlying network. As a first step toward this vision, we present a declarative debugging schema for modern network software amid its rapid evolution: the user only needs to answer "yes/no" questions about the software's intended behavior, leaving procedural inspection and bug localization entirely to the debugger; meanwhile, new language features—arisen with emerging applications—are seamlessly supported through a novel use of partial evaluation, which automatically incorporates these features into the declarative debugging process.

Keywords: Network troubleshooting · Algorithmic debugging · Partial evaluation · Declarative networking

1 Introduction

Modern networks have outgrown our tools for debugging them: a proliferation of network Domain Specific Languages (DSLs) in Software-Defined Networks (SDNs) and programmable networks have been developed, along with lightning-fast verification tools in hyper-scale data centers, yet troubleshooting [5,12,15,16,21,32,42] still mainly depends on ticket systems. These systems log, record, replay, and analyze live events, largely overlooking newly accumulated "software"— namely, abstract models and system software. We see this not only as a limitation but also as a missed opportunity. Is it possible to directly

N. Amin and J. Arias (Eds.): PADL 2026, LNCS 16401, pp. 181–198, 2026.
https://doi.org/10.1007/978-3-032-15981-6_11

pinpoint a faulty line in the control software? Can we leverage abstract models, especially executable ones already present in verification tools, to locate the root cause of faults at fine granularity in the control logic, shedding light on the operational network?

One might be tempted to trace the root cause within a model using the verification tool itself: it employs techniques akin to those of a debugger—such as static and dynamic analysis—and many verification tools generate counterexamples when checks fail, providing a natural starting point for debugging. However, verification focuses on exhaustively and efficiently checking predefined properties under specific assumptions or constraints, whereas debugging emphasizes usability. It must support programmers—no two alike—and diverse symptoms—often unexpected. The completeness of verification—a multitude of uninteresting counterexamples can cancel the real issue—can render debugging cumbersome. Additionally, performance optimizations—such as meticulously crafted internal representations—can make it harder to relate back to the source model. In general, debugging with a verification tool requires the user to connect the dots: the onus falls on them to refactor a troubleshooting task into a sequence of checkable properties that fit within the constraints of the tool, relying heavily on their insights into both the network and the tool's internal workings (Sect. 2.1).

On the other hand, network DSLs present new challenges. Unlike standardized general-purpose programming languages, network DSLs are typically extensions of a base—often a general-purpose—language, with features that continually evolve to keep pace with emerging applications. For instance, *network datalog* [27,28] adapts datalog for distributed computation of network protocols by introducing a specialized data type augmented with a location specifier @ in order to generate efficient query plan. *Network optimized datalog* [10,29] is specifically designed for scalable verification by incorporating a more compact packet representation and an accelerated packet manipulation implementation into Z3 Datalog. Although these optimization-oriented features often do not impede debugging with existing methods, this is not always true. *Fauré-log* [24], also an extension of datalog, supports partial network modeling—such as forwarding with arbitrary link failures—by introducing a `condition` construct. The new `condition` abstracts away the complexity of conditional reasoning from the programmer but embeds it into the language itself, altering the standard semantics and evaluation of Datalog, and thereby requiring an understanding of its implementation for effective debugging. The very language feature that simplifies programming can complicate debugging (Sect. 2.2).

In response to these opportunities and challenges, we argue that the software accumulated in the control plane and verification tools offers a valuable vantage point for troubleshooting—if, *when things go bump in the night, someone who wasn't involved in writing the software and isn't familiar with the DSL or verification tools can still pinpoint the exact culprit line in the software to guide diagnosis.*

As a first step to achieve this, we propose declarative debugging for network models and control software, designed to evolve with the underlying languages and their features. Inspired by declarative debugging—a provably correct framework originally developed for Prolog [33] and widely adopted across major programming paradigms [4,7]—we illustrate how essential network troubleshooting can be transformed. In this approach, the user need to answer only "yes/no" questions about the network state, leaving the procedural inspection and bug localization entirely to the debugger. Moreover, we develop a novel application of partial evaluation [3,19,26] to effectively integrate new language features into debugging as they emerge. This enables the process to adapt gracefully to ad-hoc language extensions. While partial evaluation is typically used to optimize programs by removing costly features, our innovation applies it to eliminate language features that hinder debugging. We implement both the declarative debugger and partial evaluation using Prolog meta-programming, evaluating them on a rule-based network DSL called `vanilla` with *fauré-log*-like extensions for partial modeling. The `vanilla` language allows us to focus on the core challenges of network troubleshooting in DSLs, but our approach is not limited to this tentative language; rather, it is broadly applicable thanks to the generality of declarative debugging and partial evaluation. We also discuss the limitations of declarative debugging in network troubleshooting, particularly due to its distributed nature, along with a potential remedy through program slicing.

2   Motivation

This section makes the case for declarative debugging for evolving network DSLs, illustrated through two concrete cases that also serve as running examples in Sect. 4 and Sect. 5.

2.1   Need for Debugging Beyond Verification

We use the Batfish verification tool to illustrate the need for a dedicated debugger. Batfish [11] is a static network verification tool that provides built-in troubleshooting support. An example troubleshooting scenario (simplified) is shown in Fig. 1: Network N in the center interconnects a customer network C and a provider P, while controlling access to its internal subnet 1.2.3.4/24, which is reachable only by the customer (C). To block traffic from P, n_3 is configured to drop the packets to 1.2.3.4/24. To enable connectivity with C, n_1 and n_2 are configured with flow entries that forward traffic from C (e.g., c_2) to 1.2.3.4/24. The problem is that n_1 is configured with multipath routing by default: as n_1 sends packets from c_2 to 1.2.3.4/24 through both neighbors n_2 and n_3, so c_2 experiences intermittent connectivity. Batfish facilitates root cause analysis of such multipath inconsistency by building a comprehensive model of the network, including flow entries and the protocols that generate them—a knowledge base generated as a by-product during its verification with datalog—which can be iteratively queried.

Batfish knowledge base makes it easier to compare the network's states against the intended values, sparing the user from re-running the entire network.

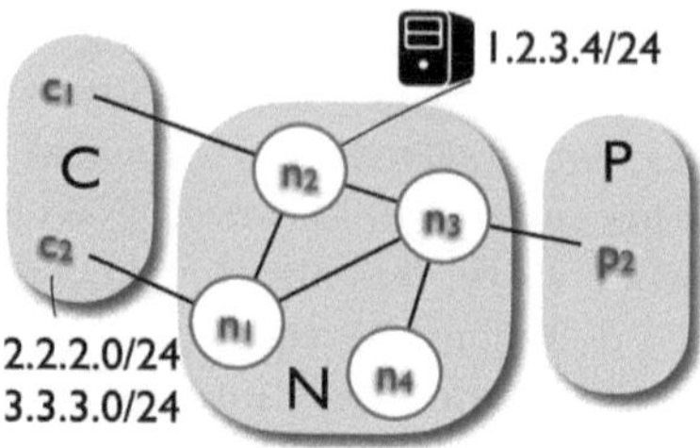

Fig. 1. troubleshooting multipath inconsistency of N.

This contrasts with traditional "echo (print) debugging", where the programmer must iteratively insert print statements into key parts of the source code and re-run the program to observe the values of relevant variables. Nevertheless, Batfish still falls under the "tracer"-style of debugging [8,34]—the burden of identifying which parts to inspect still rests entirely on the user, relying on their insights into the operational semantics of the object program (Batfish knowledge base). Note that even this primitive form of debugging support was lost when Batfish implementation transitioned from datalog to Java, where performance was prioritized over debugging capability [2].

Objective: We seek a more usable debugger, one that requires the user to provide only the intended meaning of the network, while delegating all procedural comparisons with the network implementation—including what to inspect, in what order, and under what scenarios—to the debugger itself (Sect. 4).

2.2 Challenge from Evolving DSL

We use the *fauré-log* DSL to illustrate the challenge from evolving language features in debugging. *Fauré-log* [24] is an extension of datalog that makes network modeling with partial information—such as forwarding under link failures—particularly simple. It enhances the Horn clause (rule) $A : -B_1, \cdots , B_n$ by adding an explicit condition C, resulting in a *fauré-log* clause of the form $A :- B_1, \cdots , B_n, [C]$, meaning that the head A is true when the conjunction of the body B_i is true under the condition C. As an example use of *fauré-log*, consider the access control (ACLs) configurations in the presence of link failure in Fig. 2 (a), inspired by Cisco fast rerouting [20]. The backup links $1 - 3$ and $2 - 4$ (dashed) are used only when the primary links $1 - 2$ and $2 - 3$ (bold) fail. Two access control lists (ACLs)—`acl1` and `acl2`, each permitting only a subset of packets—are consistently configured on the primary and backup links so that only packets allowed by both ACLs can reach 4 under any link failure. Fully specifying this network—the combined effects of the ACLs and all possible link failure scenarios—requires only five *fauré-log* rules: each forwarding arrow (both solid and dashed) corresponds to exactly one *fauré-log* rule.

```
n2(S,D) :- n1(S,D), acl1(D), ['X12=1']. % forwarding from n1
    to n1 when the primary link (1-2) is up
```

```
2   n3(S,D) :- n1(S,D), acl1(D), ['X12=0']. % forwarding from n1
        to n3 when the primary link (1-2) fails
```

Listing 1.1. Specifying the access control configuration under link failures in *fauré-log*

Listing 1.1 shows the *fauré-log* rules for the two forwarding arrows $(1->2$ and $1->3)$: ni(S, D) says a packet header (S, D) is admitted at ni, acl1(D) matches destinations in the first access control list, and X12 is a so-called c-variable [24] that encodes the link state of $1-2$—allowing concise modeling of forwarding with link failures. Programming with *fauré-log* is simple because the interactions of link failures and ACLs are hidden from the programmer and handled entirely by the *fauré-log* evaluator, which modifies standard datalog evaluation and integrates it with satisfiability checking of conditions. But precisely because of this, debugging becomes harder. Consider the buggy configurations in Fig. 2(b, c): acl1 is missed from the backup link $1-3$ in (b), while the misplacement of acl2 on $2-3$ (instead of $3-4$) in (c) is subtler—the error remains latent until the seemingly unrelated primary link $1-2$ fails. To troubleshoot such bugs, especially that in (c) that involves specific combination of link states and ACLs, debugging techniques for Horn clauses alone are no longer sufficient—debugging now requires a proper understanding of how the new *fauré-log* conditions are evaluated!

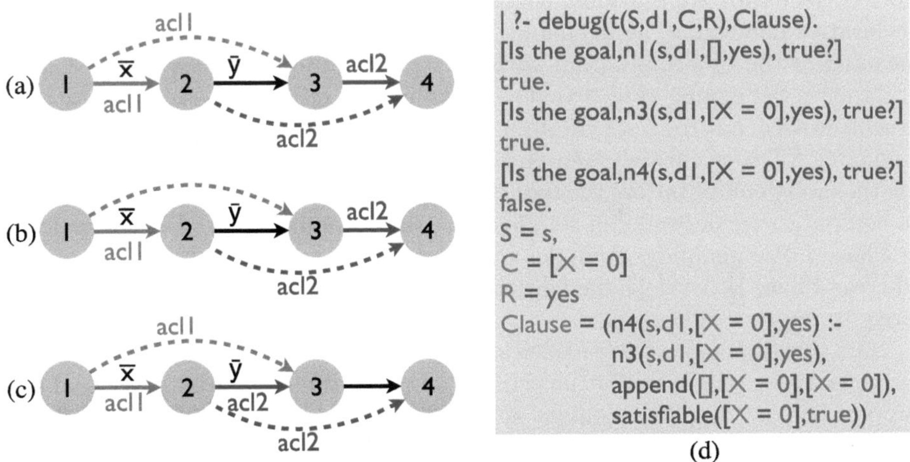

Fig. 2. (a) correct configuration, (b/c) two buggy configurations, (d) a declarative debugging session for (c).

Objective: We seek a more reusable debugger, one that remains effective as new language features are added on the fly, allowing users to enjoy the ease of programming with these features without worrying about—during debugging—their implementation logic, which is (ideally automatically) imbued into the debugger itself (Sect. 5).

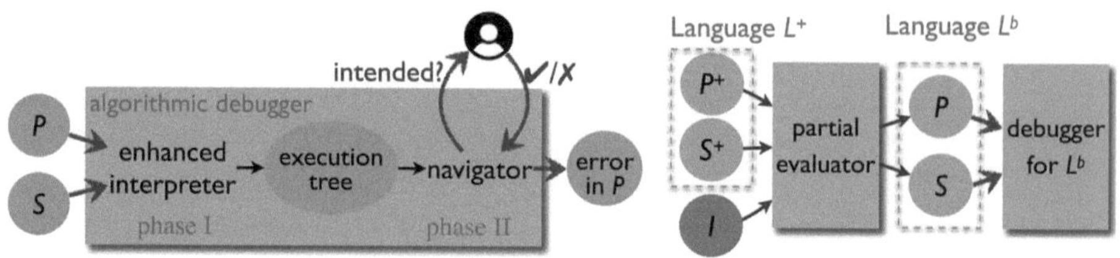

Fig. 3. (left) classic declarative debugging, (right) reusing declarative debugging amid the ongoing proliferation of network DSLs.

3   Approach

Given a network program written in some language—such as a modeling language of a verification tool or an SDN DSL—we propose a network troubleshooting method by adopting algorithmic debugging [4,33] in combination with partial evaluation [8,19]. Algorithmic debugging asks an oracle (typically the programmer) questions like "Is y a correct output for (a sub) procedure p on input x", while automatically comparing the program's intended behavior as obtained from the oracle with the real computation, in order to locate the precise culprit line. A computation is deemed the culprit if it has produced an erroneous result from correct subcomputations. Algorithmic debugging is more widely known as declarative debugging, as it enables the user to concentrate on the declarative meaning of the object program without manual procedural inspection. Classic declarative debugging (Fig. 3 (left)) works in two phases: Phase I generates an execution tree ET from a symptom S—an unintended output—while Phase II navigates ET to accurately pinpoint the error. ET is a data structure representing the faulty computation: the root corresponds to S and each intermediate node (a computation) depends on its children (sub-computations). ET construction in Phase I often employs compiler instrumentation or interpreter enhancement, whereas Phase II develops navigation strategies and questions of varying granularity to improve efficiency.

The new dimension we consider in network DSLs is the multitude of new language features, which exhibit no signs of stopping their evolution. Our goal is to support the ongoing development of new features without having to rebuild the debugger for each one. Our key insight and assumption is that the logic responsible for handling these new features can be *automatically* extracted from their implementation and refactored into debugging through partial evaluation [37] (Fig. 3 (right)): When the new features of L^+ are interpreted (or implemented) in a base language L^b by an interpreter program I written in L^b, we partially evaluate I with respect to an object program P^+. This process produces a specialized interpreter [13] tailored exclusively to P^+—effectively a program that behaves like P^+ but without the L^+ features—thereby yielding an equivalent L_b program, denoted by P. (S^+ is transformed into S in L^b similarly.) Debugging P^+ for S^+ now reduces to debugging P for S, thereby allowing use to reuse the L^b debugger for L^+ features.

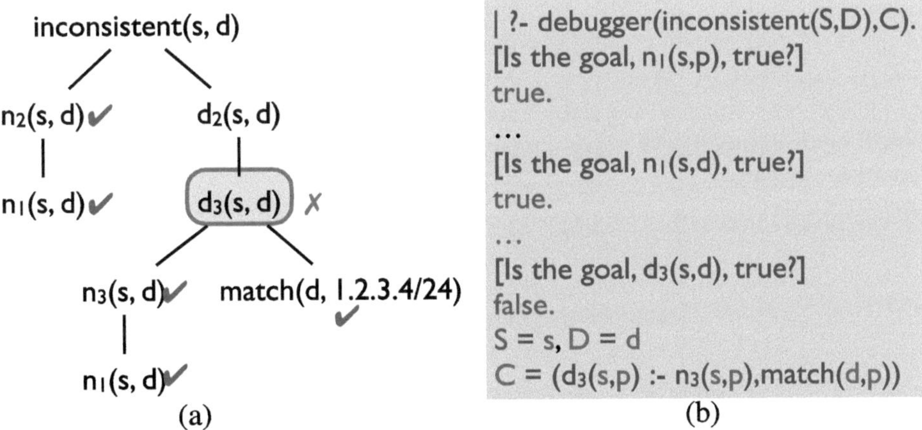

Fig. 4. (a) the execution tree, (b) debugging session with repeated question concerning n1.

We present a proof-of-concept prototype that uses Prolog [23, 25, 37] as both the implementation language for the classic debugger and as the base language. Prolog is a powerful meta-programming tool, wherein both data and programs are Prolog terms, making it particularly easy to develop the debugger (as enhanced meta-interpreters) and the partial evaluator (through program transformations). Our object network DSL is a minimal rule-based DSL: it is as expressive as standard Horn clauses, making it suitable for modeling essential network behaviors (Sect. 2.1). The rule-based syntax is also convenient to extend for handling link failures (Sect. 2.2). Our design and selection of a tentative language—rather than opting for a general-purpose language (e.g., Prolog or Java) or existing DSLs (e.g., Pyretic [31] or P4 [1])—enables us to concentrate on enhancing the usability and reusability of the debugger. By steering clear of the complexities inherent in more established languages, we achieve a more streamlined base debugger (Sect. 4) and a more principled approach to incorporating new language features (Sect. 5).

4   Declarative Debugging

This section develops a classic declarative debugger for a language called `vanilla`, and shows its effectiveness in troubleshooting multipath inconsistency.

4.1   A Vanilla Declarative Debugger

Our network language, called `vanilla`, is minimal and features one single construct: rules of the form `rule(Head, Body, Name)`, it is essentially the Horn clause `Head : −Body`, augmented with a rule name `Name`. In the `Body`, conjunctions is denoted by the infix operator `&`, applied to individual goals that are placed inside the postfix operator `is_true`. By implementing `vanilla` rules as a Prolog term (Listing 1.2), they are processed more explicitly and cleanly (the equivalent Horn clauses are accessed in Prolog at runtime via the extra-logical `clause` predicate that complicates debugging). Extending `vanilla` is also straightforward, enabling us to evaluate our partial evaluation method for debugging new language features.

```
1  rule(inconsistent(S,D), n1(S,D) is_true & d1(S,D) is_true,
       con1). % equivalent to inconsistent(S,D) :- f1(S,D),
       d1(S,D).}. Similar rules con2,con3 omitted
2  rule(n2(S,D), n1(S,D) is_true, fw12). % fw13,fw32 omitted
3  rule(d3(S,D), n3(S,D) is_true & match(D,p) is_true, drop3).
4  rule(d2(S,D), d3(S,D) is_true, drop23). % drop12, drop13
       omitted
5  rule(n1(s,d), empty, source1).
6  rule(match(d,p), empty, eq).
```

Listing 1.2. A `vanilla` program for the Batfish example in Fig. 1

Listing 1.2 gives a (simplified) `vanilla` program for the network in Fig. 1: Line 1 states that inconsistent forwarding for packets (from source S to D) is detected if they are both forwarded and dropped at the same node, n1. Similarly, rules (con2, con3) capture inconsistency at node n2, n3. Line 2 (`fw12`) encodes forwarding from n1 to n2 (`fw13` and `fw31` do likewise for other node pairs). Line 4 encodes the propagation of missing packets (`di`) from node i, similar to forwarding, if they are otherwise reachable. Line 3 encodes the packet filter for destination p implemented by n3, such that packets to p arriving at n3 (denoted by n3) will be dropped (d3). The last two rules (`source1` and `eq`), with empty bodies, are facts—where the heads are trivially true—indicating that packets to some prefix d matching the filter condition are injected at n1.

```
1  debugger(A, Clause) :- solve_pt(A,Proof),
       locate_clause(Proof, Clause).
2  % solve_pt(Goal, ET), Goal is computed with the execution
       tree ET
3  solve_pt(empty, true). % matching facts
4  % matching bodies (single, or multiple)
5  solve_pt(A is_true, Proof) :- solve_pt(A, Proof).
6  solve_pt((A is_true & B), (ProofA, ProofB)) :- solve_pt(A,
       ProofA), solve_pt(B, ProofB).
7  % matching rules
8  solve_pt(A, (A :- Proof)) :- rule(A, B, Name), solve_pt(B,
       Proof).
```

Listing 1.3. A `vanilla` debugger (fragment)

Implementing the classic declarative debugger [4,33] for `vanilla` is straightforward (Listing 1.3): The top procedure `debugger/2` takes as input a symptom A and identifies a faulty clause `Clause` in the `vanilla` program defined by `rule/3`. The key part is `solve_pt`, an enhanced interpreter that "runs" the input symptom `A`, and generates the execution tree `Proof`—note that it resembles the 3-line Prolog meta-interpreter known in folklore [17], but has a cleaner structure that processes rules in a more uniform manner due to the rule design of `vanilla`.

4.2   User Experiences and Effectiveness

Figure 1 (left) shows the execution tree corresponding to the buggy computation for `inconsistent(s, d)`, where the computation node is labeled according to the user's answers during the debugging session (right). The location of the bug— the faulty rule $C = (d3(s, d) : -n3(s, d), match(d, p))$—is flagged by the debugger because it corresponds to a node that produces incorrect results from otherwise correct ones (i.e. all of its children are correct). The usability of our debugger can be further enhanced by improving the quality of questions [4]—for example, by reducing their number, avoiding repetition, allowing users to skip difficult ones, and grouping semantically related questions. Listing 1.4 shows an enhancement that eliminates repeated questions (Fig. 4(b)): it modifies `query_goal/2` by introducing `known/2` that records user answers during the debugging session, leveraging Prolog's extra-logical predicate `assert`, which dynamically updates the debugger state.

```
1  % old_query_goal(Goal, Answer) :- writeln(['Is the goal',
       Goal, 'true?']), read(Answer).
2  query_goal(Goal, Answer) :- known(Goal, Answer).
3  query_goal(Goal, Answer) :- not known(Goal, Answer),
       writeln(['Is the goal', Goal, 'true?']), read(Answer),
       assert(known(Goal, Answer)).
```

Listing 1.4. Two enhancements for question quality

5   Future-Proof to Evolving DSL

This section introduces a novel technique for reusing our debugger with new language features by automatically integrating them into the execution tree via partial evaluation. Specifically, we extend the `vanilla` debugger (Sect. 4) for new language features to enable declaratively diagnosis of networks in the presence of link failures.

5.1   Background: Link Failures and *fauré-log* Extensions

The new language features we address is inspired by *fauré-log* [24] which is briefly reviewed in the following. *Fauré-log* is a datalog-like language that supports conditional tables (i.e. c-tables), a structure that makes it particularly convenient to model and analyze networks under arbitrary link failures. A c-table allows variables to occur in the table entries and introduces an additional column of conditions over the variables. The idea is to use the variables to denote information with proper attributes but currently unknown, and to use the conditions to characterize legitimate information. To see the strength of c-tables, consider the fast rerouting configuration employed by Cisco to combat link failures [20] (Fig. 5): The nodes $1, 2, 3, 4, 5$ are abstract addressable routing/forwarding entities, the bold arrows between the nodes show the primary links that we want to protect, and the dashed arrows are backup links that will be used as a detour when failure occurs. The many possible forwarding behaviors, due to arbitrary failures, can be described in a single c-table once and for all. As shown in the c-table F (Table 1): the schema F(node, node) says packets arrived at the first node are to be forwarded to the second; the three c-variables $\bar{x}, \bar{y}, \bar{z} \in \{0, 1\}$ denote the state of the four protected links—0 means the link fails while 1 means normal.

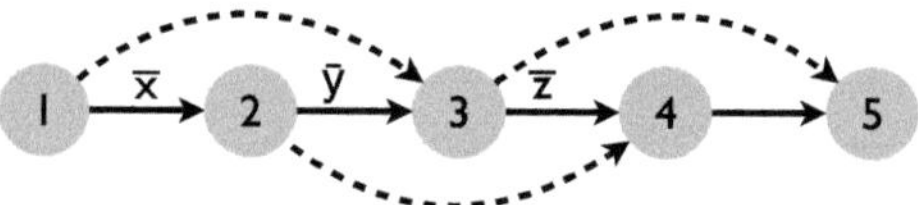

Fig. 5. Fast rerouting under link failures: protected links encoded by $(\bar{x}, \bar{y}, \bar{z})$.

Table 1. F represents for all (possible) forwarding behaviors; R represents reachability under combinations of failures.

F	node	node		R	source	dest	
1	2	$\bar{x} = 1$		1	2	$\bar{x} = 1$	
1	3	$\bar{x} = 0$				$\cdots$	
2	3	$\bar{y} = 1$		1	5	$\bar{x} = 1 \wedge \bar{y} = 1 \wedge \bar{z} = 1$	
2	4	$\bar{y} = 0$		1	5	$\bar{x} = 0 \wedge \bar{z} = 1$	
	$\cdots$			1	5	$\bar{x} = 0 \wedge \bar{z} = 0$	
				1	5	$\bar{x} = 1 \wedge \bar{y} = 0$	
				2	3	$\bar{y} = 1$	
						$\cdots$	

A significant property of c-tables is their completeness: the answers to a query over a c-table can always be represented by another c-table [18]. Such queries can be implemented by a straightforward extension to SQL. For example, joining two c-tables T_1 and T_2 can be obtained by concatenating every tuple $t_1 \in T_1$ and $t_2 \in T_2$ and associating it with $\varphi_1 \wedge \varphi_2 \wedge \varphi(t_1, t_2)$ where φ_1 (φ_2) is the condition associated with t_1 (t_2), and $\varphi(t_1, t_2)$ is a condition that states the equality between join attributes in t_1 and t_2. *Fauré-log* incorporates similar c-table semantics into datalog. Rules q_1, q_2 in Listing 1.5 gives a recursive program that takes F as input and computes the reachability R shown in Table 1. Formally, a *fauré-log* query q^F over c-tables with schema $\mathbf{R^F}$ are a finite collection of rules of the form:

$$H(u)[(\wedge_{i=1}^n \varphi_i) \wedge (\wedge_{i=1}^m C_i)] : -B_1(u_1)[\varphi_1], \cdots , B_n(u_n)[\varphi_n], C_1, \cdots , C_m.$$

where B_i's are relations in $\mathbf{R^F}$; the u, u_i's are tuples that contain both regular variables and symbols (constants or c-variables), φ_i's are the conditions associated with B_i's, and C_i's are explicit comparisons (i.e. $=, !=, <, >$ etc.). *Fauré-log* carefully mediates between two types of variables: the regular variables in *fauré-log* (denoted by usual $x, y, z, \cdots$) are processed by the usual datalog unification; c-variables representing unknown values in the c-tables, on the other hand (denoted by $\bar{x}, \bar{y}, \cdots$), are treated as constants during unification but as variables when checking the satisfiability of conditions. The introduction of c-variables makes it particularly easy to query networks under failures. Rules q_3, q_4, and q_5 in Listing 1.5 illustrate intuitive characterizations of link failure patterns as conditions over the c-variables.

```
1  % reachability as recursive query
2  q₁: R(f,n₁,n₂)[φ]  :- F(f,n₁,n₂)[φ].
3  q₂: R(f,n₁,n₂)[φ_F ∧ φ_R]  :- F(f,n₁,n₃)[φ_F], R(f,n₃,n₂)[φ_R].
4  % examples of failure patterns
5  q₃: T₁(f,n₁,n₂)[φ ∧ x̄ + ȳ + z̄=1 ]  :- R(f,n₁,n₂)[φ], x̄ + ȳ + z̄=1.
     % reachability under 2-link failure
6  q₄: T₂(f,2,5)[φ ∧ ȳ = 0]  :- T₁(f,2,5)[φ], ȳ=0. % reachability
     between 2 and 5 under 2-link failure, one of the failure
     must be (2,3)
7  q₅: T₃(f,1,n₂)[φ ∧ ȳ + z̄<2]  :- R(f,1,n₂)[φ], ȳ + z̄<2. %
     reachability to 1 with at least 1-link failure
```

Listing 1.5. *Fauré-log* offers intuitive and flexible reachability analysis under failures for free

5.2 Partially Evaluating vanilla⁺

We now show how to gracefully adapt algorithmic debugging to support *fauré-log* semantics. To simplify the discussion, but without loss of generality, we use vanilla⁺—an extension of vanilla that incorporates a subset of *fauré-log* features—as a working example to illustrate our partial evaluation method. In vanilla⁺, the vanilla rule/3 predicate is extended to rule(Head, Body , Condition, Name) where the new Condition field is a list of equations and inequalities over c-variables ranging over integers. The meaning of a vanilla⁺ rule is that the Head is computed from the Body only when the conjunction of equations and inequalities in the Condition field holds true. Listing 1.6 provides examples that intuitively capture network behavior under link failures (Sect. 2.2): Line 1 states that if packets can reach 1, and the primary link $1 - 2$ is up, then they can be inferred to reach 2. Line 2 states that packets move from 1 to 3 when the primary link fails, provided that they also match the ACL list p2. Line 3 presents a more interesting use of `Condition`: it defines a query (named `test`) that asks which packets can reach 4 when exactly one link fails ($X12 + X23 = 1$).

```
1  rule(n2(S,D), n1(S,D) is_true, ['X12=1'], fw12).
2  rule(n3(S,D), n1(S,D) is_true & acl(D,p2) is_true, ['X12=0'],
      fw13).
3  rule(q(S,D), n4(S,D) is_true, ['X12+X23=1'], test).
```

Listing 1.6. vanilla+ rules modeling reachability with link failures

Interpreting the new vanilla+ features requires satisfiability reasoning over the `Condition` field and its proper integration in rule processing. For example, Listing 1.7, lines 2–3, shows rule processing enhanced with condition manipulation for a goal `A` that matches the head of a vanilla+ rule solve(A, Condition, Result): when `A` has an answer, `yes` is returned along with the additional `Condition` under which the answer holds. Unlike the vanilla interpreter in Listing 1.3 (line 8), it has two cases due to the additional condition manipulation using `satisfiable/2`, which returns `yes` (or `no`, respectively) depending on whether a list of equations and inequalities is satisfiable or not. Here, rule processing and condition manipulation are intertwined: only when an answer is found for the body, will the condition of the rule be jointly considered for satisfiability (line 3).

```
1   % (fragment) an enhanced interpreter, matching rules
2   solve(A,bottom,no) :- rule(A,B,C,Name),
        solve_body(B,bottom,no).
3   solve(A,CA,R) :- rule(A,B,C,Name), solve_body(B,CB,yes),
        append(C,CB,CA), satisfiable(CA,R).
4   % controlling partial evaluation with fold/unfold
5   should_unfold(rule(H, B, C, N)).
6   should_unfold(solve_body(G, C, R)).
7   should_fold(solve(n1(A,B),C,R), n1(A,B,C,R)).
8   should_fold(solve(n2(A,B),C,R), n2(A,B,C,R)).
9   % specializing the interpreter for rule(n2(S,D), n1(S,D)
        is_true, ['X12=1'], fw12).
10  n2(X,Y,Z,yes) :-
        n1(X,Y,U,yes),append(['X12=1'],U,Z),satisfiable(Z,yes).
11  n2(X,Y,Z,no) :-
        n1(X,Y,U,yes),append(['X12=1'],U,Z),satisfiable(Z,no).
12  n2(X,Y,Z,no) :- n1(X,Y,U,no),append(['X12=1'],U,Z).
```

Listing 1.7. Partially evaluating vanilla+ interpreter with respect to program in Listing 1.6

Partial evaluation is a controlled sequence of fold/unfold transformations, originally introduced in functional programming [3,6]. Intuitively, unfold replaces a procedural call by its definition (body), while fold is the reverse that replaces an instance of a procedure by a call to it. For example, in partially evaluating the interpreter for line 1 of Listing 1.6: `rule` is unfold meaning that the interpreter is now specialized for (instantiated to) line 1. Similarly, `solve_body` is pre-processed by replacing the call with its procedural body (not shown). On the other hand, the `should_fold` (line 7) folds the procedure $n1(A, B, C, R) : - solve(n1(A, B), C, R)$. Fold pushes the arguments carried by the interpreter when evaluating the $vanilla^+$ rule—the interpreter finds R as an answer to $n1(A, B)$ under the condition C—down into an equivalent Prolog program that no longer contains any $vanilla^+$ constructs, which is shown in Listing 1.6 (the last three lines). Note that the resulting Prolog program explicitly encodes the link state semantics buried in the $vanilla^+$ rule (line 1). More generally, specializing the $vanilla^+$ interpreter for a specific $vanilla^+$ program involves recursively applying `fold`/`unfold` transformations until no further progress can be made, provided that the appropriate set of `fold`/`unfold` definitions is given.

5.3   Debugging with Link Failures

We have implemented a declarative debugging toolkit of $vanilla^+$ with XSB [43]. It contains a $vanilla^+$ interpreter, a generic partial evaluator, and a few facilities: the $vanilla^+$ interpreter uses a satisfiability reasoning module for handling $vanilla^+$ `Condition` that is built with the constraint package `clpr` for solving linear equations and inequalities over integers. The partial evaluator uses additional `fold`/`unfold` specifications to specialize the interpreter for any $vanilla^+$ programs.

Figure 2(d) shows the debugging session of our tool for Sect. 2.2: Assume that three classes of packets are injected into n1, identified by their destinations d1, d2, d3; acl1 (acl2) allows only d1, d2 (d2, d3, respectively), with the intention that only packets to d2 (allowed by both ACLs) can reach n4. The symptom is that packets destined for d1 slip through due to the misplacement of `acl2`. The buggy configurations is captured by a 5-rule $vanilla^+$ program: each forwarding arrow corresponds to a rule similar to line 1 or 2 in Listing 1.6. Our toolkit first partially evaluates the interpreter, transforming $vanilla^+$ program and the symptom. For example, the 5-rule $vanilla^+$ program for the buggy configuration in (c) is transformed into a Prolog program with 43 rules. The error in the resulting Prolog program for the symptom is then returned by the `Clause`, correctly identifying that `acl2` is missing from n3, as shown in Fig. 2(d) (we modified the variable name automatically generated by our partial evaluator to X).

6   Limitation

Our approach complements tools for live network troubleshooting; however, its effectiveness relies on an accurate underlying model, which lies beyond the scope of this research. The rest of this section discusses a limitation of applying algorithmic debugging—designed for traditional software—to distributed networks. The key idea and underlying assumption of algorithmic debugging is that an erroneous computation is one that produces an incorrect output from a set of correct input computations, whose correctness—and, indeed, the intended meaning of the program as the set of valid program states—can be determined *independently* for each computation. network In the distributed context of networks, however, it is not always easy—if even possible—to decide the truth value of a state predicate *in isolation*.

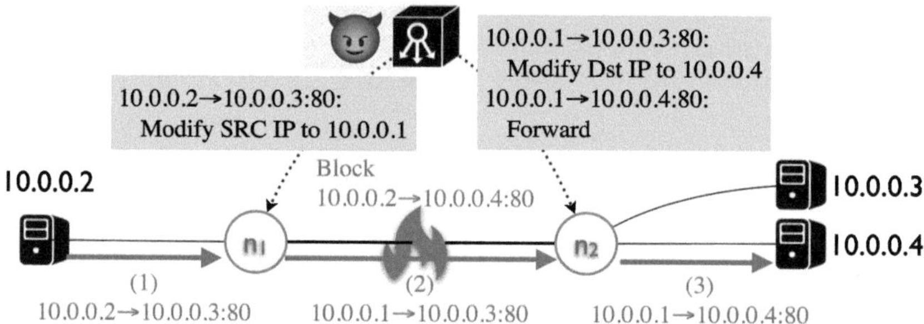

Fig. 6. Bypassing the firewall through coordinated header modification rules at n_1 and n_2.

To see the subtlety, consider the *coordinated* attack in Fig. 6 inspired by the dynamic flow tunneling scenario in [30]: the network consists of one SDN controller (top), two switches (n_1, n_2), and a firewall in the center. The intended security policy of the firewall is to block traffic from the outside host 10.0.0.2 to the internal web server 10.0.0.4 on port 80. By default, n_2 delivers traffic from 10.0.0.1 (Source IP) to 10.0.0.40 (destination IP) on port 80 to the server. An adversary launches an attack in two steps: first, it—through the SDN controller—installs rules into n_1, n_2 that modifies packet headers as follows: at n_1 (n_2, respectively), the source (destination, respectively) IP address of the packet is rewritten to 10.0.0.1 (10.0.0.4). Next, the attacker injects traffic at 10.0.0.2 with source 10.0.0.1 and destination 10.0.0.3. As shown in red across the three phases, the collaborative modification rules the attacker installed allow this traffic to evade the firewall.

A possible model of this attacking scenario is a program computing network states, defined by $n_1(\text{IP}_{\text{SRC}}, \text{IP}_{\text{DEST}}), n_2(\text{IP}_{\text{SRC}}, \text{IP}_{\text{DEST}}), n_f(\text{IP}_{\text{SRC}}, \text{IP}_{\text{DEST}})$, which indicate the packets present at n_1, n_2, and the firewall. Algorithmic debugging of this program then reduces to determining the truth values of these computation results. Obviously, $n_f(10.0.0.1, 10.0.0.3)$ is correct (true), but the assignments to $n_1(10.0.0.2, 10.0.0.3)$ and $n_2(10.0.0.1, 10.0.0.3)$ are less clear: Making both true allows the attack traffic, making both false would unnecessarily block otherwise admissible traffic, and assigning only one as false seems arbitrary. The fundamental issue is that $n_1(10.0.0.2, 10.0.0.3)$ and $n_2(10.0.0.1, 10.0.0.3)$ constitute a bug only when they are simultaneously true—their values must be considered jointly. We argue that, in general, the program states manipulated by a network model do not always constitute an atomic semantic unit and therefore require an extension of existing algorithmic debugging techniques.

7 Related Work

For a long time, the networking community has relied on only primitive troubleshooting tools such as ping and traceroute, requiring operators to manually monitor and inspect the states of distributed network elements (e.g., routers). The emergence of software-defined networking (SDN) [9,38] and programmable networks [22,39] has opened the door to applying software debugging techniques in networking, leading to network analogs of breakpoints [15,16]. In this paper, we introduce into networking the more sophisticated concept of algorithmic debugging, providing—for the first time—a formal framework for error localization along with tools that automate much of the effort traditionally required in trace-based debugging.

Algorithmic debugging, originating from the seminal work of [33] on debugging Prolog, has since evolved into a rich line of research. Existing efforts primarily focus on improving usability and scalability, ranging from reducing the number of user queries and grouping them into semantically related sets [4], to optimizing search strategies for faster error localization, and integrating techniques such as program slicing [35] and abstract interpretation [8] to handle realistic, large-scale programs (e.g., compilers with hundreds of thousands of lines of code). We address a unique challenge that has received little attention—namely, the presence of diverse non-standard language features and new semantics in networking. To the best of our knowledge, we are also the first to employ partial evaluation as a systematic approach to extend algorithmic debugging to new language features on the fly.

In the context of debugging Prolog-like languages, it is also worth noting provenance-based methods [40,41,44], which use post-mortem lineage graphs that are tightly coupled with datalog. We argue that, in contrast, we make novel use of techniques that are more widely applicable. Algorithmic debugging has been successfully applied across diverse programming paradigms (e.g., Haskell and Java), while partial evaluation has become a standard optimization technique in compiler research for mainstream programming languages.

8 Conclusion

This paper introduces declarative debugging as a means to transform network software troubleshooting: it requires only the user's declarative interpretation of the network, while automating the procedural comparison with actual execution and seamlessly incorporating new language features by partial evaluation. We demonstrate its usefulness in diagnosing typical network forwarding with link failures, written in a tentative, rule-based DSL called `vanilla`, by a preliminary implementation in Prolog. But the ideas of declarative debugging and partial evaluation are not limited to logic programming languages. We argue that our rapid development of declarative debugging with `vanilla` serves as a first step towards declarative troubleshooting of modern networks characterized by a proliferation of DSLs that present distinctive language challenges, such as the trade-off between intermediate representations and concrete protocols [14], and the placement of computation across control and data planes [36]. We call on the declarative programming community to take a more active role in addressing these challenges.

References

1. Bosshart, P., et al.: P4: programming protocol-independent packet processors. SIGCOMM Comput. Commun. Rev. **44**(3), 87–95 (2014). https://doi.org/10.1145/2656877.2656890
2. Brown, M., Fogel, A., Halperin, D., Heorhiadi, V., Mahajan, R., Millstein, T.: Lessons from the evolution of the batfish configuration analysis tool (2023). https://doi.org/10.1145/3603269.3604866
3. Burstall, R.M., Darlington, J.: A transformation system for developing recursive programs. J. ACM **24**(1), 44–67 (1977). https://doi.org/10.1145/321992.321996
4. Caballero, R., Riesco, A., Silva, J.: A survey of algorithmic debugging. ACM Comput. Surv. **50**(4) (2017). https://doi.org/10.1145/3106740
5. Chen, M., Kiciman, E., Accardi, A., Fox, A., Brewer, E.: Using runtime paths for macroanalysis. In: Proceedings of the 9th Conference on Hot Topics in Operating Systems, vol. 9, p. 14. HOTOS'03, USENIX Association, USA (2003)
6. Debray, S.K.: Unfold/fold transformations and loop optimization of logic programs. SIGPLAN Not. **23**(7), 297–307 (1988). https://doi.org/10.1145/960116.54020
7. Drabent, W.: On feasibility of declarative diagnosis. Electron. Proc. Theor. Comput. Sci. **385**, 193–200 (2023). https://doi.org/10.4204/eptcs.385.20
8. Ducassé, M., Noyé, J.: Logic programming environments: dynamic program analysis and debugging. J. Log. Program. **19–20**, 351–384 (1994). https://doi.org/10.1016/0743-1066(94)90030-2, https://www.sciencedirect.com/science/article/pii/0743106694900302
9. Feamster, N., Rexford, J., Zegura, E.: The road to SDN. Queue **11**(12), 20 (2013)
10. Fogel, A., et al.: A general approach to network configuration analysis. In: Proceedings of the 12th USENIX Conference on Networked Systems Design and Implementation, NSDI 2015, , pp. 469–483. USENIX Association, USA (2015)
11. Fogel, A., et al.: A general approach to network configuration analysis, NSDI 2015. USENIX Association, USA (2015)
12. Fonseca, R., Porter, G., Katz, R.H., Shenker, S., Stoica, I.: X-trace: a pervasive network tracing framework. In: Proceedings of the 4th USENIX Conference on Networked Systems Design & Implementation, NSDI 2007, p. 20. USENIX Association, USA (2007)
13. Gallagher, J.P.: Transforming logic programs by specialising interpreters. In: Proceedings of the 7th European Conference on Artificial Intelligence, ECAI 1986, vol. 2, pp. 313–326. North-Holland (1986)

14. Giannarakis, N., Loehr, D., Beckett, R., Walker, D.: NV: an intermediate language for verification of network control planes. In: Proceedings of the 41st ACM SIGPLAN Conference on Programming Language Design and Implementation, PLDI 2020, pp. 958–973. Association for Computing Machinery, New York (2020). https://doi.org/10.1145/3385412.3386019

15. Handigol, N., Heller, B., Jeyakumar, V., Maziéres, D., McKeown, N.: Where is the debugger for my software-defined network? In: Proceedings of the First Workshop on Hot Topics in Software Defined Networks, HotSDN 2012, pp. 55–60. Association for Computing Machinery, New York (2012). https://doi.org/10.1145/2342441.2342453

16. Handigol, N., Heller, B., Jeyakumar, V., Mazières, D., McKeown, N.: I know what your packet did last hop: using packet histories to troubleshoot networks. In: Proceedings of the 11th USENIX Conference on Networked Systems Design and Implementation, NSDI 2014, pp. 71–85. USENIX Association, USA (2014)

17. Hill, P.M., Gallagher, J.: Meta-programming in logic programming. In: Handbook of Logic in Artificial Intelligence and Logic Programming: Volume 5: Logic Programming. Oxford University Press (1998). https://doi.org/10.1093/oso/9780198537922.003.0010

18. Imieliński, T., Lipski, W.: Incomplete information in relational databases. J. ACM 31(4), 761–791 (1984). https://doi.org/10.1145/1634.1886

19. Jones, N.D.: An introduction to partial evaluation. ACM Comput. Surv. 28(3), 480–503 (1996). https://doi.org/10.1145/243439.243447

20. Juniper networks, Fast Reroute Overview (2018). https://www.juniper.net/documentation/en_US/junos-space-apps/connectivity-services-director4.1/topics/concept/fast-reroute-understanding.html

21. Kandula, S., Mahajan, R., Verkaik, P., Agarwal, S., Padhye, J., Bahl, P.: Detailed diagnosis in enterprise networks. In: Proceedings of the ACM SIGCOMM 2009 Conference on Data Communication, SIGCOMM 2009, pp. 243–254. Association for Computing Machinery, New York (2009). https://doi.org/10.1145/1592568.1592597

22. Kfoury, E.F., Crichigno, J., Bou-Harb, E.: An exhaustive survey on P4 programmable data plane switches: taxonomy, applications, challenges, and future trends. IEEE Access 9, 87094–87155 (2021). https://doi.org/10.1109/access.2021.3086704

23. Körner, P., et al.: Fifty years of prolog and beyond (2022)

24. Lan, F., Gui, B., Wang, A.: Faure: a partial approach to network analysis. In: ACM Workshop on Hot Topics in Networks (HotNets) (2021)

25. Lloyd, J.W.: Foundations of Logic Programming, 2nd extended edn. Springer, Heidelberg (1987)

26. Lloyd, J., Shepherdson, J.: Partial evaluation in logic programming. J. Log. Program. 11(3), 217–242 (1991). https://doi.org/10.1016/0743-1066(91)90027-M, https://www.sciencedirect.com/science/article/pii/074310669190027M

27. Loo, B.T., et al.: Declarative networking: Language, execution and optimization. In: SIGMOD 2006. ACM (2006). https://doi.org/10.1145/1142473.1142485

28. Loo, B.T., Hellerstein, J.M., Stoica, I., Ramakrishnan, R.: Declarative routing: extensible routing with declarative queries. In: SIGCOMM 2005 (2005). https://doi.org/10.1145/1080091.1080126

29. Lopes, N.P., Bjørner, N., Godefroid, P., Jayaraman, K., Varghese, G.: Checking beliefs in dynamic networks. In: 12th USENIX Symposium on Networked

Systems Design and Implementation (NSDI 2015), pp. 499–512. USENIX Association, Oakland (2015). https://www.usenix.org/conference/nsdi15/technical-sessions/presentation/lopes

30. Porras, P., Shin, S., Yegneswaran, V., Fong, M., Tyson, M., Gu, G.: A security enforcement kernel for OpenFlow networks. In: Proceedings of the First Workshop on Hot Topics in Software Defined Networks, HotSDN 2012, pp. 121–126. Association for Computing Machinery, New York (2012). https://doi.org/10.1145/2342441.2342466

31. Reich, J., Monsanto, C., Foster, N., Rexford, J., Walker, D.: Modular SDN programming with pyretic. USENIX Login **38**(5) (2013)

32. Scott, C., et al.: Troubleshooting blackbox SDN control software with minimal causal sequences. In: Proceedings of the 2014 ACM Conference on SIGCOMM, SIGCOMM 2014, pp. 395–406. Association for Computing Machinery, New York (2014). https://doi.org/10.1145/2619239.2626304

33. Shapiro, E.Y.: Algorithmic Program DeBugging. MIT Press, Cambridge (1983)

34. Silva, J.: Debugging techniques for declarative languages: profiling, program slicing and algorithmic debugging. AI Commun. **21**(1), 91–92 (2008)

35. Silva, J., Chitil, O.: Combining algorithmic debugging and program slicing. In: Proceedings of the 8th ACM SIGPLAN International Conference on Principles and Practice of Declarative Programming, PPDP 2006, pp. 157–166. Association for Computing Machinery, New York (2006). https://doi.org/10.1145/1140335.1140355

36. Sonchack, J., Loehr, D., Rexford, J., Walker, D.: Lucid: a language for control in the data plane. In: Proceedings of the 2021 ACM SIGCOMM 2021 Conference, SIGCOMM 2021, pp. 731–747. Association for Computing Machinery, New York (2021). https://doi.org/10.1145/3452296.3472903

37. Sterling, L., Shapiro, E.: The Art of Prolog (2nd edn.): Advanced Programming Techniques. MIT Press, Cambridge (1994)

38. The Future of Networking, and the Past of Protocols. http://www.opennetsummit.org/archives/apr12/site/talks/shenker-tue.pdf

39. Why does the Internet need a programmable forwarding plane. https://tinyurl.com/29859hrn

40. Wu, Y., Haeberlen, A., Zhou, W., Loo, B.T.: Answering why-not queries in software-defined networks with negative provenance. In: Proceedings of the Twelfth ACM Workshop on Hot Topics in Networks, HotNets-XII, Association for Computing Machinery, New York (2013). https://doi.org/10.1145/2535771.2535799

41. Wu, Y., Zhao, M., Haeberlen, A., Zhou, W., Loo, B.T.: Diagnosing missing events in distributed systems with negative provenance. SIGCOMM Comput. Commun. Rev. **44**(4), 383–394 (2014). https://doi.org/10.1145/2740070.2626335

42. Wundsam, A., Levin, D., Seetharaman, S., Feldmann, A.: OFRewind: enabling record and replay troubleshooting for networks. In: Proceedings of the 2011 USENIX Conference on USENIX Annual Technical Conference, USENIXATC 2011, p. 29. USENIX Association, USA (2011)

43. XSB homepage. https://xsb.sourceforge.net/

44. Zhou, W., Sherr, M., Tao, T., Li, X., Loo, B.T., Mao, Y.: Efficient querying and maintenance of network provenance at internet-scale. In: Proceedings of the 2010 ACM SIGMOD International Conference on Management of Data, SIGMOD 2010, pp. 615–626. Association for Computing Machinery, New York (2010). https://doi.org/10.1145/1807167.1807234

Solving Hard Combinatorial Optimization Problems with PyQASP

Damiano Azzolini[1]($\boxtimes$) [ID], Nicola Leone[2] [ID], Giuseppe Mazzotta[2] [ID],
and Francesco Ricca[2] [ID]

[1] University of Ferrara, Ferrara, Italy
`damiano.azzolini@unife.it`
[2] University of Calabria, Rende, Italy
`{leone,giuseppe.mazzotta,francesco.ricca}@unical.it`

Abstract. Answer Set Programming with Quantifiers (ASP(Q)) extends classical ASP to naturally capture problems within the polynomial hierarchy (PH). Recently, the formalism has been enriched with weak constraints to express both local and global optimization criteria, enabling the modeling of problems in Δ^P_{n+1}. In this paper, we present the first implementation of ASP(Q) with global weak constraints, built on top of the state-of-the-art ASP(Q) system PYQASP, based on an upper-bound improving strategy that effectively guides the search toward optimal solutions. Experiments demonstrate that our approach can be effectively applied to solve hard optimization problems.

Keywords: Answer Set Programming · ASP with Quantifiers · Weak Constraints · Optimization

1 Introduction

Answer Set Programming (ASP) [12,30] stands as one of the most expressive and practically successful paradigms for declarative problem solving. Its combination of a highly expressive modeling language [18,22] and efficient solving technology [1,9,20,28] has made ASP a powerful tool for encoding and solving a wide range of combinatorial and optimization problems [13,19,31,32,34].

ASP has been recently extended to handle problems across the entire Polynomial Hierarchy (PH) through the Answer Set Programming with Quantifiers (ASP(Q)) formalism [6]. Inspired by Quantified Boolean Formulae, ASP(Q) extends standard ASP by introducing quantification over answer sets of ASP programs, allowing the nesting of an arbitrary number of ASP programs to naturally encode problems at any level of the PH.

Building on this foundation, ASP(Q) has recently been enhanced to handle preference and optimization tasks via weak constraints [33], analogous to the mechanism used in standard ASP. Within ASP(Q), weak constraints can be employed locally, inside individual ASP subprograms, or globally, to express

N. Amin and J. Arias (Eds.): PADL 2026, LNCS 16401, pp. 199–217, 2026.
https://doi.org/10.1007/978-3-032-15981-6_12

preferences across quantified answer sets. The ability to model global weak constraints is particularly significant, as it enables the natural and compact encoding of optimization problems in classes such as Δ_{n+1}^P, substantially extending the practical applicability of the framework [33].

In recent years, ASP(Q) has attracted growing interest, with emerging applications in areas such as outlier detection [10] and probabilistic reasoning [7,8], among others [6,24,25]. This success stems not only from the theoretical expressiveness of the formalism but also from the availability of efficient evaluation tools, such as QASP [4] and PYQASP [23], which evaluate ASP(Q) programs and compute quantified answer sets effectively.

Despite these advances, existing systems do not yet support weak constraints, limiting the ability to exploit the full power of ASP(Q) in practical optimization scenarios. Implementing weak constraints in a real system is therefore a crucial step toward enabling real-world applications that rely on preferences and multi-level optimization, bridging the gap between the theoretical potential of ASP(Q) and its practical use in complex reasoning tasks.

In this paper, we fill this gap by presenting the first implementation of ASP(Q) with global weak constraints, built on top of the PYQASP system [4]. Our approach adapts and extends the methodology used in state-of-the-art ASP solvers for handling weak constraints [3]. This enables ASP(Q) to efficiently deal with multi-level optimization tasks. More precisely, we adopt an upper-bound improvement strategy that iteratively refines ASP(Q) programs to search better solutions (i.e., quantified answer sets) until no further improvement is possible, thereby establishing optimality to compute optimal quantified answer sets for problems lying beyond NP.

We carried out an extensive empirical evaluation covering several representative problems from the literature, including abductive reasoning, logic-based optimization, and graph-theoretic benchmarks. The obtained results are very promising, showing that the proposed approach is both practical and effective in tackling complex optimization problems in the higher levels of the PH.

2   Preliminaries

2.1   Answer Set Programming

Syntax. A *variable* is an alphanumeric string starting with an uppercase letter. A *constant* is either a number or an alphanumeric string starting with a lowercase letter. A *term* is either a variable or a constant. A *standard atom* is an expression of the form $p(t_1, \ldots, t_n)$ where p is a predicate of arity n and $t_1, \ldots, t_n$ is a list of terms. A *standard literal* is either a standard atom a or its negation *not a* where *not* stands for *negation as failure*. An *aggregate element* is an expression of the form $t_1, \ldots, t_k : l_1, \ldots, l_n$, where $t_1, \ldots, t_k$ is a list of terms and $l_1, \ldots, l_n$ is a conjunction of standard literals. An *aggregate atom* is an expression of the form $f\{e_1; \ldots; e_m\} \succ T$ where $f \in \{\#sum, \#count\}$, e_i is an aggregate element, with $1 \leq i \leq m$, $\succ \in \{\geq, >, \leq, <, =\}$, and T is a term referred to as *guard*. An *atom* is either a standard atom or an aggregate one. A *literal* is either an atom a or its negation *not a*. A *rule* is an expression of the form $h :\!\!- l_1, \ldots, l_n$ where h is an standard atom, referred to as *head*, which can be also omitted, and $l_1, \ldots, l_n$, with $n \geq 0$, is a conjunction of literals, referred to as *body*. A rule with an empty head is said to be a *hard constraint*; whereas a rule with an empty body is said to be a *fact*. A rule is said to be *safe* if each variable appearing in it, appears also in some positive standard literals in its body [17,26]. A *weak constraint* is an expression of the form $:\sim l_1, \ldots, l_n$ $[w@l, t_1, \ldots, t_k]$, where $l_1, \ldots, l_n$ is a conjunction of literals, referred to as *body*, w and l are terms, referred to as *weight* and *level* respectively, and $t_1, \ldots, t_k$, with $k \geq 0$ is a list of terms. The notion of safety extends also to weak constraints, and so a weak constraint is said to be *safe* if each variables appearing in it appears also in some positive standard literals of its body. An ASP *program* is a finite set of safe rules and weak constraints. A program is said to be *plain* if it does not contain weak constraints. An ASP expression ϵ (i.e., atoms, rules, constraints, etc.) is *ground* if it contains no variable. Given a ASP program P, the *Herbrand Universe*, denoted as U_P, is the set of all constants appearing in P; whereas the *Herbrand Base*, denoted as B_P, is the set of all possible ground standard atoms that can be obtained from predicates in P and constants in U_P. Let $r \in P$ be a rule (resp. a weak constraint), *ground(r)* denotes the ground instantiations of r that can be obtained by properly substituting variables in r with constants in U_P [15]. Similarly, *ground(P)* denotes the union of *ground(r)*, for each $r \in P$.

Example 1. Let P be the following ASP program:

```
d(1).       d(2).
a(X):-d(X),not b(X).
b(X):-d(X),not a(X).
:- #count{X:a(X)}>1.
:~ a(X). [X@1]
```

Here *ground(P)* is the following program:

```
d(1).       d(2).

a(1):-d(1),not b(1).
b(1):-d(1),not a(1).

a(2):-d(2),not b(2).
b(2):-d(2),not a(2).

:- #count{1:a(1);2:a(2)}>1.

:~ a(1). [1@1]
:~ a(2). [2@1]
```

Semantics. An *interpretation* $I \subseteq B_P$ is a set of standard ground atoms. A positive (resp. negative) standard ground literal $l = a$ (resp. $l = not\ a$) is true w.r.t. I, denoted as $I \models l$ if $a \in I$ (resp. $a \notin I$); otherwise it is false, denoted as $I \not\models l$. A conjunction of standard ground literals $l_1, \ldots, l_n$ is true w.r.t. I, denoted as $I \models l_1, \ldots, l_n$, if $I \models l_i$, for each $i \in \{1, \ldots, n\}$. Given a set of ground aggregate elements $S = \{e_1; \ldots; e_n\}$, $Eval(I, S) = \{(t_1, \ldots, t_k) \mid t_1 \ldots, t_k : l_1, \ldots, l_n \in S, I \models l_1, \ldots, l_n\}$. Moreover, $I(S)$ denotes the multi-set $[t_1 | (t_1, \ldots, t_k) \in Eval(I, S)]$. A ground aggregate atom $a = f\{e_1; \ldots; e_n\} \succ t$ is true w.r.t. I, denoted as $I \models a$, if $f(I(S)) \succ t$ holds; otherwise it is false, denoted as $I \not\models a$. A positive (resp. negative) literal $l = a$ (resp. $l = not\ a$) is true w.r.t. I, denoted as $I \models l$, if $I \models a$ (resp. $I \not\models a$); otherwise it is false, denoted as $I \not\models l$. A ground rule $r = h :\text{-} l_1, \ldots, l_n \in ground(P)$ is satisfied w.r.t. I, denoted as $I \models r$, if $I \models h$ whenever $I \models l_1, \ldots, l_n$. I is said to be a *model* of P if $I \models r$, for each $r \in ground(P)$. Given a model M of P the FLP-reduct [26], denoted by P^M, is the program obtained from $ground(P)$ by removing all those rules in P having their body false w.r.t. M. M is an *answer set* of P if M is a $\subset$-minimal model of P^M. We denotes with $AS(P)$ the set of answer sets of the program P. P is said to be *coherent* if $AS(P) \neq \emptyset$; otherwise P is *incoherent*.

Example 2. Consider the program P from Example 1. Intuitively, the rules of P models a choice between $a(X)$ or $b(X)$, for each $d(X)$. Then, the hard constraint imposes that it is not possible to have more than one $a(X)$. Thus, the answer sets of P are $M_1 = \{d(1), d(2), b(1), b(2)\}$, $M_2 = \{d(1), d(2), a(1), b(2)\}$, $M_3 = \{d(1), d(2), a(2), b(1)\}$. $\qquad\qquad\square$

Given an answer set M of P, the set of *weak constraints violations* is defined as $ws(P, M) = \{(w, l, \boldsymbol{t}) \mid :\sim l_1, \ldots, l_n\ [w@l, \boldsymbol{t}] \in ground(P), I \models l_1, \ldots, l_n\}$. Given an integer l, the cost of M at level l is defined as $\mathcal{C}(M, l, P) = \sum_{(w,l,t) \in ws(P,M)} w$. Let M_1, M_2 be two answer sets of P, then M_1 is *dominated* by M_2 if there exists an integer l such that $\mathcal{C}(M_2, l, P) < \mathcal{C}(M_1, l, P)$ and for each $l' > l$, $\mathcal{C}(M_2, l, P) = \mathcal{C}(M_1, l, P)$. An answer set M of P is also an *optimal* answer set of P if it is not dominated by any answer set of P. We denote by $OptAS(P)$ the set of optimal answer sets of the program P.

Example 3. Consider the program P from Example 1 and its answer sets from Example 2. Here, that M_1 does not violate any weak constraint, so $ws(M_1, 1, P) = \emptyset$. On the other hand, M_2 (resp. M_3) violates exactly one weak constraint in $ground(P)$ which is $:\sim a(1)\ [1@1]$ (resp. $:\sim a(2)\ [2@1]$). Thus, in this case $ws(M_2, 1, P) = \{(1, 1)\}$ and $ws(M_3, 1, P) = \{(2, 1)\}$. Whereas for each $l \neq 1$, $ws(M_1, l, P) = ws(M_2, l, P) = ws(M_3, l, P) = \emptyset$.

This means that $\mathcal{C}(M_1, 1, P) = 0$, $\mathcal{C}(M_2, 1, P) = 1$, and $\mathcal{C}(M_3, 1, P) = 2$. Whereas for each $l \neq 1$, $\mathcal{C}(M_1, l, P) = \mathcal{C}(M_2, l, P) = \mathcal{C}(M_3, l, P) = 0$.

Thus, we can conclude that both M_2 and M_3 are dominated by M_1 and so they are not optimal answer sets. Whereas M_1 is dominated neither by M_2 nor by M_3, and so, M_1 is the only optimal answer set of P. $\qquad\qquad\square$

2.2 ASP(Q) with Global Weak Constraints

An ASP(Q) program is an expression of the form:

$$\Box_1 P_1 \cdots \Box_n P_n : C : C^\omega \tag{1}$$

where for each $i \in \{1, \dots, n\}$, P_i is a plain ASP program and $\Box_i \in \{\exists^{st}, \forall^{st}\}$, C is a plain and *stratified* ASP program (i.e., it contains no recursive rules involving negation [17]) which possibly contains hard constraints, and C^ω is a set of weak constraints defined over atoms in B_{P_1}. An ASP(Q) program is said to be *existential* if $\Box_1 = \exists$; otherwise it is *universal*. Let P be a program and $M \in AS(P)$ then $fix_P(M)$ denotes the following set of facts and hard constraints:

$$\{a \text{ :- } \mid a \in M\} \cup \{ \text{ :- } a \mid a \in B_P \setminus M\}$$

Moreover, given an ASP(Q) Π of the form (1), we denote by $\Pi_{P,M}$ the ASP(Q) program obtained Π by substituting the program P_1 with $P_1 \cup fix_P(M)$ (i.e. $\Box_1 P_1 \cup fix_P(M) \cdots \Box_n P_n : C : C^\omega$). We are now ready to define the semantics of ASP(Q). The coherence of ASP(Q) program is defined inductively as follows:

- $\exists^{st} P : C : C^\omega$ is coherent if and only if there exists $M \in AS(P)$ such that $C \cup fix_P(M)$ is coherent.
- $\forall^{st} P : C : C^\omega$ is coherent if and only if for each $M \in AS(P)$, $C \cup fix_P(M)$ is coherent.
- $\exists^{st} P \; \Pi$ is coherent if and only if there exists $M \in AS(P)$ such that $\Pi_{P,M}$ is coherent.
- $\forall^{st} P \; \Pi$ is coherent if and only if for each $M \in AS(P)$, $\Pi_{P,M}$ is coherent.

Let Π be an existential ASP(Q) program, then $M_1 \in AS(P_1)$ is a *quantified answer set* of Π if and only if $(\Box_2 P_2 \cdots \Box_n P_n : C : C^\omega)_{P_1, M_1}$ is coherent. We denote by $QAS(\Pi)$ the set of quantified answer sets of Π.

Example 4. Let us consider the following ASP(Q) program Π:

```
%@exists // Program P1
a(1) :- not b(1).        b(1) :- not a(1).
a(2) :- not b(2).        b(2) :- not a(2).
%@forall // Program P2
c(1) :- not d(1).        d(1) :- not c(1).
c(2) :- not d(2).        d(2) :- not c(2).
%@constraint // Program C
:- a(1), a(2), c(2).
```

In this case, the program $P1$ has four answer sets $M_1 = \{a(1), a(2)\}$, $M_2 = \{a(1), b(2)\}$, $M_3 = \{b(1), a(2)\}$, and $M_4 = \{b(1), b(2)\}$. Let us consider M_1 and answer set of the program $P_2' = P_2 \cup fix_{P_1}(M_1)$. Here, there exists $M = M_1 \cup \{c(1), c(2)\} \in AS(P_2')$ such that $C \cup fix_{P_2'}(M)$ is incoherent, and so M_1 is not a quantified answer set. On the other hand, if we consider M_2 then for each $M \in AS(P_2')$, with $P_2' = P_2 \cup fix_{P_1}(M_2)$, $C \cup fix_{P_2'}(M)$ is coherent as $a(2)$ is false w.r.t. M. Thus, M_2, as well as M_3 and M_4, are quantified answer sets of Π. $\Box$

Let $M \in QAS(\Pi)$ be a quantified answer set, and l be an integer then the cost of M at level l is defined as $\mathcal{C}(M, l, \Pi) = \mathcal{C}(M, l, P_1 \cup C^\omega)$. Given two quantified answer sets $M_1, M_2 \in QAS(\Pi)$ then M_1 is *dominated* by M_2 if there exists an integer l such that $\mathcal{C}(M_2, l, \Pi) < \mathcal{C}(M_1, l, \Pi)$ and for each $l' > l$, $\mathcal{C}(M_2, l, \Pi) = \mathcal{C}(M_1, l, \Pi)$. M is also an *optimal quantified answer set* if M is not dominated by any $M' \in QAS(\Pi)$.

Example 5. Let Π be the ASP(Q) program from Example 4 where C^ω contains the weak constraints $:\sim b(1).[1@1, 1]$ and $:\sim b(2).[1@1, 2]$. Here, the cost of M_2 (resp. M_3) at level 1 is equal to 1 as only $b(2)$ (resp. $b(1)$) is true w.r.t. M_2 (resp. M_3). Conversely, the cost of M_4 at level 1 is 2 as both $b(1)$ and $b(2)$ are true w.r.t. M_4. Thus, M_2 and M_3 are the two optimal quantified answer sets of Π. $\square$

3   Computing Optimal Quantified Answer Sets

The classical approach used in the ASP context for optimal answer set search can be classified into three categories: *upper-bound improving, lower-bound improving*, and *mixed* [2,3]. More precisely, upper-bound improving algorithms start by solving an input program P by ignoring weak constraints. Then iteratively search for an answer set that dominates the previous found one (i.e., an answer set with a smaller cost). As soon as no better answer sets are found, then the last computed one is proved to be optimal. On the other hand, lower-bound improving algorithms follow the opposite approach. First, weak constraints are transformed into hard constraints. If there exists an answer set, then it is also optimal as it does not violate any weak constraint (note that w.l.o.g. weights can be assumed to be positive). If no answer sets exist, then weak constraints are iteratively relaxed and the lower-bound is increased by the minimum weights of the relaxed weak constraints. In this way, as soon as an answer set is found, it is also optimal. Finally, mixed strategy combine the two techniques until the upper and lower bounds coincide, and so optimality is proven. Based on such methodologies, in this paper, we propose an upper-bound improving algorithm for computing optimal quantified answer sets.

To this end, we start by introducing a rewriting technique which transforms weak constraints into rules, so that weak constraints' violations can be modeled by means of fresh atoms.

Definition 1. *Let P be an ASP program. Then $opt(P)$ denotes the program obtained from P by transforming each weak constraint $:\sim l_1, \ldots, l_n$ $[w@l, t_1, \ldots, t_k]$ in P into a rule of the form $opt(w, l, t_1, \ldots, t_k) :\text{-} l_1, \ldots, l_n$, where opt is a fresh predicate not appearing in P.*

Intuitively, the $opt(\cdot)$ transformation encodes weights and levels as terms of a fresh atoms appearing in the head of the rule. As a result, if a weak constraint is violated (i.e., its body is true) then the corresponding atom is derived. The following example will better clarify how the transformation works.

Example 6. Let us consider the program P from Example 1. Given an answer set M of P, for each atom of the form $a(\cdot)$ which is true w.r.t. M, the set of weak constraints violations, $ws(P, M)$, contains the tuple $(\cdot, 1)$. Similarly, $opt(P)$ allows to capture weak constraints' violations as atoms over predicate opt:

```
d(1).       d(2).
a(X):-d(X),not b(X).
b(X):-d(X),not a(X).
:- #count{X:a(X)}>1.
opt(X,1):- a(X).
```

Here answer sets of $opt(P)$ are $M_1' = M_1 = \{d(1), d(2), b(1), b(2)\}$, $M_2' = \{d(1), d(2), a(1), b(2), opt(1,1)\}$, and $M_3' = \{d(1), d(2), a(2), b(1), opt(2,1)\}$.   □

From Examples 3 and 6, one can observe a one-to-one correspondence between the tuples in $ws(P, M_i)$ and the atoms of the form $opt(\cdot, \cdot)$ in M_i', for each $i \in \{1, \ldots, 3\}$. This correspondence is formally captured in the following proposition.

Proposition 1. *Let P be an ASP program. Then $M' \in AS(opt(P))$ iff $M' = M \cup W$, with $M \in AS(P)$ and $W = \{opt(w, l, \boldsymbol{t}) \mid (w, l, \boldsymbol{t}) \in ws(P, M)\}$.*

From Proposition 1, it is possible to compute and check the cost of an answer set at each priority level by means of ad hoc aggregate atoms. More precisely, we denote by $OptAt(P)$ the set of atoms in $B_{Opt(P)}$ over the predicate opt. Let l be an integer, then $S(l)$ denotes the set of ground aggregate elements of the form $w, t_1, \ldots, t_k : opt(w, l, t_1, \ldots, t_k)$, for each atom $opt(w, l, t_1, \ldots, t_k) \in OptAt(P)$. Let c be an integer and $\succ \in \{>, \geq, <, \leq, =\}$, then $Aggr(P, l, \succ, c)$ denotes the aggregate atom $\#sum\{S(l)\} \succ c$. Intuitively, $S(l)$ contains each atom modeling a weak constraints' violation at level l with the respective weight assigned to it (i.e., the first term of each atom). Thus, using a sum aggregate on $S(l)$ it is possible to compute the cost of the answer set at the level l and check if it satisfies a given threshold c.

Proposition 2. *Let P be an ASP program, l and c be two integers denoting, respectively, a priority level and a cost threshold, and $\succ \in \{=, \geq, >, \leq, <\}$ be a comparison operator. Then, for each $M \in AS(P)$, $C(M, l, P) \succ c$ holds iff $M \subseteq M' \in AS(opt(P) \cup \{ \text{:- not } Aggr(P, l, \succ, c)\})$.*

We are now ready to introduce our upper-bound improving algorithm for computing optimal quantified answer sets reported in Algorithm 1.

Given an ASP(Q) program Π of the form $\square_1 P_1 \ldots \square_n P_n : C : C^\omega$, the main idea behind Algorithm 1 is to iteratively refine the answer sets of the program P_1 according to the cost assigned by weak constraints in C^ω until the optimality criteria is met. More in detail, Algorithm 1 starts by computing the program P as the union of the program P_1 and the global weak constraints C^ω (line 2). Then, the ASP(Q) program Π' is obtained from Π by replacing P_1 with $opt(P)$ (line 3). Intuitively, these two steps allow the inclusion of the global weak constraints (i.e., C^ω) in the program P_1 and, more importantly, to

---

Algorithm 1: ComputeOptQAS

Input : An ASP(Q) program Π of the form $\square_1 P_1 \cdots \square_n P_n : C : C^\omega$
Output: An optimal quantified answer set M

1 begin
2 $P := P_1 \cup C^\omega$
3 $\Pi' := \square_1 opt(P)\square_2 P_2 \cdots \square_n P_n : C$
4 $M := solve(\Pi')$
5   **if** $M = \bot$ **then**
6 $\lfloor$ **return** $\bot$
7 $Levels := \{l \mid opt(\cdot, l, \cdots) \in OptAt(P)\}$
8 $OptCost := \emptyset$
9   **while** $True$ **do**
10 $opt\_l := max(\{l \in Levels \mid \nexists \langle l, \cdot \rangle \in OptCost\})$
11   **if** $opt\_l = \bot$ **then**
12 $\lfloor$ **return** M
13 $ActualCost := \{\langle l, c \rangle \mid l \in Levels, \mathcal{C}(M, l, P) = c\}$
14 $bounds := \{ \text{:- } not\ Aggr(P, l, =, c) \mid \langle l, c \rangle \in OptCost\}$
15 $bounds := bounds \cup \{ \text{:- } Aggr(P, opt\_l, \geq, c) \mid \langle opt\_l, c \rangle \in ActualCost\}$
16 $\Pi' := \square_1 opt(P) \cup bounds\ \square_2 P_2 \cdots \square_n P_n : C$
17 $M' := solve(\Pi')$
18   **if** $M' = \bot$ **then**
19 $\lfloor$ $OptCost := OptCost \cup \{\langle opt\_l, c \rangle \mid \langle opt\_l, c \rangle \in ActualCost\}$
20   **else**
21 $\lfloor$ $M := M'$

---

model weak constraints violated by the quantified answer sets as atoms over the predicate opt.

At this point, Algorithm 1 proceeds by searching for a quantified answer set of Π' (line 4). Intuitively a quantified answer set M of Π', from Proposition 1, corresponds to a quantified answer set of Π which has been extended with atoms over predicate opt. As a result if such M does not exist (i.e. $M = \bot$) then the algorithm returns $\bot$, which means no quantified answer set exists and so neither optimal ones. On the other hand, if such a quantified answer set M exists, then an optimal quantified answer set exists as well and will be obtained by iteratively improving M. To this end, Algorithm 1 collects all such integer l appearing in some weak constraints in the set $Levels$ and initializes the set $OptCost$ that will be used to store the pairs $\langle l, c \rangle$ where l is level and c is the optimum cost at level l. At this point, the upper-bound improving loop starts. At each iteration, Algorithm 1 computes the highest level, opt_l, such that an optimum cost for this level has not been found yet (i.e., $\nexists \langle opt\_l, c \rangle \in OptCost$, line 10). If such level does not exists (i.e. $opt\_l = \bot$) then no further level to optimize exists and so M is the optimal quantified answer set (line 12). Otherwise, Algorithm 1 computes the cost of M at each level l and store it as pair of the form $\langle l, c \rangle$ in the $ActualCost$ set (line 13). At this point, the hard constraints needed to improve the cost of M are constructed and stored in the set *bounds* (lines 14 and 15). Observe that the algorithm at each iteration selects opt_l as the highest level that has not reached the optimum value yet. Thus, for each pair $\langle l, c \rangle \in OptCost$, $l > opt\_l$ which is the current optimization level, and l has already reached its optimum value. Given that, for each pair $\langle l, c \rangle \in OptCost$, a constraint of the form $:\text{-} \ not\ Aggr(P, l, =, c)$ is added to *bounds* to impose that the cost at level l must be equal to its optimum value that is c. Finally, from the pair $\langle opt\_l, c \rangle \in ActualCost$, the constraint $:\text{-} \ Aggr(P, opt\_l, \geq, c)$ is added to *bounds* to impose that the cost at level l cannot be greater than or equal to c that is the current cost obtained at level l, and so it must be smaller. At this point, the ASP(Q) program Π' is refined by substituting the first subprogram with $opt(P) \cup bounds$. Then, Algorithm 1 searches for a quantified answer set M' of the refined Π'. If such M' does not exists (i.e., $M' = \bot$) then the level opt_l has reached its optimum that is the cost stored in $ActualCost$ (i.e., $\langle opt\_l, c \rangle \in ActualCost$, see line 18). On the other hand, if this M' exists then the previous quantified answer set M is dominated by M' and so M is overwritten by M' (line 21).

4 Experiments

In this section, we present an empirical evaluation aimed at assessing the performance of the proposed approach in solving hard optimization problems beyond the NP class. In particular, Algorithm 1 has been implemented on top of the PyQASP systems that is currently the state-of-the-art ASP(Q) system and is available online.[1]

The experiments were executed on a machine with Intel(R) Xeon(R) CPU E7-8880 v4 @ 2.20 GHz running Debian Linux (4.9.0-19-amd64), with memory and time limits of 8 GB and 800 s, respectively.

4.1 Problems and Benchmark Suite

Our evaluation covers different problems taken from multiple domains [16,21,36]. In what follows, we describe how such problems have been modeled, and we provide a description of the benchmark suite used in our evaluation.

Logic-Based Abduction [21]. The Propositional Abduction Problem (PAP), is defined as a tuple of the form $\mathcal{A} = \langle V, T, H, M \rangle$, where V is a set of variables, T is a consistent propositional logic theory over variables in V, $H \subseteq V$ is a set of hypotheses, and $M \subseteq V$ is a set of manifestations.

A *solution* for $\mathcal{A}$ is a set $S \subseteq H$ such that $T \cup S$ is consistent and $T \cup S \vDash M$. Among the possible solutions to $\mathcal{A}$, denoted by $sol(\mathcal{A})$, it is possible to define a preference relation $<$ (e.g., cardinality-minimal) which allows to define the set of optimal solutions to $\mathcal{A}$ as $sol_<(\mathcal{A}) = \{S \in sol(\mathcal{A}) \mid \nexists\ S' \in sol(\mathcal{A})\ such\ that\ |S'| < |S|\}$. Solving PAP is beyond NP [21], so ASP(Q) is a perfect candidate to encode it [33].

---

[1] https://github.com/MazzottaG/PyQASP.git (7f809bd).

We first focus on the computation of optimal (i.e., cardinality-minimal) solutions to PAP. This problem can be modeled with an ASP(Q) program with 2 quantifiers that uses global weak constraints.

```
%@exists % Program P1
sol(X):-h(X),not nsol(X).
nsol(X):-h(X),not sol(X).

tau(X,t):-v(X),not tau(X,f).
tau(X,f):-v(X),not tau(X,t).

sat(C):-pos(C,X),tau(X,t).
sat(C):-neg(C,X),tau(X,f).
:-clause(C), not sat(C).
:-sol(C), not sat(C).

%@forall % Program P2

tau_c(X,t):-v(X),not tau_c(X,f).
tau_c(X,f):-v(X),not tau_c(X,t).

sat_c(C):-pos(C,X), tau_c(X,t).
sat_c(C):-neg(C,X), tau_c(X,f).
:- clause(C),not sat_c(C).
:- sol(C),not sat_c(C).

%@constraint % Program C
:-m(C), pos(C,X) tau_c(X,f).
:-m(C), neg(C,X) tau_c(X,t).

%@global % Program Cω
:~s(X). [1@1,X]
```

This ASP(Q) encoding assumes that an instance of PAP is encoded as a set of facts over the predicates v, *pos*, *neg*, *clause*, h, and m. That is, each variable $x \in V$ is encoded by a fact of the form $v(x)$. For each clause $c \in T$ of the form $(l_1 \vee \ldots \vee l_k)$, there is a fact *clause*(c) and a fact for each negative (resp. positive) literal $l_i = \neg x$ (resp. $l_i = x$) of the form *neg*(c, x) (resp. *pos*(c, x)). Similarly, each positive (resp. negative) manifestation x (resp. $\neg x$) is encoded by the fact *pos*(c, x) (resp. *neg*(c, x)), while $m(c)$ encodes the identifier of the manifestation set. Finally, each hypothesis $x \in H$ is represented by a fact of the form $h(x)$.

Thus, given an instance of PAP, the first subprogram guesses a candidate solution $S \subseteq H$, represented by atoms of the form $sol(x)$ for each $x \in S$ and verifies the satisfiability of $T \cup S$. To this end, a truth assignment τ for the variables in V is guessed (i.e., the atom $tau(x, t)$ (resp. $tau(x, f)$) denotes that the variable x is assigned true (resp. false) by τ) and then hard constraints enforce that all clauses in T and all the selected hypotheses must be satisfied.

The second subprogram computes all truth assignments τ' that satisfy $T \cup S$, following the same approach described above. Finally, the last subprogram C checks whether τ' satisfies $T \cup S \models M$. Since each τ' satisfies $T \cup S$, the hard constraints ensure that all positive and negative manifestations are satisfied with respect to τ'. Thus, a quantified answer set corresponds to a solution of PAP.

To minimize the cardinality of the solution, the global weak constraint adds a penalty (of 1) for each hypothesis included in the solution. Hence, by minimizing the cost of the quantified answer set cost we obtain an optimal solution to PAP.

Another interesting task concerning PAP is to study the relevance of each hypothesis w.r.t. optimal solutions to PAP [21]. More precisely, an hypothesis $h \in H$ is *relevant* if h appears in some optimal solutions; *irrelevant* if h does not appear in any optimal solution; *necessary* if h appears in every optimal solution; and *dispensable* if h does not appear in some optimal solutions.

The *relevant/irrelevant* property can be checked by updating the global weak constraints, as follows

```
%@global  %  Program  C^ω
:~s(X).  [1@2,X]
:~check(X),not  sol(X).  [1@1,X]
```

Here, two priority levels are required. At the highest priority level, we minimize the length of the solution; at the lowest priority level, we introduce a penalty if the checking hypothesis is not included in the current solution. As a result, optimal solutions to PAP excluding the checking hypothesis will be dominated by those including it. Consequently, if there exists an optimal quantified answer set with cost 0 at level 1, then the checking hypothesis is relevant. Conversely, if the cost of the optimal answer set at level 1 is 1, the checking hypothesis is irrelevant, as all optimal quantified answer sets exclude it.

Similarly, we can verify whether an hypothesis is necessary or dispensable.

```
%@global  %  Program  C^ω
:~s(X).  [1@2,X]
:~check(X),sol(X).  [1@1,X]
```

In this case, the weak constraint at level 1 adds a penalty whenever the checking hypothesis is included in the current solution. As a result, optimal solutions to PAP including the checking hypothesis will be dominated by those excluding it. Thus, if there exists an optimal quantified answer set with cost 0 at level 1, then the checking hypothesis is dispensable. Conversely, if the cost of the optimal answer set at level 1 is 1, the checking hypothesis is necessary, as all optimal quantified answer sets includes it.

Minmax Clique [16]. Given an undirected graph $G = \langle V, E \rangle$, let I and J be two finite sets of indices, and $(A_{i,j})_{i \in I, j \in J}$ a partition of V. We write J^I for the set of all total functions from I to J. For every total function $f \colon I \to J$, we denote by

G_f the subgraph of G induced by $\bigcup_{i \in I} A_{i,f(i)}$. The MINMAX CLIQUE problem is defined as:

$$\min_{f \in J^I} \ \max\{|Q| : Q \text{ is a clique of } G_f\}.$$

Intuitively, the MINMAX CLIQUE problem aims at computing the total function $f \in J^I$ such that the size of the largest clique in the induced subgraph is minimum. Such a problem can be encoded in ASP(Q) as follows.

```
%@exists % Program P1
f(X,Y) :- setJ(Y),setI(X), not nf(X,Y).
nf(X,Y) :- setJ(Y),setI(X), not f(X,Y).

selected(X) :- f(X,Y), setJ(Y).
:-setJ(X), not selected(X).
:- f(X,Y1), f(X,Y2), setJ(Y1), setJ(Y2), Y1!=Y2.

ind_n(Z) :- v(X,Y,Z), f(X,Y).
ind_e(X,Y) :- edge(X,Y), ind_n(X), ind_n(Y).

inClique(X) :- ind_n(X), not outClique(X).
outClique(X) :- ind_n(X), not inClique(X).
rm(X):- ind_n(X), inClique(Y), X!=Y, not ind_e(X,Y).
:- inClique(X), rm(X).
:- outClique(X), not rm(X).

size(C):-#count{X:inClique(X)}=C.

%@forall % Program P2
inGTClique(X) :- ind_n(X), not outGTClique(X).
outGTClique(X) :- ind_n(X), not inGTClique(X).

rmGT(X) :- ind_n(X), inGTClique(Y), X!=Y, not ind_e(X
    ,Y).
:- inGTClique(X), rmGT(X).
:- outGTClique(X), not rmGT(X).

%@constraint % Program C
:- size(C), C<#count{X:inGTClique(X)}.

%@global % Program C^ω
:~size(C). [C@1]
```

Here, we assume that the input graph $G = \langle V, E \rangle$ is represented as facts of the form $e(x,y)$ for each edge $\{x,y\} \in E$. Then, the sets I and J are encoded as facts of the form $inI(i)$ and $inJ(j)$, for each $i \in I$ and $j \in J$. Finally, each partition $A_{i,j}$ is encoded as facts of the form $v(i,j,x)$ for every $x \in A_{i,j}$.

Given a problem instance, the first subprogram guesses a total function f, represented by atoms $f(x, y)$, mapping $x \in I$ to $y \in J$ and computes the subgraph induced by f selecting the vertices in each partition $A_{x,f(x)}$ for $x \in I$ ($ind\_n(x)$ and $ind\_e(x, y)$ vertices and edges of the induced subgraph). Then a maximal clique of the induced subgraph is guessed, and its size is computed as an atom $size(c)$, where c is the count of vertices v included in the clique (i.e., atoms of the form $inClique(v)$).

As maximal cliques are not necessarily the largest ones, the second quantifier explores all maximal cliques in the induced subgraph and, finally, the constraint program C enforces that the size of the clique computed in the first subprogram (i.e., $size(c)$) cannot be smaller than the size of any other maximal clique.

As a result, each quantified answer set corresponds to a total function $f \in J^I$ and one of the largest cliques in the subgraph induced by f. To compute the function f that minimizes the size of the largest clique, the global weak constraint assigns a penalty equal to the size of the clique to each quantified answer set.

Maximum Term Deletion [36]. Given a formula φ in disjunctive normal form (DNF), the MAXIMUM TERM DELETION problem [36] requires to compute the maximum number of terms of φ that can be deleted from it while maintaining equivalence to φ. This problem can be encoded in ASP(Q) as follows.

```
%@exists % Program P₁
remove(T):-term(T), not keep(T).
keep(T):-term(T),not remove(T).

removed :- remove(I).
:- not removed.

%@forall % Program P₂
tau(X,true):-var(X),not tau(X,false).
tau(X,false):-var(X),not tau(X,true).

%@constraint % Program C
sat_o:-lit(T,E1,V1,E2,V2,E3,V3), tau(E1,V1), tau(E2,
    V2), tau(E3,V3).
sat_s:-lit(T,E1,V1,E2,V2,E3,V3), tau(E1,V1), tau(E2,
    V2), tau(E3,V3), keep(T).

:-sat_o, not sat_s.
:-sat_s, not sat_o.

%@global % Program Cᵂ
:~ keep(T). [1@1,T]
```

We recall that a formula φ in DNF is a disjunction of terms, where each term is a conjunction of literals of the form $l_1 \wedge \cdots \wedge l_k$. Without loss of generality, we restrict our modeling to 3-DNF formulas, where each term contains exactly three literals ($k = 3$). In our encoding, each term of φ is encoded by a fact $term(t)$ and the literals within the term are encoded by a fact of the form $lit(t, x_1, v_1, x_2, v_2, x_3, v_3)$ where, for each $i \in 1, 2, 3$, x_i is the variable appearing in the i-th literal, and v_i is a Boolean value indicating its polarity: *true* if the literal is positive ($l_i = x_i$) and *false* if it is negated ($l_i = \neg x_i$).

Thus, given a 3-DNF formula φ, the first program guesses a subset of terms that should be removed from φ ensuring that at least one term is removed. More precisely, an atom of the form $remove(t)$ (resp. $keep(t)$) denotes that the term t has been removed from φ (resp. kept in φ). Then, the universal quantifier iterates over possible truth assignment τ of variables in φ. In particular, $tau(x, true)$ (resp. $tau(x, false)$) denotes that the variable x is assigned to true (resp. to false) by τ. Finally, the program C checks that φ is satisfied by τ iff the simplified formula (i.e., considering only retained terms) is satisfied by τ.

Thus, a quantified answer set is a subset of terms that can be removed from φ while remaining equivalent with φ in its original form. To maximize this set, the global weak constraint assigns a penalty of 1 for each term that is maintained.

Benchmark Suite. The benchmark suite is built on top of the above ASP(Q) encodings. We obtained three benchmarks from the Propositional Abduction Problem, namely *opt-abduction*, *relevant-hyp*, and *necessary-hyp*. *opt-abduction* refers to the task of computing cardinality minimal solutions to PAP, while *relevant-hyp* and *necessary-hyp* refer to the task of verifying whether a given hypothesis is, respectively, relevant/irrelevant or necessary/dispensable. For these three benchmarks, we consider different instances taken from the literature [35] including formulae up to 9851 clauses and 3284 variables, for a total of 294 instances. For each instance, we randomly sampled up to 10 hypothesis to construct *relevant-hyp* and *necessary-hyp* benchmarks. Concerning the Minmax Clique benchmark, namely *minmax-clique*, instead, we considered all the instances used in a previous evaluation of the ASP(Q) system [23]. Finally, for the Maximum Term Deletion problem we constructed a benchmark made of different formulae obtained by random formulae generators [5]. The *max-term-del* benchmark includes formulae with 6 up to 20 variables and 10 up to 100 terms.

4.2   Experiment Results

Table 1 summarizes the results of our experimental evaluation, providing an overview of performance for each benchmark. For each benchmark, the table reports the total number of instances (Tot. inst.) along with statistics for solved and unsolved instances. For solved instances, it shows the number of successfully solved instances (Solved #inst), the total number of quantified answer sets computed (Solved #qans), the total execution time (sum t.), and the average memory usage (avg m). For unsolved instances, it reports the number of cases exceeding the time limit (Timeout #inst., with corresponding quantified answer sets #qans) or the memory limit (Memout inst).

As can be observed, the considered problems are computationally demanding, as polynomially many ASP(Q) solver calls may be required in the worst

Table 1. Obtained results.

Bench.	Tot. inst.	Solved				Timeout		Memout inst.
		#inst.	#qans	sum t.	avg m.	#inst.	#qans	
opt-abduction	294	127	502	14.438,36	443,93	167	512	0
necessary-hyp	853	846	3348	139.922,20	556,17	7	107	0
relevant-hyp	853	822	3504	145.318,48	536,35	31	210	0
max-term-del	80	45	248	5.085,73	62,52	35	56	0
minmax-clique	45	28	15	3.118,92	1.195,03	15	1	2

case to compute an optimal quantified answer set. Furthermore, proving unsatisfiability of the refined program is necessary to reach optimality and this can be particularly demanding when the number of candidate quantified answer sets below the cost threshold is large.

In general, PYQASP successfully solved up to the 60% of the instances among the opt-abduction, max-term-deletion, and minmax-clique benchmarks, demonstrating its ability to handle computationally demanding optimization problems that go beyond NP. A closer analysis of the time-out cases highlights two distinct performance patterns. For opt-abduction, the most computationally expensive phase is the proof of optimality. PYQASP was able to compute a number of quantified answer sets comparable to those of the solved instances within the time limit. This shows that the system is highly effective in exploring the search space and steadily progressing toward optimality, even when the final proof could not be completed within the allotted time. In contrast, for the minmax-clique benchmark, the main challenge lies in computing even a single quantified answer set. Among the 15 time-out instances, only one quantified answer set was generated, and two instances run out of memory. This is mainly due to the QBF-based encoding adopted by PYQASP which in this case produces hard to evaluate formulae. The max-term-del benchmark, instead, exhibited both patterns. For most of the unsolved instances, PYQASP was unable to compute any quantified answer set, while for the remaining ones, the main challenge was to prove optimality. This highlights the inherent difficulty of such problems, yet PYQASP proves to be an effective solution overall.

For the necessary-hyp and relevant-hyp benchmarks, we focused exclusively on instances already solved in opt-abduction. This choice ensures a meaningful evaluation, as assessing whether a hypothesis appears in some or all optimal solutions of a PAP instance is only relevant when at least one optimal solution can be computed within the time limit. PYQASP solved nearly all instances in both benchmarks, showing that multi-level optimization can be effectively handled using the proposed upper-bound improving strategy. Furthermore, the addition of a second optimization level introduces a marginal overhead (only a few instances exceeded the time limit) confirming the robustness and scalability of PYQASP when dealing with problems featuring multiple optimization layers.

5   Related Works

Answer Set Programming (ASP) has proven highly expressive, capturing problems up to Δ_3^P through the combination of the saturation technique [22] and weak constraints [14]. However, saturation-based encodings are often not intuitive [29] and can be computationally demanding for state-of-the-art ASP solvers.

Among related formalisms with available implementations, it is worth mentioning the stable-unstable semantics [11] and the quantified answer set semantics [27]. To the best of our knowledge, none of these currently support weak constraints or other optimization constructs, and no tools exist to practically handle such reasoning tasks. In principle, the methodology introduced in this work could serve as a foundation to incorporate optimization statements into these frameworks. For detailed comparisons between ASP, ASP(Q), and these formalisms, we refer the reader to the existing literature [6,27].

ASP(Q) [6,33] extends ASP to model problems across the entire PH and it is supported by efficient solvers such as QASP [4] and PyQASP [23]. Such systems are at the core of the proposed methodology as ASP(Q) programs are iteratively evaluated for converging to the optimum cost.

The proposed methodology is inspired by the upper-bound improving strategy employed in standard ASP systems [2,3]. At a high level, it leverages the principle of iteratively improving previously found solutions, that are answer sets in standard ASP setting, and quantified answer sets in ASP(Q). Thus, the main difference between the two approaches lies in the fact that ASP(Q) involves nested quantifiers, corresponding to multiple ASP programs rather than a single one. Consequently, the approach proposed for ASP cannot be applied by simply computing an optimal answer set for the first program and then checking ASP(Q) coherence; instead, the first subprogram must be refined iteratively until incoherence of the ASP(Q) program is detected.

6   Conclusion

Modeling and efficiently solving optimization problems beyond NP remains a major challenge in computational logic, as many relevant problems lie at higher levels of the PH [36]. ASP(Q) provides a highly expressive language for modeling both decision and optimization problems across the entire PH [6,33]. Moreover, the availability of efficient solvers, such as QASP and PyQASP, enables the practical solving of problems in these complexity classes [7,10,25].

A key limitation of existing systems was the lack of support for weak constraints, which prevented the efficient handling of optimization problems. In this work, we extend PyQASP to support global weak constraints, thus enabling efficient solving of problems that are hard for the Δ_{n+1}^P complexity class. Our approach is inspired by upper-bound improvement strategies used in standard ASP solvers [2,3], which iteratively improves previously found solutions until no better ones exist, thereby proving optimality. We evaluated the proposed methodology on challenging problems from multiple domains, and the results demonstrate its effectiveness.

As future work, one can approach local weak constraints, and explore whether alternative strategies, such as lower-bound improvement and mixed ones, can be adapted to the ASP(Q) setting.

Acknowledgments. This work was supported by the Italian Ministry of Industrial Development (MISE) under project EI-TWIN n. F/310168/05/X56 CUP B29J24000680005; and by the Italian Ministry of Research (MUR) under projects: PNRR FAIR - Spoke 9 - WP 9.1 CUP H23C22000860006, and Tech4You CUP H23C22000370006.

References

1. Alviano, M., et al.: The ASP system DLV2. In: Balduccini, M., Janhunen, T. (eds.) LPNMR 2017. LNCS (LNAI), vol. 10377, pp. 215–221. Springer, Cham (2017). https://doi.org/10.1007/978-3-319-61660-5_19
2. Alviano, M., Dodaro, C.: Anytime answer set optimization via unsatisfiable core shrinking. Theory Pract. Log. Program. **16**(5-6), 533–551 (2016). https://doi.org/10.1017/S147106841600020X
3. Alviano, M., Dodaro, C., Marques-Silva, J., Ricca, F.: Optimum stable model search: algorithms and implementation. J. Log. Comput. **30**(4), 863–897 (2020). https://doi.org/10.1093/LOGCOM/EXV061
4. Amendola, G., Cuteri, B., Ricca, F., Truszczynski, M.: Solving problems in the polynomial hierarchy with ASP(Q). In: Proceedings of LPNMR. LNCS, vol. 13416, pp. 373–386. Springer, Cham (2022). https://doi.org/10.1007/978-3-031-15707-3_29
5. Amendola, G., Ricca, F., Truszczynski, M.: Generating hard random boolean formulas and disjunctive logic programs. In: Sierra, C. (ed.) Proceedings of the Twenty-Sixth International Joint Conference on Artificial Intelligence, IJCAI 2017, Melbourne, Australia, 19–25 August 2017, pp. 532–538. ijcai.org (2017). https://doi.org/10.24963/IJCAI.2017/75
6. Amendola, G., Ricca, F., Truszczynski, M.: Beyond NP: quantifying over answer sets. Theory Pract. Log. Program. **19**(5–6), 705–721 (2019). https://doi.org/10.1017/S1471068419000140
7. Azzolini, D., Mazzotta, G., Ricca, F., Riguzzi, F.: Most probable explanation in probabilistic answer set programming. In: Proceedings of the Thirty-Fourth International Joint Conference on Artificial Intelligence, IJCAI 2025, Montreal, Canada, 16–22 August 2025, pp. 9049–9057 (2025). https://doi.org/10.24963/IJCAI.2025/1006
8. Azzolini, D., Riguzzi, F.: Probabilistic answer set programming with discrete and continuous random variables. Theory Pract. Log. Program. **25**(1), 1–32 (2025)
9. Beiser, A., Hecher, M., Unalan, K., Woltran, S.: Bypassing the ASP bottleneck: hybrid grounding by splitting and rewriting. In: IJCAI, pp. 3250–3258. ijcai.org (2024)
10. Bellusci, P., Mazzotta, G., Ricca, F.: Modelling the outlier detection problem in ASP(Q). In: Cheney, J., Perri, S. (eds.) PADL 2022. LNCS, vol. 13165, pp. 15–23. Springer, Cham (2022). https://doi.org/10.1007/978-3-030-94479-7_2
11. Bogaerts, B., Janhunen, T., Tasharrofi, S.: Stable-unstable semantics: beyond NP with normal logic programs. Theory Pract. Log. Program. **16**(5-6), 570–586 (2016). https://doi.org/10.1017/S1471068416000387

12. Brewka, G., Eiter, T., Truszczynski, M.: Answer set programming at a glance. Commun. ACM **54**(12), 92–103 (2011)
13. Brewka, G., Eiter, T., Truszczynski, M.: Answer set programming: an introduction to the special issue. AI Mag. **37**(3), 5–6 (2016)
14. Buccafurri, F., Leone, N., Rullo, P.: Enhancing disjunctive datalog by constraints. TKDE **12**(5), 845–860 (2000)
15. Calimeri, F., et al.: Asp-core-2 input language format. Theory Pract. Log. Program. **20**(2), 294–309 (2020). https://doi.org/10.1017/S1471068419000450
16. Cao, F., Du, D.Z., Gao, B., Wan, P.J., Pardalos, P.M.: Minimax Problems in Combinatorial Optimization, pp. 269–292. Boston, MA (1995)
17. Ceri, S., Gottlob, G., Tanca, L.: Logic Programming and Databases. Surveys in Computer Science (1990)
18. Dantsin, E., Eiter, T., Gottlob, G., Voronkov, A.: Complexity and expressive power of logic programming. ACM Comput. Surv. **33**(3), 374–425 (2001)
19. Dodaro, C., Galatà, G., Khan, M.K., Maratea, M., Porro, I.: An ASP-based solution for operating room scheduling with beds management. In: Fodor, P., Montali, M., Calvanese, D., Roman, D. (eds.) RuleML+RR 2019. LNCS, vol. 11784, pp. 67–81. Springer, Cham (2019). https://doi.org/10.1007/978-3-030-31095-0_5
20. Dodaro, C., Mazzotta, G., Ricca, F.: Blending grounding and compilation for efficient ASP solving. In: Marquis, P., Ortiz, M., Pagnucco, M. (eds.) Proceedings of the 21st International Conference on Principles of Knowledge Representation and Reasoning, KR 2024, Hanoi, Vietnam. 2–8 November 2024 (2024). https://doi.org/10.24963/KR.2024/30
21. Eiter, T., Gottlob, G.: The complexity of logic-based abduction. J. ACM **42**(1), 3–42 (1995). https://doi.org/10.1145/200836.200838
22. Eiter, T., Gottlob, G.: On the computational cost of disjunctive logic programming: propositional case. Ann. Math. Artif. Intell. **15**(3–4), 289–323 (1995)
23. Faber, W., Mazzotta, G., Ricca, F.: An efficient solver for ASP(Q). Theory Pract. Log. Program. **23**(4), 948–964 (2023). https://doi.org/10.1017/S1471068423000121
24. Faber, W., Morak, M.: Evaluating epistemic logic programs via answer set programming with quantifiers. In: HYDRA/RCRA@LPNMR. CEUR Workshop Proceedings, vol. 3281, pp. 78–89. CEUR-WS.org (2022)
25. Faber, W., Morak, M., Chrpa, L.: Determining action reversibility in STRIPS using answer set programming with quantifiers. In: PADL. Lecture Notes in Computer Science, vol. 13165, pp. 42–56. Springer (2022)
26. Faber, W., Pfeifer, G., Leone, N.: Semantics and complexity of recursive aggregates in answer set programming. Artif. Intell. **175**(1), 278–298 (2011)
27. Fandinno, J., Laferrière, F., Romero, J., Schaub, T., Son, T.C.: Planning with incomplete information in quantified answer set programming. TPLP **21**(5), 663–679 (2021). https://doi.org/10.1017/S1471068421000259
28. Gebser, M., Kaminski, R., Kaufmann, B., Ostrowski, M., Schaub, T., Wanko, P.: Theory solving made easy with clingo 5. In: ICLP (Technical Communications). OASICS, vol. 52, pp. 2:1–2:15. Schloss Dagstuhl - Leibniz-Zentrum fuer Informatik (2016)
29. Gebser, M., Kaminski, R., Schaub, T.: Complex optimization in answer set programming. TPLP **11**(4–5), 821–839 (2011)
30. Gelfond, M., Lifschitz, V.: Classical negation in logic programs and disjunctive databases. New Gener. Comput. **9**(3/4), 365–386 (1991)

31. Grasso, G., Iiritano, S., Leone, N., Lio, V., Ricca, F., Scalise, F.: An ASP-based system for team-building in the gioia-tauro seaport. In: Carro, M., Peña, R. (eds.) PADL 2010. LNCS, vol. 5937, pp. 40–42. Springer, Heidelberg (2010). https://doi.org/10.1007/978-3-642-11503-5_5
32. Marek, V.W., Truszczynski, M.: Stable models and an alternative logic programming paradigm. In: The Logic Programming Paradigm - A 25-Year Perspective, pp. 375–398 (1999)
33. Mazzotta, G., Ricca, F., Truszczynski, M.: Quantifying over optimum answer sets. Theory Pract. Log. Program. **24**(4), 716–736 (2024)
34. Niemelä, I.: Logic programs with stable model semantics as a constraint programming paradigm. Ann. Math. Artif. Intell. **25**(3–4), 241–273 (1999)
35. Saikko, P., Wallner, J.P., Järvisalo, M.: Implicit hitting set algorithms for reasoning beyond NP. In: KR, pp. 104–113. AAAI Press (2016)
36. Schaefer, M., Umans, C.: Completeness in the polynomial-time hierarchy: a compendium. SIGACT News **33**(3), 32–49 (2002)

Author Index